RUPERT SMITH

The Utility of Force

The Art of War in the Modern World

ALLEN LANE
an imprint of
PENGUIN BOOKS

ALLEN LANE

Published by the Penguin Group
Penguin Books Ltd, 80 Strand, London WC2R ORL, England
Penguin Group (USA) Inc., 375 Hudson Street, New York, New York 10014, USA
Penguin Group (Canada), 90 Eglinton Avenue East, Suite 700, Toronto, Ontario, Canada M4P 2Y3
(a division of Pearson Penguin Canada Inc.)
Penguin Ireland, 25 St Stephen's Green, Dublin 2, Ireland (a division of Penguin Books Ltd)
Penguin Group (Australia), 250 Camberwell Road,
Camberwell, Victoria 3124, Australia (a division of Pearson Australia Group Pty Ltd)
Penguin Books India Pvt Ltd, 11 Community Centre,
Panchsheel Park, New Delhi – 110 017, India
Penguin Group (NZ), cnr Airborne and Rosedale Roads, Albany,
Auckland 1310, New Zealand (a division of Pearson New Zealand Ltd)
Penguin Books (South Africa) (Pty) Ltd, 24 Sturdee Avenue,
Rosebank, Johannesburg 2196, South Africa

Penguin Books Ltd, Registered Offices: 80 Strand, London WC2R ORL, England

www.penguin.com

First published 2005
1

Copyright © Rupert Smith and Ilana Bet-El, 2005

The moral right of the author has been asserted

Typeset in Linotype Sabon by
Palimpsest Book Production Limited, Polmont, Stirlingshire
Printed in Great Britain by Clays Ltd, St Ives plc

A CIP catalogue record for this book is available from the British Library

ISBN 0–713–99836–9

To all those who followed me or took my direction
when I thought these thoughts

Contents

Preface

This book has been forty years, and then three, in the making: a life in military service, and a period of reflection.

From the time the 1991 Gulf War ended until I left the army in 2002 I was asked if I was going to write a book, and on each occasion I said no. Sometimes I asked my questioners what the book was to be about, and they would answer along the lines of, 'You have done so much, surely there is a story to tell.' I took from these answers that they expected some account, chronological with anecdotes of personalities and events encountered along the way, and the more the telling uncovered a fresh angle on events, the better it would be. I have not kept a record in such a way as to be at all confident of telling such a story, even if I had thought about my service as source material for such a book.

Then, just before I retired, I was standing amidst a number of people, glass of wine in one hand, sandwich in the other, indulging in the hospitality of a learned institute prior to giving a seminar on, as I recall, 'The prospects for a European Defence Identity', when I was asked the question again. My reflex response was the usual denial. One of those who heard the question and answer was a great historian, a man whose writings and wisdom I admired; he said, 'Don't say no, now. When you have retired write a report to self and then you will know if you have something you want to write for others to read.' From that conversation on I have reflected on this advice, and while I have not, as such, written that report to self, I have thought at length about what might be included in it.

What do I report about? What have I to say about where or when I have served that is not already part of the record? After each event reports were written by me and others about all salient issues: those involved, the situation, the actions taken, the equipment or lack of it, and so on. Why repeat myself? Or did I, deliberately or not, leave something unsaid? These thoughts, or as one of my French comrades would say *thinks*, have slowly distilled into one report entry:

On every occasion that I have been sent to achieve some military objective in order to serve a political purpose, I, and those with me, have had to change our method and reorganize in order to succeed. Until this was done we could not use our force effectively. On the basis of my lengthy experience, I have come to consider this as normal – a necessary part of every operation. And after forty years of service, and particularly the last twelve, I believe I have gained an understanding of how to think about this inevitable and crucial phenomenon of conflict and warfare. The need to adapt is driven by the decisions of the opponent, the choice of objectives, the way or method force is applied, and the forces and recourses available, particularly when operating with allies. All of this demands an understanding of the political context of the operation, and the role of the military within it. Only when adaptation and context are complete can force be applied with utility.

In stating the foregoing I am not raising the old cry of armies preparing for the last war. Indeed, armies do not prepare for the last war, they frequently prepare for the wrong one – if for no other reason than that governments will usually fund only against the anticipated primary threat as opposed to risk, and the adversary will usually play to his opponents' weakness rather than strength. For example: when we deployed to the Gulf in 1990 we went in circumstances that lay outside the parameters of British defence policy since the late 1960s. As a result only the very oldest equipment had been designed to operate in a desert. The more recent acquisitions had been designed to work only in north-west Europe – and therefore none had sand filters, a vital necessity in desert warfare – and within a concept of battle associated with that great confrontation, the Cold War. In this grand scenario the armies of the West, mobilized and under NATO command, would conduct a forward defence, while the air forces, in the main those of the United States, attacked the Warsaw Pact columns and the Soviet heartland, first with conventional high explosive and then with nuclear weapons. This was to be total war, and it was for this we were organized, particularly in the fields of supply, maintenance and medical support. But our aims in the Gulf in 1991 were limited; the war was not total. In addition, the British forces were deployed as minority partners in a coalition dominated by the United States and without the mechanisms of political control that have been evolved over the years by NATO. On the plus side, Iraq's generals – or was it only Saddam Hussein? – chose to fight in such a way and on such terrain that they played to many of the strengths of the US and NATO way of war, particularly in the use of air power. And so, in these circumstances it was necessary to adapt our method and organization, concentrating on those to do with land warfare and its support, while continuing to play to our strengths in the air.

Change or adaptation is also required when the objective that is to be achieved by military force is different from that prepared for. In the case of the Gulf War this was not necessary since the objective for the actual use of military force, as opposed to its threat, was very similar to that we had prepared for in Europe: the destruction of the Soviet Operational Manoeuvre Groups being much the same as the destruction of Saddam's Republican Guard. Thus much of the preparation for the tactical battle in north-west Europe was still applicable. However, when military force is expected to be deployed to achieve an objective different from that prepared for, such as the coercion of President Milosevic of Serbia to hand over the province of Kosovo to an international administration, then this will also affect the nature of the battle and require an adapted or new method of operating, as well as changes to the process of command and organization.

Perhaps the most extreme example of this change of objective is to be found in the employment of the British army in Northern Ireland, where it is operating in aid of the constabulary. Indeed, in British army jargon this type of operation goes under the heading of Military Aid to the Civil Power. The long history of such operations, founded in the days of empire and practised frequently in the retreat from empire, has meant that for the British army many changes in tactical method and organization have become institutionalized and applied as similar situations are identified. In other words, the British army has been in a constant state of change and adaptation for good operational reasons. However, it has retained much the same organization throughout this period, adapting its formations and units to each and every operation. Doctrine has been used more to justify the basic organization than to explain why the adaptations have worked.

All armies are facing the need for transformation, particularly those of NATO and the former Warsaw Pact, but currently this is a debate concerning technology, numbers and organization – not how these forces are to be fought, and to what purpose.

I have spent many years thinking about, practising and implementing the use of force, and what I have to report is an approach to considering the use of military force and then applying it to achieve one's purpose. I am penning this report at a time of global security concerns, when military force is being considered or actually used in a wide range of scenarios, often with allies. Even a few examples reflect the complexity of these scenarios: terrorism, proliferation of weapons of mass destruction, peace making, peacekeeping, control of the mass movement of people, environmental protection, or the protection of availability of some scarce resource, be it energy, water or food. There are many more, possibly less obvious, examples, but the point remains the same: military force is considered a solution, or part of a solution, in a wide range of problems for which it was not originally intended or configured.

I began my military service in 1962 and was commissioned an officer in 1964; in training and theory I was therefore a product of the industrial war machine deemed necessary for the Cold War. And yet, possibly barring my experience in the 1991 Gulf War, all the military operations I have participated in and commanded were not those of industrial war. As a result, I have spent many years bringing re-configured forces into situations seeking a solution – most especially during the final decade of my forty years' service, when I held senior command in a number of major international theatres, starting with the British Armoured Division in the Gulf War of 1991, UNPROFOR in Bosnia in 1995, the forces in Northern Ireland 1996–8, and as the NATO Deputy Supreme Allied Commander Europe (DSACEUR) from 1998 to 2001. With the exception of my time in Northern Ireland I was commanding forces of other nations – nineteen in NATO in addition to partnership countries; nineteen in UNPROFOR, including contingents from Bangladesh, Malaysia, Russia, the Ukraine and

Egypt – and being commanded by officers of other nations representing either their own nation or an international organization. In addition, I have had staff officers on my teams from any number of other
nations, including Pakistan, Russia, Australia and New Zealand. I
have led forces against both states and those non-state actors that are
now so predominant in our modern military operations. At the same
time, my service has afforded me detailed insight into the forces and
capabilities of many of the militaries of the world, including the most
prominent.

Between 1992 and 1994 I was the Assistant Chief of the Defence
Staff, responsible for the oversight of all the UK's operations. Here, as
in all my deployments throughout the decade, I was working closely
with those concerned with achieving the overall political objective so
as to apply force to best advantage. In other words, I worked in tan-
dem with diplomats and politicians, civil servants and officials of the
UN and other international organizations, implementing the largely
political mandates handed down to me. It was this insight into the civilian national and international decision-making processes that I took
with me into subsequent commands, and which led me to realize there
was a dissonance between the organization of existing forces and their
operational activity. No less, it became obvious to me that the extant
theories of military organization and application and the unfolding
realities were wide apart. No more was I part of a world of wars in
which the civilian and military establishments each had its distinct role
in distinct stages. The new situations were always a complex combination of political and military circumstances, though there appeared to
be little comprehension as to how the two became intertwined – nor,
far more seriously from the perspective of the military practitioner,
how they constantly influenced each other as events unfolded. I therefore set about trying to understand this matter, first and foremost for
my own purposes in command. It was through these musings that I
realized we were now in a new era of conflict – in fact a new paradigm
– which I define as 'war amongst the people'; one in which political and
military developments go hand in hand. This understanding greatly
aided me in my military work. In my period of reflection post-
retirement, it was this theoretical idea that was the background to my
unwritten report to self. Ultimately the two merged into this book.

The Utility of Force is intended to explain how force can be used to greater utility – as both a conceptual and practical discussion. Indeed, I must emphasize practicalities: my service record is one of practical experience at all levels of command and in a wide range of circumstances. This point is significant because alongside theory there is also a need to understand the practicalities of the use of force and the realities of operations and combat. Indeed, I have come to see that this lack of knowledge often compounds the lack of understanding of conflict: the politicians quite rightly expect the military to respond to their requirements, but too often do so without any comprehension of the practical considerations of the matter, let alone conceptual ones. If force is to continue to be used, and to have utility, this situation must change.

The book follows a chronological development, but is a thematic discussion rather than a definitive history. Indeed, its three major parts may be read separately as extended individual essays, or else together as a multifaceted examination. I make no claim to a comprehensive telling, but rather a reflection, my own, on the world I lived in for many years, on the tools and methods I was given and trained to use, on the confrontation and conflicts I experienced, and on the different approaches I ultimately arrived at within them. To this extent I must emphasize I have made every effort to refer either to the military as a whole or to the individual services when relevant, but I am aware that there may be places in which I use the term 'army' in a collective sense for all military services – in these cases to the air and the naval services I offer my sincere apologies. I have also used the male pronoun throughout as a matter of simplicity. A note on sources may also be of use: this is not a work of definitive research. Facts, figures and narrative tales of the past are offered only as examples of the analyses and themes, and sourced only where a specific quotation makes this necessary. There are also technical issues: force and its uses is a subject of some breadth. However, in seeking to bring my ideas to a wider audience I have tried to avoid using military jargon or technical terms, although in some cases this has been unavoidable. To those with no interest in such matters, I offer George Orwell's excellent advice to his readers in explaining the intermingling of political and military concepts in his book *Homage to Catalonia*:

If you are not interested in the horrors of party politics, please skip; I am trying to keep the political parts of this narrative in separate chapters for precisely that purpose. But at the same time it would be quite impossible to write about the Spanish Civil War from a purely military angle. It was above all a political war.

Finally, I wish to emphasize this is a work of interpretation rather than an academic monograph – and it is in such a spirit I recommend it be read.

Part of my reluctance to write in the first place is that I distrust memory; my own as much as others. I am not suggesting we lie deliberately, but the moment an event has occurred and we know its outcome we are prone to reorder and reinterpret the information and decisions we took in light of the outcome. This very natural human characteristic is evident to anyone who has filled in an insurance claim after they have damaged a car. It also leads to the phenomenon of: 'Failure is an orphan and success has a thousand fathers'. Keeping this in mind, I must emphasize I have drawn on my memory to illustrate the points I am making, not in order to provide a record, and I ask that those who were there with me at the time and have another memory bear with me in this indulgence.

Over the years I have encountered and been privileged to work with many people – literally thousands – who have either knowingly or unknowingly contributed to my understanding of force and forces. To them all I owe a debt of thanks and I have dedicated this book to those who took my lead or direction as we endeavoured by force of arms to impose our will on our opponents. I would also like to acknowledge and thank the many staff colleges, academic institutions and intellectual fora that have given me a platform to introduce and develop my ideas.

The creation of this book was aided and abetted by many. Wilfrid Holroyd was an eloquent and speedy researcher, who managed to cover great swathes of history with due aplomb. Thanks also to those long-suffering friends who read the early drafts and whose comments and encouragement guided the revisions, most especially Dennis

Staunton, John Wilson, Chris Riley and Laura Citron – who for two critical months in the final stages of producing a manuscript also helped keep the household nearly sane. All errors and misjudgements are, however, entirely my own. I am in debt to Professor Nigel Howard, whose explanation of Confrontation Analysis and Game Theory at a seminar in 1998 excited my interest. Our subsequent discussions helped me to order my thoughts and the lessons I had learned previously into a coherent structure with the result that, for the first time, I was able to understand my experiences within a theoretical model which allowed me to use them further. Michael Sissons, my agent, always believed in this project – even if it took time to become presentable. At Allen Lane Stuart Proffit, my commissioning editor, provided unfailing and good-humoured support and advice which did much to shape this book. Liz Friend-Smith made contact with Stuart and the world of Penguin very smooth. Thanks also to Trevor Horwood for polishing the manuscript so effectively, and to John Noble for the comprehensive index, a fascinating read in itself. Finally and primarily, this book would not have been written if it had not been for Ilana Bet-El, my partner and an author, historian and journalist. Her enthusiasm for the project gained a publishing contract in the first place, my efforts having failed to pass even my agent, and has sustained us both subsequently throughout the process of producing a manuscript – and then painfully correcting it. Her skills, knowledge, analytical capability and insights, and contribution to our debate are in evidence on every page.

Introduction: Understanding Force

War no longer exists. Confrontation, conflict and combat undoubtedly exist all round the world – most noticeably, but not only, in Iraq, Afghanistan, the Democratic Republic of the Congo and the Palestinian Territories – and states still have armed forces which they use as a symbol of power. None the less, war as cognitively known to most non-combatants, war as battle in a field between men and machinery, war as a massive deciding event in a dispute in international affairs: such war no longer exists.

Consider this: the last real tank battle known to the world, one in which the armoured formations of two armies manoeuvred against each other supported by artillery and air forces, one in which the tanks in formation were the deciding force, took place in the 1973 Arab–Israeli war on the Golan Heights and in the Sinai Desert. Since then thousands more tanks have been built and purchased, especially by the groups of nations in NATO and the then Warsaw Pact. Indeed, by 1991, when the extended event known as the Cold War ended, NATO allies were estimated to have over 23,000 tanks between them whilst the Warsaw Pact states had nearly 52,000. Yet over the past thirty years armoured formations have either supported the application of air power and artillery, as in the 1991 and 2003 wars in Iraq or in Chechnya in 2000, or else their units and sub-units have been committed piecemeal, often to provide heavily protected infantry support vehicles in urban operations such as those now undertaken by coalition forces in Iraq or by Israel in the Occupied Territories. But use of the tank as a machine of war organized in formation, designed to do battle and attain a definitive result, has not occurred during three decades. Nor, for that matter, is it ever likely to occur again, for the wars in which armoured formations could and should be used are no longer practical.

This reality is now acknowledged by some military planners who are advocating rapid and light forces. However, such advocacy largely refers to the circumstances of modern battle – but within an outdated concept of war. And yet it is the entire concept of war that has changed: it has shifted into a new paradigm.

Since the events of 11 September 2001 there has been much discussion of Samuel Huntington's theory of the clash of civilizations, a discussion which has been useful in trying to come to terms with the motives of terrorists and their horrific activities. But in order to understand the true implications of these to the world in which we live, and most certainly for understanding how the premises of war in all its wider definitions have changed, one may be better served in applying Thomas Kuhn's theory of scientific revolutions. Kuhn noted that all scientific communities – in this case military thinkers – practise within a set of received beliefs that are rigidly upheld, to the extent of suppressing novelties that are subversive to them. A shift occurs when an anomaly finally does subvert the existing traditions of scientific practice. This is a revolution, what Kuhn calls 'a paradigm shift' that necessitates both new assumptions and the reconstruction of prior assumptions – which is the main reason it is strongly resisted.

Reflecting upon war, it is clear the current shift in paradigm began with the introduction of nuclear weapons in 1945, and the point in which it became dominant was in 1989–91, at the end of the Cold War – a title that is a gross historical misnomer, since it was never a war but rather a prolonged confrontation; but for the sake of clarity I shall conform to it. For it was the introduction of nuclear power that made industrial war practically impossible as a deciding event; indeed, the Cold War was conducted within the concept of mutually assured destruction (MAD). None the less, strategic planners, in support of this concept, developed forces within the old paradigm of industrial war – but in parallel, and often with the same forces, they were fighting other wars such as those in Vietnam and Algeria: increasingly nonindustrial wars against non-state opponents. In other words, the Kuhnian anomaly occurred possibly as early as 1945, and whilst acknowledged by the political and military leaderships as a reality its true significance was resisted by military planners, not least because there was little choice: integral to MAD was the credibility of the prospect of cataclysmic total war. The ending of the Cold War unmasked the new paradigm that had long been lurking, although it was not necessarily comprehended as such. Indeed, the ensuing debate of the past fifteen years has generally settled on the organization and development of forces and resources within the old paradigm.

It is now time to recognize that a paradigm shift in war has undoubtedly occurred: from armies with comparable forces doing battle on a field to strategic confrontation between a range of combatants, not all of which are armies, and using different types of weapons, often improvised. The old paradigm was that of interstate industrial war. The new one is the paradigm of war amongst the people – and it is the background to this book.

I am aware that the term paradigm has become something of a catchphrase in our times, usually intended as a synonym to a proven model. To be absolutely clear, I do not use it in that sense, but rather in the way Kuhn defined paradigms, as 'universally recognized scientific achievements that for a time provide model problems and solutions to a community of practitioners'. The paradigm of interstate industrial war clearly served the military and political communities in such a capacity, but it is now time to comprehend the paradigm of war amongst the people in the same way.

War amongst the people is both a graphic description of modern war-like situations, and also a conceptual framework: it reflects the hard fact that there is no secluded battlefield upon which armies engage, nor are there necessarily armies, definitely not on all sides. To be clear: this is not asymmetric warfare, a phrase I dislike invented to explain a situation in which conventional states were threatened by unconventional powers but in which conventional military power in some formulation would be capable of both deterring the threat and responding to it. War amongst the people is different: it is the reality in which the people in the streets and houses and fields – all the people, anywhere – are the battlefield. Military engagements can take place anywhere: in the presence of civilians, against civilians, in defence of civilians. Civilians are the targets, objectives to be won, as much as an

3

opposing force. However, it is also not asymmetric warfare since it is also a classic example of disinterest in the change of paradigms. The practice of war, indeed its 'art', is to achieve an asymmetry over the opponent. Labelling wars as asymmetric is to me something of a euphemism to avoid acknowledging that my opponent is not playing to my strengths and I am not winning. In which case perhaps the model of war rather than its name is no longer relevant: the paradigm has changed.

Nation states, especially Western ones and Russia but others too, all send in their armies, their conventionally formulated military forces, to do battle – to have a war – in these battlefields, and they do not succeed. Indeed, throughout the past fifteen years both the Western allies and the Russians have entered into a series of military engagements that have in one way or another spectacularly failed to achieve the results intended, namely a decisive military victory which would in turn deliver a solution to the original problem, which is usually political. This is basically due to a deep and abiding confusion between *deploying* a force and *employing* force.

In many cases forces have been deployed and then force has not been employed. The UN in the Balkans is an example: by 1995 there were tens of thousands of UN troops based mostly in Croatia and Bosnia, but they were barred by the Security Council resolutions that placed them there from using any actual military force. As Commander UNPROFOR in Bosnia in 1995 I spent a lot of time trying to explain to a range of senior figures in the UN and in various capital cities precisely this issue: that keeping over 20,000 lightly armed troops in the midst of the warring parties was strategically unsustainable and tactically inept; that presence alone amounts to little. Or, as I used to put it to my international stakeholders, you become a shield of one side and a hostage of the other.

In other cases force has been employed but with little if any effect, as in the no-fly zones over Iraq in the years preceding the 2003 war, when targets were constantly being hit by coalition aircraft far away from the media glare (apparently known amongst some pilots as 'recreational bombing'), but to very little consequence with regard to the continuing horrors of the Saddam Hussein regime. Sometimes great force has been employed, as in the case of the Gulf War of 1991 or in Chechnya in 2000, and the result has been less than strategically conclusive: the military operation was a success, but the essential strategic problem remained unresolved. On other occasions force has been applied in such a way that the method and its purpose is difficult to explain to allies and the public at large, as in Kosovo in 1999, when a bombing campaign anticipated to last a week or so stretched over seventy-eight days and eventually involved hitting civilian infrastructure in Serbia proper rather than Kosovo – even if it turned out to be the Chinese embassy in Belgrade, a hit for which I was *personally* blamed by the Beijing press – in order to attain the retreat of the Milosevic forces. Or, as in the last war in Iraq – which caused a great rift amongst allies before, during and after its engagement, and to this day – when the actual military campaign was brief but the aftermath and its entanglement in civilian life was lengthy and messy.

In all these cases military force may have achieved a local military success, but frequently this success failed to produce its political promise: there is no decisive victory. In other words, throughout these fifteen years statesmen, politicians, diplomats, admirals, generals and air marshals have had difficulty both in applying military force to advantage and in explaining their intentions and actions. For example throughout 2003–4 the Israelis were wrestling with the same problem, as were the coalition forces in Iraq. This endemic problem is the result of the shift in the paradigm of war and the continued resistance to it: politicians and soldiers are still thinking in terms of the old paradigm and trying to use their conventionally configured forces to that end – whilst the enemy and the battle have changed. As a result, the utility of the effort is minimal: the force may be massive and impressive, but it is not delivering the required results, nor indeed any result that is in proportion to its assumed capabilities. As with the difference between deploying and employing a force, this reflects a lack of understanding of the *utility* of force – which is the core issue at stake, and the subject of this book.

It may be as well to begin this investigation with a discussion of military force, since it is common to all paradigms of war – and unfortunately is often commonly misunderstood. Force is the basis of any military activity, whether in a theatre of operations or in a skirmish between two soldiers. It is both the physical means of destruction – the bullet, the bayonet – and the body that applies it. It has been so since the beginning of time. Indeed, the essence of force and its military uses are identical now to that described in the Bible, Sun Tzu's *Art of War*, the Greek or Nordic myths, and just about any historical book on battle and warfare.

Military force when employed has only two immediate effects: it kills people and destroys things. Whether or not this death and destruction serve to achieve the overarching or political purpose the force was intended to achieve depends on the choice of targets or objectives, all within the broader context of the operation. That is the true measure of its utility. It follows that to apply force with utility implies an understanding of the context in which one is acting, a clear definition of the result to be achieved, an identification of the point or target to which the force is being applied – and, as important as all the others, an understanding of the nature of the force being applied. Imagine a landslide that needs to be cleared from a road. The objective is the pile of rocks, the context is the surrounding hills that are unstable, including the villages upon them and the infrastructure of electricity, gas and water that surrounds the area. The definition of the result to be achieved is a clear road, as quickly as possible. The pile of rocks on the road is the target to which force is to be applied. That leaves the basic question as to the nature of the force: should it be mechanical diggers or explosives? Each poses a promise of a solution, but possibly at different speeds and costs – the explosives would be quicker, but may set off another landslide; the diggers would be safer, but slow. Either option would deliver a clear road, but the utility of each would be different.

Military force is applied by armed forces composed of men, materiel and their logistic support. The capability of these armed forces to act is never merely an inventory of the three but rather a function of their organization, and always in relation to the opposing forces, the circumstances of the time and the specific battle. This is because the enemy in any fight is not inert or merely a constant object of plans. The enemy is *always* a reacting being that not only has no intention of falling in with your plans, but will actively be setting out to foil them – whilst making plans of his own at the same time. The enemy is an adversary, an opponent, not a sitting target. Response and adjustment are as much part of

6

a plan of attack unfolding as the original blueprint. Without fully comprehending this, most military activity, at every level, will never be clear to the onlooker. Indeed, I have learned this at personal physical cost: I was blown up. In Northern Ireland in 1978, in concentrating my company's efforts on the IRA's principal activities and threats (I believe successfully), I lost sight of the need to keep learning. I did not credit them soon enough with an ability to change the nature of their attack on my forces, as opposed to improving their capacity to continue with what they were doing. In the event, they ran a device into the market place of Crossmaglen when a market was in process, which they had not done before. The radio-controlled bomb was carefully designed and placed to have only the most local effect; I and another officer, on a day I thought predictably safe, were caught in the blast and fireball. I had failed to realize that my enemy had a free, creative mind and was not thinking nor going to think like me. From that point on I tried to construct all my operations, in Ireland and elsewhere, so as to learn continuously what my enemy was intending to do rather than assuming knowledge.

An armed force may be made up of either regular or irregular forces, but there is a difference. A regular force is employed to serve a political purpose decided upon by a lawful government, which instructs the military, as a legally sanctioned and formed body answerable to that government, to apply the force. A regular force is therefore legal, deadly and destructive. An irregular force can be just as deadly and destructive, but operates outside the state, and therefore the laws of that state. However, their irregularity does not in itself put them beyond the protection of international law. Irregular forces range from the gangs of organized crime through resistance and terrorist organizations to guerrilla forces and even some structured as armies, such as the Vietcong towards the end of the Vietnam War.

An armed force is essential to any independent geopolitical entity that is part of the international system, yet it must always be made legal – converted into a regular military force. Over the centuries emperors, kings, princes and democratic governments have pondered this aim since all have faced the same problem: how to have an armed force available to advance and protect their interests, at an affordable financial and political cost, and in such a way that it does not threaten them. Historical circumstances have produced solutions different in their detail but all with four common attributes, all authorized and rooted in the structure of the legal recognized state – which is what sets them apart from irregular forces:

- an organized military body,
- an hierarchical structure answerable to the highest in the entity or the state,
- a legal status to bear arms and to have a separate disciplinary code,
- centralized funding for the purchase of warlike materiel.

These four attributes are all apparent in the military forces of today across the globe, and are indeed their underpinning. Together, they ensure a military force works cohesively and legally – but also entirely separately from society. A force draws its members from society, and exists in order to serve it, but nevertheless in order to preserve its identity it functions with its own codes in parallel to society. It can be seen that over time irregular forces are brought under control by the political body, often with difficulty – in an attempt to make the force regular.

The conversion of an irregular force into a regular force is equally important from the public perspective: we tolerate this lethal body within our society because it is under the control of our elected leaders and so operates within the law. In conflict zones around the world, from the Balkans to the Democratic Republic of the Congo (DRC) to Afghanistan, it is sometimes difficult to see when a regular military force has lost its legitimacy and reverted to being an armed irregular force, whilst in some cases an irregular force is transiting towards legitimacy and becoming a regular military force. It is easy enough to see that a drug-funded warlord in Afghanistan heads an irregular force, but is the PLO, when operating in Gaza or the occupied territories, a regular or irregular force? Or when elements of the old Yugoslav army, a regular force known as the JNA, became the Bosnian Serb Army (BSA) in Bosnia in 1991, did this formation become an irregular force or was it another regular force? This problem of identifying the regularity of a force applies to any armed independence movement and to the vast majority of our conflicts today, and it is one the international community has yet to grapple with coherently, as we shall see in the third part of this book. For the majority of our conflicts involve the legitimacy of the sides and their causes, including their military forces. In Bosnia, for example, the international community did not recognize the Bosnian Serbs as a separate entity, which is why it was difficult to define the legitimacy of the BSA.

In the Western world we live in an age of growing uninterest in all aspects of military force. Whilst the horrors of 11 September 2001 induced a renewed public interest in security, and in the US a vast increase in defence spending, in overall terms since the end of the Cold War public discourse on matters military has mostly been relegated to debates on defence budgets and the legality and morality of the use of force – whilst discussion of the actual meaning of force, and its utility, has become nearly obsolete. Indeed, the public international outcry and discourse in the lead-up to operation Iraqi Freedom, the invasion of Iraq by a US-led coalition in March 2003, reflected that in many ways deciding the morality and legality of the use of force automatically defined its utility: if it was moral and legal it would be successful and deliver the desired result; if not the inverse would be true. Yet this cannot be so; whilst the application of force for immoral reasons or in an illegal way is not to be countenanced, it is also not a sufficient manner in which to understand a core reality: we the people need a force as a basic element of our lives for two generic overarching purposes – defence and security. Put more particularly, or even personally, to defend our homes and ourselves, and to secure our interests. Like every other aspect of force, these two purposes are eternal – which means that in times of peace as in times of war the maintenance of a force can never be entirely dismissed, even if it is expensive; nor can a focus upon the morality and legality of the use of force supplant the very basic need to understand its utility.

In recent years, especially since the end of the Cold War, the basic deadly purpose of a military force has become obscured and its independent nature, as defined by its four basic attributes listed above, has often been misunderstood in popular Western perception, especially as wars have become media events far away from any ongoing social reality. This obscuring and misunderstanding is equally true of the politicians who seek to both deploy and employ military forces for humanitarian and policing purposes for which they are neither trained nor intended. This does not mean that the hierarchical and disciplinary attributes of a force cannot be adapted for wider use, nor that weapons should not be used other than for purely military activity between armies. However, it is necessary to understand that in many of the circumstances into which we now deploy, our forces as a *military force* will not be effective. The coalition forces in Iraq were a classic example of this situation: their effectiveness as a military force ended once the fighting between military forces was completed in May 2003. And though they then went on to score a series of victories in local skirmishes, they had greatly diminished – if any – effect as an occupation and reconstruction force, which had become their main mandate. They were neither trained nor equipped for the task, and therefore could not fulfil it. To use the parlance of this book, there was little utility to the force.

The pursuit of both defence and security is adversarial, emanating from confrontations apparent and potential. Confrontations between people with differing interests and priorities are endemic within all societies. When those societies that are called states confront one another over some issue, and this cannot be resolved to the satisfaction of both parties, and they seek to resolve the matter by force of arms, we call the resulting conflict war – even if it is currently inappropriate, as stated at the start – the objective of both sides being to establish their respective versions of peace. Generally, excepting self-defence, the use of military force is seen as an act of last resort to be entered into only after all other measures to achieve a resolution have been exhausted. Over the past centuries states have developed laws and protocols to manage these conflicts – generally known as the Geneva Conventions – together with military and governmental institutions to conduct them. Once at war the adversaries, whilst expected to obey the Conventions, do not have to play by the same rules of the game; indeed, much of generalship involves arranging to play on a pitch, in a style and to rules that suit your side and disadvantage the other. Furthermore, and unlike all other socially acceptable behaviour except some sports, wars and fights are not competitions: to be second is to lose.

Wars and conflicts are conducted at four levels – political, strategic, theatre and tactical – with each level sitting within the context of the other, in descending order from the political; it is this that gives context to all the activities of all the levels aimed at the same objectives, and enables coherence between them. The first, political, level is the source of power and decision. This level has always existed in that armies enter combat not merely because two or more of them happen to be hanging around an empty battlefield and decide to fill in some time but because an issue between two or more political entities cannot be settled in other ways and therefore military means are resorted to. Historically, the political and military leaderships of a state or entity tended to be identical, since it was usually the prince or king who both made the policy and led his army – if only nominally. With the evolution of nation states throughout the nineteenth century the political and military leaderships became separate in democracies and have remained so to this day. The position of the Queen in the UK and the US President in relation to their nations' armed forces, although each constitutionally different, reflects the historical unity of the political and military leaderships. In modern conflict it is the political leadership that controls the military – and it is there that the purpose of entering into the conflict is decided. This decision must be taken in relation to the threat posed to whatever it is that is valued – be it territory, sovereignty, trade, resource, honour, justice, religion, or anything else. Like any other major decision, in life as in war, it can be taken only after an evaluation, first of the risk of the threat materializing, and second of what is actually risked if the threat succeeds. For example, when faced with the ultimatum of 3 September 1939, giving him two hours to begin withdrawing his troops from Poland or else be at war with Britain, Hitler knew the threat would materialize, but clearly deemed it not sufficiently threatening to his plans and actions. Conversely, Chamberlain and his government, having watched Hitler first take the Sudetenland then march into Poland, knew the threat was materializing before them, with the distinct possibility of it reaching the British Isles – and therefore knew what was at risk. Other than negotiating with Hitler or simply waiting for his forces to arrive, there was no option other than to issue an ultimatum, and then go to war.

It is during this analysis of threats and risks that the role of military force is introduced, in terms of what it is expected to achieve and the manner of its achievement. The purist will argue that this should be decided early in the debate, but in practice this only occurs with an imminent threat. In the main this policy debate is about anticipated threats and unfolds much like decisions about insurance: we know we need some, but not so much as to inhibit life today to cover some distant prospect that may not occur. None the less, since the policy provides the nest for the strategy, in peacetime the strategist must still be involved with the formulation of the former. For it is he who brings the harsh realities of combat to the debate and the product of his efforts is to be found in the quality, morale, adaptability, equipment and quantity of the forces available to his successors when faced with an opponent.

Having made a decision at the political level to enter conflict, activity moves to the strategic level in which the political purpose of having recourse to military force, either as a potential or in the actual use of force, is translated into military formations and acts. This translation then gives rise first to the existence of the force itself, and subsequently to its deployment and employment. However, it must never be forgotten that the political considerations provide the context within which the strategy rests. Therefore the relationship between the political and strategic levels must always be very close, to the point of engaging in continuous reassessment and debate, which does not stop until the overall purpose or aim is achieved. At the same time, it must always be remembered that the political objective and the military strategic objective are not the same, and are never the same: the military strategic objective is achieved by military force whilst the political objective is achieved as a result of the military success.

It is the task of the strategic commander to understand fully the object of his endeavours and the forces and resources available to him, to the degree that he can select his aim. The word aim encompasses more than a task or objective: it is both a target and the direction of all senses on that target so that one's strength or force is focused to hit that target with the greatest accuracy and effect. The strategic aim can be difficult to define and yet it is essential to do so. Without an aim firmly linked to the political purpose it is difficult to use force to advantage, because the commander does not know what outcome or effect must be achieved in order to support the achievement of the overall political purpose.

Devising the strategy to achieve the aim involves striking a series of compromises. There is no such thing as a perfect strategy or even plan; indeed, to seek such perfection is to forget or deny that the enemy is not inert and has a free creative part in the conflict which is directly opposed to one's own. As such, one should be seeking to devise a strategy that is better than his in the circumstances. Nor is the expression of a strategy a carefully crafted plan, but rather a desired pattern to events. As I put it in a directive to my commanders in November 1990, prior to our departure to the Gulf for the 1991 war with Iraq: 'Command in war rarely involves the rehearsal of a carefully laid plan. The enemy, who is missing in peace, is taking every step he can to destroy the coherence of our organization and plans. It is the will and the method of overcoming the enemy that decides the outcome.'

A strategy therefore is an expression of the aim and its links to the overall purpose and the context of the conflict, together with the limitations on action that flow from that political purpose in the circumstances. It will describe the desired pattern to events together with the measures intended to achieve this pattern, and it will allocate forces and resources. Finally, it should appoint the necessary commanders and state their responsibilities and authorities. The compromises are in the main centred on the nature of the pattern to events and the allocation of forces and resources to achieve them. The test of a good strategy is that it achieves its object without the necessity for battle. As Sun Tzu put it: 'What is of supreme importance in war is to attack the enemy's strategy; next best is to disrupt his alliances; next best is to attack his army.' However, these adversarial affairs rarely allow one strategy to be so successful over the other.

Attacking the army brings us to the tactical level, where we find battles, engagements and fights. The scale of these events covers both the individual action and the collective. They range from the great sea battles such as Trafalgar or air battles such as the Battle of Britain to a submarine sinking a battleship, for example the *Belgrano* in the Falklands War, or a dogfight between two aircraft over Kent in 1940. On the land the scale incorporates events from the battle of the Somme to some brief skirmish in a Belfast or Basra alley. Indeed, a battle is made up of a whole series of engagements on a variety of scales: individual, fire-team, sub-unit, unit and formation. There is no end of permutations in the manner these are played out, in varying combinations of weaponry, battlefield terrain and weather, and in the face of an opponent who is taking active measures to do unto you as you intend to do unto him.

The essence of all tactics is fire and movement, and the basic tactical dilemma is to find the correct balance between how much effort to apply to striking the opponent to achieve the objective and how much to countering his blows. In many ways, tactical warfare is akin to the art of boxing – and I hold both clearly to be an art. The combatants require physical fitness, a degree of skill and enduring courage in the face of an opponent's blows. On this basis each party guards and strikes, seeking to break through the other's defence so as to deliver telling combinations of punches and ideally a knockout blow. The combinations are drilled into the boxer by long practice. His art is in forcing his opponent to leave a vulnerable spot unguarded and recognizing the opportunity in time to take violent advantage of it. All this is true and necessary in battle too, especially the drill of combination blows. But Queensberry rules do not apply, and the art of tactics is more like a lethal brawl in the gutter where there are no rules or referees, and where low cunning matched with the maximum use of force available wins the day. I use these analogies to emphasize that tactics is not only about the manoeuvre of a force; it is about the application of force, lethal force, to an opponent and avoiding his intentions to do the same. The outcome of tactics is simple: kill or be killed. The successful tactician must be more nimble and move faster relative to his opponent, so as to bring fire to bear in telling quantities. To do this he may well use fire and obstacles, natural and man-made, to delay or suppress the enemy's ability to move.

Finally, we come to the level that links the tactical to the strategic: the theatre or operational level. In our modern circumstances I think theatre is a better description, and in the main I shall use it from now on – largely because of the widespread use of the term 'operational' for a variety of activities in the military and civilian worlds. The theatre or operational level of war is conducted in the theatre of operations – a geographical area containing in its military and political totality an objective that on achievement alters the strategic situation to advantage. For example, the 1944 D-Day landings in Normandy were an operation in their own right that changed the strategic reality: Western Europe could now be liberated and Germany conquered. To be clear: an operation in a theatre is not merely a collection of tactical battles that take place within a defined geographic area. The theatre commander must make the plan, his campaign, which designates the path towards his final objective – given to him by the strategic commander – and orchestrates the activities of his command to achieve tactical objectives that take the command as a whole in the designated direction. The theatre commander has to understand the political context of his theatre, comprising as it will the politics of the area in question, those of his political and strategic masters, and of his force – particularly with multinational forces, as is more frequently the case, when the political and strategic components become multiplied and often entangled.

My own commands throughout the 1990s offer a good example of the levels of war. In 1990–91, in command of a British division subordinated to VII US Corps in the Gulf, I was a tactical level commander – and so was my corps commander, Lieutenant General Fred Franks. The theatre commander, General Norman Schwarzkopf, and his subordinate generals had to understand the political and strategic context of the deployment of my formation, and take this into account in its employment, which they did. In 1995, as Commander UNPROFOR, I was in effect a theatre commander. The politics of the conflict in Bosnia, and those of the troop contributing nations to my command, were such that they defined the theatre. The overall force commander – since UN forces were also deployed in Croatia and Macedonia, thereby necessitating a central commander – was based in Zagreb. He found himself in limbo: neither a strategic commander nor able to command the three theatres simultaneously. This is because the UN is an organization without a permanent military structure. It therefore has no capacity to create a strategic command, which is why it can never offer a serious option for the use of military force. Between 1996 and 1998, as General Officer Commanding (GOC) Northern Ireland, I was clearly a theatre commander directly answerable to the Chief of the General Staff (CGS), my strategic commander in London. When I became the NATO Deputy Supreme Allied Commander Europe (DSACEUR) in November 1998, I was a commander at the strategic level of an alliance, albeit a deputy to the supreme commander. Additionally, as the senior European commander in NATO – which is always the case with the DSACEUR, since the SACEUR is always an American – I was the strategic commander of the nascent EU force. Finally, as GOC and in my NATO and UN roles I spent much time interacting with the political levels, in theatre and in capitals, which I did not do as a tactical commander. Such divisions of labour and authority, not always clearly understood by those enmeshed in them, are the realities of modern command.

Much more will be said of all levels of operation throughout the book, since they are the frameworks within which force is applied. However, at this point it is important to understand two basic and largely obvious points: first, it is the political level that makes the decision to enter conflict, and it is the political level that decides to stop it; the military implement both of these decisions. Second, all activities sit within the overall context of a given strategy, and when the fight begins each engagement nests within the greater engagement of the superior commander; the achievement of each commander contributing, at least in theory, to the achievement of his superior. The understanding of the context of a particular operation is as important as understanding the superior commander's intentions, so as to ensure there is coherence of the effects of action at each level – each contributing to the other. However, in our modern circumstances most fights do not go to the strategic level: war amongst the people is mostly a tactical event, with occasional forays into the theatre level – yet we still persist in thinking of them as wars, which will deliver decisive victories and solutions. It is important to understand why.

Our understanding of the use of military force is based in large measure on the old paradigm of interstate industrial war: concepts founded on conflict between states, the manoeuvre of forces en masse, and the total support of the state's manpower and industrial base, at the expense of all other interests, for the purpose of an absolute victory. In the world of industrial war the premise is of the sequence peace–crisis–war–resolution, which will result in peace again, with the war, the military action, being the deciding factor. In contrast, the new paradigm of war amongst the people is based on the concept of a continuous criss-crossing between confrontation and conflict, regardless of whether a state is facing another state or a non-state actor. Rather than war and peace, there is no predefined sequence, nor is peace necessarily either the starting or the end point: conflicts are resolved, but not necessarily confrontations. For example, the Korean War ended in 1953, but the confrontation with North Korea remains unresolved; or, more recently, the bombing and military action against Serbia following its abuse of the Kosovars ended in 1999, but there is still no decision on the final status of Kosovo and the confrontation between Serbia and the international community remains in place.

War amongst the people is characterized by six major trends:

- **The ends for which we fight are changing** from the hard absolute objectives of interstate industrial war to more malleable objectives to do with the individual and societies that are not states.
- **We fight amongst the people,** a fact amplified literally and figuratively by the central role of the media: we fight in every living room in the world as well as on the streets and fields of a conflict zone.
- **Our conflicts tend to be timeless,** since we are seeking a condition, which then must be maintained until an agreement on a definitive outcome, which may take years or decades.
- **We fight so as not to lose the force,** rather than fighting by using the force at any cost to achieve the aim.
- **On each occasion new uses are found for old weapons:** those constructed specifically for use in a battlefield against soldiers and heavy armaments, now being adapted for our current conflicts since the tools of industrial war are often irrelevant to war amongst the people.
- **The sides are mostly non-state** since we tend to conduct our conflicts and confrontations in some form of multinational grouping, whether it is an alliance or a coalition, and against some party or parties that are not states.

These six trends reflect the reality of our new form of war: it is no longer a single massive event of military decision that delivers a conclusive political result. This is because the relationship between the political and military factors has also greatly changed. Whilst the four levels of war have remained intact, and it is still the political leadership that makes the decision to use force, our world of confrontation and conflict means that the political and military activities are constantly intermingled throughout. To understand any modern conflict, therefore, both must be examined in parallel – since they will evolve and change together, impacting the one on the other. Only when the use of force is analysed in this way will it have utility.

Military force does not have an absolute utility, other than its basic purposes of killing and destroying. Every confrontation or indeed conflict is different, not only in location and sides but in nature, especially in our era of humanitarian interventions or military operations amongst the people, such as those in Afghanistan in 2002 and Iraq in 2003. Force can be used to advantage only if its utility in the circumstances is understood and the force comprehended. To do this it is necessary to understand military forces, since they are the medium through which force is applied. There does not exist a generic 'military force'. There may be more standard, even generic types of resources: land, sea and air forces; special forces of various kinds; fighter and bomber aircraft; carriers and submarines; missiles and artillery; tanks and machine guns; and a variety of weapons systems and technological aids in our current era. These are all important components, but they are just that: components, to be selected by a commander for a specific force. And each force is specific – to a period, to a state, to a war, to a single theatre of war, possibly to a battle. Even a standing force is specific: a result of the factors of the time of its formation. For at base, it must be understood that battle is an event of circumstance, and therefore every element of force must be understood as a product of the circumstances in which it was created or used. The battle of Waterloo was the battle it was because it took place in 1815 in Wallonia; because Napoleon raised an army of a certain size and Wellington and Blücher had the armies they did; because Napoleon devised one plan and fought his forces in a certain way, whilst his two opponents devised their plan and fought their forces in another way – and so on. If the battle had taken place a month later it is possible all these factors would have been different – this dependence on the circumstances of the day, and understanding their significance, is the true framework of military activity.

The basic act of forming a military force requires the massing of troops and materiel. But this would not in itself produce a usable force. The men and materiel must be found from society in such a way that they are affordable and are suitable in quantity and quality. Some nations rely on conscription, others on volunteers for their manpower; some seek equipment of the greatest sophistication and apparent power whilst others have older, simpler equipment. And yet, as we have seen in many recent military engagements, possession of modern sophisticated equipment does not necessarily lead to victory. And that is because every single force, anywhere in the world, is constructed in accordance with a purpose: a defence and security policy and a military doctrine, which demands certain amounts of troops and materiel of specific qualifications, that all interlock into a coherent force. And the greater the coherence the greater the chance of the force succeeding in battle. As we will see throughout this book, lack of coherence – whether in purpose or between purpose and force – is a major reason for the failure of forces.

Beyond geography, money has always been the greatest deciding factor in the structure of a force. Even the size of a population and the availability of potential troops have been secondary to financial considerations: you can always buy in extra force if money is no problem. Historically, in the formation of forces money has usually represented a balance of investment between the actual or anticipated purpose of the military force and the costs to society, immediately and over time. The most obvious costs are money and manpower, and these must be estimated not only as they exist when a force is being formed, but also in costs to a society's overall and continued well being. For example, the force cannot take all the people who would be needed for the harvest or the maintenance of the economy, since both the force and society would starve; or else not all horses can be requisitioned, since the harvest would probably languish rotting in the fields; or indeed, even in total war not all factories can be devoted only to weapons manufacturing since the basic needs of society must be catered to if it is not to collapse. In short, the formation of a force must reflect a realistic balance of investment from available and future resources. This logic dictates that if people are cheap and horses dear the foot soldiers – the infantry – will predominate; if a population is small but comparatively rich the cavalry or artillery rather than the foot may dominate;

or if labour is expensive a standing force will be less well armed, since the price of arms production is high.

All these considerations are still true today, when weapons are manufactured globally and are theoretically available to all: a force must represent the correct balance between the available and future resources of a state. For if the costs of manufacturing or purchasing the weapons and maintaining the force are so great as to become a burden that adversely affects the economy of the society, then at best the society fails to prosper and at worst the leaders have destroyed the very thing they sought to defend. We now tend to see this outcome as a mark of an under-developed society, and also of an undemocratic society, since people will always seek prosperity over military strength, unless their survival is under threat. Maintaining an expensive and large military machine can therefore be assured only in very rich democratic societies such as the US or else in those societies in which the population is under threat – either externally, as in democracies such as India or Israel, or else internally, as in despotic regimes such as North Korea or even Iran.

Like many other aspects of force, striking the balance of investment has exercised kings, princes and governments since time began. Various measures have been tried more or less successfully to manage the dilemma. The more technical arms, for example the artillery or the warships, were held centrally by the monarch, since they were very expensive and had no commercial use and therefore it was not possible to take them up from trade or enter into some contractual relationship with the private citizen. No less, kings did not want powerful weapons or vessels to get into the wrong hands. Equally, however, the balance of investment must always reflect the basic structure of a society. Even if assets can be bought in, the core logic of a force is based on the people and place from which it comes: a land-locked country will not usually have a navy; a poor country will have fewer arms than a rich one; a populous state will have a larger army than a less populated one.

In deciding on the balance of investment governments have always been careful to differentiate between defence and security – as noted, the perennial purposes for which forces exist. In essence, the balance has usually been struck at the point in which peace is cheapest to maintain or attain. This point is found by including in defence only those items that are absolutely necessary to the existence of the entity or the state, leaving all else to be secured by a mixture of measures, military, diplomatic and economic. For example, Britain from the seventeenth century to the Second World War defended the British Isles and its maritime trade by maintaining a strong navy. Its army and at the very end its air force was kept at the minimum to secure the Empire, it being judged that in a time of crisis the navy could prevent the loss of the kingdom for long enough for a suitable army to be formed. It was for that reason that the British standing army was – and still is – traditionally small. This military strategy was then complemented by other measures: diplomacy was centred on maintaining a balance of power in Europe such that no single state dominated the north coast of Europe and should it come to war there would be an ally on the continent. This defence and security policy, to give its modern name, worked pretty well barring a number of glaring episodes: in the American War of Independence Britain lost its American empire, in part because the threat from France demanded the navy's priority; in the Napoleonic Wars, when it took nearly ten years for the direct threat of invasion to be destroyed at Trafalgar and another ten for Napoleon to be defeated – during which time Britain was never able to raise and sustain an army big enough to open more than a secondary front; the Crimean and Boer Wars both found the army lacking, with victories bought in campaigns marked by spectacular failures before lessons were learned, followed by military reforms; and it took from 1914 to 1917 for Britain to raise the army that won the First World War. But Britain is just one example. Now that the certainties of the monolithic threat of the Warsaw Pact are over, all European states – including those of the Warsaw Pact – face a similar dilemma.

Our history books reflect common features in the development of almost all armed forces. For example, armies are, or were, divided into foot, horse and guns, they have 'siege trains', and 'commissariats'. Navies have developed lighter scouting and escort vessels together with ever bigger battleships, and air forces have fighter and bomber forces. Navies and air forces are equipment driven: they are organized and evolve as their equipment demands and technology dictates. The organization of armies, on the other hand, tends to reflect the geography and nature of the societies from which they are drawn. For example, the Mongol Horde and the Boer Commando were the forces they were – exceedingly effective mounted infantry – because both were drawn from societies that lived in secluded small groups on the open plains, dependent on their horses and their skill with bow and rifle, respectively. The same can be seen with armies today, drawn as they are from their societies and reflecting their strengths and weaknesses. The higher educational levels of the west European armies, the expectations of their societies as to how soldiers should be treated and employed, all dictate the nature and operating method of those forces. At the risk of a gross generalization, they are technologically dependent, require considerable resources to keep them in the field comfortably, and their political masters tend to not be prepared to risk them.

The balance between the various components of a force and between the three services – land, sea and air – will either dictate how best to employ the force, or else reflect that a commander has decided how he wants to fight and has designed his force accordingly. On the whole, most standing forces are formed in anticipation of being used in defence and therefore it is the former case, of best employing the force as it stands, that applies. This is especially true in our current circumstances, when most major Western and former Soviet militaries are still configured for the now defunct concept of defence from the Cold War, and hence need to be constantly adapted for the new perceptions of threat, such as terrorism, and for the operations of war amongst the people into which they are sent repeatedly.

It is to the standing force of a state or a nation that the strategic commander will therefore most often have recourse for the creation of a specific force to undertake an operation. These are the means of applying force. The strategy derived from the political decision to go to conflict should provide the end to which it is to be applied, whilst the commander must devise the way. These three elements of ends, ways and means are eternal to the use of force, and if they are not clearly defined, and the balance between them correctly struck, there is very little chance of success in any military operation – a matter to which I will return throughout this book in one way or another.

*

There are five critical factors when handling a force at the strategic and operational levels, regardless of whether it is for defence or security, big or small, relying on catapults or computer-guided missiles:

- **Forming** The physical creation of a force: the actual amassment of troops and materiel into a coherent structure. Even within standing forces, but especially in multinational endeavours, an actual force has to be created to serve the specific purpose of an operation. Apart from doing this continuously to maintain NATO's Balkan operations, I was the first NATO DSACEUR specifically designated as commander of the nascent EU force decided on by the political level in St Malo in 1998. This meant working with the EU High Representative Javier Solana, NATO and the nations to produce a viable European capability, engaging each and every Chief of Defence in Europe in order to get a commitment for men and materiel.
- **Deploying** The movement and placement of the force to the theatre of operations in readiness for immediate action.
- **Directing** The overall element that covers all others: the ability to have an overview and decision powers over all aspects of the fight; in other words, the ability to use the force to decide the political and military outcome of the campaign. As a negative example, it is quite clear that the UN may be able to do one or more of the other elements, but it cannot direct a force at any level, which is why it cannot be considered a serious military option in time of need.
- **Sustaining** I have said in many lectures at staff colleges, 'Don't start a battle you can't supply'. In the US Civil War the Confederates took on the North without having a sufficient industrial base to sustain their war. When the North realized it could out-produce the South it began to conduct what became the first industrial war. Sherman's March was a deep attack to destroy the capacity of the South to sustain the fight.
- **Recovering**. There should be an old adage that says: Don't send out a force you can't get back. The ability to return a force is integral to its successful use – though it must be emphasized that the decision to return the force always lies with the political level, even

if all military objectives have been successfully attained. And whilst it is the direct opposite of generating and employing a force, its recovery is no less important since it implies finishing a job and thereby either leaving at a successful end or else finding a replacement. It is precisely the problem the US and the UK faced in Iraq in 2003 having declared victory, since neither was able to leave without dire consequences, as there were no apparent replacements. The force was therefore stuck. In this they were not unlike the Crusaders, who went to relieve the Holy Land and ended up occupying it – or indeed Israel in 1967, which sought to relieve the pressure upon it by taking the West Bank and Gaza from Jordan and Egypt and has since ended up occupying the territories with their Palestinian populations.

Within these five functions the event known as a war or an operation will take place, with the actual action apparent mostly at the two levels below the political and strategic: the theatre and the tactical. Indeed, these five elements are true to any military force that has ever been created. As noted, they are applicable to any size of force – but at the same time it is important to note that size must not be confused with available forces to manoeuvre, nor the size of force that may be manoeuvred. There may be 20,000 troops in a force, for example, but that does not mean they can be used as a whole. A multinational force reflects this issue in its worst extreme: each national contingent, to a greater or lesser extent, will have its own supporting tail, duplicating in many cases those of other contingents, thereby making the 'tooth to tail' ratio for the same number of men less efficient than that of a purely national force. In addition, each contingent can usually only conduct its own tactical engagement, meaning the overall force commander has to manoeuvre his force as a collection of smaller national groupings rather than a single coherent force. As an example, if the contingents are of battalion strength, and they are found from three nations, the force commander must manoeuvre and fight his force as three separate battalion engagements instead of fighting them as a brigade – which he could do if they were all from the same nation. It is important to understand this, both for its organizational impact and particularly because it dictates the maximum size a tactical objective can be. Following on the above example, therefore, the force commander can be confident of attacking only objectives that can be won by a battalion, whilst in comparison the national force commander can select targets that can be won by a brigade.

Since the end of the Cold War force has been used time and again, yet failed to achieve the result expected: it has been misapplied, whilst in other cases leaders have shrunk from applying it because they could not see its utility. All the while they have intended to achieve a decisive victory which would resolve the problem they faced, usually political. As I write we are conducting a so-called War on Terror – one intended to deliver a decisive victory over terror according to the leaderships who declared it – but by the end of this book I hope to have shown that this is a statement without useful meaning, at least in terms of describing the conduct of this confrontation. It is one in which the terrorist is demonstrating a better understanding of the utility of force in serving his political purpose than those who are opposed to him – both political leaders and military establishments. This has also been the case in other interventions of the past fifteen years, such as the US in Somalia in 1993 or the UN in the Balkans throughout 1991–5. It is probably without useful meaning to suggest such situations can forever be avoided – but I do believe it is possible to apply force to a far greater purpose in our modern circumstances than is currently the case. This is the final purpose of the detailed investigation I offer here into the utility of force.

Military fights are brutal because force is applied by military forces armed with lethal weapons. When unleashed, they will kill and destroy. That is what they are trained to do – and that is actually what we, civil society, ask of them. However, this is an unspoken contract, which is encased within the clear frameworks of war and peace that have evolved over the ages, but most especially in the past two centuries. And the fact these no longer suit the reality in which we live does not stop us from rearranging reality into the frameworks we know.

The paradigms of war are of great importance because they are the structures, conceptual and factual, through which force is applied, whilst military forces are the means with which force is applied. Our bane today is a conception of force and formulated forces within the paradigm of interstate industrial war, whilst our conflicts are those of the paradigm of war amongst the people. What follows is therefore a discussion of both – reaching into the past in order to explain the present and the future. Starting from Napoleon it explains the evolution of the paradigm of interstate industrial war, the long shift in paradigm between 1945 and 1989, the new paradigm of war amongst the people since 1991 to the present and, finally, prospects for the future.

The major conflicts and developments of the past 200 years are the context for our understanding of the utility of force. However, as I noted right at the start, force and its uses are eternal. Armed conflict is a human condition, and I do not doubt we will continue to reinvent it from generation to generation. It is highly unlikely we will ever totally remove it. This being the case, in order to defend and secure ourselves better, we must improve the utility of our force.

PART ONE

Interstate Industrial War

I

Foundation: From Napoleon to Clausewitz

Our understanding of military forces, military operations and wars stems from the nineteenth century, when the paradigm of interstate industrial war was forged. The Napoleonic Wars were its starting point, and it evolved throughout the century as its two crucial elements came into being and matured: states and industry. The American Civil War, the German wars of unification, and finally the two world wars of the twentieth century all contributed, amongst other events, to the military development of the paradigm, each in its way. I am not a professional historian, but I am a student of history, and have often used writings of and about the past not just to learn and understand how issues were handled in times past but also to test my own ideas about how to handle the matters I faced when in command and in the field. The study of history will tell you why you and your adversary are where you are now: it will establish in broad political terms the context in which both of you will take the decisions that lead you into the future. This study begins with establishing the chronology of events so as to understand the 'march of time' and to recognize cause and effect. Once one understands these facts one can begin to comprehend the decisions taken by the various actors, not necessarily to judge them but to understand why they were taken, in those circumstances and at that time. This is how one can begin to understand the story, 'His Story', that each of us individually and in our social groups carries in our head as the context for the decisions we take in the present.

Our subject here is the history of force, which must start with basic structures: the military structures that apply force. The point of departure is the last decade of the eighteenth century, as the French Revolution moved France from a violent mess towards the early if violent workings of a citizen state. From this movement was born what we recognize to this day as modern military forces, largely through the leadership of one man: Napoleon. On the whole our armies, navies and air forces – for in essence air forces as military entities were in one way or another spawned from the other two services – still carry much of the structure and organization Napoleon created when he remodelled the armies of France and set out to conquer Europe. His flair and boldness in the face of convention was remarkable. Indeed, in a period marked by rigidity of thought and operations, Napoleon's use of force was very innovative: he positively gloried in organizational mobility and operational flexibility – and in combining these two fluid concepts with the contrasting ones of mass and heavy weapons. However, it was in the way he formed and used his armies within a new strategic model that his great victories were won: his understanding of the utility of force was supreme.

To understand Napoleon's innovations, their durability and relevance to our use of force, it is best to start with the birth of the citizen army which provided both the sheer bulk necessary for his strategies and the new model of manpower: national soldiers. No longer were these serfs in uniform fighting for the king; these were French patriots fighting for the glory of France. Napoleon did not initiate this innovation, since the concept of conscription as universal military service in time of need may be traced back to ancient Egypt, whilst the idea that the citizen had a duty to the state to serve as a soldier was a product of the ideas of *liberté, égalité and fraternité* that underpinned the French Revolution. All and everyone joined together as French citizens, for each other and for the glory of France. In military terms this allowed the introduction of the *levée en masse*, which effectively means conscription, the new French citizen having a duty to defend the state. The first *levée* of 300,000 men – called to defend the homeland against the threat of foreign and émigré invasion – was in 1793, the year Napoleon was promoted to general. During the revolutionary wars the proportion of annual *levées* varied according to circumstances and military needs, but was largely a back-up to the voluntary recruitment process of the period. This, however, soon showed its limits, especially as Napoleon commenced on his Italian wars. As a result the Directory voted the Jourdan-Delbrel law on 5 September 1798, which mandated all Frenchmen aged between twenty and twenty-five years to undertake a period of military service. The law was based on Article 9 of the 1795 Constitution of the citizen's duties, which stipulated that each and every citizen owed his services to the homeland and to the protection of liberty, equality and property. It was the official birth of the citizens' army.

It was Napoleon who realized the immense potential inherent in the *levées* as a steady source of manpower, and it was therefore he who regulated the system and made sure it became a fixture of national life. On 29 December 1804, as Emperor of France, he passed a decree detailing the process of conscription throughout the French *départements*. From then on the annual number of conscripts was decided on a yearly basis by Senate decree, and the civil and military authorities of the 130 *départements* were responsible for drawing up lists and recruiting fixed numbers of conscripts, for a fixed period of time. It was this system that ensured a steady volume of manpower to the army – and it was this system, with many changes and variations, that was the framework within which conscription remained a fixture of life in France more or less constantly until it was officially suspended by President Chirac in 2001, nearly two centuries later. The military planner of today would recognize it as the basis of any modern conscription system – yet for the time it was an absolute revolution: establishing and maintaining a standing army not through money, or duty to a lord, or penal servitude, or professional qualifications, but rather through universal service on the basis of citizenship and gender.

The annual *levées* provided the backbone of Napoleon's Grande Armée: between 1800 and 1814 an estimated 2 million men were recruited through them to serve under the French flag. This was a colossal number, a force unprecedented in human history – yet it still reflected the potential rather than the absolute power of conscription since the impressive total still represented only about 36 per cent of eligible conscripts from the relevant age group and 7 per cent of the total population; it was indeed but the testing ground of the new paradigm of war. A hundred years later during the First World War, in 1914–1918, at the apex of the paradigm, France raised 8 million soldiers through conscription, representing 20 per cent of the population. This comparison also reflects upon another issue, that of mass. Both figures reflect mass in the sense of bulk or very large numbers; however, this word is also used by the military to denote a concentration or density of forces relative to the opponent. For example, one would say of a commander: he massed his artillery, all twenty pieces, on the main axis of his attack, thereby achieving an overwhelming barrage in support of the initial attack. Napoleon himself used mass in both senses – being the first to create a mass army in modern times, yet throughout his battles he amassed his forces in various ways to achieve victory in battle. As industrial war evolved and became pervasive, the duality increased – since armies became a matter of mass that could then be amassed in density. Understanding the dual meaning of mass in industrial war is therefore an important measure for understanding the application and utility of force within it.

Though Napoleon focused on mass, it would be wrong to suggest he was interested only in the quantity of soldiers for his campaigns. He understood that this bulk of manpower also needed to be willing; that the popularity of the fight was crucial to its success – and he therefore took great care to nourish the idea and image of the fighting patriot, with rousing speeches and great gestures of sharing and solicitude. As he once put it: an emperor confides in national soldiers, not in mercenaries. Many commanders before him had cared deeply for their soldiers and shared their destiny, but Napoleon was probably the first to present his vision to them as a joint national venture in which they all had an equal part as citizens. Indeed, he had respect for his soldiers, both rank-and-file and officers, and shared with them his plans and visions before making demands upon them. For example, in 1805, on the eve of the battle of Austerlitz, Napoleon rode over fifty kilometres, much of the time along the ranks of his army, tiring out horses and staff to inform his troops of the next day's battle plan. This direct show of leadership, the setting of each man's goal as equal to his own, and the show of confidence ensured a high morale, and undoubtedly contributed to their success in the battle.

*

It would take many years for mass conscription to spread throughout Europe as a patriotic expression of duty and allegiance to a state – largely because it is a measure dependent on a citizen state, and these were only to develop across the continent in the wake of the Napoleonic Wars. In the meantime, the *levées* allowed Napoleon to conscript large armies and to continue to do so for nearly twenty years, which meant he could risk losing an army, or at least substantial numbers of men, in a single decisive strategic action, without necessarily contemplating defeat. His opponents of the *ancien régime* were in no such position, with armies made up of men well described by the Duke of Wellington: 'People talk of their enlisting from their fine military feeling – all stuff – no such thing. Some of our men enlist from having got bastard children – some for minor offences – many more for drink.' Moreover, without conscription these men were not available in a steady stream, nor could they be rapidly replenished if lost. For Napoleon's enemies, therefore, to lose the army in a battle was to lose the war. In his manpower Napoleon had a major strategic advantage – which he complemented with a second: firepower. Napoleon, an artilleryman by training and early experience, understood the power of the guns – he is reputed to have said that God is on the side with the best artillery – and as far as his industrial and scientific base would permit, he developed an impressive artillery arm. The numerical, and to an extent technological advantage of these pieces was, according to contemporary accounts, put to awe-inspiring and literally awful effect. He usually massed his guns into a 'grand battery' on the axis of his attack, and used their power to batter a path into his enemies' defence for his assaulting infantry columns. Apart from the destructive effect of their fire, the psychological effects of being exposed to this lethal punishment without being able to respond tested his opponents' leadership, morale and discipline – on occasion to breaking point. It is a measure of the respect the British had for the French artillery that whenever possible Wellington deployed on a reverse slope, the one out of sight, or had his infantry lie down – as he did with the Guards at Waterloo.

Napoleon never explicitly defined in writing a precise strategic vision of war or military operations, though he did leave his *Maxims*, which include ideas that have now become basic, such as 'The passage

from the defensive to the offensive is one of the most delicate operations of war' or 'March divided, fight united'. His was a practical
rather than a theoretical type of military genius, and it focused upon
one basic precept: decisive destruction of an opposing force. With his
mass manpower and early industrial firepower, Napoleon implemented this precept through his innovative use of force: attacking the
enemy's main strength directly; closing with and destroying an opponent's main force in the field. As a general rule the strategic military
aims of the wars of the previous century had not been of such a decisive nature, if for no other reason than that the forces were similarly
matched and, as noted, no side wanted to risk losing theirs in totality
since it would take years and vast sums to rebuild and replace them.
These were known as 'wars of manoeuvre' in which commanders
sought to achieve positions of advantage with limited forces and logistic support, in order ultimately to serve negotiations. Napoleon
utterly changed this approach to war. As he noted in his *Maxims*, his
goal was to destroy enemy equilibrium through a 'careful balancing
of means and results, efforts and obstacles'. He saw the central objective as the annihilation of field forces, and deemed this sufficient to
break the enemy's will to resist; the rest was of a secondary nature.

The victories of Napoleon's army were the result of this conceptual
shift, which was startlingly new and for many years enabled him to
achieve rapid victories. Speed and flexibility were at the core of his
campaigns; but most significantly, Napoleon planned his campaigns
as a whole: planning, marching and fighting were connecting
parts of the whole. To him the approach to the battle was integral to
the battle itself, rather than it being a necessary but separate activity
that preceded the engagement, as was the prevailing convention.
'Approach' is to be understood here as both the planning process leading to the battle and the setting of the context for the battle, which
would include such activities as an intelligence operation, diplomacy,
and political and economic measures. This period of 'approach' often
lasted months, as all possibilities to reach the ideal battle situation
were weighed against each other – followed by the actual physical
movement towards the battle. In order to realize this overall approach
in practical terms his forces had to be organized to move quickly and
in a way that did not indicate their intentions. This is one of

Napoleon's greatest achievements, one which I have called 'organizational mobility', implemented through the introduction of another, significant innovation: the *corps d'armée*, an all-arms miniature army in itself, which could operate independently from other corps and would join with them only to fight the battle. Since the Grande Armée was sufficiently large to be able to fight simultaneous campaigns in different theatres of war, Napoleon would make the strategic allocation of forces to each theatre, and it was the army in each that was then subdivided into corps. Each of these then subdivided into divisions and brigades.

Since the *corps d'armée* and the use Napoleon made of this idea were crucial to his armies' success, it is worth explaining them further. The seventeenth- and eighteenth-century armies were composed of infantry, cavalry and artillery troops, or foot, horse and guns, as they are known in the business. And while they were organized into units, such as regiments and battalions, and then grouped into divisions and brigades, the force as a whole moved and was fought as a single entity. The subordinate commanders had relatively little latitude or freedom of action. Napoleon took this whole entity and, to use the modern jargon, task organized it: each corps was composed of foot, horse and guns – one or several infantry divisions, plus cavalry, artillery and baggage trains, ambulances, and any other or all the elements of a military force as necessary. A corps was made up of an appropriate mix suitable for the specific mission at hand, and large enough to stand an engagement until help arrived from another corps. And precisely for this reason, no corps was ever more than a day's march from another. Napoleon summarized the corps' role in a letter to his stepson Eugène de Beauharnais, himself a general, by explaining that a *corps d'armée* of 25–30,000 men could remain isolated:

Commanded by a good officer, it can choose to engage in battle or avoid it, and can manoeuvre according to circumstances without endangering itself, because it cannot be forced into an engagement, and can therefore also withstand fighting on its own for a long period of time. Well led, the *corps d'armée* must always be warned of an enemy approach and must never agree to be forced into combat by a larger enemy army. The corps commander must always be at the avant-garde of his unit to direct the engagement, and should never delegate this responsibility. He is the only one to know of the commander-in-chief's intentions, the position of the other army corps and the relief he can expect from every one of them, and the moment when the army will be able to reunite in order to fight a battle.

This is a most interesting description, which reflects a *corps d'armée* that was not small – on numbers alone the present British army could produce approximately three. And it is worth noting how important Napoleon considered the commander to be; how he had to be in the correct place to make decisions, including crucial ones such as whether to actually fight or not.

The Napoleonic corps would advance on a number of separate routes, which made for faster movement overall – rather like adding new motorways and back routes to the same destination – as opposed to the conventional practice, still used by his opponents, of keeping the army together and marching on a single route or along a single axis. By 'marching divided', sending off corps on different roads, Napoleon increased their ability to 'march on their stomachs' by living off the land, there being fewer people foraging on any one route, with the consequent reduction in logistic and supply units in each corps. In fact, Napoleon was to a large extent making a virtue out of a necessity: given his huge armies and the distances they travelled, lengthy convoys of supplies would have been both expensive and impractical. However, his enemies were exactly thus encumbered – and since each of them was structured as a single fighting entity, none could break up and march on several routes without risk of being attacked by Napoleon's corps, each of which had all the necessary fighting elements. Moreover, since these armies were relatively large they could not rely only on foraging en route, and therefore had large supply units running long lines of communications, carrying vast quantities of rations. By comparison, Napoleon's armies sustained supply lines only for munitions and senior officers' personal requirements, and carried relatively few rations. The army that marched to the Danube in 1809, for example, set out with only eight days' rations. The combination of these organizational measures gave Napoleon speed relative to his opponent – which is the measure of organizational mobility.

The choice of routes on which Napoleon's corps advanced to battle was carefully calculated beforehand and coordinated in execution, the object being to confuse the enemy as to the true aim or target, to force him in this way to show his hand, and to seize an opportunity when it presented itself. Overall, the marching corps usually imparted the impression of disunity, but in reality the entire army was carefully dispersed along a single line of operations in one or other of a number of meticulously devised formations, of which the most usual was the '*bataillon carré*' or square, ready for rapid 'concentration' within the space of one or two days once attainment of the desired battle situation seemed possible. A line of operations describes in broad terms, often spatially, the direction and focus of a force's collective effort towards an operational objective, whilst a number of routes may serve a single line of operations, and are allocated to specific formations. Perhaps the best example of the two in action was at Jena, where the Prussian army was destroyed in 1806. Seeing the opportunity of achieving his operational objective, and having defined his line of operations, Napoleon moved and concentrated his army along a number of routes at twice the speed anticipated by the Prussians and forced them into battle a day earlier than they expected. As a result they were destroyed in detail: a crushing example of his operational use of speed and therefore his maxim, 'March divided, fight united'.

The very idea of the *corps d'armée* allowed Napoleon the organizational mobility to implement the maxim, since these self-contained and more or less independent formations allowed him an unprecedented level of operational flexibility. Variations in the width and depth of deployments illustrate this. At the beginning of a campaign the front would usually resemble a long cordon, though not apparently a continuous one. In September 1805, for example, the Grande Armée facing the third coalition covered a 200-kilometre front between Strasbourg and Würzburg; in 1812 the 600,000-strong Grande Armée stretched more than 400 kilometres along the Vistula river. Once an advance began a screen of light cavalry would protect and disguise operations. As campaigns progressed the deployment would shrink or expand, in order to tackle natural obstacles or to confuse the enemy. At the same time, the composition of the major formations was adjusted, whether to fulfil immediate needs, or in order to deceive the enemy; during a campaign the commander in theatre could create a new brigade, add or move a division or even create a new *corps d'armée*. As Austrian intelligence discovered in Austerlitz in 1805, these last-minute structural changes proved very difficult to follow, since in the space of a few days any information collected could be invalidated by further sudden change.

As the corps moved closer to the opposing force, they would concentrate at an increasing pace. Marches were crucial to this end, and indeed integral to Napoleon's concept of war. As he noted in 1809, 'I have destroyed the enemy merely by marches.' Examples of epic marches abound: in 1805 General Davout drove the leading division of the third corps from Vienna to Austerlitz, a distance of 140 kilometres, in two days. Allowing a little time for sleep this means his laden men and horses maintained a speed of four to five kilometres an hour over poor roads for two days. A decade earlier, in 1796, during the first Italian campaign, General Augereau marched his division over a distance of eighty kilometres in thirty-six hours to reach the field of Castiglione in time to help defeat Wurmser's Austrian troops. Or indeed at Jena, in 1806, Napoleon had his troops at a distance considered two days' march away from the Prussians – but as noted, in order to surprise them he ordered his army on a forced march over a single night, and thereby gained a definitive advantage and decisive victory.

Throughout these endeavours we can see Napoleon's emphasis upon flexibility and organizational mobility – which is why he favoured lighter, dispersed armies, since they could assemble quickly and march rapidly – and also the degree to which it rested upon his marshals (chief generals) and officers, those who led beneath him. Rather like him, they were mostly drawn from the people rather than the aristocracy, and selected to a large degree on merit. Indeed, to the extent understood in the societies of the time, they were professional. In this way Napoleon created an army with a high and enduring morale, proud of its professionalism and prowess, confident in itself and its leader, and organized and trained to fight as he intended. He attended personally to the overall campaign plan, often going into considerable detail. In implementation, he gave his subordinates considerable freedom to take advantage of his organizational innovations

– and at the same time he maintained overall direction, collecting the information from the field of action by special liaison officer so as to reallocate priorities, forces and resources accordingly. Since his opponents, especially for the first fifteen years of his campaigns, were still operating within rigid conventions of organization and structure, including strict hierarchical command and control by a prince or duke, Napoleon's modus operandi was literally stunning.

A significant part of Napoleon's genius lay in his distinction between the use of force and the utility of force – and his ability to put the former at the service of the latter. The structural and conceptual changes he introduced in the use of force – uniting in one single exercise the approach, the march, the manoeuvre and the battle, based on the flexibility of the *corps d'armée* system – therefore also gave his forces new utility within his overall strategic aim: to achieve the political objective by a single crushing military act. As should be obvious by now, this was not the way in the preceding two centuries, when wars were a separate but linked part of continuing diplomacy, and were therefore not intended to achieve a decisive end. Seen within the broader context of what is known as the balance of power, if wars were resorted to, they were conducted within the clear strategic aim and understanding that everyone's power was to be preserved, at one level or another. Rulers and states remained intact even if land was sometimes ceded. Napoleon completely refuted this premise. His strategic political aim was precisely to change rulers and states, largely in order to make them part of his empire. His genius lay in marrying the military means he created and the method he devised of using them to achieve the end: the decisive defeat of the enemy force. This usually wrought the desired strategic defeat, even if rulers remained nominally in place, as with Prussia after Jena where the king remained in situ, but as ruler of a client state. Conversely, the decisive defeat of the Russians at Friedland in 1807 led to the Treaty of Tilsit in which the two became allies. This achieved a balance on Napoleon's eastern borders, but this was not sufficient for him: Russia remained a threat and he still found it necessary to seek the strategic decision in 1812.

Napoleon succeeded in his strategy for nearly twenty years, until he himself was militarily and politically annihilated. In so doing, he redefined the strategic aim of war. It was he who decreed that the first duty of the strategist is to select the aim of the military force in support of, and in order to realize, the political purpose. Napoleon appreciated this maxim fully, first of all by understanding that conscription allowed him to lose large numbers of men – a division, a corps or even two or three – and still remain viable. But conscription purely in the sense of manpower was not enough – technically his enemies could have built bigger armies, and as the wars proceeded many of them did; nor was even the creation and use of the mass manpower in the *corps d'armée* sufficient. Rather it was conscription as the reflection of a new state, the conscription of citizens and patriots, which was the decisive difference, since it meant that the whole state and its machinery were mobilized: he could now engage the opponent's main force directly with a high probability of success, and by comprehensively and rapidly destroying his ability to resist would break his will to continue the struggle. This he usually did, and the exceptions proved to be his undoing: his opponents did not comply with his strategic use of force.

Napoleon's armies failed in Spain because the Spanish will to resist was not broken and the guerrilla war ensued. Indeed, this long struggle was the start of that which I define as the 'antithesis' to the paradigm of interstate industrial war – an important model in itself which will be discussed in Part II. The British took this opportunity to open a continental theatre and reinforced their Portuguese and Spanish allies. Throughout the whole of the Peninsular campaign Wellington carefully handled his British and Portuguese army by trading space and time – conceding territory and refusing battle except on his terms – so as to avoid being drawn into the decisive engagement Napoleon's forces sought until it suited him. The Russians likewise refused the decisive battle in 1812, preferring to trade Moscow for their army, which in turn harried Napoleon's retreating forces into a catastrophic defeat. And throughout the Napoleonic Wars Britain, safe behind its maritime shield, could not be brought to a decisive battle unless Napoleon gained maritime superiority, which the British victory at Trafalgar ensured he never did. Each of these cases also proved that the Napoleonic, and subsequently the industrial way of war depends on constant access to all the resources of the state, and becomes increasingly difficult to conduct as resources become reduced. After Trafalgar the British blockade of the continent slowly eroded France's ability to sustain its wars since it could not supply them. This situation, coupled with the Peninsular War that came to be termed by Napoleon as a 'running sore' that bled his armies, was terminally aggravated by the defeat of 1812. For it was after the retreat from Russia that Napoleon found he could no longer sustain his 'manpower production', or conscription, since the number of men available through the *levées* was not sufficient. And as his resources waned, so he was driven back west of the Rhine and forced to sue for peace.

The sea and the steppes provided the strategic space to refuse the Napoleonic battle at operational level in the same way that the rugged theatre of the Iberian peninsula allowed the guerrillas and Wellington, each in their way, to manoeuvre tactically – and in a manner superior to Napoleon's forces. These failures were for two major reasons. First, Napoleon was the political leader and strategic commander of his armies; he was also usually the theatre commander and often for the major battles the senior tactical commander. However, he could not discharge all these roles simultaneously, especially in Spain and at sea, and those who were replacing him in command were not of his standing: there was only one Napoleon. Second, there were operational reasons for the failures. Napoleon's use of force was not equally effective at all levels of war; he had a mass army, but even divided into corps his tactics were not always effective. It is important not to confuse the way an army fights, its tactics and firepower, with its organization. The two are separate though closely related issues. Ideally, the organization must suit the tactics or alternatively the tactics must suit the organization. Factors such as communications, supply, suitable leaders and, at a higher level, multinational forces – such as the coalitions formed against Napoleon – often require the tactics to suit the organization. Tactics and firepower are also separate but closely related: firepower is in the possession of a force and it has measurable characteristics, such as explosive and kinetic effects, quantity, rapidity, rate, range and trajectory. Tactics is the application of firepower – by means of procedures and drills in manoeuvre decided by the commander – that lowers the opponent's guard and destroys him on the battlefield. The tactical engagement is the heart of the battle. Given his victories, it is clear Napoleon was an adroit tactician no less than a strategist. None the less, in an investigation into his overall use of force it is important to understand his flaws. Napoleon's innovations gave him the advantage at the operational level, but the British could beat his forces at the tactical level: where Napoleon understood mass, the British understood firepower.

In the days of the musket there was an understandable tendency to believe that the number of men in the ranks was a measure of the available firepower – that masses of men equalled masses of fire. However, for masses of men to produce effective fire there is a need for a decision, in the midst of battle, as to timing, quantity and the target of the fire. It is because all decisions are taken and implemented under fire that there is a need for the force to have undergone appropriate drills and procedures – a necessity true to this day, regardless of the number of men. Without these drills and procedures commanders will fail to move their commands fast enough in relation to the enemy to bring effective fire to bear and thus retain the initiative – in other words, be the ones dictating events. This is one of the most basic and eternal characteristics of an army at a tactical level. When we watch a formal parade, such as a Trooping of the Colour, we are watching the rehearsal of the battle drills of the Wellingtonian army. Through these impressive manoeuvres of great blocks of men marching we can see even today the facility with which a large number of men can be moved in and out of line. If one imagines the troops were to use the arms with which they march – though not the automatic rifles of today, rather the muskets of the past – it is possible to understand the effect of volleys of infantry fire. For the greatest sustainable firepower absent automatic weapons can be obtained by deploying the troops in a line of two ranks (two parallel lines), each rank firing in turn: the first kneels and loads whilst the second fires on command; whilst the second is loading the first fires on command, and so on. It is a continuous barrage, in which the sum of the individual projectiles is massed into a powerful force. The tactic is well recreated in the classic 1960s film *Zulu*, about an attack on a colonial outpost in Africa in the 1890s. Wave after wave of Zulus are mown down by two ranks of infantrymen firing on command. As a result, their outpost is saved: a tactical victory.

So although Napoleon's innovations gave him the advantage at theatre level or on campaign, his armies were less effective at the tactical level since he could not always translate his mass of men into an effective mass of firepower. Indeed, in most encounters the British forces had the edge: the Wellingtonian drill was undoubtedly superior. Achieving this edge took time and Britain never produced an army big enough to take on the French without support. Nevertheless, in the Peninsular Wars and at Waterloo the British army and its allies under British command were able to win the tactical battle, since at that level the British had superior organizational mobility. To understand fully the value of this superiority in the tactical battle it is necessary to understand two other concepts: width/depth and dispersion/concentration. A commander can deploy a force in two ways: in width or in depth, sometimes referred to as in line or in column. With width he gains the greatest sight of the enemy, can bring fire to bear over the greatest area and has the greatest number of opportunities to attack the enemy. Against this, however, his line is much easier to penetrate at any given point, it is difficult to control and he cannot reinforce success easily. With depth he has the reverse of these advantages and disadvantages. A concentrated force is strong at the point of concentration, and is easy to command and supply; however, it is difficult to move, is a single target, and cannot see what is happening elsewhere. Moreover, for the commander it is also difficult to choose the right place to concentrate. Once again dispersion has the reverse of these advantages and disadvantages. However, it is not the deployment of the force that matters, but the effect of its fire. For men armed with short-range direct-fire weapons, such as the musket or rifle, their deployment can be considered as representing the effect of their fire. But with weapons of greater range and capable of firing over greater obstacles, such as artillery, one must consider where the fire is to be effective, and then deploy accordingly. The capacity of artillery and similar weaponry to shift its effective fire from width to depth, from concentrating its mass on to a single target or to disperse its fire onto a number of them, at speed and without moving the gun line, is the great value of that arm to the tactician. Air forces are similarly important today to the theatre commander. Fortunately for his enemies, at the time of Napoleon, artillery was only just beginning to gain its modern characteristics, and air power was an unrealized dream. The essence of tactical skill is to be able to move rapidly from one to the other, from width to depth, and to disperse or concentrate as appropriate.

It should now be possible to understand the British tactical superiority over Napoleon's forces: they were organized and drilled to move on the battlefield in relatively small groups in comparison to the French. They could therefore move swiftly from line, where the maximum fire was achieved at the greatest rapidity by firing volleys, or from successive ranks to column to exploit a success or move elsewhere. They could concentrate in a square and produce a high density of fire or disperse in small detachments. And the flexibility was compounded by the small British army being very well drilled – which Napoleon's mass and willing conscript army was often not. Wellington favoured the tactics of forcing the French to attack him; as described above, he would use the ground to protect his force from the artillery. In so doing he was playing to the French use of mass: great columns of infantry would advance once the artillery were thought to have softened up the defence – only to be met by the volleys of the British infantry. In such circumstances massed firepower defeats massed manpower.

The Napoleonic battlefield movements I describe may seem simple and easy; in practice they were confusing, complex and lethal. General Chambray, a contemporary French observer, reflects this reality well:

The French charged with shouldered arms [i.e. not firing] as was their custom. When they arrived at short range, and the English line remained motionless, some hesitation was seen in the march. The officers and NCOs shouted at the soldiers, 'Forward; March; don't fire'. Some even cried, 'They're surrendering'. The forward movement was therefore resumed, but it was not until extremely close range of the English line that the latter started a two rank fire which carried destruction into the heart of the French line, stopped its movement, and produced some disorder. While the officers shouted to the soldiers 'Forward: Don't fire' (although firing set in nevertheless), the English suddenly stopped their own fire and charged with the bayonet. Everything was favourable to them; orderliness, impetus, and the resolution to fight with the bayonet. Among the French, on the other hand, there was no longer any impetus, but disorder and surprise caused by the enemy's unexpected resolve: flight was inevitable.

*

Napoleon's defeats were important, especially for an understanding of the use of force, but his victories over fifteen years were of much greater significance and were astounding by any measure. Moreover, even when finally defeated, Napoleon's military vision endured: his enemies ultimately all reformed their armies, and whether knowingly or unknowingly did so within the parameters he established. And this was necessary, since the armies facing the French had problems with both their officers and the ranks. The Prussians are an excellent example of this, and an important one, since their reforms within the Napoleonic model both refined it and created another innovation: their general staff.

Like many of the armies that faced the French, the Prussian army was composed of men thrown into the service and held in check by the fear induced through the power of fierce discipline, symbolized by the frequent use of the lash. The French conscript army also used fierce discipline – but it was not based on coercion by terror. Most of the other recruits to the Prussian army were foreigners, as the home population was deemed more useful tilling the land, working and paying the taxes that would enable the princes to raise such armies. In 1742, Frederick the Great decided that as a general rule, two-thirds of infantry battalions should be composed of foreigners, the remaining third being Prussians. As a result, most battalions were filled with deserters from foreign armies, prisoners of war, criminals and vagabonds, recruited through cunning, violence and the lure of gold. Only savage discipline could hold this heterogeneous mass of soldiers together, without which they would promptly desert. Indeed, desertion was the main concern of military leaders: Frederick II began his *General Principles on the Conduct of War*, written between 1748 and 1756, with fourteen rules to avoid desertion; tactical and strategic considerations often had to be subordinated to the need to prevent it. As a result, troops were formed in tight lines, scouting patrols were rarely used, and chasing a defeated enemy army was extremely difficult. Marching, let alone attacking by night, or establishing camps close to forests, had to be avoided. Soldiers were ordered to watch over their comrades for potential deserters, in times of peace as at war. Even civilians faced heavy penalties for failing to detain deserters and hand them in to the army.

Consider these troops in contrast to Napoleon's conscripts: troops provided constantly by law, troops willing to fight, troops who could therefore be trusted in any kind of march or manoeuvre. The difference was immeasurable – and it extended to the officer class too. As opposed to Napoleon's new professionals, the Prussians were still largely led by men defined by class rather than capability. Some were foreigners but most were aristocrats drawn from the ranks of the Prussian Junkers. In his writings, Frederick II repeatedly stated that commoners should not receive a commission since their minds tend to be turned towards profit rather than honour. But even families of noble blood were often reluctant to send their sons to the army: although a military career could in time prove to be both glorious and profitable, the academic level of most military schools was hardly superior to primary education. As a result, the average Prussian officer was rarely well educated – a situation which impacted upon the level of Prussian command.

The inadequacies of the Prussian army had already been exposed in the period 1792–5 when, as part of the first coalition, it encountered the then pre-Napoleonic French revolutionary army of mostly untrained volunteers, and lost. These initial losses led to the creation of a war college, the *Kriegsakademie*, for the study of military theory and practice, headed by one of the most significant reformers of the Prussian army, General Gerd von Scharnhorst. As an experienced soldier, he was already fascinated by these mostly untrained lowly conscript soldiers and unknown officers, often too of lowly origin, that fought so well and defeated the professional armies of Europe. He and other Prussian military reformers understood the operational flexibility resulting from the idea of the *corps d'armée* relatively quickly, but then came to realize this was not enough: there was a bigger issue at stake than military organization. It was Scharnhorst who sensed that in some unclear way it had to do with the new revolutionary state – that it was a political issue – which needed far more insight and comprehension than most officers possessed. To begin to broach this complicated matter Scharnhorst introduced liberal studies to the syllabus of the *Kriegsakademie*, which was an important step in itself, but one that did little to truly reform the army. This was not surprising, given the immensity of the task: the Prussian army was too big and too heavy, its columns like those of Austria and Russia marching only a few miles a day, their existence tied to thousands of cumbersome supply wagons. The army's tactics too were outdated: recruits were drilled in rigid and slow automated rhythms, in anticipation of a battlefield in which soldiers would deploy in stiff, inflexible lines before firing volleys against volleys fired from an enemy's equally stiff, inflexible lines. It was this army – facing Napoleon's more flexible tactics, mass, rapid movement with willing soldiers of high morale, and a focused strategy of decisive victory – that was vanquished at the battle of Jena in 1806. An impressive display of Napoleonic strategy, the battle is not well known – as is Waterloo, for example – which is ironic since it was the defining experience for a generation of Prussian officers, and especially, as we will see, for one Carl von Clausewitz.

Alarmed by the devastating French victories over Austria and Russia in 1805, Prussia mobilized for war in 1806, somewhat overconfident in its capabilities: both the nation and the army were ill prepared psychologically. Napoleon responded quickly, and his Grande Armée – in this case some 200,000 strong, organized in a number of corps and deployed *en carré* on a converging axis – began moving in early October. His aim was a decisive victory over King Frederick William of Prussia. From the start the campaign did not go well for the Prussian forces. Marshal Murat and Marshal Bernadotte's corps soon crossed the river Saale and forced General Tauenzien's division to fall back on General Prince Hohenlohe's army. Meanwhile, Marshal Lannes achieved a small but stunning victory at Saalfeld, defeating Prince Louis Ferdinand's corps, killing its commander and taking 10,000 prisoners. With Prussian morale already plummeting, on 10 October the army under Napoleon's command found Hohenlohe's rearguard occupying the Landgrafenberg plateau above the town of Jena. Napoleon decided to deploy Marshal Lannes' corps and the Imperial Guard on this plateau to hold down the enemy's centre. Marshal Augereau was sent on the right and Marshal Ney on the left to outflank the Prussians on both sides. Meanwhile, Marshal Davout's corps were sent marching north towards Apolda to complete the encirclement. Napoleon spent part of the night personally supervising the building of a mountain road, to bring troops and artillery pieces up to the plateau. At dawn, the French army was deployed to form a front a mile and a half long. As the dense fog cleared in mid-morning, Hohenlohe, who had believed he was fighting a flank guard, realized his mistake. From cover, the French soon started pounding his forces, which were concentrated on open ground, as he awaited reinforcements. In the early afternoon, Napoleon ordered the advance, committing his 40,000-strong reserve. Facing a gigantic advancing mass of 90,000 infantry and cavalry supported by artillery, Hohenlohe's troops fled. Before 4 p.m., the battle was over. Half of the French soldiers had not even fired a shot.

Napoleon was convinced he had achieved the decisive victory over the Prussians. In fact, Frederick William had departed the day before with 70,000 troops, heading towards the Magdeburg fortress. The real clash came when this army encountered Marshal Davout's isolated corps close to Auerstadt. Twenty-six thousand men strong, it only included some 1,500 cavalrymen and forty-four pieces of artillery. The first encounter with Prussian forces came when 600 of Blücher's cavalry – the same Blücher of subsequent Waterloo fame – galloped out of the fog. The Prussians then launched four successive cavalry charges, each 2,500 men strong. The French troops, who had formed in battalion squares, withstood the assaults. Division after division of Prussian troops were thus checked, and Davout was forced to commit his only reserve: a single regiment. Napoleon had judged the strength and organization of Davout's corps correctly. At noon, Frederick William decided to fall back in order to join up with Hohenlohe's army and resume fighting the next day. To his dismay, instead of an army, he was faced with a mass of fugitives fleeing the battlefield of Jena, which he had no option but to join. He left behind 3,000 prisoners, including Clausewitz, and 10,000 dead. Davout had held at bay a force three times the size of his own – for which Napoleon congratulated him but, imperial legend *oblige*, he ordered that henceforth the two battles would be remembered only as the battle of Jena.

The Prussians were comprehensively defeated because in his campaign Napoleon had approached them in a way from which they could not deduce his intentions in time to react to them. When the armies were in contact he moved faster than they expected and from directions they did not expect, so that when they did react they did so on the basis of a false understanding of the battlefield. Furthermore, their ponderous centralized procedures for command and the insistence that orders were to be obeyed to the letter meant that those closest to the French, who could see what was actually happening, were neither empowered to act nor sufficiently informed to act appropriately. This lesson is still greatly significant. In the 1991 Gulf War, when the armoured division I commanded was some eighteen hours into its attack into Iraq, my reconnaissance force reported Iraqi armour moving towards us. A little later, when weapons had been moved into range, these armoured units were destroyed. The prisoners we took told us they had been moving to counter-attack the breach we had made the day before in the obstacle of deep minefields along the Iraqi border about 100 kilometres away. As such, their commanders were reacting to an event that had happened some eighteen or twenty-four hours previously and 100 kilometres back.

The peace settlement came only in 1807 at Tilsit, signed on 25 June between Napoleon and the Tsar, ally of the defeated Prussian king, on a specially constructed raft anchored in the exact midstream of the river Niemen in East Prussia. In the settlement Prussia lost half its population and territory and effectively became a French satellite. In addition, the Prussian forces were constrained to no more than 42,000 men, with limits on the numbers allowed in each arm or service. Such diminishment and strictures were a further blow for the army, which was still stunned from its humiliating defeats at Jena and Auerstadt. None the less, it was through implementing these strictures that reform was achieved, to lasting effect: over years a different army came into being, with its new 'thinking soldier', the innovative idea of a general staff, and ultimately the theories of *On War*. These three linked together produced a doctrinal energy, and the nervous system to carry it, that would enable Prussia and then Germany to evolve through the following hundred years – and create a model of command that came to be emulated by many of the leading militaries in the world. This would establish an understanding of the organization and application of force that dominated the battlefield through two world wars – and possibly to this day. And it began with the painful reforms post Jena.

General Scharnhorst headed the endeavour, backed up by an impressive coterie of generals who realized the need for total reform:

of the army, of its officer class and of its operations. At a structural level, the Prussian reformers created six corps, following the French *corps d'armée* system. Each contained the three types of forces, artillery, infantry and cavalry, and each was organized in brigades some 6–7,000 strong. They then turned to the issues of men and arms. In order rapidly to increase the army's numerical strength without openly flaunting the 1807 treaty, the permitted complement of recruits was drafted and rigorously trained for a few months, then sent back home, ready to be called up in time of need – and the next full complement was then called up and trained likewise. This was another emulation of the French system, in this case conscription of physically able men – though with a distinct difference: this was not universal conscription nor, as will be discussed below, was this the conscription of willing patriots of a citizen state, since such a state did not yet exist in Prussia; rather, it was selective conscription for short-term service. As such the Prussians effectively redefined the purpose of conscription: Napoleon was using his *levées* to sustain his armies in wartime – the citizen was called up to replace the losses of war. The Prussians used conscription to create an army which was small in peacetime but which was also a machine to train men who returned to civil life as soldiers waiting for war – and who could therefore expand the army in time of need. A final change to the army structure was the suspension of the principle of promotion through age in an attempt to instil meritocracy in the ranks. Ability and professionalism became the defining attributes.

Armaments had been heavily depleted at Jena. Repair workshops were therefore created, the main manufacturer in Berlin was enlarged so as to produce 1,000 muskets per month, a new factory was established in Neisse and weapons were purchased from Austria. In three years more than 150,000 firearms became available. Field artillery pieces also needed to be replaced. The eight Prussian fortresses remaining after Tilsit furnished the material to build new ones and factories were reorganized to produce them. In three years the army had field artillery to support forces of 120,000 men. By 1809 the Prussian army had been completely reorganized and its rules, regulations and structure altered. By 1812 these changes enabled Prussia to field an army officially only 42,000 strong but which expanded within the space of a few months to a fully armed force of nearly 150,000. This new conscript army fought successfully in the final Napoleonic campaigns of 1813–15, and as a consequence its structure remained the model for Prussian and then German armies in the decades that followed.

The new Prussian army was a much more flexible and responsive organization than its predecessor. None the less, it had to be reformed within the Prussian state as it existed: an old-style monarchy. The reformers were therefore faced with a dilemma: how to fight a mass army, the French, driven by a national revolutionary ideology, if not with another mass army driven by another national revolutionary ideology? In order to raise such an army it was necessary to inspire and draw the people under arms – or, as the reformers put it, to elicit the 'endless forces not developed and not utilized [that] slumber in the bosom of a nation.'* Yet such a step could well lead to the democratization of the state and the destruction of the monarchical system through revolution. The officers in charge of remodelling the army were reformers, not revolutionaries, and wished to avoid such an outcome at all costs. This issue was to dog the Prussian military enterprise until a law of universal conscription was finally passed in the 1860s, as both a precursor to and part of the wars of German unification that ultimately produced a large state with a fully developed concept of nationality and nationalism, drawing men to patriotic service. In the interim, and especially in the post-Jena period of reforms, the reformers' attempted solution was to try to ally the traditional dynastic legitimacy of the Prussian king, which had been the driving force of the previous army, to a new emphasis on 'national legitimacy' or national pride. This had initially been created by a binding and collective dislike of France and Napoleon following the humiliating defeats – and was then strengthened by the Prussian victory at Leipzig in 1813. This national pride was an idea that the wider population could support and therefore willingly agree to give military service for. In this way it was possible to introduce conscription, even though it was not yet a citizen state. At the same time it was also possible to preserve the traditional social

---

* Quoted in David Thomson, *Europe Since Napoleon* (Pelican Books, 2nd edn, 1983), p. 120.

structure, in which princes and the dukes answerable to the king led the armies in the field (unlike the French, who supplanted those aristocrats they had not already guillotined with more professional soldiers) and the Junkers provided the officer class.

Against this background, the Prussian reformers also dealt with the vital issues of command and leadership. The changes that had already begun with the establishment of the *Kriegsakademie* now took on greater urgency and depth. Officers were recruited on talent, trained on substance – academic and intellectual syllabi as well as military – and promoted on merit rather than by class, family background or royal clientism. It was the beginning of Prussian military profession-alization. As a result, the new brigades and their sub-structures quickly came to be commanded by young and talented leaders. But these leaders and their men were also all of a new model: thinking soldiers who followed the spirit of a command rather than its letter; who were capable of understanding the unfolding battle and respond-ing. Indeed, one way of viewing the disaster at Jena was precisely that of officers strictly following orders rather than taking necessary initia-tives within their framework, and of ranks following rigid drills. The 'thinking soldier' was not a concept unique to Prussia, and had been actively pursued by the British. Admiral John Byng of the Royal Navy had been tried and executed for failing this test in 1756; he had pre-ferred to follow the letter of his orders rather than their spirit (as a result, the French fleet escaped his clutches). It was an important mile-stone. In line with Voltaire's famous comment that, 'In this country, it is thought good to kill an admiral from time to time, to give courage to others,' Byng's execution had a galvanizing effect on the British officer corps, since it made plain that rank mattered little if an officer failed to fight. A lot might go wrong during an attack on the enemy, but the only fatal error was not to attack at all. General Moore's reforms and training of the Light Division 1799–1801, were similarly to encourage the active involvement of the rifleman as a 'thinking soldier' on the battlefield. As he put it, the aim was to 'train the judge-ment of the officers, so that, when left to themselves, they may do the right thing. They should have no hesitation in assuming responsibility.' What in time made the Prussian pursuit of the concept of the initiative-taking soldier remarkable was its marriage with another of the post-Jena innovations: the general staff. This body sought to address what had been perceived as a disastrous drawback in the Prussian performance throughout the Napoleonic campaigns, namely the lack of a central structure that could coordinate not only among the various military formations but also between the political and military leaderships. In the above description of the battle of Jena, for example, note how the French forces were commanded by marshals whilst the Prussians were all led by princes and dukes – each with his own force, each answering only directly to the king. The need for coherence and professionalization was overwhelming if the Prussian army was to be victorious in the future.

A staff has always been an integral element of any military formation, since every commander has need of assistants; in the Prussian army, for example, each of the princes and dukes had a staff. Until the Napoleonic Wars staffs tended to be devoted to administration, combining the workings of a large household with formal military issues such as supplies, legal systems, organization of troop formations and the carrying of messages in battle. Staff officers were not specially trained, nor were they usually called upon to counsel the military commander. As in other areas, Napoleon wrought the initial change – largely due to his new *corps d'armée*. With such a dispersed system it became very necessary to have a central body that could act as a form of nervous system connecting all the corps. His solution was a new but not entirely efficient organization of a general staff. As with conscription, it originated in a haphazard arrangement initiated by the Revolution which he liked and then institutionalized. The new mass armies with their equally new commanders needed men to instil order in these well-meaning but wholly disorganized formations. Louis Berthier, a professional soldier who had served in the old imperial army, was the most significant of these. Assigned to the Army of Italy in 1795, he had remarkable skill for organization and centralization – a fact recognized by Napoleon when he took up command. Berthier became head of Napoleon's military planning staff, responsible for troop supply, personnel and supplies, but his true brilliance lay in an ability to translate the many orders of the emperor into easily understood messages to subordinates. His staff became the central body that organized, aided and passed on directives to all parts of the Grande Armée. But military planning was only part of the duties of Napoleon's staff, which also combined the functions of a personal household and an imperial administration. This was its main flaw. With the emperor as the sole source of direction, its efficiency diminished as the scale of warfare and his empire increased.

The Prussian model for a general staff was inherently different from the French, aimed at creating a wide yet detailed basis for professional planning and command. As such it was conceived by Scharnhorst as an institution of kindred ethos with the *Kriegsakademie*, and when it was established in 1808 he naturally assumed the role of its first chief. In this capacity he focused upon integrating the new, well-trained middle-ranking officers of common education that the war college was producing into a central body. The Defence Law of 1814, which created permanent staffs for the divisions and army corps, further enhanced the joint utility of the *Kriegsakademie* and the general staff: by linking up the central body of direction with the fighting formations, a nervous system manned and run by officers of common training started to evolve. This also helped resolve the problem of how to preserve the authority of the monarchy while conducting war with citizen soldiers: by matching a professional general staff, which reached from the strategic to the tactical level, with those appointed to command by the monarch, the royal authority was paralleled with professional competence. Over time this common ethos would be ever more emphasized, as a measure for creating commanders of identical training, thinking and capabilities, all versed in the details of every plan and contingency. However, the routine tasks of the staff and the basis of most professional careers were mapmaking, gathering intelligence, preparing mobilization plans and coordinating railway schedules. For the main purpose of the general staff was preparing for war, mostly at the tactical level. This purpose was clear to the reformers who founded the general staff, but not necessarily to the broader Prussian military, especially the old guard of senior commanders. Following the premature death of Scharnhorst in 1813, and the end of significant campaigns following the defeat of Napoleon in 1815, there was a waning of interest in military reform. As a result, the general staff lapsed in significance within the German military for some decades – and more profound reflection was still left to the *Kriegsakademie*, and most especially to the body of ideas formulated by one of its chief graduates and subsequent directors, Carl von Clausewitz.

The combination of Napoleon's extraordinary strategic vision and the fundamental reforms of the Prussian army he defeated was undoubtedly crucial in creating our understanding of the use of force: Napoleon's actions led to our modern concept of War – the wars with a capital W still conjured up in the media, and those most of us still assume are waged – in which we seek the definitive political result by force of arms, whilst the Prussian reforms ultimately produced a remarkable military machine which became the template for many of our modern militaries. However, it is possible that Napoleon's significance would not have been understood, nor the meaning of the reforms endured, but for one man: Carl von Clausewitz. It was he who properly understood that Napoleon presented not just a bigger or stronger force – but a completely different one, which fought for different strategic aims. It was he who translated this understanding into the monumental *On War*, thereby codifying Napoleon's actions within a theoretical construct and thereby also describing the Prussian reforms. In so doing he created one of the most important and enduring texts of military philosophy ever written.

Carl Philipp Gottlieb von Clausewitz was a professional soldier who rose to the rank of major general, but whilst he twice served as Chief of Staff in large fighting formations he never attained high operational command. He was, however, an exceedingly experienced officer, who had his baptism of fire at the age of thirteen in 1793 as part of the first-coalition forces which fought back the French Revolutionary armies. He subsequently saw action throughout the Napoleonic Wars, including the 1806 battle of Jena in which he was wounded and fell prisoner. Apart from leaving him with a lifelong dislike of all things French, his year of incarceration and subsequent convalescing left him outside the initial body of military reformers that changed the Prussian army after the Jena humiliation. He was further excluded owing to a year serving in the Russian army during the 1812 campaign, having resigned from the Prussian army together with thirty brother officers in protest at the Franco-Prussian alliance signed that year. He was readmitted to the Prussian general staff in 1815, but owing to his perceived disloyalty was awarded neither a command nor a strategic position. Instead, he served as director of the Prussian military college, the *Kriegsakademie*, where he devoted himself to teaching and his writings. In 1830 he was appointed Chief of Staff to the Prussian army, at a time of brief preparation for war in response to the uprisings in France and Poland. No sooner had that danger passed than cholera swept the land from the east, and Clausewitz was tasked to organize a *cordon sanitaire* to check its advance. The mission was not a success and he himself succumbed in November 1830, at the age of fifty-one.

Clausewitz craved senior command all his life, as is apparent from his letters to his wife. But owing partly to his relatively lowly birth to a non-Junker family and partly to his brief defection in 1812, he never achieved it. In any event, he was judged ill suited to high command in the field. As a contemporary, General Brandt, said of him after his death: 'as a strategist he would have greatly distinguished himself . . . [but] he wanted the art *d'enlever les troupes*'.* Suitability to command is a complex issue, to which I will return in the next chapter; here I will simply emphasize that Clausewitz was unique. Many officers make minor if significant theoretical advances, but only he wrote *On War*: a magnum opus of eight books. He may not have led large armies on the battlefield, but his understanding and analysis of both was supreme. Some of Clausewitz's writing is specific to the armies of the day: in reading him one must make allowances for the fact that his insights predate the breech-loading rifle, the railway, the aeroplane, the tank and the radio. None the less, much of his writing remains relevant – which shows he understood the true essence of war, the reason *On War* is enduring.

Clausewitz was greatly influenced by General Gerd von Scharnhorst, the Prussian military reformer, whom he encountered in 1801, when at the age of twenty-one he attended the *Kriegsakademie* as a student. He quickly became one of Scharnhorst's disciples and best students – graduating head of his class in 1803 – sharing his focus upon Napoleon and his innovations. In this way Clausewitz under-

---

*J. J. Graham (col.), 'Brief Memoir of General Clausewitz', in Carl von Clausewitz, *On War* (Penguin, 1985), p. 96.

stood at a very early age that the study of the new French armies and their campaigns was imperative. Even as he fought these armies he immersed himself in studying them in detail – during his twelve years as director of the war college he wrote original studies of most of the Napoleonic campaigns – and continued to do so until his death. From these detailed investigations and reflections emerged *On War*. It was brought to publication posthumously in 1832 by his admiring wife, who noted in her original preface that he had worked on ideas and drafts for the book since 1816. In fact, Clausewitz died before he finished revising all eight books as a whole, and he himself recorded in notes of 1827 and 1830 that the later works demanded a revision of the former. In particular he noted that there were other forms of war than that between nations and/or states, and that whilst theoretically absolute violence was called for in war, there were reasons – depending on its political purpose – to moderate violence. These issues will be examined in Part III of this book.

Clausewitz's theory of war contains a number of concepts, but given they are discussed in eight volumes I will dwell here strictly on the three concepts I deem relevant to this narrative. First, I give primacy to his idea of the 'remarkable trinity' of the state, the army and the people, which to me means the government, the military – all the armed forces – and the population. Clausewitz came to derive this formulation from a clear understanding that the Napoleonic form of war, the massive military event with a decisive outcome, was now to become the prevailing mode. As he put it:

Will this always be the case in the future? From now on will every war in Europe be waged with the full resources of the State, and therefore have to be fought only over major issues that affect the people? Or shall we again see a gradual separation taking place between government and people? Such questions are difficult to answer, and we are the last to dare to do so. But the reader will agree with us when we say that once barriers – which in a sense consist only in man's ignorance of the possible – are torn down, they are not easily set up again. At least when major interests are at stake, mutual hostility will express itself in the same manner as it has in our own day.*

* Carl von Clausewitz, *On War*, ed. and trans. Michael Howard and Peter Paret (Princeton University Press, 1976), p. 593.

Based upon this conceptual insight, he put forward the triangular relationship, one in which all three sides are equally relevant – and in which all three must be kept in balance if war is to succeed. As we will see in subsequent chapters, this trinity is crucial to all forms of war, to this very day. To this extent I do not agree with some who dismiss Clausewitz and his trinity as irrelevant: it is my experience in both national and international operations that without all three elements of the trinity – state, military and the people – it is not possible to conduct a successful military operation, especially not over time. This is due to the second basic Clausewitzian concept relevant here, to which the trinity is linked, that of the primacy of policy: 'War has its root in a political object, then naturally this original motive which called it into existence should also continue the first and highest consideration in its conduct.'* Unfortunately, this clear idea has become lost, indeed contradicted, by the frequent use of the title of the section heading that follows it: 'War is a mere continuation of policy by other means.' This has led to two common misunderstandings. First, that there is a point at which policy as politics and diplomacy is stopped and war commences, whereas Clausewitz makes absolutely clear, in the quote above and elsewhere, that these are parallel activities. And second that the political and military objectives are identical, whereas Clausewitz emphasizes that the two are definitely separate but wholly related. Equally, however, I think one must also understand his use of the word 'political' to be altogether a wider definition than that associated with the governance of states – as they existed in his time, or our modern nation states. It is the activity and interaction of both the formal and informal political entity. The warlord in modern Angola, for example, empowered by trading diamonds and with his own armed force, has a political purpose, however informal, underpinning his actions. He is using his force to establish a political position, and using force whilst conducting a political or economic negotiation: these are concurrent activities.

The third concept from *On War* that I have found of great practical value is the description of war as the product of both a 'trial of strength' and a 'clash of wills':

* Section 23, ch. 1, bk 1 (Penguin edn, p. 119).

If we desire to defeat the enemy, we proportion our effort to his powers of resistance. This is expressed by the product of two factors which cannot be separated, namely, *the sum of the available means* and *the strength of the Will*.*

This is another clear understanding drawn from the experience of Clausewitz's age, when Napoleon realized what could be achieved with the massed strength of the state. The eighteenth-century 'wars of manoeuvre', which were deeply entwined with diplomacy, tended to be a clash of wills. But by crushing the enemy's main force in an anni-hilating battle, Napoleon won the trial of strength – and the will of the state collapsed thereafter. This concept became basic to the para-digm of interstate industrial war – and remains a tenet of military thinking to this day. However, as we shall see in Part III of this book, in our current circumstances it is actually the will of the people that is often the objective being sought – yet there is still a tendency to use overwhelming military force in the belief that winning the trial of strength will deliver the will of the opponent. But Clausewitz empha-sized the two factors equally, not just the one over, or in sequence to, the other – meaning it is well to examine each situation to decide on the relationship between them.

The continuum and combination of Napoleon's vision, Prussian mili-tary reform and Clausewitz's theoretical insights undoubtedly laid the framework for both the new forms of forces and the application of force. These were the basis of the paradigm of interstate industrial war – together with the political element: in the French Revolution the people became a political force, and military force became a means for directly achieving a political end. Indeed, Napoleon ensured it became *the* means, and as Clausewitz predicted, his way of war prevailed. For through his victorious encounters with other armies over two decades he ultimately came to influence them. Such shifts reflect an underlying truth, which is eternal rather than Napoleonic: war is an imitative and reciprocal activity. In order to defeat an opponent in a long war one becomes more and more like him, and both sides end up feeding off the other. The form of the imitation will reflect the particular society

* Section 5, ch. 1, bk 1 (Penguin edn, p.104); italics appear in the original.

and its aims in engaging in the specific war, but nevertheless it will copy the basic idea in large measure. So, by the end of the second decade of the nineteenth century we find most of the armies that participated in the wars against Napoleon showed the basic attributes of his forces:

- The emergence of mass conscripted citizen armies reinforced by technology
- The destruction of the enemies' main force as the strategic aim
- The holding of large numbers of reserves in peace and the creation of new armies in war
- The hierarchical division of armies to allow for control and rapid movement
- Professionalism and meritocracy tied to the command of the armies' divisions
- Professional training within a doctrine of war

The three qualities of force as being decisive, total and framed within the trinity of the government, the people and the military would constantly evolve throughout the nineteenth century, clearly establishing thereby the paradigm, and ultimately reaching their culmination in the two world wars of the twentieth century. The need to achieve a decisive outcome made it necessary to pursue war through the trinity, in which all three elements were understood to be interlinked: it would no longer be possible to wage war without the support and participation of the people, from the soldiers of the mass army to the workers who would fund it. But war could only be declared for political aims by the government – which gradually became of the people – and professionally directed by the military, which needed a mass army to implement the new kind of war. Since each of these three elements was equally crucial, industrial war ultimately became total. Indeed, 'total war' should not be associated only with the two world wars. It is a term that originated with Clausewitz's interpretation of Napoleon's strategies and the way he implemented them. In each state and in each war the balance between the three elements of the trinity was different, but the logic that connected them was identical and as the century progressed became stronger: throughout Europe nation states evolved, citizens claimed rights, governments were elected. Patriotism and nationalism became common sentiments, and stirred competition among nations. The political causes of total war were being laid.

As of 1815 these basic structures led to the development of institutions to support them, fuelled by government thinking that followed a circular logic: In order to defend our state and advance our interests, we need armed forces. To win, we have learned from Napoleon that we must fight wars with all available resources. To this end we need to be able to mobilize a mass army with considerable reserves. But to mobilize we need to have a strategic plan so as to know what is required, in what order, and to what purpose. However, to have a strategy, we need an enemy. It is most logical to choose the worst case, and therefore be prepared for all lesser events. The worst case will always be our strongest neighbour – against whom we must therefore defend ourselves . . . This institutional logic, which is in place to this day, led to the development throughout continental Europe of military forces with the following characteristics:

- *Conscription* In order to have a pool of trained and available manpower to expand the forces in the event of war, the male population was conscripted in peace as well as war. By the mid nineteenth century France and Prussia had a high proportion of civilian reservists, as did most European states by the end of the century. The length of conscription varied from state to state and from period to period, but the conscripted individuals, who then became reservists, and the units composed from them, were always trained and organized for one type of war, that of the worst case, which could only be the defeat of the threat posed by the strongest neighbour. Since every neighbour was conscripting a similar army, the result could only be total war of state against state.

- *Mobilization* The evolution of the nation state and leaders elected by the people meant that governments, mindful of the economic consequences of total war – the cessation of regular economic activity in order to support the war – were reluctant to take a decision to open hostilities until the last practical moment. This led to the development of sophisticated mobilization plans to assemble the serving conscripts and trained reservists, which theoretically allowed the very last safe moment for going to war to be identified, taking the least possible time, and the machinery of government to take the decision. After all, if the economy and people were now working for the war, there had to be a central authority organizing this effort. In addition, and in order to ensure it was indeed the 'last safe moment' to disrupt the economy and the people, who were also becoming the electorate, military intelligence agencies expanded in a way hitherto unknown: they were tasked with gathering information as precise as possible on issues such as the enemies' parallel capabilities in terms of men and materiel, mobilization plans and movement toward borders.

- *Professionalism* To run the conscription machine, a production line of trained and organized manpower, a professional officer corps was required to manage and direct its efforts. The professional training of these officers tended to focus on the acts of moving these vast conscript forces to battle and executing a predetermined plan. In addition, the senior level of the officer corps became closely associated with government in the capital, for reasons not of prosecuting war but of preparing the nation to conduct total war. To do this the military needed to gain an adequate share of the national economic cake in time of peace.

- *Technological development* With the conscription of a nation's manpower came the realization that its industries were part of the total war effort. Each nation sought technology that outperformed that of its opponents. This was particularly evident with naval forces. During the nineteenth century every navy embarked on a quest for superiority in numbers and firepower in preparation for the decisive fleet engagement, the equivalent to the Napoleonic decisive land engagement. In addition, all military forces took advantage of the improvements in communications that came with the industrial revolution, the railway and the telegraph.

These characteristics of military forces and their associated institutions would become thoroughly established during the nineteenth century – and indeed are present in most societies to this day, regardless of whether a state maintains a conscript or a professional army. And they can all be traced back to Napoleon.

*

Napoleon met his match at Waterloo in 1815. To the last his forces were superb and his use of force masterly, but in the final campaign he failed. It was a trial of strength won by Wellington's allied army reinforced by Blücher's Prussian forces that led to the breaking of the French will to continue – a decisive military defeat in service of a political strategic aim, the restoration of the *ancien régime*. His opponents beat him on his terms: it was the end.

2

Development: Iron, Steam and Mass

Battle is an event of circumstance, no matter how much planning, exercising and drill precede it. The chances of victory are undoubtedly increased with proper preparation, but ultimately opponents fight the battle of the day: on another day, in the same location, with exactly the same forces, they would fight another battle in different circumstances. All decisions that commanders make in a battle, therefore, are those of the circumstances on that day. Napoleon understood this fact. He knew that his organization – the setting of authority and responsibility, the grouping of forces and resources, and the allocation of tasks – directly related to his mobility, and that in the face of an adversary this was not a constant; his organization for battle must always adapt. By understanding the 'approach' to be part of the battle he planned to dictate the most favourable circumstances in which to engage and with his 'organizational mobility' he was able to achieve this time and again – and for this reason he was not only a visionary, but a great commander.

Command is a crucial element in the use of force, for it is the commander who will decide both the structure of the forces and the use of force. If he does this well, and understands the place of force within the broader political strategic objective, his force will also have utility. The commander is therefore vital to understanding force. He is the personification of the force he commands. His aptitude for war and his character, his morale and his will to triumph are the essential ingredients that weld and focus the will and effort of his command to win. The commander is the source of the commands' driving logic and the application of this logic to the achievement of its object. It is he who makes the military decisions, and should carry all authorities to do this; in turn he is responsible for the outcome, win or lose. Just as the levels of war are different so are the demands of command at each level; the commander at each level is also necessarily dependent on the actions and decisions of those above and below him in the hierarchy. As a result, it is most important if a force is to succeed that commanders at all levels share a common doctrine, by which I mean a way to think about the matter rather than a way to deal with it, so that there is coherence of view, interpretation and expression from the strategic to the tactical levels.

Command in war is exercised in the face of an opponent and in adversity. So is leadership. The difference between the two is that the leader says 'come on', while the commander says 'go on'. As long as those being led trust the leader's competence to find the way, recognize the end and look after them, they follow. The commander has a more difficult task: the people he sends out must trust that they know the way and recognize the end, and are capable of looking after themselves along the way – but equally that they will be supported on the way, and that the end is of value. The selection of those to send, and achieving this level of trust, are the primary duties of the commander. As a result, it is the leader who applies force on the battlefield, but it is the commander who unleashes and directs it – and all those in his command must trust that his understanding of force will allow them to conquer.

The next duty of the commander is to judge between conflicting imperatives as they arise. To do this he must have knowledge of the subject but his is the view of the generalist, the general, not the expert. He will have experts on his staff and in his command, and they will help him form his plan. But all planning is compromise; there is no such thing as the perfect plan, only the best compromise of competing priorities in the circumstances – circumstances that in war include the enemy, who is making every effort to frustrate your endeavour. The commander also strikes and accepts compromises in his command: not all his men and officers will be perfect, and he must accept this fact and plan accordingly. Up to a point in the hierarchy of the service the very competent officer can do some of the work that others cannot do: he compensates with his skill for the inefficiency of others, largely by closely supervising the points of weakness in his command. He is usually promoted as a result. But then comes a point in the hierarchy where the span of command is too great. At this point the commander must learn to tolerate, in the engineering sense, inefficiency; this is not something he has been promoted for – and some indeed fail. An obituary to Arthur Rudolph, a scientist who developed the Saturn 5 rocket, well illustrates the need to tolerate inefficiency: 'You want a valve that does not leak and you try everything possible to develop one. But the real world provides you with the leaky valve. You have to determine how much leaking you can tolerate.' To achieve maximum utility, the commander must therefore accept the reality of his subordinates and cast his plan according to his judgement of them and their capacities. If a man is good for 80 per cent it is folly to give him a job that demands 90 per cent. He will fail and it will be the fault of the commander, who demanded more than that officer could give. Moltke the elder, the chief of the Prussian and then the German general staff, probably put it best in saying: 'An order shall contain everything that a commander cannot do by himself, but nothing else.' It is up to the commander to know what his subordinates are capable of when giving the order.

The commander must be exceedingly knowledgeable of his forces: the people, the structures, the capabilities. If he has forces from other services under his command, he must familiarize himself with the structures and organizations he is taking on; to judge their strengths and weaknesses, and plan to play to the first and guard the second. To fully assimilate the significance of these matters, the commander needs to have an understanding of logistics – the science of efficient movement and storage – since the movement of mass and the execution of a campaign is almost wholly a logistical matter. Without understanding the logistics a commander may find himself fighting a battle he cannot supply – or, as happened with NATO forces in Kosovo in 1999, ordering more aircraft to be deployed without first having ramps to put them on, a mistake quickly rectified by the generosity of a then new NATO ally, Hungary. An actual battle may be an event of circumstance, but not all circumstances need be of the moment. Much of the degree and nature of risk of a venture can be reduced to a logistic calculation.

Above all, the commander is the primary source of morale for his command. I define morale as that spirit that triumphs in adversity: it is a product of leadership, discipline, comradeship, confidence in self, and in the commander and his staff. Without high morale amongst his forces, especially in war, a commander stands little chance of success. Equally, the commander must sustain his own high morale – for it is that which will help him endure the isolation of decision, and those grinding days and nights during which he assumes the risks and uncertainties. It is what enables him to carry his burden: the knowledge he is responsible for the lives under his command – and that if he is to achieve his objective he has no way of being certain to save them. Indeed, the only certainty of a commander's plans is that there will be casualties.

The essentials of these points have been constant to commanders through time. In his age Napoleon undoubtedly embodied them, especially in his ability to handle his staff and forces, but above all in that he created a new army and was for many years victorious. Napoleon's greatness as a leader and commander was epitomized when, after he escaped from exile on Elba and landed in France, many of his previous command and much of the citizenship rallied to him despite their previous experiences of war culminating in defeat. For me, this is remarkable.

Napoleon and Clausewitz were the two most important figures in forging the paradigm of interstate industrial war through a new understanding of the use of force. They were unique in being a pairing of a commander and a theorist, and in that they did not work together; indeed, they were on opposite sides. Subsequently it was a combination of commanders and political leaders who did much to shape the paradigm in the nineteenth century: President Abraham Lincoln and General Ulysses S. Grant in the US, and Prince Otto von Bismarck and General Helmuth von Moltke (the elder) in what was first Prussia, later Germany. Both Lincoln and Bismarck had a deep and instinctive understanding of the ability of force to achieve a political aim with a decisive military victory; both Grant and Moltke had the capability to shape and use military forces to deliver that decisive victory. Above all, all four had the unflinching determination to stay the course through to victory, however long and arduous, and even in the face of public and political distrust – because for each of them there were hard objectives of nationhood at stake. It was these political and military fusions, coupled with the immense industrial innovations of the nineteenth century, that did much to advance and reconfigure the use and utility of force in a manner recognizable to this day.

A measure of Napoleon's innovations and Clausewitz's theoretical insights is that they transcended their pre-industrial times, largely because neither was concerned with models of war so much as its essence. None the less, it is amazing that their contributions were based on tenets that were to become obsolete within a few years owing to technology. The Napoleonic Wars were nearly the last to be conducted using muskets, which had been in use for centuries, and to utilize marches and supply lines relying on bullocks and horses, or communications based on messengers, both of which had been in use for millennia. Within decades the breech-loading rifle and the brass cartridge revolutionized tactics, steam power and the railway were introduced, extending war in every way, and communications were fundamentally changed with the invention of the telegraph. These changes in weaponry, transport and communications, three basic elements of war, materially changed the way force was used in the nineteenth century.

Steam power and its application to vessels and vehicles was the true innovation in transport, which ultimately revolutionized strategy, logistics and, more generally, the way wars were fought. First, and often overlooked, came the use of steam power in oceanic transport. This allowed western European states, their offshoot in North America, and at a later stage Japan, to project their military power to previously inaccessible regions of the earth. This is especially true of Britain, which possessed the greatest merchant fleet in the world in addition to the most powerful navy. The transition to steam enhanced this power, and confirmed Britain's view of itself as a maritime rather than a land power. It also explained the need to include within the empire expedient locations: steam demanded coal, so coaling stations were established in locations such as Aden, which was on the strategically vital route to India. The benefit to Western sea power derived from steamships was illustrated during the first Opium War (1840–42), when a fleet of twelve British gunboats inflicted a crushing defeat on the last great empire relying on sail: China. A decade later, Commodore Perry's US expedition to Japan set a textbook example of gunboat diplomacy. Without firing a shot, Western military technical superiority succeeded in opening up the fiercely isolationist Tokugawa Japan. In other words, steam allowed for the swift and decisive projection of force far afield – whilst for the target it magnified the threat of force by bringing it closer, thereby making it more real and credible.

The second innovation was, of course, the application of steam power to transportation on land: railway networks radically altered the way wars were fought. From 1825 to 1900, the length of railway tracks within Europe grew from almost nothing to nearly 300,000 kilometres, cutting through all of the continent's natural barriers including the Rhine, the Danube, the Alps and the Pyrenees. In a continuing feat of engineering prowess, tunnels were dug and bridges built in order to enable this achievement. In Britain, quickly followed by Belgium, the early phase of railway expansion focused on linking factories to ports. France and Prussia soon followed suit, and the network then began expanding eastwards so as to encompass the predominantly agricultural areas of Austria-Hungary and Russia into a common economic system. By the turn of the century, capital cities in the industrialized core of continental Europe were within twenty-four hours of all other capitals in this area – which meant potential battlefields were within like proximity.

Time and distance, two of the factors in planning for war, had become much shorter in comparison to the era of the marching army. Napoleon, as we have seen, to surprise the enemy sometimes held forced marches that lasted days rather than weeks; with the new modes of transportation this became the norm. The mass conscript armies could now be rapidly delivered to a front line and, as significantly, kept supplied with food and ammunition.

The development of the locomotive conceptually expanded the world, making it accessible to the individual and states alike. Large states such as the USA and the Russian Empire now found it possible to exert effective political, economic and military control over the immense stretches of land to which they laid claim. Expansion of empires and colonial wars were also transformed (and, in some cases, enabled) by the introduction of the railways, since they allowed the nations of western Europe, Britain and France in particular, to establish control over the interior of Africa, using coastal trading posts already in their possession as bases. Before the advent of the railway, every major colonial military expedition had to rely on waterways or advance supply posts: animals and men could carry only a limited load, and after a short period of time – eight days for an ox, for example – they consumed the whole of it. Railways changed the equation: provided the railway was developed to stay in contact with the force, or the force remained in contact with the railway, it could receive as many supplies as were available for it from the home economy.

Accompanying these innovations in transport was the invention of the telegraph, which brought the ability to convey instructions and requests for information to and from the far-flung outposts of empire. In the military, general staffs and their overseas commands acquired the capacity to remain in continuous communication. This revolution in communications technology permitted a degree of centralized direction unheard of in the days when envoys or military commanders on the spot were required to make extemporaneous decisions that could determine the outcome of campaigns or even entire conflicts. As we have seen, Napoleon could not control events in theatres distant from him. For the theatre in which he was operating he could devolve decisions to his corps commanders within the overall plan, and with his system of aides de camp (ADCs) and messengers remain in control, but the system was too slow and cumbersome to handle the other theatres. The telegraph heralded the advent of the era of truly centralized control: from now on there would exist the communications to collect the information and issue orders, railways could deliver men and materiel to several fronts, and priorities between fronts could be reassessed and forces and resources reallocated accordingly. This enabled the birth of the operational or theatre level of war.

In every major European country, general staffs were quick to appreciate that the rules of the game had changed. If foreign passenger trains could now reach their capitals within a day, so could troop transports. The German army set up its own department to exploit rail transportation to its full potential in times of war. As other countries followed suit, the frontiers of France, Austria, Russia and the German Reich were equipped with the infrastructure necessary to receive large numbers of troops from the rest of the country should the need arise. On the German border, platforms a mile long that could receive several troop trains at a time sprung up at small rural stations. Guns, armaments and ammunition were to be transported in large quantities by the same means. The consequences of this new relation to distance gave strategic reach and became dramatically apparent during the military operations conducted at the turn of the century. The locomotive and the steamship rendered military forces more massive and more mobile. Gone were the long marches and risky sea voyages that depleted the strength of fighting men long before they reached the battlefield.

The Boer War was an example of this new reality. Between 1899 and 1902, in an unprecedented projection of military might across the ocean, Britain transported and maintained 250,000 men at a distance of 6,000 miles in the southern tip of Africa to subdue the army of the Boer Republics. In 1904, though with a less favourable outcome to itself, Russia conveyed an army of comparable size 6,500 kilometres by rail across the forbidding wastes of Siberia, to engage the Japanese forces in Manchuria. Such prodigious feats of strategic transport erased the traditional barriers of space and time that preserved the isolation of the world's land masses from one another. The entire globe at the beginning of the twentieth century had become a single entity, knit together by the network of transportation and communication represented by the railways, the steamship and the telegraph. And within this entity the civilian and military structures of each nation had become deeply intertwined. In the event of war the railways would be requisitioned and the people called up to expand the military – and without them both economic life would cease, or be put in the service of the military. The nations were becoming ripe for world wars.

After decades of preparation, when war broke out in 1914 the main belligerent nations faced up to the logistic challenge. Sixty-two French infantry divisions – each comprising approximately 15,000 men – and a further 87 German, 49 Austrian, and 144 Russian divisions were concentrated close to their respective borders within a month of the outbreak. Several million horses also accompanied this unprecedented deployment. Germany alone transported almost 1.5 million men and their equipment to the Belgo-French border between 1 and 17 August. The nations of the Entente Cordiale achieved much the same feats on the other side of the front. In the East, the Russians responded rapidly and were able – initially at least – to surprise the German general staff by launching an attack on both East Prussia and Galicia in August.

But the radical changes wrought by innovations in transport stopped at the railway station. Though steam power and the telegraph had improved strategic and theatre level movement, its effects on the tactical level were limited to sustaining the large forces of the industrialized states in place. Once soldiers deployed from the railheads they became soldiers of yore, marching with heavy loads on their backs and their supplies carried in carts. Thus it was in the American Civil War, and thus it remained in the First World War.

Railways allowed for the mass transportation of men to the battlefield, but it was the new mass-produced forms of weaponry that transformed the face of battle. For if the railroads delivered forces to the front, it was the kinetic force of the weaponry these forces applied that brought about the decisive victory they sought. But unlike the rapid growth of railways, in the case of weapons the developments were comparatively slow. The relatively long period of continental peace that followed the 1815 Congress of Vienna gave armies much-needed time to recover and reform, but also had a stultifying effect on the application of technological change to the military sphere: since the prospect of a large-scale European war appeared remote, government funds dried up. As a result, the majority of inventions and innovations which might have been used in weaponry remained limited to civilian applications, and military authorities paid little attention to these developments until the middle of the century.

Until the nineteenth century, the greatest drawback of firearms was that they were both slow to use and easily affected by rain. Muzzle-loading muskets required soldiers to use valuable time in the heat of battle, when they were particularly vulnerable to attack, ramming in powder and ball, whilst flintlock mechanisms were difficult to ignite in damp conditions and at the mercy of a sudden change of weather. The advantage of rifling the barrel – creating a spiral of grooves on its internal surface – was well known, but for rifling to work the ball had to fit snugly. The force on the ramrod necessary to load a rifle was greater than that for a musket, which led to rifles taking longer to reload than muskets and thus a slower rate of fire. In addition, and bearing in mind the ever-present consideration of the burden on the Treasury of equipping the soldier, rifles were a great deal more expensive than muskets.

The first step towards improvement came with Edward C. Howard's discovery of 'fulminating' materials in 1799, which could explode or ignite when struck. A few years later Reverend Alexander Forsyth, a keen game shooter, developed the percussion lock, patented in 1807, followed by the percussion cap in 1814. The latter led to the creation of the self-contained cartridge and this in turn allowed for the invention of the breech-loading weapon. The first practical breech-loading sporting gun was developed in 1812 by Samuel Pauly, a Swiss gunsmith based in Paris. With its drop-down barrel firing a self-contained cartridge, Pauly had invented a weapon that worked like a modern sporting shotgun – but it took nearly fifty years to find a military market for the idea of the breech loader.

In the meantime advances were made in the design of the projectile. A Frenchman, Captain Minie, designed an elongated bullet that expanded on being forced up the barrel by the propellant. This allowed for the barrel to be rifled and for the bullet to be a loose fit as it was loaded and then to grip the rifling upon firing. For the same rate of fire there was an increase in accuracy and the bullets also had much greater effective range than the old design. The consequence of this was to increase the power of the infantry in relation to both the artillery, who had to stand further off and thus were less lethal, and the cavalry, who received more rounds more accurately as they endeavoured to close with lance and sword.

But once arms could be reliably loaded in the breech, rifled barrels and metallic cartridges became the standard and accuracy and range improved further. The needle gun was invented by Johann Nikolaus von Dreyse and adopted by the Prussian army in 1848. The father of all bolt-action rifles, this rifle took its name from the long firing pin, which passed through the paper cartridge to strike a cap in the base of the bullet. The bolt could be slid backwards and forwards by the firing soldier to open or close the breech to reload rapidly. The French developed their own bolt-action rifle, the Chassepot, as a response. These two weapons, used in the 1870 Franco-Prussian War, were the first used to equip whole armies with breech-loaders.

Percussion ignition also led to the development of the modern revolver. In 1818 a hand-rotated flintlock revolver was patented in the US. The mechanical rotation of the cylinder by a spring was a key innovation, as was the use of a spring to force the cylinder into contact with the barrel and avoid leaking gas. In 1836 Samuel Colt came up with a sturdy design that made use of these recently discovered features. More importantly, his design allowed for standard parts to be manufactured. To that point each weapon had been made by a skilled artisan, each part tooled to fit the specific weapon. By standardizing parts Colt allowed for production-line manufacture and repair in the field using interchangeable parts. The means of war were truly being industrialized. When the US went to war with Mexico in 1846, the efficiency of this weapon was soon demonstrated. A decade later, in 1857, Smith & Wesson produced a rimfire cartridge revolver with an open frame and a simple robust revolving cylinder. Weapons derived from these were soon adopted by all of the world's major armies.

Following the invention of the percussion cap and breech loading, the need to increase the rate of fire was approached in two ways. The first involved developing a magazine to hold extra cartridges, fed individually into the breech by manually working the breech block or bolt by a lever or rotating action. The second involved increasing the number of barrels on the weapon. The American Civil War spurred innovation, and in 1862 Richard Jordan Gatling took out a patent on the gun he invented, which was adopted by the US army in 1865 and sold all over the world. The Gatling gun's six barrels were mounted on a revolving frame based on a central axis. The loading and firing arrangements were behind these rotating barrels. Operated by hand crank, it was entirely mechanical. In Europe, the French army equipped itself in 1869 with the Belgian Mitrailleuse, which comprised twenty-five rifle barrels mounted around a cylinder casing. The breech block slid back to allow a plate of twenty-five cartridges to be dropped into the weapon, which was also operated by hand crank. A decade later, in 1879, the British chose the Gardner machine gun, a two-barrelled weapon operated by a crank which could fire 10,000 rounds in twenty-seven minutes – the equivalent to about a hundred men firing rapidly with the breech-loading rifle of the day.

The French had the Mitrailleuse in their inventory in 1870 when they fought the Prussians. It is interesting how little advantage they gained from this weapon, particularly when one recalls the necessity for troops to move in close order so as to remain under the control of their commander in the days before radio, thus presenting an excellent target. The French understood the weapon as a form of artillery, perhaps because it looked like a small gun and the artillery had the technological knowledge to maintain the equipment, and failed to take advantage of its attributes: a high rate of concentrated aimed rifle fire from one position applied best into the flank of the attacker. It is no good acquiring technology if it is not used to advantage, which may require adapting your organization and tactics accordingly. Alternatively, if there are good reasons not to adapt, then you should question whether it is necessary to burden yourself with the new technology. Most armies, including the British, have failed to learn this lesson – particularly in the field of modern communications.

These early hand-cranked machine guns were followed closely by designs where the power of the propellant in the cartridge provided the power for the weapon to reload itself. This was made possible with the improvement in the propellants being used. The smokeless powder based on nitrocellulose was superior to the old gunpowder: in addition to not obscuring the target from the firer and indicating his position, it was more powerful and consistent in effect. Within eighty years of Forsyth perfecting the percussion lock, Hiram Maxim had designed the automatic machine gun, an extraordinary rate of progress if one compares it with the slow advances in the field of firearms during the previous four centuries. Maxim had the idea of tapping into the energy liberated when a cartridge was fired. He exploited it and came up with a design that utilized the recoil of the gun to perform the actions of loading and extracting the cartridge from an ammunition belt. A few years later, in the United States, the Colt company equipped the army with a machine gun that used the gas behind the bullet as a driving force. Meanwhile, in Europe, Skoda developed the first blowback mechanism, a system in which the gas pressure blowing the cartridge case out of the chamber was used to drive the breech block back against a powerful spring. These three systems, recoil, gas and blowback, have dominated machine-gun manufacture ever since, and as the propellants became more stable so accuracy improved. At the same time, rapid advances also took place in the field of artillery. The development of a reliable breech-loading system allied with rifled barrels, a development spurred on by the 1854–6 Crimean War, led to the production of the Armstrong gun in the US and of Whitworth's English hexagonal-bored barrel gun. In Germany, Krupp designed a 1,000-pounder for the 1867 Paris exhibition, which returned to bombard the city in 1870.

The appearance of the ironclad warship armed with heavy guns brought with it the need for the investment of large sums of money in the defence of harbours and naval bases. Evidence of the expenditure can still be found in many places along the south coast of Britain, particularly the forts around Portsmouth and Plymouth that were built in the 1860s in case Britain should go to war with France again – and known as 'Palmerston's Follies' since they were never needed. Similar fortifications exist on America's eastern seaboard, constructed against the contingency of a British or French attack. As a result, guns, submarine mines and early types of torpedoes became important instruments of defence; only later did the latter two reveal their full potential as offensive weapons. The development of quick-firing marine artillery was a response to the need to improve on machine guns as a defence against fast torpedo boats. As these fast boats became bigger and stronger, heavy-calibre quick-firing weapons were needed to defeat them. These could not be made to operate in exactly the same manner as machine guns because of the extra weight of the mechanism and ammunition, but the idea of using the force of the propellant was adapted to achieve a high rate of fire. In the late 1880s Hotchkiss in France and Nordenfelt in Sweden both produced 47mm and 57mm guns, firing thirty and twenty-five rounds per minute, respectively.

The system was then perfected and adapted to field guns, the most famous of which was the French 75mm, created in 1897, which made use of hydraulics to control the gun's recoil. And as the gun carriage was now more stable, accuracy was improved. However, the artillery was still placed well forward on the battlefield so its commanders could see their targets and direct the fire. This exposed the gun crews to rifle and counter-battery fire, but the more stable carriages made it practical to fit a protective shield. By the turn of the century the current characteristics of the artillery piece were fixed: breech loading, a recoil system and crew protection.

By the end of the nineteenth century this array of weaponry was available to all industrialized nations: steam-powered warships with very powerful long-range guns; fortification of both ports and borders making use of the developments in naval gunnery; rifles capable of sustained rates of aimed fire to effective ranges in excess of 800 metres; machine guns capable of producing from one weapon the same fire as whole groups of men; and accurate, rapid-firing field artillery guns. The designs and principles upon which these weapons operated are essentially unchanged today, and the visual forms of force reflected by them remain those within which we still conceive of the battlefield: they have become iconic. Yet in many cases neither the weapons nor the battlefield exist any more. Take the example of personal weapons. The soldier has always had a personal weapon – he has frequently been identified by its character; for example, 'archer', 'lancer', 'grenadier' or 'rifleman'. Artillery and later the armoured vehicle were initially supporting arms for the foot and horse, whose actions dominated the battlefield. Yet through industrialization and improved communications these supporting arms have come to dominate the battlefield and our perception of it: we now count armies not by their rifles, but rather by the number of men under arms or by 'combat power' – the volume of war-making equipments and systems. For many, these are the tools of real war. Yet the AK-47 and the machete continue to kill people by the millions: they are the tools, as we shall see, of war amongst the people. But these are not weapons systems. They may be lethal, but they are not part of the iconic images and understanding of industrial war.

Then there is ammunition, for above all it is the bullet that kills.

Skill is, of course, an essential element in dispatching that bullet effectively, but it is still the bullet that kills – or the bomb, or the missile. At the lower tactical levels of command one operates on the assumption that bullets are in continuous supply, but everyone is conscious that it is only an assumption. A rifleman can discharge all that he can carry in only a few minutes, and his commander must then either replace him or resupply him. It is therefore up to the commander to either strictly define or limit a soldier's task to the ammunition he carries, or else ensure he is steadily replaced or resupplied. As you rise in command, you become increasingly concerned about the bullets rather than the rifles, and all other weapons, since they are the force being propelled and applied. For example, in Zimbabwe in 1980, as part of the British Military Advisory and Training Team (BMATT) to Prime Minister Mugabe, we were forming battalions from the two tribally based guerrilla armies that had been part of the formation of the new state. This was being done on the infrastructure of the former Rhodesian army. I had urged the ex-Rhodesians to equip the new battalions with their rifles, which fired NATO standard ammunition that only they had, rather than leaving them with the AK-47s that they had acquired in the bush, and for which there was no shortage of ammunition, both declared and undeclared. The Rhodesians could not conceive of letting 'these Terrs [short for terrorist] have our weapons'. As a result, when seven of these new battalions mutinied and started to kill each other on a tribal basis, we had the greatest difficulty in shutting down the violence, fuelled as it was by a ready supply of ammunition.

A significant point of industrial war, and one of the few relevant to this day, is that of industry itself. Most discussions of industrial war tend to overlook the subject, either assuming it is understood as a default of the title, or else simply ignoring it. However, industry is absolutely integral to industrial war, not merely in the sense of the industrial revolution enabling it, but in the very existence of industry as economic enterprise. Money has always been made from war in one way or another, but usually in the activities surrounding it – money lenders or banks financing monarchs in their wars, tradesmen selling wares to armies as they marched, blacksmiths shoeing cavalry horses and weapon builders making armaments. For all we know Goliath bought his armour from Philistine Armouries Ltd rather than making it himself, and that is the point: in earlier times enterprises served war but were not integral to it, but industrial war is not possible without industry, for both its output and its commerce. By the late nineteenth century industrial competition came to fan the flames of war, whilst defence industries enabled the war itself. To be sure, the element of shareholder profit may be reduced or even eliminated from the equation by making the industry state owned, as all totalitarian regimes have shown, and most democracies in time of war too – when the state assumed ownership or simply founded its own defence industries to equip its armies. However, the element of employment can never be deleted in any type of regime: defence industries provide jobs, which fuel economies and provide the means in peace to defend them in war. And in industrial war economies battle each other as much as armies.

There is a truly symbiotic relationship between industrial war and industry. Indeed, some of the most important firms to become integral to industrial war hail back to the very start of the paradigm. Eliphalet Remington developed his first gun in his father's forges in 1816, and soon moved into the firearms business. The company evolved and grew from conflict to conflict, especially during the US Civil War and the two world wars, and is still a significant manufacturer of guns and ammunition, and a supplier of the US military. The Mauser Company also dates back to a small industry in the Black Forest, founded in 1811, that grew alongside German military expansion and its various wars. It exists to this day – as a subsidiary of Rheinmetall – still manufacturing weapons such as the Mauser BK-27 cannon used in the Eurofighter jet. Krupp, the major German arms manufacturer, also started out in 1811 – in the midst of the Napoleonic Wars – when Friedrich Krupp founded a steel factory in Essen. On his death in 1826 his son Alfred took full charge of the faltering concern at age fourteen. He rapidly made a fortune supplying steel for the railways and manufacturing cannons. The outstanding performance of Krupp guns in the Franco-Prussian War of 1870–71 allowed the firm to become the chief supplier to the Second Reich whilst also supplying the armies of nations all around the world. The next Krupp generation, under

...lrich Alfred Krupp's leadership, was further enriched by the rise ...he German navy and the need for armour plate. By the time ...edrich Alfred's elder daughter, Bertha, inherited control of the firm in 1902, it employed more than 40,000 people. Her husband, Gustav von Bohlen, affixed Krupp to his name and soon took over the running of the company; by the outbreak of the First World War he had gained control of the German arms manufacturing sector. His factories created U-boats as well as the famous Big Bertha, a heavy-calibre howitzer which was used for the shelling of the fortress of Liège in Belgium. His company also produced the Paris gun, a long-barrelled gun that could fire up to 120 kilometres.

The terms of the Treaty of Versailles obliged Krupp to re-centre his activities around the production of agricultural machinery, which he did in the 1920s. In May 1933 Hitler appointed Krupp as chairman of the Adolf Hitler Spende, an industrialist fund administered by Martin Bormann. The same year, Krupp began producing tanks in what was officially part of an agricultural tractor scheme. He was soon building submarines in Holland whilst other new weapons were developed and tested in Sweden. Within a few years, the firm had become a major part of the German war machine and was equipping the armies of the Reich from German factories. After the outbreak of the Second World War Krupp built factories in countries under German occupation and made use of the slave labour provided by concentration camps. This included a fuse factory inside Auschwitz, and a howitzer factory in Silesia. In 1943, Gustav was succeeded by his son Alfred, who was later convicted of war crimes at Nuremberg. An Allied order to break up the company in 1953 languished for lack of a buyer, and Alfred eventually managed to restore the family fortunes although the Krupp dynasty died with him in 1967. Krupp is now merged with Thyssen, another major commercial steel and iron dynasty that evolved throughout the nineteenth century – one which supplied arms manufacturers, but did not establish such an industry of its own.

Vickers of the United Kingdom is another excellent example of the symbiosis between industry and war. Formed in 1867, though the company origins can be traced back to 1828, it was based initially in Sheffield, where its head office was attached to the steelworks by the river Don. The company did not have a London address until it

acquired the Maxim Nordenfelt Guns and Ammunition Co. Ltd in
1897. In 1911 it was felt that a stronger presence was needed near
Whitehall, which had become the company's major customer, and the
head office moved from Sheffield to Westminster. In its early years
Vickers concentrated on the production of high-quality steel castings.
By the start of the twentieth century, however, it was producing a wide
range of military equipment. Vickers expanded into other areas,
acquiring the Wolseley Tool and Motor Car Company and building
the first British submarine in 1901. By 1910, fifty-six vessels had been
built. Vickers also created the Vickers 303 machine gun, which served
the British army from 1912 to 1968. During the First World War, British
railway artillery was almost entirely developed by the Armstrong and
Vickers factories. The army specified heavy guns and the two firms
utilized whatever excess naval barrels they had in their factories. Vickers developed a 12-inch howitzer mounted on rail and wheel mounts
to respond to Krupp's challenge on the continent. During these years
the company developed a wide variety of military aircraft, producing
one of the first designed to carry a machine gun, the FB-5 Vickers
Gunbus. It was a Vickers Vimy that completed the first non-stop
Atlantic crossing in 1919. In 1927 Vickers merged with the greater part
of the company Armstrong-Whitworth of Newcastle to form Vickers-
Armstrong. The Armstrong company had developed on similar lines
to Vickers, producing a range of different guns, before expanding
into naval ships and the car and truck business. In the lead-up to the
Second World War, Vickers-Armstrong played a major role in
rearming the British military. One of the company's most famous
designs was the Valentine infantry tank, which was produced in
greater number than any other British tank in the Second World War.
Post-war Vickers was responsible for the production of the first British
nuclear submarine and the first British V-bomber. In 1999 Vickers
merged with Rolls-Royce – yet again a company that prospered
through defence manufacture, for whilst it is best known for its
luxury motor cars it was the engines it made for fighter aircraft in both
world wars that made great fortunes for the company. Engines for
military aircraft remain a significant element of the business.

These are but a few examples from many in the West. However, as
industrialization spread across the globe, defence industries sprang

up in every corner, becoming the ultimate enablers of industrial war. Industrialization enabled industrial war, which in turn sought industrial solutions, solutions that were provided by industry – which needed industrial war to survive. Indeed, as noted above, Krupp manufactured and sold to all nations, not only Germany, and this trait remains to this day with all defence industries: they are commercial enterprises, basic to war but financially answerable to shareholders. There are now safeguards in many states against arms sales to states that may use them against one's own, or against civilian populations – but such laws are not always enforced. In addition, many weapons and systems are openly traded amongst nations by major industries; these are mostly no longer state owned, and as commercial enterprises they need to provide profit to their shareholders. And so the symbiotic relationship is still in place: the commercial ventures feed off the political will to prepare for war and the ability to make war is dependent on the output of industry. Yet the political will is waning, and in some states is no longer present, whilst the industries remain large economic concerns, job providers and profit makers. To survive they need the preparations for war to continue. Outside the US, which still heavily funds defence industries, it is a symbiotic relationship in crisis.

The American Civil War that broke out in 1861 was the first major conflict to incorporate the new developments in transport, communications and weaponry, and the first to be fully fought within the new paradigm: it was pursued in order to uphold a political vision by force, and it was won by a decisive and brutal defeat of the enemy. This was a clear clash of wills decided in war by an immense trial of strength: the North, by destroying the capacity of the South to make war as it chose, broke its will to continue. It was the first industrial war, and while both sides belonged to the same nation, they formed themselves into two separate entities on the political and military battlefield – each comprising the crucial trinity of people, state and army. The war they fought was an important milestone in the evolution of interstate industrial war, not least because of its subsequent influence on the American way of war, and because of the many European observers dispatched from across the Atlantic. The conclusions they took back from their strong impressions of the battlefields may not always have been correct, but none the less had enormous impact on the evolution of total war in Europe.

For the North, and especially President Lincoln, the political aim of the war was clear: to maintain the Union and the power of the elected government over all the states. There was no compromise position. The strategic military objective was therefore to destroy the power to act independently of the Confederates generally and the government in Richmond specifically. The South, having declared an independent Confederacy, and realized it to all intents and purposes, had only to keep it in being in order to achieve its political aim. Its strategic military objective was therefore to keep the Union forces out of the South by defeating their armies. The story of the war was that the Confederates initially succeeded, winning one tactical victory after another – but unfortunately for them, Lincoln understood the nature of total war. Harnessing the industrial and logistical superiority of the North to the cause, through the extensive network of railways, industrial output and conscription, he sought decisive victories that would be sufficient to break the South's will to resist. In this he ultimately found an excellent military counterpart, General Ulysses S. Grant, who matched his political understanding of force with a military one.

From the very beginning, the North controlled all the large cities. It was more than twice as populous as the South: except for New Orleans, all towns containing more than 100,000 inhabitants lay within states loyal to the Union. Its industry was strong and dynamic, amounting to nearly ten times the size of Southern industry, and it had important financial reserves. The North also controlled most of the navy and it rapidly developed the ability to match the threat posed by the ironclad Confederate warship CSS *Virginia* by building a semi-submersible ironclad ship of its own, USS *Monitor* – a forerunner of modern submarines. Henceforth its naval supremacy lay uncontested. The South's industry was at an embryonic stage and in 1861 its railway network was less than half the size of the North's. The number of guns and firearms in the Confederate army was less than a third of those possessed by the Union forces. On the other hand, at the outset of the war, the Confederates were particularly strong in the military and ideological spheres. Many high-ranking officers and well-trained soldiers chose to fight in the Southern army, and the will to protect their way of life instilled the people with a sense of patriotic fervour, which led to volunteers joining up in their thousands. This was not the case in the North, where the war was unpopular and in 1862, for the first time, the US army had to resort to conscription. The Confederacy also enjoyed the benefits of a discreet level of diplomatic support from Britain and France, eager to protect their cotton supplies – though this was of little value without maritime supremacy.

Hostilities broke out after Confederate forces captured Fort Sumter in April 1861, a fortified island commanding the entrance to Charleston harbour in South Carolina. At the time, both sides expected a short conflict, but it was not to be. The Southern armies under General Robert E. Lee proved hard to beat. For three long years the North struggled to find the right commanders, form the right army and find the winning way – but nevertheless prevented the South from winning. From this experience it became apparent that the North had the strategic advantage in national terms, and provided they could stop Lee from exploiting his tactical victories they could, by a process of attrition at the tactical level, exhaust the South to the point of defeat on the battlefield. This, however, threatened to be a lengthy process, and the unpopularity of the war pushed Lincoln and his commanders to look for solutions that could hasten the South's demise. One of these solutions was the destruction of the enemy's industrial capabilities: a form of total war that brought it into the civilian realm by destroying infrastructure, workplaces, agriculture and everything that supported the enemy war effort.

In March 1864 Ulysses S. Grant was promoted to lieutenant general, at that time the highest rank in the United States army, and President Abraham Lincoln effectively made him the strategic commander of the Union army. Grant rapidly devised a plan aimed at decisively defeating the Confederacy, through an offensive that would put simultaneous pressure on as many fronts as possible. Four concurrent operations were planned in order to prevent the numerically inferior Confederate troops from concentrating on any single battlefield. The aim was to force Southern armies to engage in combat on all four fronts and simultaneously destroy them, or at least materially reduce them. Major General William T. Sherman headed a fifth operation: to attack deep into the South, with the aim of destroying its capacity to make war. Initially he intended to defeat the Army of Tennessee commanded by General Joseph E. Johnston around Dalton. He soon came to realize that whilst his troops outnumbered Johnston's by almost two to one, his enemy's strong entrenchments meant that the Northern army might be held off for a long time. And so, instead of attacking Dalton, he covered the position (or marked it strongly, in football terms) and concentrated on surrounding Atlanta and isolating the town by cutting off its rail links. Shortly after the last railroad into Atlanta was demolished, Confederate forces began evacuating the city, destroying what they could not take with them. The remainder of the army, under General Hood, then escaped.

Instead of losing time pursuing the enemy army, Sherman decided to cut his way across Georgia to the coast, where he could expect naval support and supplies. On his way, he planned to destroy the resources of the state and therefore the people's will to fight. He and Grant believed that marching a foraging army across Southern territory, far away from rail links and supply chains, was not only possible, but would also prove to be devastating to the Confederate war effort, in both domestic and international terms. A force of 60,000 able-bodied, battle-hardened soldiers thus departed from a burning Atlanta in November 1864, as the remainder of Sherman's army was sent northwards. With the smouldering ruins of Atlanta behind, and only a few thousand reserves, militia and a small body of Southern cavalry between them and the ocean, Sherman's army moved across Georgia with his troops divided into two wings protected by cavalry on the flanks. Like Napoleon's *corps d'armée*, these two wings followed separate paths in four parallel corps columns that covered an area varying from twenty to sixty miles in width. This formation allowed his troops both to cover a wide front and to gain in speed. Sherman's army then laid waste to central Georgia, destroying railroads, farms, factories and everything Confederates could use in their war effort. His forces burnt plantations, shops and crops alike. A sixty-mile-wide swathe of ruin lay behind the army's 285-mile drive to the sea. After making contact with the navy, Sherman stormed the city of Savannah on the coast. In a famous dispatch, he then presented Lincoln with the city and its armaments, as well as thousands of bales of cotton.

Sherman's march to the sea was one of the major events of the Civil

War and it played a significant role in the Union's ultimate victory. For what he commanded was not just another front in which he engaged the opposing forces, nor was it a rampage; rather, it was a very deliberate act, stemming from a strategic decision to destroy the material base of the South. The march signalled the future direction of industrial warfare, both in the targeting of the enemy's industrial and economic infrastructure, and in the development of an industrial base at home. Although up to the very last days of the war Southern armies managed to inflict defeats upon Northern troops – ironically the last battle was an isolated Southern victory in Texas – the inadequacy of their industrial base condemned the Confederate troops. And the inadequacy was underpinned by their inferior rail capability in a war that was in many ways dictated and decided by railways. On the eve of the war, in 1860, the American railway network, stretching over 30,000 miles of track, was already longer than the rest of the world's combined networks. But from the start Northern armies controlled a network of tracks more than twice the size of the Confederacy's. This allowed them to make use of resources throughout their territory, transporting armaments, ammunition and even beef from the Chicago slaughterhouses to the front. Logistically, the South stood at a disadvantage, and the Union's high command therefore deduced correctly that a vital part of their strategy should be aimed at destroying Southern communications. Northern soldiers were instructed to pull up every stretch of Confederate track they came across and in 1863 Brigadier General Herman Haupt, the commander in charge of the Union's military rail system, produced a detailed instruction manual to teach federal cavalrymen how to wreck a railroad behind enemy lines, quickly, thoroughly, and scientifically. The impact on the South's network was compounded by its industrial inability to replace the tracks. Southern raiders behind federal army lines also proved proficient at destroying railroad tracks, but these were rapidly replaced by the North's booming rail industry. In fact, the Union's railway network actually expanded during the course of the war.

But industry affected every aspect of the Civil War. As we have seen, the war gave a great impetus to the development of weapons – the breech loader was introduced, artillery shells improved, lines for the mass production of rifles and ammunition were developed and warships were armoured. Armoured trains towing armoured carriages containing light guns and riflemen came into service. The South, lacking in such extensive weaponry, sought to defend its harbours and estuaries with mines and torpedoes developed by local industry. The experiences of the Civil War also demonstrated the indispensability of the electric telegraph both in the administration of the force as a whole and in directing and controlling operations. In addition to the commercial systems in place at the beginning of the war, more than 15,000 miles of lines were laid for military purposes. President Lincoln rarely missed his daily visit to the telegraph-room of the War Department – a foretaste of the future. However, as with the railways, the telegraph was still a strategic and operational tool: it did not penetrate the tactical levels of military operations. Commanders at these lower levels still depended on communicating face to face, by dispatch rider or runner, or by flag or bugle. Once the troops left the train they moved at the speed of a laden man – and to communicate, and then be controlled, men had to be close together. Tactically these conditions favoured the defence, and soon entrenchment and breast works became a feature of the battlefield.

The American Civil War had an important impact on warfare, since it exposed a new use of force, outside the battlefield – and its utility. Industry allowed for new forms of weapons and new modes of transport, which were clearly crucial; but it was Lincoln and Grant's strategy of using these against the South's means to make war rather than directly against the enemy soldier which brought the victory. Force had a new utility. But there was more. If we take Clausewitz's trinity and apply it to the Civil War we can see that the South lost because the North, with its superior industrial capacity, reduced the strength of the Southern army relative to its own by attrition, and with Sherman's march reduced the capacity of the people and their industrial base to make and sustain the war. The combination led to a loss of will by the Confederacy to continue, and it sued for peace. The North, on the other hand, under Lincoln's leadership and resolve, had harnessed the people, industrially and through conscription, to the army. This trinity provided the framework for victory, and one which also established a basic concept of interstate industrial war: process. For in order to marshal the trinity in the way of the North, it became necessary to have a strong national organization which could mobilize the entire state. By the end of the war the North had created such an organization that dealt with the war within a process that began with the generation of a military strategy based on a political policy; drawing up the resulting mobilization plans; maintaining and adjusting the strategy and the plans over time; and interfacing with other departments of government, most especially the Treasury, over funding the strategy. After the war other nations that already had their own capabilities came to realize that a winning process such as that of the North could be made feasible only by the creation of a permanent bureaucratic machinery to handle it, whether in peace or war – and above all to interface between the military and civilian authorities. This machinery quickly established itself into new institutions which evolved into government ministries capable of implementing the strategy both in preparation and in time of need – and therefore over the projected disruption to the economy of a total war. The institutions evolved over time to become known as ministries of defence. In modern times such institutions have been emulated to an extent on the international stage by organizations such as NATO – which always work around a process but now tend to be far less effective than the original models, not least, as we shall see in Part III, because they cannot identify an enemy around which to form a strategy, and without a strategy it is impossible to make a plan to use force. The process within them is therefore stalled.

The Civil War also established the US way of war: the clear under-standing that industrial ability decides a war, if not a battle, became embedded in the national way of war – as did the concept that seek-ing the decisive defeat of the enemy by destroying his means to make war is equal to scoring a decisive victory in the field. For at the end of the day it was the South, understanding their effort was no longer sustainable, that sued for peace. As such, industrial war, especially as practised in the Civil War, is less an art than a search for the technical solution and a process, which is frequently the case with the US way of war to this day.

I have found an understanding of these matters, and especially the North's strategic development, of considerable use in understanding my US ally over the years. Understanding your ally does not rest on a specific so much as a general comprehension. A good example of this was during my tenure as deputy commander of NATO (DSACEUR) with a US supreme commander (SACEUR), General Wesley Clark. I arrived approximately three months before we started the 1999 bombing in Kosovo, to find a replica of the process that had led to the Dayton Accords in 1995 being played out, in a completely different set of circumstances, over Kosovo. The US was leading the diplomatic engagement, NATO air power – predominantly that of the US – was being used as a threat to back up diplomacy, and the draft agreement that President Milosevic was to sign bore a close resemblance, down to similar paragraph numbering and certain phrases, to the military annexe of the Dayton Accords. Having been the UN commander in Bosnia in 1995, the process was wholly familiar to me, as were the technical means: air power. Yet I also realized that this was now seen by the US as an institutional process, to be followed through to success, even if it was not entirely appropriate to the circumstances. This was the US way of war. In essence I saw my role as DSACEUR, on behalf of the alliance and in particular the European allies, to recognize where the assumptions on which this process had worked in 1995 did not apply four years later in another setting – and to highlight them to my US colleagues whilst at the same time finding suitable solutions. Wesley Clark managed admirably the difficult task of matching the process to the reality, to his personal cost. For my part, I tried to match the supporting measures – the operations in Macedonia and Albania, the generation of forces to enter Kosovo, and my advice as a deputy commander – to reconciling the differences in the allied points of view with the discontinuities between the process and the reality. In effect, my focus was really upon reconciling some of the allies to the slow progress of this process – in Bosnia the bombing and continued threat of force worked within days; in Kosovo it extended over seventy-eight days – which caused a weakening of allied resolve. This was a deep discomfort with the US way of war, and the significance of process within it. In this context I recall I wrote, 'In any event the pivotal position of US Forces is obvious and the position of US Commanders is assured. We must support the US Commanders in their positions, only the US can unseat them; carping in the corridors will weaken the command like a cancer.'

*

As did their US counterparts, the many European scouts who were observing the Civil War's battlefields learned many of the basic lessons of industrial war. They came away with the realization that whilst at a tactical level military talent was undoubtedly crucial, industrial might was also a necessary component of strategic success. They saw the value of the breech-loading weapons and other technical developments – especially the French and Germans, who were already developing their own versions of them, and who therefore benefited from the opportunity to see these innovations in action. And they were deeply impressed by the need for a successful 'railway strategy', which, as we have seen, greatly abetted the ultimate victory of the North. Governments in Europe, learning from the US example, became ever more enmeshed in the process and machinery enabling total war and laid increasing emphasis upon the strategic importance of railways. By 1860, half of Prussia's railways were already run by the state. Twenty years later, this sector was perceived as such a vital part of national defence that imperial Germany brought all railways into public ownership. This was not by whim or chance. The German wars of unification illustrated the superiority of rail over road movements when conducting large-scale military campaigns. It only took a week and twelve trains to deploy the Prussian Guard Corps, based in Berlin, to the Austrian front in 1866. This enabled the Prussians rapidly to concentrate a superior force and overpower the enemy. The French defeat in 1870, due partly to inferior logistics, underlined the point – and reflected that henceforth any state that did not combine its mobilization procedures with its transport policy would risk invasion at the hands of one that did.

The importance of the German wars of unification of 1864–71 extended far beyond the increased and sophisticated use of the railways: they further evolved both the military and political understanding of the use of force, by reflecting the idea of war as a decisive act to achieve a political purpose, and an activity governed by the trinity of people, state and army. As already noted, the relationship between the three is never constant, and in the German case the army was the dominant element. It used the people to create the state, since conscription was as much a tool for nation building as a way of manning the army. Indeed, the idea that all citizens have a duty to serve the state in the armed forces was turned round from its original configuration: in the French Revolution free citizens volunteered and then were conscripted to serve their state, whilst in late-nineteenth-century Germany, by serving in the army the individuals helped forge the state of which they became citizens. Moreover, citizenship was maintained by the conscript, once his period of service terminated, by being placed in the reserve – ready at all times to serve the state, which thereby also gained the ability rapidly to enlarge its military forces in times of war or crisis when the state was under attack.

The dominance of the military in forging the German nation was a result of a clear political decision to use force and an empowerment of the military, especially through an expansion – indeed, a near reconfiguration – of the general staff. This was made possible by two men who clearly understood force and its utility: Otto von Bismarck and General Helmuth von Moltke (the elder). Both were staunchly conservative men who strove for Prussian greatness; both were visionary strategists in their own fields; and like all great strategists, both matched their vision with the capacity to put it into practical effect. Above all, both were as one on the need to use force to achieve a decisive victory – though, as we shall see, they notoriously clashed on the roles of the military and political leaderships in time of war. And whilst Bismarck created the political conditions for this endeavour, largely by engineering the causes of the three wars of unification and keeping the Prussian leadership and public steady throughout the process, Moltke moulded and guided his forces through the battles, delivering three decisive and total victories.

Bismarck, a Junker landowner by birth and breeding, began his political career with a deep belief in the Holy Alliance of Austria, Prussia and Russia, and the dominance of Austria in German affairs. It was upon this ticket that in 1851 he was elected to the federal Diet in Frankfurt – dominated by Austria – only to decide within two weeks of being there and experiencing Austrian leadership that in fact the only way ahead was the independence of Germany headed by Prussia. Moreover, he was convinced of the need for a military solution to the leadership of Germany, since to his mind Prussia could attain supremacy only through a general reconfiguration of the European map. In other words, in order for Prussia to be great, Austria and

France had to be diminished as the leading Great Powers. His was not a popular opinion or voice with the Prussian king, Friedrich Wilhelm IV, and it was not until his brother Wilhelm I assumed the throne in 1861 that Bismarck became prime minister. This happened in 1862, in the midst of an intense dispute between monarch and Diet on military reform: the long-standing tensions between reformers and conservatives, and between military and civilian leaderships, that had their roots in the post-war reforms discussed in the previous chapter, had finally come to a head. The liberal-dominated Diet was refusing to pass a budget aimed at reforming the army's structure and augmenting its size to an extent that would effectively implement universal military service in Prussia, instead of the rotating short-term service solution of the post-war reforms. Bismarck solved the issue by dispensing himself from parliamentary consent, arguing that since none of the chambers of the Diet agreed, the state should continue functioning independently. In so doing he gambled on the fidelity of the Prussian administration – and succeeded. On 30 September 1862 universal conscription became law, but for a clear purpose from Bismarck's perspective, as his address to the Chamber of Deputies, the upper house of the Diet, made clear: 'The great questions of our day cannot be solved by speeches and majority votes . . . but by blood and iron.' There could be no doubt the new Prussian prime minister saw force as the best route to political decision.

With the army bill made law Bismarck set about remaking Germany and the European map. In this he needed a military counterpart who understood the utility of force in the way he did, and found one in the incumbent Chief of the General Staff, Field Marshal Helmuth von Moltke (the elder; the younger, his nephew, held the same position when the Great War broke out in 1914). Many grand titles have been attached to Moltke and most of them are well deserved, for in essence he was the greatest military organizer of the nineteenth century after Napoleon. He was a product of the post-Jena reforms to the Prussian military in that he was a graduate of the *Kriegsakademie* – and one of the best at that – which was then under the direction of Clausewitz. Indeed, in later life Moltke attributed his stunning victories in the wars of German unification to the guidance he had received from *On War*, and there is no doubt that both his military practice and his explicit discussions of military theory reveal a mind thoroughly grounded in the concepts of Clausewitz's writings, though far more focused upon practical organizational matters than preoccupied with strategic abstractions. And this for good reason: Moltke became Chief of the General Staff in 1857, and assumed command of a staff that had become nearly irrelevant. As noted in the previous chapter, after the initial burst of enthusiasm when it was created by the reformers, the general staff lapsed in significance and organization, rejected by the old guard of the army. It was Moltke's job to both revive and make relevant this central staff, for he realized that without it the Prussian military would not have the intellectual or professional knowledge to match Bismarck's ambitions to create Germany by force, and a resulting German army.

His approach to this project was framed in a basic dictum: 'In war as in art there exist no general rules; in neither can talent be replaced by precept.' And so he sought men who, while having all the characteristics of good staff officers – diligent, hard working and exact – had in addition the intellectual qualities to rise above the narrow and particular to comprehend the whole. From within this highly trained group he sought the commanders of the future, and appointed them throughout the army to act with a single purpose and as the supreme commander would, even if he were not there in person. The fundamental change wrought by this approach is viable to this day and apparent in successful military organizations around the world. The basis for this success is ensuring the commanders at every level are operating to the same doctrine, and that the staff as a whole are operating to common methods and procedure.

There are two methods to achieving this end. The first is that the staff put the commander's direction into effect. This requires the commander to make an early decision, if only as to the information he requires in order to make a subsequent decision, and subordinate commanders to be told the result required (get the unit over the river by dawn) rather than what to do (build a bridge at X by midnight) – since the latter requires more detailed work in the superior headquarters. In this first case staffs tend to be small and the responsible staff officer deals directly with his commander. The second method leads the commander to his decision. Having obtained, by a more or less formal process, the commander's guidance, options will be worked up for him to choose from. In this contingency staffs are larger and there are more branches, since there is more work to be done; and the work is directed and overseen by a Chief of Staff who stands between the commander and his staff. The former system tends to informality, the latter to formality. The more a military core is operating to a single doctrine comprehended in its depth, the more it is possible to use the informal system because one can delegate responsibility for implementation with confidence.

In practice headquarters reflect the nature of the commander they serve and the activity they are dealing with. Nevertheless, they will be based on one or other of the two models. As examples, the British army's system is based on the first model and the system used by the US army and the NATO allies is based on the second. I have commanded using both methods on different occasions and been commanded by headquarters using one or other of them. As a commander it is important to understand which method the headquarters is designed round and to act accordingly, or at the least acknowledge the consequences of not doing so. To my mind the first, more informal system is suited best to the tactical level: it is smaller, more agile and produces rapid results, provided the commander is well forward and decisive. The other, more formal system is better at the theatre and strategic levels: it is more thorough, can handle a wide range of issues at the same time and, with a good Chief of Staff, can anticipate and plan ahead. In the 1990–91 Gulf War, my armoured division headquarters was organized on the British model – and was noticeably smaller than the US divisional HQ. This was a function of national preference and philosophy. It took us some time to learn that the many plans emanating from the superior US corps HQ and flanking US divisional HQ were but contingencies; indeed the Americans often referred to them as 'plays', as in American football, since they were not 'the plan' or concrete orders. I had one staff officer to deal with all this paper where an equivalent US HQ had a branch of about five officers. There were other differences in the systems: decisions were taken about different matters at different levels, but as a general rule responsibility and authority were found lower in the British HQ. On the staff a British captain often carried the authority of a US colonel. Jargon was also different. My ADC, a personal staff officer usually of junior rank, would occasionally use this to advantage when he discovered that his US ally's ADC was an assistant divisional commander in the rank of brigadier general – who was entitled to order his own helicopter, which my ADC was not. This did not stop him telephoning the US command for a helicopter, and getting one. In reality these were super-ficial differences, which definitely had to be viewed as such. On the whole I thought of the matter rather like electrical equipment: we had different plugs and worked on different voltages, but all our equip-ment needed to run together. By the time we had fully deployed I had some seventy officers and men with the necessary communications as 'transformers' and 'adaptors' to various points of the US command, from the HQ on my flanks to the logistic HQ in the port at Al Jubayal. This enabled the operation to run smoothly, but it was at a cost to the rest of the British military: all these men had to be found from other units in Britain and Germany, which were expected to continue to function without the manpower and equipment. Without conscrip-tion or any other steady stream of manpower, sustaining operations becomes a matter of robbing Peter to pay Paul as well as command and professionalism.

Moltke, in re-creating the Prussian general staff, tended towards the first, more informal method of organization: the general staff were intended to put an operation into effect and to ensure tactical co-herence. But first he had to create the staff. To this end he turned to the *Kriegsakademie*, and arranged that each year 120 officers were sent to it after being selected from the entire Prussian officer corps on a competitive basis. Only forty usually finished the entire, much re-invigorated course, and of these Moltke chose twelve to serve on the general staff after further training. This included as much practical input as possible, including planning for hypothetical battles and analysing past campaigns. Both exercises are now standard practice in military academies around the world, but at the time they were great innovations. After these theoretical studies the chosen officers spent some years alongside Moltke in headquarters and field exercises with troops, followed by a period of duty with regiments. This completed the training of senior staff officers, who henceforth spent their careers rotating between assignments in the general staff and regimental duty.

Between campaigns the staff spent its time exercising and formulating plans, often in minute detail, for the next war. Every element of military activity was examined, each plan and contingency constantly analysed and revised, every formation and unit configured and standardized down to the last item – ensuring a trained soldier, but especially a trained officer, could move seamlessly from unit to unit. Through this intensive and highly detailed programme of inculcation Moltke created a body of staff officers and commanders who in thinking and understanding came close to being identical to him and each other, thereby ensuring that when dispersed amongst regiments and in battle they created a coherence – a nervous system – that enabled the Prussian military body to perform as one, without the need for detailed orders from higher commanders. Equally, senior commanders could and did assign missions to subordinate commanders, but left the manner of completion to them in the knowledge that it would be within the same core ethos. Over time the outcome of these activities also came together into another innovation of Moltke's: a coherent military doctrine, best reflected in his 1869 *Instructions for Large Unit Commanders* – a document which, in spirit at least, has inspired most operation manuals of Western militaries to this day.

In many ways Moltke was evolving further Napoleon's ideas of organizational mobility and operational flexibility – and ultimately therefore the understanding and use of force. For the core idea behind his restructuring of the general staff was the creation of a true nervous system based on the dichotomy of decentralization and centralization: the decentralization of the command structure in order to achieve speed in decision and the making of the most appropriate decisions for the circumstances, coupled with centralized direction and doctrine. We have already seen in the case of Napoleon how, when engaged, making a decision and acting on it faster than one's opponent causes the latter to act on false information and therefore inappropriately. The best way of achieving speed and appropriateness is by ensuring information and orders have to travel the least distance both physically and hierarchically, since the information has the best chance of being correct if the man making the decision is near to the matter in hand. In other words, the commander on the ground rather than the central command – which means decentralization of decisions. But to be successful and to concentrate the efforts of an army, all the decision making must, as already noted, be working within the same doctrine and towards the same objective. Napoleon empowered his senior commanders and gave them considerable authority, but none the less remained the sole source of direction and doctrine. In the system Moltke created, there was a core doctrine and the concept of decentralized command encompassed every element, from mobilization to battle, enhanced by the focused and meticulous central planning capabilities of Moltke's staff. Indeed, even with the business of mobilization, Moltke designed a system which could bring massive numbers of troops to bear at crucial junctures in a matter of weeks. This represented a much faster method than before. Each Prussian army corps commander was put in charge of the mobilization of his own formation, with the assistance of the civil authorities in his district. This decentralization of execution was matched by centralized direction of purpose. In case of war, the first step was the mobilization of men and horses for the field army. At the same time, depot troops would begin to amass: each infantry or artillery regiment formed a depot battalion, each cavalry regiment a depot squadron – in other words, still more decentralization. The mobilization of the reserve and garrison troops took place immediately after that of the field army. With universal conscription in law, a general plan of mobilization could be drawn up and annually amended by the general staff, incorporating the systematic use of the telegraph and railways to move troops and supplies to the projected theatres of operation. As noted, the military greatly influenced the development of the railways, stipulating, for example, the need for certain high-volume east–west routes and the length of platform necessary to allow for the rapid entrainment and detrainment of troops. With such a method of command, matched to the appropriate organization applied at the strategic level, Moltke achieved the ability to move his state from peace to war faster than his opponents – another form of organizational mobility.

From the original concept that emanated from the post-Jena reforms, Moltke made the Prussian general staff a reality. And it was this sophisticated machine, matched with a doctrine of speed of decision making at both the tactical and strategic levels, and the concentration of force for a decisive strike that he brought to bear in support of Bismarck's strategy for Prussian supremacy and German unification through the use of force. These joint visions unfolded in a threefold sequence from 1864, when Prussia and Austria went to war together against Denmark, with the objective of splitting the Danish controlled duchies of Schleswig-Holstein between both attacking powers. For Bismarck, apart from achieving this aim the enterprise was to consolidate his internal position and to show that his expansion plans for the nation and his path of iron and blood were the only ones viable for Prussia. Moltke devised a plan based on his doctrine of central planning coupled with decentralized command, which indeed delivered a decisive victory – though not exactly in the way he wished. For whilst he was seen as a near 'demigod' by his own staff and some politicians, many of the old guard in the Prussian military resented him and as before derided the general staff as intellectual upstarts. Many of his directives were therefore modified or even ignored by some commanders; but a decisive victory was delivered none the less. Through the Treaty of Gastein, imposed on Denmark in August 1865, Austria gained control of Holstein, whilst Prussia seized Schleswig and the Duchy of Lauenburg. The next step was a move against Austria, which had successfully thwarted Prussian attempts to unify German states under its leadership in the 1850s. Bismarck saw war as necessary to push Prussia's rival out of the scene and diminish it in stature. In 1866 he succeeded in using a diplomatic dispute to provoke Austria into declaring war on Prussia. Following the earlier victory, this time Moltke had far more control over all his commanders since he both planned and personally directed the action. Prussia mobilized with great speed against Austria and its south German allies, entering Austria in three large columns on a broad front. This enabled the Prussians rapidly to concentrate a superior force and overpower the enemy, whose efforts to mobilize were much slower. As noted, it took only a week and twelve trains to deploy the Prussian Guard Corps, based in Berlin, to the Austrian front. At Königgratz in Bohemia, Prussian troops fought a decisive battle. Superior organization, the use of the needle gun and (as often in war) a certain amount of luck gave the victory to Prussia. As a result, the Seven Weeks War, as the

Austro-Prussian War came to be known, was a triumph for Bismarck and Moltke's general staff.

The first of Bismarck's objectives was fulfilled: Austria was permanently eliminated from the direction of German national affairs. Now only the south of Germany and the disputed provinces of Alsace and Lorraine remained outside Prussia's realm. In 1870 Bismarck engineered another war, this time against France – seeking to unite the German people against the traditional enemy. The fate of Alsace and Lorraine, which had belonged to the Holy Roman Empire until the seventeenth century, was used to stir up nationalistic sentiment. The south German states took the bait and joined Bismarck in his crusade against the French, which had been cunningly conned into declaring war on Prussia. Having established himself with the two victories, Moltke's status was now indisputable; no one dared to challenge his plan for the campaign. This time he did the opposite to his successful attack in Austria and chose to enter France with his army largely concentrated on a narrow front – reflecting thereby all the strengths of the general staff's capabilities. Thorough study of the railways in eastern France had led to the conclusion the French could concentrate their forces in only two areas, Metz and Strasbourg. The best option for Prussia was therefore to attack with all their forces each of the French concentrations in turn, approaching in such a way that the enemy remained divided and each part was unable to aid the other. The staff drew up a meticulous plan to implement this operational manoeuvre, which unfolded from 16 July, three days before the start of the war, when mobilization was declared. On the ninth day, 24 July, about 500,000 men had already been mobilized, so nearly doubling the size of Prussia's peacetime army of 300,000. Concentration of the field army near the frontier began on the same day. By 3 August, day nineteen, the whole field army, some 440,000 strong, was concentrated alongside its materiel. In the process, nine railways were given up entirely to the movement of armies: three for the south and six for the north German armies. The average haul during this phase of concentration was about 400 kilometres.

As Moltke and his general staff had anticipated, the French could not match the Prussian speed or system of mobilization and so began operations before the reserves and complete equipment had reached the active army. As a result the French mobilization effort was never completed. The first of the French forces were soon pinned down around Metz and engaged in two great battles: Vionville-Mars-la-Tour on 16 August and Gravelotte-St-Privat on 18 August, from which the Prussians emerged victorious. At this point the strengths, literally, of Moltke shone through. At the end of the battle, seventy years old yet having been on his horse all day and twice unsheathing his sword in the face of the enemy – an extreme measure for a supreme commander to take, denoting imminent danger – he dictated an order to split his army: one group was sent north-west towards the border fort of Sedan to attack the French force commanded by Napoleon III that was based there. The other was directed west towards Paris, at great speed, to exploit the victories of the past days, and he continued to contain the forces concentrating around Strasbourg to his east. The French at Sedan, cut off from reinforcements by the German march on their capital, fought extremely well but were none the less defeated. The Prussian victory was overwhelming. The French emperor abdicated and fled to England whilst France lay torn apart by conflicting political and social factions that devolved into civil war, which focused on the communards' uprising in Paris. In the German states, victory stirred patriotic spirits to the point of obliterating past resentments against Prussia, and the south German states chose to enter voluntarily the Prussian-led new German state. In May 1871 the German Empire – the Second Reich – was declared, and Wilhelm I was crowned as its emperor in Louis XIV's Hall of Mirrors at Versailles. The political aim of German unification had been achieved, exactly as Bismarck, now its Chancellor, had predicted and intended – by force.

In military terms, it was Moltke, his strategy and campaign, and his general staff that truly conquered in each of the three wars. The speedy concentration of a mobilized force allowed the Prussian theatre commander to seize and retain the initiative and dictate events, forcing his opponents to react within his plan. This resulted in early and decisive victories, which led directly to the achievement of the political purpose: the inclusion of territories and German-speaking people within the Prussian monarch's sovereignty. The achievement was enabled through the process of the industrial approach to war, from the mass of troops produced by universal conscription through mobilization and the amassment of men and materiel on the battlefield. And the general staff, the graduates of the *Kriegsakademie* and Moltke's meticulous training, showed their mastery both of the 'industrial process' of mobilization, the movement and supply of the mass of men and materiel on the battlefield, and the coordination of the tactical handling of the German forces. The senior commanders, all trained in the same school and assisted by the same staff, made decisions faster than the French, decisions that were focused to a single purpose and within a common doctrine. Their opponents were as good as – and sometimes better than – the Prussian soldiers and commanders at the tactical level, and often equally or better armed; but this was insufficient to counter the superior operational method the Prussians had for the handling and coordination of their army.

The battles of all three wars reflected both the old and the new. They retained many Napoleonic features, particularly the manoeuvre of large formations of men in close order. The lack of battlefield communication persisted since the telegraph was immobile, and thus so did the need for close-order formations to achieve control and focus firepower. On the other hand, the battles were also more evolved, as evidenced by the appearance of new weapons and the wider use of the telegraph: it allowed for rapid communication between the political and strategic levels in Berlin and the field commanders; until, that is, the advancing columns thoughtlessly tore down the cables, as they did in the war with Austria. But while the tempo of political and strategic events had quickened, those on the battlefield remained tied to the speed that a laden man could march, and his supplies moved at the speed of the horse-drawn wagon. In other words, the railways delivered the mass armies and weapons to the battlefield, but once away from the railheads it was back to the previous modes of transportation. And whilst the cavalry remained on the battlefield, it lacked firepower; and faced with increasing rates of aimed direct fire from the new breech-loading rifles, it became more and more a reconnaissance force and less and less a force of shock and decision as it had been in Napoleonic times. It was indeed a transitional battlefield.

The decisive victories of the Prussian forces reflected the military worth and superiority of the general staff, especially in mobilizing forces and designing the application of force; and in the years that followed most continental armies adopted their model of a planning staff backed up by universal conscription. In the new German Empire the prestige of the general staff and admiration for the military became supreme, effectively deciding a dispute which had emerged during the wars between Moltke and Bismarck over leadership in time of war. Moltke drew a distinct boundary between politics and strategy, claiming diplomacy was paramount until the start of hostilities when military necessity reigned supreme. He and his generals resented Bismarck's interference in military operations, found him to be basically rude and boorish and derided what they deemed his risible advice. Equally, Bismarck, in his view of war as a forceful means of achieving a political end, demanded that statecraft remain supreme at all times. He found the military masters to be narrow professionals, uncomprehending of – or uninterested in – diplomacy and politics. There had been strong clashes over the issue throughout the three wars, but over time – indeed, after two world wars – Bismarck was proved to be correct. After Moltke, the general staff slowly evolved into a body that concentrated on the tactical and operational matters at the expense of the strategic and political issues. The admiration in which Kaiser Wilhelm II later held it meant that it became the de facto centre of German policy making, but without, by this time, the fundamental capabilities for the task. The Great War proved to be a disaster for Germany and a disaster for Europe. And the significance of the general staff's contribution to this disaster was underlined in the 1919 Treaty of Versailles, which specifically dictated its dismemberment and prohibited its re-creation – probably the only peace treaty ever to focus upon a staff as a threat.

By the end of the Franco-Prussian War the paradigm of interstate industrial war was nearly complete; in the years and wars to come it would be refined, and industry and technology would furnish it with ever more destructive weapons. But the core structures were all in place: in just seventy-five years – an insignificant period in historical terms, especially with regard to warfare – many aspects of war had been completely changed. Napoleon's startling innovations in the nature of war had become generally accepted within his lifetime; the establishment of the Prussian general staff as early as 1808, as a measure of response to his decisive victories, reflected this fundamental change. Within another twenty years Clausewitz had codified these innovations into a new theory of war. Thirty years later the protagonists in the American Civil War were implementing these changes on an increasingly industrialized battlefield, as was Moltke in the organization of armies. Moltke's subsequent implementation of his methods and structures in the German wars of unification brought the conduct of war and armies to a point of extreme efficiency – and became a model for emulation, even to this day. And within all of these developments, the use of force evolved, growing ever stronger and more destructive, and applied in new ways to different ends. Mainly, inter-state industrial war was a tool for creating and preserving nations – which is why decisive victories could be sought through it. There can be no more fundamental aim or need, and within this context the utility of force was absolutely clear. The German wars of unification reflect this.

The unified Germany represented a new reality: a big army with a shared military experience and reserve capacity. It was also presented with a new problem: positioned between France to the west, wanting revenge and its territory back, and Russia to the east, willing to enter into any alliance to check the German–Austro-Hungarian alliance from expanding further. In any future war it would potentially have to fight on two fronts at the same time. As we shall see in the next chapter, this strategic dilemma concentrated the minds of the German general staff on the theatre or operational level, and therefore the need to win quickly and decisively in one theatre before rapidly switching resources to the other. They knew it was not possible to match their enemies in both simultaneously. This strategic dilemma was a direct consequence of creating Germany. It is also a reflection of the point in which force went beyond its utility. As we have seen, Bismarck and Moltke, each in his way and to his purpose, had an excellent understanding of the utility of force in achieving a political aim. Within this context the Danish and Austrian wars were effectively neat little land grabs well nested within political contexts – almost foregone conclusions before fighting actually began. The Franco-Prussian War in 1870 was another matter. The political aim of the war was the unification of Germany under Prussia. To this end the defeat of the French army would by itself have led to the annexation of Alsace and Lorraine – and unification. But in going on to Paris, ensuring the collapse of the Second Empire, and then as a final humiliation the wholly political act of crowning the Kaiser in the Hall of Mirrors in Versailles – the political context of the war was exceeded.

Bismarck and Moltke did not live to see the consequences of the French humiliation – the overstretch of force utility – but ironically in later life both came to realize the limitations of force and a powerful military, and tried to warn against them. Following his final encounter with Kaiser Wilhelm II, who came to visit him in 1896 when he was already ill, Bismarck said to his aides: 'If the country is well ruled, the coming war may be averted; if it is badly ruled, that war may become a Seven Years War!' And in 1890 Moltke, having finally stepped down as Chief of the General Staff in 1888, warned the Reichstag of which he was now a member that the generals and militarists surrounding the Kaiser were agitating for a war, and when it broke out 'its length will be incalculable and its end nowhere in sight . . . and woe to him who first sets fire to Europe, who first puts the flame to the powderkeg!'

The war that broke out in 1914 proved them both correct.

3

Culmination: The World Wars

By the end of the 19th century the paradigm of interstate industrial war was complete: its core elements of mass, industry and force were in place, as were the core concepts of process and organization. Following on Napoleon and Moltke there was a wider understanding of the application of force. Moreover, industrial war had proven its utility: it had created nations and changed the map of Europe. And as the Great Powers of this new Europe vied for supremacy it became obvious that another industrial war would be fought. Commanders and staffs in all nations began laying their plans, largely based on the notions gained in the previous wars, especially the German wars of unification. But when the war came it was bigger and more forceful than could be imagined: no longer interstate, but world wide. In the world wars the paradigm was fully implemented – to the point of culmination.

The starting point is 1871, for after the Franco-Prussian War, and even more after the arms race between the Great Powers had begun in the 1890s, it was clear that sometime in the not-too-distant future – a future tangible to the many who spoke of it – there would be a war: an act of revenge by France upon Germany which could turn into an act of defence by Germany; an act of attempted hegemony by any of the Great Powers; or an act of provocation by a Great Power or an external actor that would make inevitable a war amongst them all. As the anticipation of war grew so did the web of agreements and counter-agreements amongst the nations become ever tighter and more complex, and the mutual mistrust of all the powers and their players – the politicians, the generals, the monarchs, the diplomats – grow ever stronger, to a point at which the reasoning for war overpowered any other. It was this mutually accepted reasoning that also ensured a mutually understood concept of war, at least on the European continent, as a mass event in which immense forces would do battle with immense force to deliver a decisive victory. And despite the prescient words of Moltke and a minority of other sages, it was also believed that this war, like those of German unification, would be rapid: the massed armies, the men and materiel of the states, would finally come face to face on a battlefield in a mighty confrontation which would decide in one fell swoop the rightness of one way and the wrongness of another. This would be the war to end all wars because after it one state, or possibly one union of states, and its industrial ability would be decidedly superior to the other. The paradigm of interstate industrial war would be realized to the full – and then become by implication redundant.

The logic of a war to end all wars was simple: since it had successfully reshaped the map of Europe through industrial capability, war could therefore also define its absolute dominant power. Unfortunately this simplicity was also its fatal flaw, since the possibility that industrial war could lead to absolute destruction across the map of Europe did not seem to occur to many, especially as prosperity increased all about. For as the centuries changed, the European industrial miracle that would feed the future war continued to expand, fuelled largely by its own coal and agriculture, manufacturing goods from the resources of its states and those of its empires, which were sold in its own national and imperial markets. Populations grew as health and wealth increased, and so did nation states as the dominant governing unit – or else nations aspiring to be states, especially within the Habsburg Empire. And with them grew ideas and sentiments of patriotism which often led to nationalism. The Clausewitzian trinity of people, state and army now appeared to be in near balance: this was not the Napoleonic model of the state where ideals or the emperor led the other two, nor the Prussian model of the military dominating: as war grew ever near all three were pulling together in many parts of Europe. In a mix of national pride and military enthusiasm, the idea of war as the logical crowning glory of the age was bandied about by politicians, soldiers and civilians alike. Pride in the industrial ability of a nation was also proof of its military capability, whether in ships or guns or bullets; the growth of its population was also proof of its industrial ability to put men in the field, as were the length and speed of its railways and fleets. The sheer prosperity of the age was proof of its preparedness for war. It was a logical balancing act – a delicate equilibrium kept stable by the 'balance of power'. In 1914 the equilibrium slipped and Europe went to war.

The overarching drama and horror of the First World War marked the end of a human era, a fact recognized relatively quickly – indeed within a year of the war starting, when all ideas of speed as a defining characteristic of war had been deeply buried beneath the mud of the trenches in Flanders, together with the first crop of European youth. Any mobility and operational flexibility had become entrenched, together with the mass conscript armies mobilized in 1914. With no swift and decisive victory, the use of massive force had not had utility. As the front lines became set, entire state economies and populations were mobilized in the service of the beast: interstate industrial war had become total war for the combatant nations. The product of the industrial output of two massive economic blocs created the grinding conditions of trench warfare on the western front, and the develop-ment of almost all the equipment available to commanders today. I am not going to rehearse the history or even the military history of this cataclysmic war, many excellent accounts of which exist elsewhere; I will, however, touch on both to explain the evolution of force and its utility within the major trends we have been following. The starting point is the Schlieffen Plan and its background.

Following the unification of Germany under Prussia, Bismarck sought to convince other European leaders that this new Great Power was of peaceful disposition. Understanding the strategic threat, his greatest fear was of German isolation and war on two fronts, and to avoid this outcome he was driven by two cardinal rules: averting conflicts among the powers of central Europe, and settling for 'semihegemony' as a means of ensuring German security. He set about achieving these aims of his security policy through a system of strategic alliances. Given that France was inevitably set on revenge after the annexation of Alsace-Lorraine, he turned towards his other neighbours, con-cluding alliances with Austria-Hungary in 1879 and Italy in 1882.

However, the greatest success of Bismarckian diplomacy was the secret agreement signed with Russia in 1887, the Reinsurance Treaty, the terms of which violated the spirit of the treaty with Austria-Hungary but enabled him, within the context of his security policy, to avoid war on two fronts.

Bismarck's fall from office in 1890 heralded the end of this age of cautious German diplomacy. A more aggressive attitude to relations with the other Great Powers soon emerged, backed by considerable investments in the military and naval spheres. The first casualty was the fragile Russian Reinsurance Treaty. In 1893, partly from economic motives, Russia refused to renegotiate the treaty, choosing instead to turn to France for financial assistance and military security. As the European arms race spread to the seas, Britain became increasingly worried by the growth of Kaiser Wilhelm's navy. Already strained, Anglo-German relations deteriorated in 1898 after the Reichstag passed the First Naval Bill, which allowed for the increase of the navy by seven battleships, two heavy cruisers and seven light cruisers, and were further undermined by the Supplementary Naval Act of 1900, which doubled these new additions to the fleet, and German claims on Morocco. In 1904 Britain and France entered into the Entente Cordiale, a non-binding agreement that resolved territorial disputes between them but which none the less signalled a clear shift in British policy towards France. This was underlined in 1907, when Britain joined the Franco-Russian alliance: the Triple Entente that Bismarck had wanted to avoid at all cost had come into being.

Encircled by an alliance of hostile powers, Germany now had to face the prospect not only of war on two fronts but also at sea: a new strategic challenge for the general staff. The Entente's overall superiority in numbers was evident, since the Russian Empire's reserves of manpower were immense, whilst Britain and France could potentially draw on their colonial realms as long as Britannia ruled the waves. However, for the general staff, the weakness of Russia lay in its mass: the sheer size of the Tsar's realms meant that mobilization would probably prove to be a lengthy process, especially since the Russian railway network was not as developed as those in central and western Europe. On the other hand, the Prussian and German armies had twice proved their capacity to mobilize rapidly and strike immediately after concentration had been achieved. With the help of the rail network, they believed they could attempt to destroy one opponent quickly and decisively before concentrating all their forces on the other. Count Alfred von Schlieffen, Chief of the German General Staff from 1891 to 1906, devised a rapid offensive strategy that could fulfil this goal soon after he took office. He believed German and French mobilization could be accomplished in a fortnight, whilst Russia's would probably take six weeks owing to its size and the limitations of its rail network. This left little time for the Germans to defeat France before turning their efforts towards the eastern front. The problem faced by Schlieffen was that the fortresses erected by France after 1870 to protect its new frontiers with German Alsace-Lorraine would slow down or halt the attack. He resolved this issue by deciding to attack France through Belgium, a neutral state since 1839, which would allow his northern wing to avoid the French defences. To do this, he had to move large numbers of forces over the water obstacles of the Low Countries and defeat the Belgian defences fast enough and with sufficient numbers to produce the necessary concentration of forces on the borders of France. These would then accomplish a great encircling movement through northern France and round Paris to defeat the French armies in the depth of their own country. According to the plan, in the first six weeks of war about 85 per cent of field forces would be allocated to the western theatre, whilst the remaining 15 per cent would hold the eastern front, awaiting the arrival of the Russian armies.

When war broke out on 4 August 1914 the Schlieffen Plan, with some modifications, was put into action – and it ultimately failed in execution. Reality – starting with the vast quantities of men and materiel concentrated in a relatively small space, which is a basic attribute of industrial war – overrode the plan. Even before hostilities officially commenced all the major European powers had begun the largest mobilization effort the world had ever seen. Prepared carefully in the preceding decades, plans for the gearing of society towards war stretched through most spheres of civilian life, particularly in Germany and France. The process at the heart of industrial war, established in the American Civil War, swung into action. Railways, under direct or indirect control of the state, began ferrying men, horses and materiel to the front. By 17 August the size of the German Reich's army, 800,000 men in peacetime, had been multiplied by six through the mobilization of reservists. Some 1,485,000 men had by then already been transported to the front with Belgium and France, armed and ready to engage in combat. The nations on the other side matched this achievement. Indeed, France's transportation scheme proved to be exceedingly competent; Austrian mobilization followed the same pattern of efficiency, and even the Russians surprised the Germans with the speed with which they concentrated their First and Second Armies in Poland. Enormous forces were thus in the field in a matter of weeks: at the end of August the French army comprised sixty-two infantry divisions, each 15,000 strong. The German Reich boasted eighty-seven divisions whilst its Habsburg ally totalled forty-nine. Meanwhile, in the East, the Russians raised an impressive 114 divisions. These, together with millions of horses and tons of equipment, poured rapidly onto the battlefields in far greater numbers and far quicker than Schlieffen and his staff had reckoned when they drew up the plan. The armies on all sides had learned the importance of rapid mobilization – at least to the extent of understanding that assembling forces was not sufficient: in order to apply force through them they had to be organized in the correct place and with the correct formations.

The Schlieffen Plan failed quite simply because the French defeated the German attack. That is the trouble with plans: the enemy do not as a rule cooperate with the assumptions on which they are laid. It is even more the trouble with plans which are drawn up for a contingency some time before the event – Schlieffen stopped work eight years before the war broke out – and executed by those who were not party to making them, and who do not necessarily know the assumptions on which they are based. Such was the situation in Germany. In 1906 Schlieffen had been succeeded as Chief of the General Staff by Helmuth von Moltke the younger, nephew of the great military genius of the nineteenth century. Unlike either his predecessor or his uncle, 'the nephew', as he was known, was not of a particularly bold nature – which proved to be decidedly unhelpful for the Germans. A bold plan demands boldness in execution, not incremental tinkering as events unfold. As the prospect of war became increasingly evident he reduced the number of forces in his northern wing, sending them to the eastern front, where in any case they proved insufficient when the Russians mobilized with greater speed than envisaged. On the western front the Belgians, British and French put up much stiffer resistance than anticipated, and the logistics of moving the mass of German men and materiel took longer than expected: after their initial attacks the Germans outran their transport and their heavy artillery, used to crushing advantage in earlier battles. Then Joffre and the French general staff took advantage of German overextension to snatch the operational initiative. This was probably one of the main reassessments needed but not made since the days of Schlieffen: the French were no longer weak and still licking their wounds from the defeat of 1870. They had reformed into a strong and efficient fighting machine. Under the overall and excellent command of Marshal Joffre they kept their heads, with General Foch leading the counter-attack at the Marne with the famous saying: 'My centre is giving way, my right is in retreat; situation excellent. I shall attack.' He did, and he succeeded. The Germans, on the other hand, found themselves in temporary decline. Moltke, whose command style has been compared to that of an orchestral conductor whose players disregarded his baton, lost control of his army commanders. He also lost his own position, and was replaced as Chief of the General Staff by General Erich von Falkenhayn on 14 September 1914.

A decisive victory had not been won by either side in the swift opening of the war. In its stead came a stalemate of balanced opposing forces: both sides well matched for the trial of strength and determined to win the clash of wills. As such it became evident that the end of the war, however it was achieved, would be defined in new terms. A decisive victory would not be rapid – nor probably definitive in the way of the German wars of unification, since it would involve more than the destruction of the forces in the field. This would no longer be a military clash of strength, but a far wider encounter involving the economies and people of either side.

By late October 1914 the western front had more or less stabilized on a line that ran from the North Sea to Switzerland, with Germany occupying much of Belgium and 20 per cent of France – the 20 per cent that contained about 80 per cent of its industrial strength. This line would remain more or less the same for the following four years, with massive battles producing minimal variations. It also explains one of the basic reasons the war continued, contrary to various public perceptions that it 'dragged on' futilely or became a series of pointless battles: France and Belgium were occupied. Short of capitulating to the Central Powers, there was no option but to carry on fighting. The battles were therefore neither futile nor pointless, but indefinitive – for good technical reasons.

In many ways for both sides the strategic and theatre-level problem was akin to the tactical problem of besieging a medieval castle, though on a massive scale. The besieger would dig trenches to protect himself from enemy fire, then sap or dig forward towards the defenders to get his assaulting force as close as possible and under protection. Meanwhile he would endeavour to reduce or breach the defensive barrier by fire, mines or battery. When the commander was confident he had a breach or could penetrate the barrier, and equally confident he could mass a sufficient assaulting force close enough to the breach without it being delayed or disrupted by the enemy's fire, he would attempt to take the fort. This is an example of using a 'trench system' offensively, but trenches are also used defensively. In the nineteenth century the lethality and range of the breech-loaded rifle caused infantry to use trenches as shields, and the lack of battlefield communications meant the trenches had to be linked. Unlike a shield, a trench is obviously static, so the occupant also becomes a defender of his hole – and the bigger the area entrenched, the bigger the defended locality, the greater the trench system. In most circumstances, and just like the medieval castle, one could outflank the position, surround it, and reduce it. But unlike the castle, the defender was unlikely to have the supplies or developed defences to hold out for long against a determined assault by a superior force supported by artillery. In the First World War each side entrenched: the Germans primarily as a defensive system – the besieged of the castle – and the Allies primarily as an offensive system – the besiegers. Moreover, the size of the armies and the industrial capacities of the Central Powers and the Allies were such as to fill the entire space along the front with men and sustain them there. They were able to do this with sufficient men and in sufficient depth – or to such a high density – that there was no flank to turn, the ends of the line being firmly anchored on the North Sea and the Swiss border. Since there was no flank to exploit, the attacker had to find a way to breach or penetrate the defences. In the spring of 1918 the Germans under General Ludendorff went on the offensive and breached the Allied defences, yet lacked the ability to exploit the success. Eventually it was the Allies who succeeded, and brought the war to an end. But it took more than three years of hard-won experience to develop the armies, their tactics and equipment to successfully apply military force to roll back the German defensive lines.

As the front settled in 1914, the nature of the fighting and the use of force evolved rapidly. The reasons for this were once again a direct consequence of the sheer mass of industrial total war – and the contemporary level of development of transport and communications. For the story of the western front, which became the iconic image of the war as a whole, was once again a result of the speed of strategic and theatre movement by railway being reduced to that of the marching laden man once a force moved away from the railhead, and communications being based on the telegraph and telephone or remaining a matter of runners, dispatch riders and personal contact. The operational-level problem was one of finding a way to make a gap in the line of sufficient width to be exploited to attack into the depth of the opposing defence. The railways further aggravated this problem since the defender, falling back on his railhead, could always mass forces by railway faster than the attacker moving away from his railhead could exploit any initial gain on foot. As a result of these industrial realities the war on the western front took on a wholly attritional nature. There was movement, but there was no room in which to manoeuvre. In an industrial process men and materiel were moved by rail to the line where they faced another mass. Great concentrations of forces were built up, and one side would attack – the attacker endeavouring always to breach the defences to the extent that he could flood in behind the defenders and destroy them. For weeks attack and counter-attack would cause the line to ebb and flow in an attritional exchange fed by the industrial process, which had to be run to a programme; the available communications allowed nothing else. The result was that rapid attack of one force by another in order to achieve a decisive victory quickly – the aim of interstate industrial war – was rendered impossible. The attritional stalemate of the trench lines was almost inevitable in such circumstances.

Attacks to gain ground from trench to trench were supported by the use of massive artillery bombardments. Indeed, the First World War was primarily an artillery war and the thousands of big guns deployed on each side were the prime cause of casualties. Technology followed these new developments closely: shrapnel shells, more suited to the attack of troops in the open, were soon replaced by high-explosive shells which were more effective for the destruction of trenches and earthworks. Artillery bombardments attempted to break down the integrity of the defence by attacking a number of targets. The first target was the defender himself: even if it failed to kill him, the shocking effect of bombardment sapped his spirit. The second target was the defender's environment: to destroy the trench system, sever telephone communication, breach the barbed-wire obstacles and break down the trenches themselves. The third target was to destroy the enemy guns. When the infantry assault took place the artillery was required both to keep the opponent's head down while the attacking waves closed on their objectives, and to attack the defender's reserves as he fired or moved up to counter-attack. So intense were the barrages in some cases, such as the build-up to the battle of the Somme, that the Germans called the phenomenon the battle of materiel (*die Materialschlacht*). This type of trench warfare created an endless demand for men, munitions and supplies with often no apparent gains or victories. Infantry attacks became an extremely costly affair and led to huge losses for both the attackers and the defenders. In 1916, for example, on the first day of the battle of the Somme, some 60,000 British soldiers were casualties, of which 20,000 were killed. Throughout the ongoing battle that same year in Verdun, the longest battle of the war, the French lost approximately 550,000 men and the Germans 434,000. Industrial total war, having failed to produce the promise of a quick decisive victory, was producing instead casualties at an industrial rate. It is perhaps an obvious truth that the longer men are engaged directly then the more the casualties, and the larger the number of men then the more the casualties too. As a general rule, therefore, one should try to hold most of one's force out of contact from the enemy for as long as possible, and plan to engage in many small fights very quickly. In this way, even if the conflict lasts a long time the battles do not. However, to do this one needs space and time, neither of which was available on the western front: there was no scope for operational flexibility.

In parallel to building up an industrial war machine, as its continental neighbours had done throughout the preceding century, Britain came to play a particular part in the war. Britain had always maintained the Royal Navy to defend its shores and trade and to project its power and influence, and by the end of the nineteenth century its size reflected the principle that it must be bigger than the two next largest navies in the world combined. Fear for its naval supremacy had prompted Britain to enter into the arms race with Germany in the 1880s, but the British army had remained a small volunteer force whose role can best be summed up as that of an 'imperial gendarmerie'. This army had considerable experience of 'small wars', and of raising, leading and cooperating with local native forces. There were some notable defeats, such as the battle of Islandwana in 1879, but the British, as the poet Hilaire Belloc noted, 'have got the Maxim gun and they have not'; in other words they had the industrial and technological advantage, and won their wars. In this way, throughout the nineteenth century the British, unlike the continental powers that focused on building up industrial conscript armies, used their industrial strength to develop a navy to fight again the major fleet actions such as Trafalgar, which they anticipated would defend the kingdom and empire, and to equip a small army to gain and control it.

In 1899 the armies of the Boer Republics taught them 'no end of a lesson', as Kipling put it in 'The Lesson', and though Britain was ultimately victorious the experience of its initial failures subsequently led to the Haldane Report in 1908 and extensive military reforms. By 1914 it was a very professional army, but none the less one that still relied on volunteers for its manpower. It was therefore small, just under 250,000 men, and with minimal reserves, most of them in the equally sized Territorial Army. It was because of its small size in comparison to the millions of the French and German armies that the British army did not really figure in Schlieffen's plan; in numerical terms it was not deemed a threat. Indeed, when hostilities broke out in 1914 Kaiser Wilhelm notoriously referred to it as a 'contemptible little army'. Nevertheless, the German general staff calculated the risk carefully, counting the British potential threat as minor in comparison to the possible gain of a quick win against the French. On a purely military basis they were probably correct at the time the plan was drawn up in the late nineteenth century, but it is not so clear the calculation was still correct in 1914 – not because the British had significantly increased their army, but because the Germans were not necessarily assessing the situation on the same grounds as before. It is very possible that when war broke out their political calculations of achieving hegemony in Europe were being driven by the achievement of their military strategic objective of defeating the French army before taking on the Russian one, rather than the military objective being driven by the political aim. However, the political and military aims might actually have been identical if the military institution in Berlin had indeed become the dictator of policy – as implied in the British propaganda of the time. For indeed, the Schlieffen Plan's premise of ignoring the military threat posed by Belgium and Britain, even at the expense of creating new enemies of both, reflects the supremacy of military calculations over political ones. The point is of interest because, whilst I am not suggesting that Britain would not have entered the war under the Triple Entente, the German action created a new situation, one in which Belgian neutrality was violated. As a guarantor of neutrality Britain was forced to intervene, so adding to the moral rectitude of its position and strengthening the political will of the nation in the face of an expanding involvement in the war.

For at base, whilst the army was professionalized, and despite being a signatory to the Entente, the military-political strategy in Britain in the years before the war remained one of supporting its allies with its naval power and economic means – by imposing a blockade on the Central Powers and supplying the Allies with materiel. Having not participated in any continental war since the Crimean War in the mid nineteenth century, which, like the colonial wars, did not involve the wider population, the shock of finding itself committed to a total war was immense, not just to the national psyche but also to the economy. As children's author Noel Streatfeild, born in 1895, reflected on the outbreak of war in 1914: 'The ordinary English man and woman knew nothing about war. That it would all be over soon was the first reaction. It was not in any case expected to affect the lives of the ordinary citizen. Wars were fought by soldiers and sailors, who came on leave and were made a fuss of.' Yet Britain withstood the shock. The remnants of the contemptible little army, mutilated in the battles of 1914, provided the foundation on which the war-winning army was built – at over 5 million men, the biggest army Britain has ever put in the field. And it won following close engagement with the enemy's main force.

It took until 1917 for Britain to reach its full capacity for industrial war, with the establishment of the strategy and all the institutions necessary for the 'process' to roll on continuously. The national industrial base was transformed to support the war effort, conscription was established as of January 1916, and technology harnessed to appropriate tactics. Indeed, for all participants the First World War laid the basis for a form of warfare that relied heavily on technology, and involved non-combatants through the intensive and unprecedented mobilization of society and production capacities for the war effort. Soldiers did battle in theatre whilst civilians – including for the first time many women – industry and capital participated in the greater national effort, funding, expanding and working the production lines that supplied their military forces. So integral was the civilian effort to the war that it was defined as the 'home front' – a clear sign that this was a conflict not just between armies but between nations and their economies. The people of the Clausewitzian trinity had been incorporated formally into the war.

The massive industrial output also defined the military front since the elevated level of technology, industry and communications originated from single national sources to support their national forces. In turn this established the intermediate level of war, the theatre or operational level, as the prominent one in the conduct of the war. The Italian front, the eastern front and the Middle-East front were all to a large extent independent, each with a full mix of forces and arms, led on each side by a theatre commander who was a senior general, and with the strategic command based in the headquarters and general staffs of Britain, France, Italy and Russia. However, the western front must be seen as a double theatre of operations for the first three years of war, since both France and Britain saw their part of it as their own theatre. It was only when Field Marshal Foch was appointed in over-all command of all Allied forces on the western front in 1918 that some centralized direction began, and thus a single theatre emerged. As a result, it became a theatre of war containing two operational fronts rather than national theatres of operations, though a third operation, that of Pershing's US army, was rapidly developing within the same theatre of war. This multinational organizational development was important to the direction of military force on an industrial scale, and in the Second World War, once the US entered in 1940, the Allies immediately set about creating a joint command structure based on this experience.

The nature of industrial war, and especially technological develop-ments produced on an industrial basis, created the conditions for the western front. That these conditions persisted over such a long period of time is not a little due to the unprecedented quantity of shells and bullets that mass armies devoured in ever increasing quantities. Whereas in 1870 at Sedan – the benchmark for military planners in the four decades that followed – the Prussian army had fired 33,134 rounds, in the week before the opening of the battle of the Somme in 1916 British artillery fired 1 million rounds. The need to supply armies with such massive quantities of ammunition provoked a temporary shell crisis in 1915 for the Allies. However, a programme of emergency industrialization and rapid industrial conversion in Britain, combined with the outsourcing of production to factories working at under-capacity abroad, solved the issue. The French, who expected to use about 10,000 75mm shells a day before the war (a war which was supposed to last for three or four months), were producing 200,000 per day in 1915. In 1917–18 the French supplied the American Expedi-tionary Force with 10 million shells for its French-built artillery, as well as more than two thirds of the aircraft its air force flew into combat. On the other side, the Central Powers also managed to boost their production of ammunition, despite the blockade to which they were subjected by the British fleet. The Germans used their advanced chemical industry to develop ersatz products, a solution also much favoured by the Third Reich two decades later. By doing so they increased production of explosives from 1,000 tons a month in 1914 to 6,000 in 1915.

Industrial capacity also stretched to accelerate the development of new weapons: the trench mortar and the grenade were rediscovered and brought to new levels of lethality, whilst the railway gun reached the full flowering of its brief life. Although casualty figures suggest it was far less lethal than is commonly supposed, poison gas made a startling entrance onto the battlefield when, during the second battle of Ypres in April 1915, the Germans used chlorine gas against the French formation on the British flank. The notoriety of gas can be explained by its physical effects and by the psychological impact it had on other soldiers, who from then on lived in fear of its unfamiliar effects, initially without masks and then with rapidly produced expedients that limited both the amount of air they could breathe and how much they could see. In time the use of gas became routine. The machine gun, the aeroplane and the tank were also key features of the conflict, as we shall see. These in turn led to the development of the anti-tank rifle and gun, and early anti-aircraft guns.

The mass of shells and armaments were both the logical outcome of mass industrial war and a source of salvation from it: the side that could out-invent and out-produce the other was assured victory. The British search for a technical solution found an answer in the tank, which made its first appearance on the battlefield in 1916. This armoured vehicle was intended to support the infantry by advancing with them and crushing defensive obstacles whilst providing supporting fire from its machine guns. They were mechanically unreliable and it took until 1917 to produce and sustain sufficient numbers for them to be used effectively. By the end of 1917 the British had worked out how to use them and variants were also produced to carry mortars, infantry and cargo such as ammunition or casualties.

Both sides sought by military means to attack the ability of the other to sustain war and its political will to continue. The Allies' navies imposed a blockade, but with Germany and its allies able to draw on the heartland of Europe and the Ottoman Empire for reserves, it took time to bite. The Germans attacked the British from both the sea and the air. The Royal Navy represented in its size, ships and global reach the industrial power and economic interests of imperial Britain. It was the defender of the kingdom and the Empire's communications; it was there to destroy the opposing fleet as it had done historically. In 1914 the navy had deployed as planned to cover the German navy's exits from the Baltic and North Sea ports. In May 1916 the German fleet sailed: at the battle of Jutland that followed there occurred the only major fleet action of the war. It was not decisive. The Germans withdrew to their coast and did not exit en masse thereafter. However, they had the submarine: the model of the day usually surfaced to attack its target with its gun, as torpedoes were in a very early stage of development, and were therefore more suitable for attacking merchant vessels than warships. The Germans saw their use as a means of counter-blockading the Allies and Britain in particular. By 1917 they were so successful that Britain was suffering serious food shortages. Anti-submarine measures, such as convoys, were introduced and slowly the threat was reduced to a tolerable level. The Royal Navy had the submarine too – as already noted, Vickers had built them fifty-six before the war began – but given its objective of destroying the enemy's fleet, it did not have much use for them as an attacking force at that early stage in their evolution. And whilst there was every need to impose a blockade on Germany, the latter relied more on land than sea supply, and therefore the British submarines had little maritime commerce to attack.

The second approach developed with the advance of technology and tactics on the western front, and was from the air. On both sides the target was the morale of the population, and the political will to maintain the war. Before 1914, aircraft were almost entirely limited to a reconnaissance role. At the outbreak of the war, few if any aircraft had been purpose built for military use, indeed they were not even armed: the French and the Germans, for example, relied on commandeered civil aircraft at the start of the war. As soon as hostilities broke out, the British Royal Naval Air Service (RNAS) launched operations against German airfields. Meanwhile, the Germans bombed the forts around Liège with Zeppelins. The first bombing attack on a major city occurred when a German plane flew from the Marne to Paris and dropped a few hand-grenades. In turn, the French began bombing raids on targets behind enemy lines, and the Germans responded by arming scout aircraft with machine guns. As aircraft designs improved, the fighter was born and by the middle of 1915 aerial combat was beginning. On both sides, armies were demanding more reconnaissance in order to locate enemy artillery and troops, whilst their opponents responded by sending up more and more fighter aircraft in defence. Technical developments such as the 'interrupter gear' soon allowed for machine guns to be mounted on German aircraft and fire through the propeller disc: the single-seat fighter was born. By 1916 formations of aircraft were being used to improve mutual protection, and to achieve sufficient firepower over the target area or against enemy formations. The combatant nations formed air forces which were seen as supporting arms to the battle on land and sea, with aircraft on both sides being used for reconnaissance, directing artillery fire and attacking communications. In the British case these were both the RNAS and the Royal Flying Corps (RFC). By the end of 1917 the Allies had both sufficient suitable aircraft and the tactics developed for their use to dominate the air space over the front – air superiority as it is known – on most occasions.

At first, only the Germans had the capability to conduct long-range bombing operations with their Zeppelin airships. They were able to attack London, largely due to their occupation of Belgium which gave them the geographical advantage of being closer to the enemy capital than the British were to Berlin. The attacks had an immediate psychological effect rather than a physical one, since they were sporadic, inaccurate and lacked weight. The fighter and the incendiary bullet proved a match for these hydrogen-fuelled torpedo-shaped balloons. Subsequently, bombing was to be conducted by aeroplanes. In May and June 1917 the Germans began launching raids on English soil with small formations of Gotha bombers that could each carry 400kg of bombs. The British were unable to respond in kind. And while aircraft of the Royal Navy and army sought to counter-attack, there was no force with a commander charged with the defence of the home front, and therefore in effect the morale of the people. The army was engaged in Europe and elsewhere, with the object of defeating the enemy's main force, and the navy with the blockade and defeating the enemy at sea. After an inquiry headed by the ex-Boer commando

Jan Smuts, it was decided to form a new strategic force: the Royal Air Force, the first of its kind. The air assets of the other two services were regrouped, in the midst of a war, to form a new service under its own Chief of Staff, and with its own ministry, the Air Ministry, to stand equal with the War Office and the Admiralty. The RAF was to defend the kingdom from air attacks, prosecute their own against the enemy, and support the other two services in their endeavours. In short order squadrons were moved from France and the air defence of south-east England was coherently organized. At the same time, aircraft manufacturing in Britain developed exceedingly fast, especially in comparison to Germany. Over 13,000 aircraft were produced: this, principally, was what enabled the British, and the Allies, to achieve dominance. As one commentator recently put it:

The RAF did not outfight the German air force, it overwhelmed it, filling the skies with aircraft, and allowing opponents no respite for repairs or tactical regrouping . . . [By war's end, to] their horror and despair, the German air force discovered that manufacturing standards had been allowed to slide, with the result that some of their finest new designs were seriously compromised by poor materials and slipshod construction. That was the final achievement of the new British aviation industry; not just to out-build the greatest manufacturing nation in Europe, but to so demoralize it that it could no longer trust what it produced.*

Through this massive reorganization, and coupled with the capabilities of France and assistance from the US, throughout the last year of the war the Allies entered the long-range bombing war and were also regularly launching bombing raids on Germany. The traditional boundaries of the battlefield had been extended.

The war ended in 1918 much as it began: with an innovative and massive German attack which ultimately outran its own logistical ability and was then countered by a successful Allied attack. Unlike the British, in seeking to find a method of breaching the enemy's defences the Germans did not go down the technological route, but rather

*Dean Juniper, '"Some Were Chosen": A Study of Aeroplane Procurement in the First World War', *RUSI Journal*, Vol. 149, No. 6, Dec. 2004, p. 69.

sought the solution in a change of tactics – which came to be titled 'mobile warfare'. To this end they selected and trained infantry troops as elite *Sturmtruppen*, storm troopers, soldiers who specialized in infiltration and conducting fast, hard-hitting attacks before moving on to their next target. They would mount a surprise assault after a short 'hurricane' bombardment and then move on as fast as possible into the opponent's territory. Armed with the latest weapons such as automatic rifles, light machine guns and flame throwers, they wielded the firepower necessary to overcome a defensive position quickly. The commanders of these groups had considerable freedom of action. They were directed to bypass points of resistance and then to continue deep into the British positions, seeking to destroy the coherence of the defence and to cause alarm in the rear areas. Other forces, a second echelon, would follow up and complete the destruction of the remaining defenders. This was a clear example of 'organizational mobility': the setting of authority and responsibility, the grouping of forces and resources and the allocation of tasks were all changed to allow the tactical concept of mobile warfare to be put into effect, and this mobility allowed for a different way of using force. It had taken over three years, and it was at the tactical rather than the theatre or strategic level, but the breakthrough was achieved.

In March 1918, General Erich von Ludendorff set about applying the tactics of 'mobile warfare' on a large scale by launching a major offensive on the western front. His cousin, General Oskar von Hutier, had developed and demonstrated the efficiency of the German army's infiltration tactics during the capture of Riga in September 1917. Hutier was given command of the newly created Eighteenth Army, which was charged with spearheading the German offensive. His army opened the offensive on 21 March. A short but massive artillery bombardment was followed by an attack conducted by storm troopers. By the end of the first day of the attack 21,000 British soldiers had been taken prisoner and the Germans had made great advances through the lines of the British Fifth Army. After these spectacular initial gains the push continued towards Amiens, with the British in retreat and some disorder. However, despite Ludendorff's offensive achieving the greatest advance on the western front in three years, the Germans faced the same problems as everyone else: there was always another trench to take and the further they advanced the harder it was to exploit the storm troopers' successes. The British were falling back onto their railheads, whilst the Germans were constantly advancing from theirs. After a few days the German Eighteenth Army found that it ran out of supplies as it advanced. The speed of the advance had put their supply lines under huge strain. Supply units simply could not keep up with the storm troopers. As units marched towards Amiens, the situation deteriorated: horses were killed for their meat and the mobility of the Eighteenth Army was thereby further reduced. When it reached the town of Albert discipline broke down as soldiers went on a rampage looting shops for food. Progress stopped and the attack on Amiens faltered. The advance ran out of steam and was checked by a rapidly forming defence.

The Allies rallied, and in May 1918 they launched a counter-attack, the bulk of which was British. During 1917 the British had developed the tactics to make use of the tank and the aircraft in the RFC. They had learned that it was best at the higher tactical levels to not try to exploit a gap into the enemy's depth in a single attack. Instead, they found it far preferable to chew through the opposing defences in a series of 'bite and hold' attacks, committing each fresh attack on a different axis, just as the German reserves were being committed to counter the previous one. This allowed each attack to be fully supported in its turn and meant that the defender was off balance as subsequent attacks were committed. Just as important, by attacking on a broad front rather than a narrow one all routes forward could be put to use in sustaining the attack. Operationally, the British sought to roll the front back rather than to break it – and so they did.

The counter-attack led directly to the defeat of the German army, and the end of the war. On the eleventh hour of the eleventh day of the eleventh month the Armistice was signed.

Germany and its armed forces had been a grindingly hard foe to beat. Even as the German army retreated into the Fatherland it told itself the defeatist socialist-inclined revolutionaries at home had stabbed it in the back. Just as the war started with the military apparently dictating political moves, so it ended with the military blaming defeat on the lack of popular political support. The war had been a massive trial of strength, a trial that the original Allies had ultimately won, partially assisted by the forces of the USA which had begun appearing in increasing numbers on the western front, with a promise of more money, men and materiel. But the clash of wills had been lost in the homeland – not by direct attack but by the corrosive effect of years of loss, shortages and hardship. The naval blockade imposed by Britain in 1914 had by 1918 yielded malnutrition and political unrest in Germany, eroding the confidence of the population in their leaders' vision of the future. The people had flocked or been ordered to their country's flag in their millions and had died in their millions. The anticipated rapid decisive victory was not achieved, and they had been attacked and starved in their homes. The people element of the Clausewitzian trinity effectively bailed out of the war – which is why the government and the military could no longer sustain it, and had to sue for peace. The decisive victory went to the Allies, but in many ways it was sour: they too had been starved and attacked in their homes, they too had lost loved ones in their millions. And whilst their people remained in balance within the trinity, it was clear to political and military leaders alike that it would take much to draw them into another war. For all participants, total industrial war had brought total industrial and human carnage. Between the two sides, over 65 million men were fielded – 42,188,810 by the Allies, 22,850,000 by the Central Powers; 15 million people lost their lives – over 8.5 million soldiers, and approximately 6.5 million civilians; over 21 million soldiers were wounded, and 7.5 million taken prisoner or declared missing. These numbers are so vast as to be abstract to the individual, which is precisely the point: individuals signed up to the war, either through belief or mobilization or factory work, and they all became enmeshed and eventually defeated – even those on the winning side – by its size and force.

During the four years of conflict massive amounts of force had been unleashed by massive forces such as the world had never before seen. By the end of the war the meaning of 'decisive victory' had altered from being rapid and triumphalist to slow and draining. Entering the battlefield with organizational and operational concepts derived largely from the German wars of unification, it took commanders on all sides much time to adapt and develop new ones. Britain used tanks and technology, whilst the Germans made their breakthrough with mobile warfare; both allowed for an operational flexibility that had become stuck in trench warfare. Air power had become integral to the battlefield, and had also become a strategic force in its own right. With the exception of the weapons and the systems that depend on the electromagnetic spectrum, every weapon in the inventories of our current forces made its appearance, if only in a generic form, during the Great War – including weapons of mass destruction in the form of gas. The unit commanders of 1918, with a little time to learn the communication systems, would know how to employ military units of today effectively. The structures that enabled both the creation of forces and the application of military force had expanded to the total extent of the state's capacity – and had become institutions, in both the civilian and military spheres. After the war they were largely disbanded in each nation, but nonetheless remained capable of swift resurrection in time of crisis. At the strategic level the Allies had shown that the delivery to the battlefield of mass industrial strength ultimately produced victory, but at a supremely high cost and with deep effects on society, by both direct attack and social upheaval. The force had a utility, but the cost left the people with a disinclination to engage again in such a war. The German military learned that if enormous force was to have its utility the next time it had to achieve its objective rapidly, within the nineteenth-century doctrine of Moltke the elder. For them, slow war was unsustainable. And whilst the defeated German commanders were not necessarily thinking of a future war as they left the battlefield, a lowly Austrian lance-corporal would slowly begin gathering his thoughts on the matter. The paradigm of interstate industrial war was about to move towards its final evolution – and culmination.

Once the Treaty of Versailles was signed in 1919 Europe did not appear to be set on industrial war again – at least not immediately: the nations were exhausted and all governments were concerned with internal matters. Revolution and social upheaval were in the air and all the former combatants' economies were fragile. But the Treaty, which placed all the blame for the war and a huge financial onus upon Germany, held the seeds of another conflict: after the Kaiser abdicated and fled to the Netherlands in November 1918, the shame and bitterness of defeat were never too far from the surface in the Weimar

Republic which succeeded the Reich. And it was precisely these sentiments that Adolf Hitler played to in the 1920s as the initial freedom of the new republic gave way to chaos, unemployment and hyperinflation. Promising the realization of German supremacy and war as the method for achieving it, it rapidly became clear he held what may be defined as a Napoleonic belief in the utility of force to achieve a political aim. The war he envisaged was not about nineteenth-century hegemony or colonial disputes or even revenge. Like the French emperor he was bent upon changing the map of Europe, and the world, through the use of force. And once he assumed power in 1933, he and especially his military leaders prepared for yet another round of industrial war. To this end they already had covert plans, sketched out by the secret German general staff that had been operating since 1919. For besides substantially reducing the size of the German military forces, the Treaty of Versailles specifically forbade the existence or re-creation of the general staff – probably the only treaty in the world to include such a clause, and a tribute to the strength and ability of that extraordinary body. Despite this fact, the German officer corps had set about secretly planning how they would fight the next war with a camouflaged general staff hidden in the Truppenamt (troop office), which was officially a military human-resources bureau. By 1933 they had a plan which Hitler and his cohorts could follow, both to build up the military machine and to use it to attack the enemy.

The Germans had deeply internalized the lesson that in war a standstill situation where there is tactical parity eventually benefits the side with the bigger and the more enduring industrial output. Above all, they knew costly wars of attrition not only brought the home economy to its knees but could also lead to the destruction of the sociopolitical equilibrium – as the Armistice of 1918 and the upheavals in its aftermath always served to remind them bitterly. In their analysis they recognized the value of their tactical innovations, both in attack and in defence – in which considerable initiative was granted to small groups. We have already seen the infiltration tactics of the storm troopers in attack, and its equivalent in defence was known as elastic defence, which allowed for tactical mobility in an essentially static battle of defence. Rather than a single front line, the Germans instructed their commanders to hold an area. They could withdraw from the front to any intermediate position of their area in the face of an attack, and in particular when under heavy bombardment. In this way they avoided constant exposure and unnecessary casualties, under the clear understanding that it was their duty to counter-attack at the first opportunity to re-establish the forward line. It was a flexible defence, constantly moving backwards and forwards in the circumstances, then rebounding – hence elastic defence. In effect, German commanders were seeking to draw in, attack and destroy their attackers in order to defend their line whilst avoiding the strength of the Allied artillery, rather than grimly holding a position. In order to implement both these offensive and defensive tactics, the Germans structured their forces accordingly and gave relatively junior officers the authority to act in the circumstances. For example, the commander of the unit holding the front in elastic defence had the authority – including over any commanders of units sent to reinforce him, even if they were of a higher rank – to manoeuvre his forces within his area. This idea reflects an understanding of the circumstances being the crucial factor in the battle. It also gives the lie to the myth of German rigidity, since these tactics and structures gave them the organizational mobility to resist attacks, sustaining fewer casualties than hitherto, and to achieve and develop the tactical successes of the Ludendorff offensive. Furthermore, the survivors of the storm troopers from the first war provided a core cadre of experienced professionals with whom to develop these tactics. Amongst their number were those who correctly recognized that the tank and the aeroplane could be used to advantage within this concept.

The Germans were not the only ones to see the potential of the tank and the storm troopers' tactics. During the 1920s, impressed by what they now dubbed as 'Hutier tactics', military thinkers such as Captain Sir Basil Liddell Hart in Britain, and, more significantly, the Red Army's theorists, sought to develop further these concepts of mobile warfare. Although they were still slow and plagued by technical problems, the potential of tanks had been clearly demonstrated during the First World War. As they became more reliable, theoreticians began to argue that these vehicles could prove to be the central factor in a new way of warfare. If moved rapidly enough, concentrations of tanks could break through enemy lines and cut into his rear, thus destroying supplies and artillery positions whilst decreasing his will to resist. They thought that the tank and other similar armoured vehicles could be used not so much as a supporting arm of the infantry, to help them break into defences and to support them with fire in the close-quarter battle, but in their own right, to manoeuvre and develop the battle at the speed of the vehicle rather than that of the marching man. The difference between the various armies was that the Germans had already devised command and organizational concepts which favoured the use of the new technology; others tended to envisage it as reinforcing their existing command arrangements, which had evolved to control large numbers of marching men. Put another way, the Germans saw the tank as an item of equipment to better execute the mobile tactics of Hutier, while the others saw them rather as fleets of land ships.

The next step was to think about synchronizing tank action with the infantry, artillery and the air force – a development made possible by the introduction of the radio. The Germans understood that it was the tank units that were the ones to be supported and for this to be possible the other arms had to move at the same speed. So were born the Panzer Grenadiers, armoured infantry, and the other arms, artillery and so forth were soon also equipped to move in direct support of the tanks. The Luftwaffe was deemed to have an important role to play in this fast-moving battle: to attack, to prepare the way for the armoured formations, to support them directly and, by landing airborne forces ahead of an advance, to seize important positions. The Germans, with the enthusiastic support of Hitler, whose imagination had been caught by the idea of Panzer forces as outlined in General Heinz Guderian's pamphlet entitled 'Achtung Panzer', organized their tanks and supporting forces into self-contained Panzer divisions.

Despite these organizational innovations, the bulk of the German forces in the Second World War still depended on the marching man, the horse and the railway. This was not by chance, since they had started the war in a production deficit. As early as 1933, when the Nazis assumed power, the general staff advised Hitler that the German army would be fully modernized and ready no earlier than 1944 or 1945 – a warning he dismissed. As a result, at the outbreak of war in 1939 most artillery pieces were still horse drawn, and armoured vehicles were in relatively short supply throughout the conflict; consequently infantry and artillery units would remain the majority component of the army. In addition, throughout the fighting German industry could not furnish small arms in sufficient quantities, forcing the army to rely heavily on older weapons, prizes of war and adaptations of former designs produced in conquered countries. These were not standardized or interchangeable, meaning more of each were needed and spare parts were scarce. The Allies started to crank up their war machine much later, but standardized production much earlier – their industrial output therefore had greater utility in the field.

Alongside the technical and organizational innovations and changes, the Wehrmacht was also greatly expanded. It was noted in the introduction that most standing forces are formed in anticipation of being used in defence of the homeland and therefore in time of a crisis that is not an attack on the homeland but requires a military response the question is how best to employ the force as it stands for the given objective. However, if it is the political intention from the outset to use the force offensively – to start the war, or at the least to act pre-emptively – then one can design the force to act for its primary purpose from the outset. This was the basis on which the Wehrmacht was expanded after Hitler came to power, with the developments in the described Panzer forces and the Luftwaffe. And once they had all reached a critical point, there was a need to test the new forces in their new structures in their use of force. The opportunity presented by the need to support Franco's fascist side in the Spanish Civil War of 1936–8 was therefore used as a tactical testing ground for these concepts, and the Germans found the tests to be successful.

Looking on at these increasingly ominous activities, Britain and France began to crank up their own military industrial machines, though without marked vigour. They were still not seeking war – or, as in the case of Chamberlain, for example, actively avoiding it if only to buy time. Military and civilian planners across Europe began to realize another war was inevitable – and considered that most of the industrial characteristics of the Great War, as it had come to be known very quickly after it ended, would be apparent in the next one. The 'process' of industrial war had become embedded in the nations, and it quickly took over, recreating the necessary institutions. Indeed, even in the period of immediate build-up it was clear these institutions, formed to make total war, to industrialize the national war effort and harness it to the single imperative of victory, were better organized after the experience of 1914–18. Governments had or assumed unprecedented degrees of power over their citizens, usually in the name of their defence, and this was as true of the democracies as it was of the communist and fascist states. They sought to direct and control: the people, production, supply and information. This was the 'last safe moment' to disrupt the economy and the people noted in Chapter 2 as a defining characteristic of industrial war – but writ exceptionally large: when the moment came it brought total disruption, in that every element of daily life was changed, and government took total control of much of that life. A reflection of this new organizational ability and control was apparent in Britain right from the start: during the weekend preceding the war over 3 million people, mainly women and children, were sent from cities, mostly from London, to the country. The railways were at full stretch and the stations swarmed with people, but this amazing mass was pre-designated, moved and rehoused in the course of seventy-two hours – a feat which would have taken months before the First World War.

And then war came. In the states of the Axis powers the trinity of people, army and government once again appeared to be in equilibrium, not least because the last two came close to being one. For the people, Hitler had delivered order, prosperity and a vision of greatness. These were all, of course, deeply warped and came at vast human, moral, political and ultimately military cost. The people as much as the military and the state enabled the unleashing of an awful total war that would take their world, and the peoples whom they conquered, over the edge of humanity and common life, and the paradigm of interstate industrial war to its final explosive end. In the Allied states there was an equilibrium too: people, army and government slowly and quietly rallied, dreading the battle to come, knowing in their hearts it would, like the previous one, be long and hard – but inevitable. As war was unleashed, this was simply and exactly summed up by King George VI in his full diary entry for 3 September 1939:

At the outbreak of war at midnight of August 4th–5th 1914, I was a midshipman, keeping watch on the bridge of H.M.S. *Collingwood* at sea, somewhere in the North Sea. I was 18 years of age.

In the Grand Fleet everyone was pleased that it had come at last. We had been trained in the belief that war between Germany and this country had to come one day, and when it did come we thought we were prepared for it. We were not prepared for what we found a modern war really was, and those of us who had been through the Great War never wanted another.

Today we are at war again, and I am no longer a midshipman in the Royal Navy.

*

The Third Reich was forcibly imposed upon Europe: Poland, then Denmark, Norway, the Low Countries, and finally France. The British army was defeated on the continent. In less than a year, and at relatively low cost, the Germans achieved what years of exhausting trench warfare had failed to achieve. Their preparations, based on their Panzer formations and the Luftwaffe, paid off: they appeared to have found the way to use force with great utility. When Germany invaded Poland in September 1939, its mechanized ground force, working with the close support of the Luftwaffe, was able to break through and penetrate deep behind Polish lines of defence. In 1940, in the attacks on Norway in May, and during the invasion of the Low Countries and France, the Germans made use of the same tactics once again, adding paratroop drops to shock and disorganize the defenders further. These tactics were known as *Blitzkrieg* – lightning war; they were those of rapid movement of small, well-armed groups into the enemy's depth, bypassing strong points and seeking to break the coherence of the defence before destroying or capturing its elements. The attacks were conducted and successes exploited at the speed of the armoured vehicles rather than the marching man. The defenders were organized to fight a more pedestrian battle, and therefore found themselves literally overtaken by events: their command systems effectively paralysed, their communication lines swamped with refugees and their military reserves attacked by the Luftwaffe and moving towards positions long since lost. Doubt, confusion, rumour and panic ensued.

Logistic risks were taken in conducting *Blitzkrieg*, and on occasion the Panzers had to refuel with captured fuel. However, such risks were not as great as they may seem, if one central tenet were maintained: speed. If each engagement was concluded quickly, smaller fuel supplies and reliance on captured fuel was possible owing to the very nature of battle. One can calculate with reasonable accuracy the fuel, rations, water and spare parts required to cover a given distance. It is the expenditure of these resources in a fight that is very difficult to quantify. The longer the fight, the more will be expended – and the greater the risk of calculations being wrong. Therefore, if the chosen tactics involve many small fights, each part of the greater battle but each over quickly, and if strong points that might require bigger and longer fights are bypassed, the probability of the calculations being wrong is much reduced. Furthermore, the logistic burden may be reduced by using the air force as part of the supporting firepower, since the supporting logistic train need reach no further than the airfield in the rear for the same or more firepower at the front. For this to work there is a need to win the fights quickly, ensure air superiority and make allowances for the weather; air forces, even today, cannot be guaranteed to operate in all weather conditions. The other logistic difficulty German planners faced was to move the bulk of their army fast enough to exploit and consolidate the successes of the Panzer formations. As already noted, the Wehrmacht was not fully mechanized, and as a general rule infantry divisions marched and their artillery was horse drawn. The control of traffic to bring these long columns forward without disrupting the flow of supplies to the Panzers, and establishing the priorities for movement to support the commander fighting the battle, is the true skill of operational staff work; it was shown in great measure by the German staff.

Having conquered western Europe, Hitler was faced with the same geostrategic reality that faced Napoleon: to defeat the British you must first cross to their island. The defeat of the Luftwaffe in the Battle of Britain, while not preventing air raids for much of the war, was akin to the defeat of the French and Spanish navies at Trafalgar. Britain was free from the threat of invasion. The preparedness of the RAF for this battle, the technological and industrial development of radar, aircraft and the command system, was a direct result of forming the force in 1917. By having a strategic commander responsible for the air defence of the kingdom, there was a focal point for the techno-logical developments to that end. And in the late 1930s, as money became available for rearmament, priority was given to air defence. Throughout the war the benefit of such investment was proven, espe-cially with the exemplary campaign run and maintained by RAF Fighter Command. Much is made today of the possibilities of 'net-work enabled warfare', the idea being to have a superior understand-ing of the battlefield by virtue of your ability to gather and assess information from many sources – especially in relation to that of your opponent – and to act on it. To my mind, from their reconnaissance and analysis to their ability to engage the enemy, RAF Fighter Command fought the first 'network enabled' battle.

Britain was under constant attack, but remained free. Continental Europe from the Iberian peninsula to the Balkans was now, however, controlled directly by Central Powers forces or indirectly by powers friendly to them such as Franco's Spain. Expansion was possible only to the east, and so, like Napoleon, Hitler turned his armies on Russia. Plans to give the German people *Lebensraum* at Russia's expense had been drawn up before the start of the war; if successful, they would give the Third Reich a land empire capable of facing the rest of the world. These plans did not allow for the continuing naval predomi-nance of the British, which limited German access to raw materials and petrol – a crucial failing in a protracted conflict. This factor was ignored: Hitler believed German forces could defeat Russia with a *Blitzkrieg* attack on a gigantic scale. In June 1941 Germany invaded Russia with the largest invasion force ever put together at the time. Initially, operation Barbarossa was impressively successful, and German forces reached the outskirts of Moscow by December 1941. In the long run, however, the German attempt to conquer Russia failed as the immensity of the steppes and the weather gave the Russians enough time to halt the offensive – albeit at tremendous cost. Like Napoleon's army, the German forces came up against another geostrategic reality: to defeat Russia one must be prepared to march towards the Pacific. As the Germans advanced east, the front they cov-ered became ever wider, but they lacked sufficient forces to cover it all; they lacked density. As a result gaps began to form, and as the snow began to fall, the Red Army began to counter-attack – and their successes were enhanced by the German shortage in raw materials and petrol. Barbarossa was no longer *Blitzkrieg*; it had become an old-style industrial battle.

The Allies, each in their way, began to learn how to deal with *Blitzkrieg*. For the British the proving ground was the North African campaign where after a series of victories and defeats Montgomery was given command. Blending the essence of his own experience and understanding of war with that of the Eighth Army and the desert air force, he produced a winning operational method. Montgomery organized his forces accordingly, manoeuvring at divisional strength – a larger formation than its German equivalent – and making the maximum use of his air force to isolate the battlefield, thus reducing the enemy forces in depth and depriving them of the opportunity to assist their own forces. In their own theatre the Russian commanders re-learned the lessons of the Red Army theorists culled by Stalin in the purges of the late 1930s – the structuring of mass forces and use of force at the theatre or operational level – and developed their operational method. In late 1942 the battles of El Alamein and Stalingrad showed the way, and at the same time the landings in Morocco and Algiers by the Allied First Army (operation Torch) gave US forces their own learning experience. By May 1943 the First and Eighth Armies in Africa were preparing to invade Sicily, which they did in July. In the same month the Red Army defeated the last German theatre-level attack on the eastern front in the epic battle of Kursk – for me, the true turning point of the war against Germany.

The Allies had adapted in the face of the German way of war – each attaining the organizational mobility to deploy their forces and use their force to far greater utility. In essence all arrived at similar methods, all focusing upon the operational level: in defence they accepted gaps in the line and formed defended positions capable of all-round defence. Such strong points were to hold their ground and attack the German forces attempting to follow up the initial *Blitzkrieg* assault, whilst artillery and air attacks were to support these positions and further disrupt the follow-up. Meanwhile a second echelon held in depth would be committed to destroy the initial wave of attackers who, lacking support and running low on fuel and ammunition, were vulnerable. Air superiority, or at the very least parity when there was plenty of space to move in, was essential for this to work. In attack the method was, in Montgomery's words, to 'break in' to the enemy's strong points and to draw his reserves into the 'dog fight' – attacking them by air and artillery as they moved, and then to attack in turn the enemy's depth. Each battle was carefully prepared and executed. The skill and bravery of the combatants notwithstanding, these operational methods exploited the Germans' political and strategic weaknesses, since they had to hold what they had, and if drawn into a fight they would therefore suffer disproportionate losses – in men and territory.

In contrast to the land war, the German submarine offensive proved to be very difficult to defeat and the Allies, especially the British, suffered great losses in seamen, cargo and shipping. In the North Atlantic alone 2,232 British ships were lost during the war. This battle lasted for the duration, but the turning point came in May 1943; thereafter as a rule enemy submarines were sunk at a greater rate than Allied ships. In spite of these great losses, taking the war as a whole 99 per cent of all merchantmen made port safely, a great credit to the Allied navies and the convoy system.

Since the rapid decisive victory was unattainable to either the Allies or the Axis powers, both sides continued what had been started in the First World War and attacked the other's people directly by air and indirectly by blockade, with the intention of destroying the opponent's capacity to make war and the people's will to do so. The Blitz, the developing strategic bombing operations of the RAF and US Army Air Force (USAAF), the German cruise and ballistic missile attacks, the V-weapons, were all devoted to this end. The Blitz, the German air offensive against the industrial centres and cities of Britain, commenced on 7 September 1940 and ended in May 1941. It was essentially a response to the German loss in the Battle of Britain – and was aimed at the civilian population. In 1944–5 the Germans followed up with a similar campaign, this time with the V-missiles. On the other side, the bombing of the cities of Germany and later Japan by the Allied air forces began shortly after the start of the war and gathered pace and weight from 1943. This was strategic bombing: a separate front, and for some time the only way Britain could directly attack Germany itself rather than its armies or fleets, which were then at some distance from its borders. The RAF slowly built up the capacity and the tactics to conduct ever bigger, more effective air raids. Heavy long-range bombers were produced in increasing numbers, as were increasingly heavy bombs. Great strides were made in developing radio navigation aids, radar bombing sights and electronic counter-measures. The Allied raids were aimed at destroying Germany's industrial base and the morale of its people in much the same way as the German attacks on British cities were. But the inability accurately to target the German industrial buildings meant that it was necessary to drop large quantities of high explosives and incendiaries over a wide area in order to be sure of hitting the objective.

The attacks on all the combatant populations, intended to terrorize them, had another effect: it aligned the people with those in the field. Total war was now experienced totally. This resulted in the political objective and the will to achieve it becoming extremely close to the military objective and the will to achieve it at whatever cost. The people, the state and the military were as one, on both sides. However, whilst both the Allied and the Axis bombings caused great loss of life and damage, in the end they were still a supporting activity to the major battles in the field and at sea. They were not a decisive force.

In December 1941 the war truly engulfed the world when Japan attacked the US. Like Germany, it too sought to deliver the quick and decisive blow and the bold surprise attack, in this case on the US Pacific Fleet in Pearl Harbor, Hawaii. Whilst causing great damage and loss of life and ships, the attack failed. It brought the US out of isolationism and into a war it was determined to win. The all-important US navy aircraft carriers were exercising at sea on the day of the attack, and were therefore spared – making the US entry more swift and substantial than if the Japanese attack had been better targeted. None the less, as with the Nazi conquests in Europe, there followed a similar pattern of rapid victories for Japan in Asia, but then a familiar geostrategic reality: to defeat the US Japan must first enter the North American continent and in the case of the British Empire, India must be invaded. At base, these, like the Russian steppes or the British Isles, were – and probably will always be – the greatest and most elusive prizes in the search for decisive victories by any who choose to attack them.

As the tides turned, the almost limitless reserves in labour and human life from communist Russia, combined with American capital and armaments, soon began to outmatch the German war effort. Having based their strategy on rapid strategic successes, using technology, tanks, aeroplanes and all products of industrial military might, the Germans found they had difficulty in sustaining the flow of that technology in the face of the Allies' greater productive capacity, including resources of men and materiel. Locked into a defensive posture after the battle of Kursk in 1943, they were forced into the one outcome they had sought to avoid at all costs: a war of attrition. Industry, as ever, ultimately proved to be the deciding factor: innovation and sheer bulk, of men and materiel, became the core of the competition between the opponents. After the slump of the 1930s the American economy experienced a period of extremely rapid growth: between 1940 and 1945, it expanded by 50 per cent. Armaments and military equipments were standardized and mass produced. Fifty-eight thousand M-4 Sherman tanks, which were reliable and simple to maintain, were in this way manufactured and shipped to the Allies or American troops. From mid 1941 dockyards in the US also began producing Liberty transport ships at a rate of two a day, to expand the merchant fleets and to provide Britain with reinforcements and necessary supplies. British industry was also working at full capacity, supplying its forces and the nation throughout the war. These combined efforts were made plain by the unrivalled size of the D-Day invasion fleet, and the magnitude of that operation. Meanwhile, the Russians had also entered the *Materielschlacht*. As enormous reserves of labour were mobilized, the mass production of armaments came into full swing. Most astounding of all was the relocation of the entire Russian industrial base to the east of the Urals in the face of the initial attacks of operation Barbarossa, where it immediately began functioning at full rate. Forty-two tank factories produced 40,000 T-34 tanks and 18,000 heavy tanks during the war. The Russians produced similar volumes of aircraft, which regularly harassed the Germans. Forty thousand Ilyushin II-2 Stormovik planes were built, a production run that still holds the record to this day. It was used in large formations to support the Red Army in the field, against troops, tanks and railways wherever the Soviets fought. As a result, the Russians usually had air superiority above their armies. The Stormovik was simple, almost crude, and individually no match for the Messerschmitt 109, but as Lenin put it – apparently in a discussion of tanks with Stalin – 'quantity has a quality of its own.'

Production of war materiel in Germany was maintained by ruthless prioritization of effort, and by slave labour appropriated from all occupied states, especially in the east. Moreover, although their capabilities improved throughout the war and especially in the final months, as a general rule the Allies did not have the information to target facilities accurately, nor the means to hit them precisely. But by 1943 the industrial and economic strains were beginning to become apparent in Germany, especially when the Allied bombing aimed at destroying enemy capacity began to make a mark. Hitler recognized the need to mobilize the German economy totally. Albert Speer was put in charge of this task, but his drastic attempts to reorganize the war effort were not sufficient to reverse the tide. Paradoxically, the war effort was hindered by failures inherent in the Nazi system of government. Hitler's divide-and-rule policies inevitably created problems of coordination and led to the duplication of the productive effort. This was illustrated by the ruthless poaching of labour and resources between the three armed forces, the party, Himmler's SS, and other power bases. Locked in an industrial contest and with the odds against them, the Germans intensified efforts to find a technological solution to avoid defeat – though it must be noted that all sides were seeking a technological solution. In Germany this was exemplified by Werner von Braun's work on rockets and the quest for miracle weapons (including the atomic bomb), which could perhaps save the situation at the last minute. These hopes proved to be illusory and the 'miracles' that did happen were not exploited fully. The Messerschmitt Me-262 was the first jet fighter ever produced. It first flew in mid 1942 and went into production in mid 1944. Though faster than any plane in service with the Allies, it never made an impact: few were actually produced and since the Allies had air superiority they were able to destroy most of the 262s on the ground.

From 1943 onwards the Germans and the Japanese were in retreat. Operations against them took the form of carefully prepared major offensives that exploited the breakthrough to its culminating point, usually a combination of logistic exhaustion and well-established defence works. The close-quarter battle caused casualties at the same rate as the First World War, but the difference between the wars was in the nature of the forces: the Second World War armies had proportionately fewer infantry units and more armoured, artillery, anti-aircraft and other specialist supporting arms. The air forces were also bigger and suffered heavy casualties, the RAF losing about the same number of aircrew as all the officers of all three British services in the First World War. Towards the end of the war, with the exception of Russia all sides began running out of infantry. The Germans fielded older and older men and younger and younger boys, while the British redesignated units, such as anti-aircraft regiments, for infantry combat.

By 1945 Germany was nearly returned to its pre-war borders, pressed in by large enemy armies on both east and west, and enduring the systematic bombing of its cities and communications. The occupied states in the west had in the main been liberated; but it had taken six months from the invasion at Normandy to undo what Hitler's armies had done in as many weeks. This was due to the fighting prowess of the Wehrmacht: the German soldiers, well trained and motivated till the last, fought well, strong and hard until defeated. For two long years they had been in retreat on every front, and had made the Allies pay for every yard they gained on the route to Berlin. However reprehensible the cause it served, and its own amorality, one should never question the morale and discipline of that army. In addition, the Allies faced the magnitude of the logistic endeavour necessary to bring all the men and equipment over the Atlantic and the English Channel into Europe. Nevertheless, it was a decisive victory: the Allies had produced the force of greater utility. They won the trial of strength, and broke the will of Germany. This time it was not the people who collapsed, but the government and the military. The whole regime disappeared.

By the end of 1945 the trial of the major war criminals, the principal leaders and commanders of the defeated Axis, had begun in Nuremberg. They were charged and in most cases found guilty and executed for their war crimes; crimes in which force was used against the people, innocent civilians, in gross excess. It was an important turning point: the establishment of the tribunal and the legal process became the method for deciding the immorality of these actions, and has remained with us ever since. Morality of the use of force in this way came to be defined by the legality of its use.

Decisive victory in the Second World War took even longer to achieve than the first: victory in Europe, VE Day, was 8 May, 1945, and victory in the East, VJ Day, was 15 August 1945. Once again forces of hitherto unknown magnitude had been unleashed upon the world, that applied massive amounts of force. Even more men and materiel than the First World War were involved. Around 17.5 million combatants were killed on all sides, approximately 12 million on the Allied side, including 2 million in China and 8.5 million in the Soviet Union, and 5.5 million from the Axis powers, including 3.5 million Germans and just under 1.5 million Japanese soldiers. Just over 39 million civilians were killed around the globe, including 6 million in the Holocaust, nearly 17 million in the Soviet Union and 10 million in China. In total, 56 million people were killed in the conflict. Approximately 35 million soldiers were wounded on all sides along with unestimated numbers of civilians. These were and remain incomprehensible numbers. Equally, however, we see here the most appalling reflection of the duality of mass – as bulk and as density: it was the concentration of the masses that caused a high proportion of deaths. As started in the Great War, all sides focused increasingly on the opponent's ability and will to make war as the prime target. To this end, and this was a crucial change, the battlefield was extended into every corner of a state: in its final form the paradigm of interstate industrial war took the people as its target. This was not war amongst the people of later times – this was war against the people. From the Holocaust, which declared a group of civilians as a target, to the Blitz, to the strategic bombing of Germany and Japan, and finally the atomic bomb, the Second World War removed for ever the sanctity of the non-combatant. The people, particularly in the towns and cities, were numerous and concentrated; they were easy targets, if air defences could be breached. These vulnerable masses account for the bulk of the casualties listed above. The numbers also reflect another truth: in one way or another the entire globe was affected by the war. Across continents, from the rancher in Argentina supplying beef, to the US production-line worker, through Africa and Asia, Europe and Australia, economies and lives were touched and in many cases decided by the war.

The Second World War was also a culmination of all the trends of the preceding 150 years: every element of the paradigm of interstate industrial war, from the first days of Napoleon, came to the fore. At the strategic level, and despite the tactical innovations of *Blitzkrieg*, the war was decided by the massive use of power to grind the opponent into defeat. Neither Germany nor Japan could attack the industrial heartlands of the USA and Russia, the two vast economies which, each in its way, were bent on conducting mass war. The resources of both in terms of men and materiel surpassed the Germans and Japanese who, suffering the attrition of battle and the bombing raids on the home front, were weakened bit by bit. This overarching reality was a mirror of Sherman's destructive march through Georgia, but writ large. Moreover, when defeat came to the Germans and Japanese it was a decisive victory for the Allies, in the clear Napoleonic sense. At the tactical level it was a war of empowered commanders and independent forces – units and methods that took shape in the first Napoleonic *corps d'armées* and were refined by Clausewitz then Moltke the elder. It was a war of planners and planning; of general staffs that on the Allied side combined into a Supreme Allied Command – notions which were unthought of in the eighteenth century, and yet which hark back directly to Napoleon and his visions, to the battle of Jena, and to the nascent Prussian general staff. It was a war of Clausewitzian trinities: everywhere, in all states and on all fronts, people, army and government pulled together. Without this capacity the war would never have been waged – anywhere. But unlike the preceding war, it was not the people who gave in: the military and the state in both Germany and Japan were destroyed by overwhelming force.

It was a war of gigantic mass, in which millions of men and women around the globe fought for their cause, much as the men of the first *levée en masse* in France did in the Revolutionary wars. Bulk quantities of materiel were produced by tens of millions of people – far more than the entire population of Europe in the early nineteenth century, when Napoleon was changing the face of Europe and warfare. Yet these were the direct descendants of the people who produced the first mass of artillery pieces for the Napoleonic Wars or the American Civil War. The Second World War was *the* war of the paradigm of interstate industrial war – and in its startling and horrific final act, it also ended the paradigm.

Having already ended in Europe, the Second World War ended totally after the US dropped two atomic bombs on Japan, each of sufficient power to wipe out a city. The scientific and industrial might of the USA and its British ally had created the weapon that could destroy both the opponent's ability to make war and the people at the same time. Their will was no longer relevant.

The atom bomb was the ultimate product of the elliptical loop of war as an outcome of industry, and industry in the service of war. Whilst industrial production based on technology was fuelling the conflict, constantly making it more awful and destructive, techno-logical innovation was also and always seen as the great salvation: the deus ex machina that would miraculously and instantaneously win it and thereby stop it. Like TNT or the tank in the First World War, in the second war too all sides were searching for the innovative techno-logical breakthrough that would bring the definitive victory. By 1945 it was the atom bomb.

Until the late nineteenth century, physicists believed the atom to be both indestructible and indivisible. Albert Einstein's formulation of the relativity of mass and energy opened up the prospect of releasing the energy contained within the atom. Just before the First World War German scientists were already carrying out experiments by bombard-ing mercury atoms with electrons and tracing the energy changes that resulted from the collisions. A wide range of experiments was con-ducted over the next two decades, and in 1938 Otto Hahn, Fritz Strass-man and Lise Meitner produced uranium nuclear fission at Germany's Kaiser Wilhelm Institute. A year later Meitner, from exile in Sweden, and her nephew Otto Frisch wrote a paper in which they argued that by splitting the atom it would be possible to use a few pounds of ura-nium to create the explosive and destructive power of many thousands of pounds of dynamite. Meanwhile, in the US, Leo Szilard was the first to realize that if an atom splits and sends out more than one neutron, the result could be a chain reaction: a massive energy release.

On 6 December 1941 the United States government committed $2 billion to the 'Manhattan Engineer District' aka the Manhattan Project, which was set up in great secrecy to manufacture the material to create an atomic bomb. Under the command of Brigadier General Leslie Groves and directed by Robert Oppenheimer, the members of the project formed an international cast of top-notch scientists, a large number of them recent exiles from the Axis powers. Research progressed swiftly and the first controlled, self-sustained chain reaction was produced in Chicago on 2 December 1942 by Italian Nobel Prize winner Enrico Fermi and his team: a neutron struck a uranium nucleus, thus releasing energy, which in turn had an impact on neighbouring atoms.

Across the Atlantic, scientists had also achieved great progress in the field. The British had set up a committee codenamed MAUD in the spring of 1940 to study the possibility of developing a nuclear weapon. It concluded that a sufficiently purified critical mass of uranium-235 could produce fission. The Germans had also set up a research programme after realizing the potential of the atom. German scientists took a wrong turn in their approach from the start by choosing to direct their research towards the use of 'heavy water' as a nuclear reactor moderator, which might allow them to produce plutonium for an atomic bomb. Through a series of sabotage attacks Norwegian resistance commandos, directed and supported by the British, managed to prevent the Nazi forces from transferring heavy water from the only plant in Reich-controlled territory capable of producing it. This cut off German physicists from their supplies but also had the crucial corollary impact of persuading them that they were looking in the right direction. In the end, Nazi Germany's efforts to create an atomic bomb came to nothing.

On 16 July 1945, in the New Mexico desert, the first atomic bomb was detonated. Victory in the European theatre of war had been achieved two months earlier with the fall of Berlin. In Asia, however, the retreating Japanese forces were fighting with an awful determination, in some cases greater than that of the retreating German soldiers in Europe. The number of kamikaze attacks on the Americans increased daily. Every island, every inch of land, had to be paid for with American blood, and the American public was beginning to grow tired of the stream of casualty reports. The invasion of the main Japanese islands, planned for 1 November, promised to bring terrible bloodshed, as hundreds of thousands of Allied casualties were expected. President Harry S. Truman decided to drop atom bombs on Japanese cities in order to force them to capitulate.

A special force, the 509 Composite Group of 20th Air Force, had been set up with the sole purpose of dropping the bomb. At 2 a.m. on 6 August 1945, Colonel Paul Tibbets, commanding the B-29 'super-fortress' *Enola Gay*, departed from Okinawa. At 8:16 a.m. the bomb was released over Hiroshima: the 'Little Boy' bomb was a uranium-fission weapon of about twenty kilotons of power, which carried a core of 137 pounds of Uranium 235: the ultimate exponent of techno-logical developments, of mass force, of mass power. As a terrible and unimaginable explosion shook the central section of the city, the crew of the *Enola Gay* saw a column of smoke rising fast and intense fires springing up.

The effects of the bomb were devastating. An intense flash of light was the first: anyone within a 150-kilometre radius looking in the direction of the blast was at least temporarily blinded. The second was intense heat: heat represented 35 per cent of the bomb's energy, gener-ating temperatures similar to those found at the surface of the sun. This ignited most materials and caused instant death or severe burns for anything living. The blast of the detonation represented 50 per cent of the energy of the bomb; it travelled at a rate of about 500 metres per second, sweeping everything away on its path until it even-tually weakened. Finally, the intense electromagnetic pulse generated by the detonation destroyed communications and electronic equip-ment over a large area. At the same time, particles of radioactive dust, lifted into the air by the explosion and carried by the wind, continued to damage the health of all those who came in contact with them for decades to come.

The number of casualties remains extremely hard to assess even today, especially if one attempts to include the victims of radio-activity. The immediate impact of the detonation killed around 66,000 people and injured 70,000 – out of a pre-raid population of 255,000. Of Hiroshima's fifty-five hospitals only three were usable after the blast, and 90 per cent of all doctors and nurses in the city were killed or injured. Sixty-five per cent of buildings were destroyed. By 1950, an estimated 200,000 people had died as a result of the bomb. And between 1950 and 1980, a further 97,000 died from cancers associated with the radiation caused by 'Little Boy'.

By way of a comparison, operation Gomorrah, launched on Hamburg at the end of July 1943 and conducted jointly by the Royal Air Force Bomber Command and the US 8th Air Force, was at the time the heaviest assault in the history of aerial warfare. It left 50,000 dead and a million civilians homeless; reduced half the city to rubble and nearly two-thirds of what remained of the population had to be evacuated. The destruction amounted to 250 square kilometres of the most densely built-up area of the city. Over ten days Allied aircraft dropped 9,000 tonnes of explosives and incendiaries. The point is not to compare bombing casualties but rather industrial efficiency, in which the atomic bomb was clearly superior in every way: only one was needed, delivered by one aircraft, as opposed to 3,095 sorties flown over Hamburg, in which 86 aircraft were lost and 174 damaged. These are horrific calculations, but none the less necessary for those conducting war – or seeking to stop or avert one.

Another atomic bomb with the same power as the first, 'Fat Boy', was dropped on Nagasaki three days later on 9 August, killing approximately 39,000 and injuring 25,000, out of a pre-raid population of 195,000. This, combined with the Soviet Union's declaration of war and attack on the Japanese forces in Manchuria on the same day, forced the Japanese into surrendering on 14 August.

The paradigm of interstate industrial war was literally blown to pieces on 6 August 1945. Ironically, it was ended by two of the very forces that brought it into being: industry and technological innovation. For nearly a century the pair served the towering edifice of industrial war, until the final explosion. The people – massed in their cities; the source of manpower and industrial power; the polity of the state – were now the only target worth attacking, since their cities were the most plausible objectives: constant, sitting targets of mass. And when the cities were destroyed, the forces in the field, cut off from the source of their purpose, direction and supply, could either surrender, be picked off in detail, or else concentrate and be struck with an atomic weapon. Mass industrial armies could no longer be effective in the face of a weapon of mass destruction, as the Russians came to call it. Industrial war, not to mention total war, was impossible in such circumstances. But the threat remained. That was the story of the Cold War.

PART TWO

The Cold War Confrontation

4

Antithesis: From Guerrillas to Anarchists to Mao

Conflict has been, is, and probably always will be an integral element of human society. I stated as much at the start of this book, and will revert to the theme at its end. It is vitally important to maintain the search for peace, but peace must be understood as a condition relating to conflict: not in the sense of the absence of conflict but as one in which that option is not chosen. I do not consider this situation to be good, but rather, and simply, a fact. In Part I the focus of my discussion was upon the increasingly destructive conflicts of the paradigm of interstate industrial war and the manner in which the use of force evolved within them. This historical discussion was necessary not merely as a contextual measure, but mainly because the paradigm still lives on conceptually, in our age of confrontations and reduced conflicts, despite its loss of utility after August 1945. Like the burnt-out and hollow shanties left in the wake of the atomic bomb in Hiroshima and Nagasaki, the structures of interstate industrial war were both useless and dangerous to those who sought them. None the less, like those cities, the paradigm was reconstructed, for political and pragmatic purposes; but unlike them, it never took on new life. Throughout the Cold War military and political leaders on all sides clung to it, building armies to its specifications, swearing by its redeeming capabilities in time of need. Thankfully, the need never came – if it had, the paradigm could not have functioned in its historical sense. First, because with the atomic bomb amassed armies could be no more than a target: rather than reinforcing such armies, nuclear technology as a weapon of mass destruction demands the absence of a mass as a defence; in these circumstances a large army is best used dispersed rather than amassed. And second, because 'decisive victory' came at a price that was potentially far too high to pay. In other words, the very thing fought for in interstate industrial war – the state, with its people, government and army – would be destroyed by the war.

Such realities were ignored for forty-five years, partly because of the lingering power of the idea of industrial war: in many parts of Europe it had forged the concept of the state itself. As we have seen, the map of the continent as we still know it, and the unity of the United States, were decided in the battles of the paradigm. Equally, the visual impact of industrial war was and probably still is the defining element of understanding war, especially in the public domain: cruise missiles and laser guided bombs have overlaid, but never replaced, the iconic images of armoured infantry wielding machine guns and riding on tanks. Even if the tanks are used for transport and protection rather than battle, they are still seen as the true instruments of modern war on land. But above all, the demise of industrial war was ignored because the entire underpinning of the Cold War was the need on both sides to convince the other of their willingness to go out and fight another total war, and thus deter the event, even if it appeared a contradictory plan given the consequences of total destruction. The utility of force was in its deterrence, not its application. This underpinning became a doctrine which then devolved into a dogma, an unquestionable fact, which solidified the enduring appeal of interstate industrial war long after its demise, and indeed in many ways to this day. For at the root of many of the problems we have now with the use of force and forces is their persistent structuring and use as if the old paradigm still held, at the expense of ignoring and being unfit for the new one that long since replaced it: the paradigm of war amongst the people. Indeed, as of 1945 military realities unfolded on twin parallel tracks: for even as the two sides to the Cold War were squaring up with mass industrial armies, forces of those same armies were out fighting different conflicts, with different kinds of enemies, all patently of a non-industrial nature. And it is these kinds of conflicts and enemies that we face most commonly now, in our post-Cold-War world, though we still try to mould them all back into the industrial model: to use force and forces in accordance with a dogma rather than a reality.

Understanding how these parallel worlds of conflicts and forces evolved, and how the two paradigms became intermingled, is the focus of Part II of this book. But first, there is need for a conceptual detour into the world of geography. As I noted at the start of this book, force can only have utility if used within a properly understood context. Presently this tends to mean political and military analysis – of the immediate causes of the conflict, of the enemy and his military and economic capabilities, of the possible impact upon neighbouring states and regional interests, to name but the obvious. Yet in the military we do not examine either the historical or geographical context in any great depth. And by this I mean the broader disciplines of history and geography. Military history, and as some American universities have it military geography, are important subsets of the broader disciplines, but they remain only subsets within the greater whole. Their principal importance results from the welcome fact that the profession of arms, as the pursuit of soldiering and command is rightly called, is practised by few men on few occasions. Most of the time soldiers, sailors and airmen of whatever rank are preparing for the event; they are in and of the profession, but not in practice or action. For my part I do not think I have been in action in the broadest sense for more than about six years of my thirty-seven years of commissioned service following my three years of training. And that figure includes a year in command of the UN forces in Sarajevo and three years as General Officer Commanding (GOC) Northern Ireland. The result of this lack of practice is that commanders must learn from the past by studying previous campaigns and the decisions of the commanders at the time. As we have seen, this practice was institutionalized by the Prussian-German general staffs, and has since become standard amongst the successful militaries of the world. However, I do not think the appropriate lessons will be drawn and carried forward into the present, nor the whole strategy truly comprehended, if the reader does not understand the overall historical and geostrategic context of the particular action or campaign under study.

History is the context of the battle, whilst geography is the context of the battlefield. Geography dictates the physical contours of the battlefield. Even with all the technological advances of our age, the location of a battle, and the limitations and advantages of that location – from contours through climate to the nature of the soil – will affect the battle, and very possibly its outcome. Technology has not made the globe an even surface: a missile will always be launched from one location and land in another – and both are hugely relevant to the successful application of the force. The discipline of geography therefore, as the study of the globe and its interaction with the people on it, provides us with the means to understand the battlefield and predict its nature so as to use the elements to advantage. This has always been the case. For example, the Royal Navy in the Georgian period turned to technology in the search for an accurate clock to find longitude – which, apart from improving their navigation, enabled them systematically to collect navigational data, much of which is in use on our current charts. Over centuries these and similar measures to map the earth's surface were carried out mainly for military purposes, and whilst civil society benefited from the information it was the militaries who collected it and in some cases guarded it carefully. Turkey, for example, has only recently declassified its detailed mapping, although it is still not generally available in the shops. And it is not merely a question of scientific data: postcards, literary descriptions, pamphlets – there are many sources which can supply scraps of information, especially on inaccessible locations. And all such detailed information provides a greater perspective of the battlefield, which I have found of value throughout my years in command. Indeed, as I rose in rank I found that a geostrategic analysis was of increasing value: it allowed one to comprehend the situation as a whole, and to understand the overall context of the conflict or confrontation: why it occurred physically in a certain place. In such an analysis one considers a wide variety of factors, including the major communication corridors, the availability of natural resources, regional relationships, the economies, the cultural mix and the societies' normative values and patterns of behaviour. Such geostrategic analysis shows the facts of life as it is led in that place or region, and which is the target of my force. It should be set against the historical analysis to produce a result that will help to understand one's own position in relation to that of the opponent, as well as to help predict which course of action he is likely to adopt. For example, in 1990, when planning to attack across a flat gravel desert in Iraq and then into Kuwait, I considered there was no ground of any tactical advantage whatsoever – and decided that I would not fight for the ground: if an Iraqi wished to defend a piece of desert, I would leave him there – and instead attack his commander's ability to communicate with him and supply him. This reduced my needs for infantry and for close-quarter battle, all of which reduced my anti-cipated needs for men and supplies. These in turn added to the speed at which I could move, and therefore interdict the command arrangements in the depth of the Iraqi positions.

All the battles and wars discussed in previous chapters offer examples of these contexts, not least the steppes that provided the strategic space to refuse the Napoleonic battle in Russia, and the rugged terrain of the Iberian peninsula that allowed the guerrillas a sanctuary from which to harry Napoleon's forces. Or indeed the harsh reality faced by both Germany and Japan in the Second World War, that in order to defeat either Russia or the US, there is a need to conquer each of them – in other words to conquer entire continents. An example of geostrategic factors at play can be seen by considering the geography of the Rhine valley, which stretches northwards from Switzerland to the North Sea. There are really only three corridors that allow substantial forces to cross the river Rhine: the Belfort Gap, the Mosel valley, and the line across the Low Countries, going from Liège through Aachen to the Ruhr. These geographical features were as significant to the Romans as they were to Eisenhower's generals in 1944. At the turn of the twentieth century, when Schlieffen made his plan, the exits from the two southerly corridors were guarded by substantial French fortifications, which can be seen to this day. The volume, the density of forces that could pass through these southerly corridors, was insufficient to defeat the mobilizing French defenders. The remaining corridor in the north could carry a high vol-ume of forces, sufficient to overcome the Belgian defenders and to form a powerful northerly wing to attack south, enveloping Paris and the defenders along the border. As such the Schlieffen Plan was shaped by geography, and this forced the breaching of Belgian neutrality.

The need for geostrategic comprehension is an important element of applying force with utility. It is therefore equally crucial in non-industrial warfare – such as we practice today, but which has its roots in the past. It is to these roots we now turn.

*

To this point I have focused exclusively upon interstate industrial war, but that is not to suggest there were not other kinds of wars as of the start of the nineteenth century. As we have seen, it took some time for industrial armies to develop, and in the interim many still fought in a manner closer to the 'old style' of pre-Napoleonic wars. This is especially true of most of the early colonial wars in the Far East and then in Africa, in which the weapons were still muskets or early breech loaders. However, these were conflicts in which it was the actual presence of guns, as opposed to industrially produced ones, which made the difference against the spears and arrows of the indigenous people. Moreover, in time colonial powers such as France and the Netherlands created separate armies to deal with their outposts – whilst still developing their industrial armies to deal with each other. However, in parallel to these evolutions came another: the antithesis to interstate industrial war. A counter-paradigm whose roots can be traced back to the same times, and the same wars, as interstate industrial war. Over time, this antithesis would lead to the paradigm of war amongst the people.

The origins of the antithesis lie in the Spanish countryside during the Peninsular War of 1808–14, the war or campaign Napoleon's generals lost. In 1806 Napoleon decided to impose a blockade on British trade by forcing the nations of continental Europe to close their ports to British goods. As the Portuguese refused to comply, a French army marched through Spain in November 1807 and occupied Lisbon. In February 1808 Napoleon then invaded Spain and occupied Madrid, crowning his brother Joseph king of Spain. The Spanish people rose up against the French and appealed to Britain for help – which soon arrived. But it is the people's war that is most interesting here. With their country occupied and many of their cities and towns garrisoned by the French, the people of Spain continued to fight. Two complementary wars followed: that of the people, and that of the armies. The people called their conflict a little war: a guerrilla – the combination of the Spanish word for war, *guerra*, and the diminutive suffix *-illa*. The term was coined to describe the tactics they used to resist King Joseph Bonaparte's regime: small, mobile and flexible combat groups drawn from, concealed and sustained by the people, intended to harass an enemy force superior in strength whilst avoiding any large-scale direct confrontation. The political purpose of pursuing such a war was to maintain the people's independent identity, even though occupied, by sustaining their will to continue to fight and resist. In this way they sought to recover their independence when Britain and its allies triumphed. The strategic objectives were to erode the enemy's will to continue, to gather information and to disrupt and delay enemy operations so as to weaken their resistance to the liberating forces – the Anglo-Portuguese army under the Duke of Wellington, who had arrived in August 1808 with a British expeditionary force of some 10,000 men.

Guerrilla tactics stem from the basic tenet of their forces seeking only to give battle on their terms, which entails knowing their opponent's position and strength, knowing when it is possible to isolate him from help or escape before help arrives, having the element of surprise on their side and fighting at a time of their choosing. Lacking the numerical strength and weapons to oppose a regular army in the field, guerrillas prefer to avoid pitched battles. The ambush and raid are their favoured tactical methods. Above all the guerrilla always avoids holding ground, for to do so is to invite discovery, isolation and destruction. Striking swiftly and unexpectedly, guerrillas raid enemy supply depots and installations, ambush patrols and supply convoys and cut communication lines, intending thereby to disrupt enemy activities and to capture equipment and supplies for their own use. Because of their mobility, the dispersal of their forces into small groups and their ability to disappear among the civilian population, guerrillas are extremely difficult to pin down and bring to battle: guerrilla wars evolve without a fixed front line. Their objective is to destabilize the enemy and put his resources (troops and supply lines) under strain through a continuous series of pinprick attacks over a long period, which in sum weaken the enemy materially, force him to concentrate on his own protection and erode his own resolve.

All these attributes were abundantly apparent in the guerrilla activities in the Spanish Peninsular War. The stubborn Spanish defence of cities like Saragossa tied down thousands of French troops whilst the Spanish guerrillas wreaked havoc throughout the country, tying down to rear-area security a significant number of French troops, and maintaining a constant series of attacks on the French lines of communication. In response, the full might of the Napoleonic war machine was deployed to crush the 'rebellion'. Napoleon himself briefly took personal command of his army, but in his absence the endless squabbles between his overambitious commanders and the sheer incompetence of his brother Joseph contributed to the deteriorating situation. Although on paper the French heavily outnumbered Wellington, they were never able to concentrate enough of their troops to win a decisive victory. By late 1810 some 300,000 French troops had been sucked into the peninsula, yet only 70,000 could be spared to confront Wellington; the remainder were pinned down elsewhere by threats of local insurrections and the actions of guerrillas. By 1813 Wellington's army was 70,000 strong and the resounding victories provided by his inspired generalship – aided by his Portuguese allies, the deep operation of the Spanish guerrillas and the significant amount of intelligence they provided – were crucial in driving the French from Spain.

The guerrillas depended on the people for their morale and materiel support, and to some extent for their concealment – although the terrain was sufficiently vast and wild to provide ample hiding places and room to avoid French security sweeps. The guerrilla forces were lightly armed and depended in large measure on captured powder and shot as their source of resupply. In contrast to a conventional force they were 'formless' and had no apparent formal command system. They also lacked political cohesion and expended a lot of energy and some blood quarrelling amongst themselves. Nevertheless, they kept alive the honour of Spain and the will to be free of Napoleon. Above all, the constant guerrilla activity drained the resources and diverted the attention of the French military. By 1812 the 'Spanish ulcer' or 'running sore' was costing France an average of a hundred men a day and this incremental degradation of combat power sapped the morale of the armies. With the French unable to concentrate their forces against the Anglo-Portuguese army, Wellington was able to move on to the offensive and ultimately overcome a numerically superior enemy.

Militarily, the guerrillas' use of force was tactical and it supported Wellington's theatre-level operations. On a European scale, as noted in Chapter 1, the importance of the Spanish theatre – long deemed secondary by Napoleon – proved to be crucial. After the

Grande Armée's disastrous retreat from Russia, he was more than ever in need of soldiers. In 1813, the absence of the 300,000 French troops locked in the Iberian peninsula certainly affected the course of the German campaign; whilst Wellington's crushing victory at Vitoria in June 1813, that ended the French occupation of Spain, also served to rally the wavering Prusso-Russian alliance as they faced Napoleon one last time. But this victory, and the primacy of the theatre as a whole, would not have been possible without the guerrillas. In reflecting on his miscalculation of the Spanish theatre, Napoleon once said: 'That unfortunate war destroyed me . . . All . . . my disasters are bound up in that fatal knot.'*

Guerrilla war, much like industrial war, was a model founded in the wars that preceded it. For example, in the American War of Independence, men who had learned to fight the Indians on the frontier used these Indian tactics against the British, although in time the Revolutionary Army took on more conventional tactics. Much earlier, in approximately 350 BC, Sun Tzu describes the essential tactical methods of the indirect approach. I do not suppose any of the protagonists of the day had read or even heard of Sun Tzu, but his advice in *The Art of War* 'to avoid strength and strike weakness' should be the guiding idea of the guerrilla or partisan tactician, and much else of what he wrote is a manual for the guerrilla's operational method.

There is a danger of confusing guerrilla warfare with other types of 'small wars'. As discussed above, paralleling the developments in total war were many small wars of colonization, imperial expansion and control. Some of the fighting in these resembled that of guerrilla warfare, but we must be careful in our analysis to distinguish between the tactics adopted and the geostrategic setting and political and strategic goals of the combatants. In other words, each situation must be viewed in the round rather than the specific: the tactics employed may be that of the guerrilla, but the context could very well be entirely different. The clue to this analysis lies with Clausewitz. Doubtless with the example of the Spanish in mind, after the Napoleonic Wars he argued that the

* Napoleon Bonaparte, *Mémorial de Sainte-Hélène*, Vol. 1 (Paris: Editions Garnier frères, 1961 [1823]), pp. 609–10.

weaker could prevail over the stronger. To do this the weaker opponent should aim to destroy the stronger's will to wage war, and 'partisan warfare', as he called it, could add to the erosion of that will, provided the terrain gave space and concealment, and the forces were of a suitable nature. The colonial expeditions of the nineteenth century succeeded because for the most part the polities they faced could neither conceive of acts that had an effect on the popular political will in some distant country, nor were they likely to empower the people by telling them to fight independently of the ruling authority. The locals being invaded tended to use their armed forces, if they existed as such, in an endeavour to hold ground; where faced by superior weapons such as guns they were defeated. When imperial or colonial forces did not prevail, such as the two British wars with Afghanistan in the nineteenth century, it was the imperial, invading power's will that was changed. In Afghanistan, the terrain and the country's distance from the sea, the source of Britain's power and supply, coupled with the nature of the tribes as coherent and organized, satisfied Clausewitz's criteria. As a result Britain could not find sufficient forces to achieve a dominating density. The British made two attempts to include Afghanistan in the Raj (1839–42 and 1878–90), defeating formed Afghan armies on each occasion, but these were tactical gains which could never be translated into political capital. Britain ultimately withdrew and dealt with the country's leaders rather like a medieval prince did with those on his border marches.

The Boer War which began in 1899 is another example of Clausewitz's formulation. It was also a formative experience for the British army. The Boers' citizen armies were based on mounted infantry and armed with modern weapons. Organized in small self-contained units called commandos, they moved rapidly in contrast to the ponderous British formations and both their fieldcraft and marksmanship were superior. They attacked in October and besieged the British in Mafeking, Kimberley and Ladysmith, compounding this initial success with 'Black Week' in December 1899, when the British suffered a series of defeats at Magersfontein, Stormberg and Colenso, resulting in the loss of nearly 1,000 of their soldiers and preventing them from relieving the besieged towns. However, the British held their nerve, commanders were changed, reinforcements were dispatched and the force transformed. Literally transformed: red coats were replaced by khaki. Horses were procured and mounted infantry trained, and there was a logistical reorganization of units in the field. As Kipling would once again have it:

> I used to belong in an Army once
> (Gawd! What a rum little Army once)
> Red little, dead little Army once
> But now I am M.I.!
>
> ('M.I. – Mounted Infantry of the Line')

By June 1900 the formed Boer armies in the field were defeated and the British were in possession of their state capitals, Bloemfontein and Pretoria. But the Boers, having failed in the trial of strength, did not surrender but set out to break the will of the British, and a two-year guerrilla war followed. On occupying the Boer Republics after defeating their armies Britain had achieved its stated strategic objective. There was nothing more the British could do with military force at the strategic level, but the strategic initiative was for the taking and the Boers decided to take it. Having lost sovereignty over their land, the veldt, they set out to make its occupation intolerable to the British forces, and at a cost those in Britain could not bear. To this end they adopted the tactic of the guerrilla to win the clash of wills at the strategic level by success at the tactical level. The Boers were encouraged in this strategy by a number of factors: their powerful sense of nation, familiarity with the immensity of the veldt, the political divisions within Britain over the wisdom of conducting the war at all and the support their cause received in Europe and the US. Since Britain was the supreme power at the time it ignored the pressure of the other powers. However, there were internal political divisions: the Liberal and Labour parties, the parliamentary opposition at the time, opposed the war as an excess of imperialism, but this was not reflected in the population's support for the armed forces as a whole. The general popular sentiment was that the Boer had attacked first, and in response the Empire was engaged and had sent contingents – it was therefore up to the British to show a lead and not be beaten. On the whole, however, since the British force was composed of volunteers the population was not affected by actual or potential losses, as they would have been with a conscripted force. Finally, and perhaps most significantly, at that time there was no means of putting the Boer (or any foreign) point of view to the public at large; no international media channels to present an alternative view of events to the home public. But there was internal criticism, and as time passed and the casualties mounted – in all Britain lost 22,000 men to battle and disease – opinion soured. Yet such comment was centred on the manner of the doing rather than whether the war was worth fighting at all. Indeed, as the war went on, patriotism tended towards jingoism and the more nationalistic characteristics of John Bull also made appearances. Reverting to Clausewitz, Britain's will to win was not assailed to any significant degree.

The campaign conducted against the Boer commandos was in the end successful. Tactically, with its mounted infantry, the British forces were able to match the commando at his own game and the advantage of numbers overcame any lack of natural skill and experience. The campaign involved concentrating the widely dispersed rural population: with casual brutality families were taken from their burning farms to badly mismanaged, typhoid-ridden 'concentration camps' whose disgraceful conditions were one of the major causes of criticism in London. The purpose of removing the people from their farms on the veldt was to prevent them concealing, sheltering and feeding the commandos. Once the veldt was clear, all movement could be viewed as enemy movement until proved otherwise, and the commandos, denied information and food, would have to come out of hiding as they sought these vital commodities, thus risking death or capture. The next measure taken by the British was to control communications so as to gain information that would lead them to the commandos. This was done by a system of wire barriers and blockhouses, initially based on the railway lines and connected by telephone, which crisscrossed the veldt. Finally, the areas between the barriers were patrolled heavily. As commandos sought food or to avoid capture they bumped into patrols or broke down barriers, and slowly a picture of their overall whereabouts was established. This improved the precision with which patrols were tasked, which in turn improved the British rate of success.

It was not as easy as I have made it sound: the Boer was a hard man, fighting on his own ground, and with the enduring morale and self-sufficiency of the frontiersman. Much of his ammunition and food came from raiding the British. It was not uncommon after a skirmish or battle for him to release prisoners naked, since he needed the clothes more than he needed the prisoner, whilst resupply was sometimes achieved by following ill-disciplined and profligate British patrols. At the end of two years, when peace came with the signing of the Treaty of Vereeniging in May 1902, although greatly reduced in number, starving and under pressure, there were still commandos at large to surrender. The peace was signed largely because the British had undermined the Boer will to continue. Politically and strategically the British were determined to win the war and incorporate the Boer Republics they had taken into the Empire, and the Boers knew they could not now reverse the situation. Moreover, in their actions the British had negated the Clausewitz criteria by removing the people and systematically denying the Boers the advantages of the terrain. Tactically, the Boers were losing by a process of attrition. The final and most significant factor was that the British matched their campaign with a political option for their opponents that offered a credible and better prospect than the current situation: they promised self rule, and £3 million were allocated to reconstruction of the rural economy.

The last two years of the Boer War was a supreme example of the antithesis to interstate industrial war: small operations, with a minimal amount of people, focused upon disruption rather than a decisive military victory as a means of achieving a political end. Unlike the Spanish guerrillas, the Boers were not part of a greater whole: they had no external backer and no sanctuary other than the veldt. In the two years of the guerrilla phase of the war, force was never applied for more than tactical objectives. In truth, it could not have been otherwise: the commandos only presented tactical targets, they never deployed as a whole, and because they would not do so they themselves could attack only tactical targets. The British understood this and did not attempt 'decisive operations' at theatre level. It was a war of tactical engagements won politically at theatre level – at the negotiating table.

The First World War was the next important step in the evolution of the antithesis to the paradigm of interstate industrial war – most specifically the liberation campaign, as it would now be called, fought by the Arabs of the Arabian peninsula, led by their sheikhs, to free themselves from Ottoman rule. This did not initially appear a simple proposition: the failure of the Allies' Gallipoli offensive, the surrender of British forces at Kut in Mesopotamia in April 1916 and the Turkish offensive towards the Suez Canal in 1916 all proved that Ottoman armies were still a force to be reckoned with. The British therefore built up a force in the Sinai desert, and under General Allenby developed a campaign to defeat the Ottoman armies in Palestine – with the Arab nationalist forces mounting a supporting operation. From the British point of view the Arab cause was worth supporting because it promised a great increase on the pressure that could be brought to bear on the Turks. In this regard the situation was much the same as that in the Peninsular War against the French, when the Spanish guerrillas greatly aided the conventional forces of Wellington on the road to victory.

Lieutenant Colonel T. E. Lawrence was chosen to act as advisor and liaison officer to the Arab nationalist movements. Already posted to Cairo, where he worked for British Military Intelligence, Lawrence's intimate knowledge of the Arab people, especially their culture and politics, made him the ideal candidate for the job. In October 1916 he was sent into the desert to report on the nationalist movements, and he quickly realized that the Arab political and strategic aims were 'unmistakably geographical, to occupy all Arabic speaking lands in Asia'. In *The Seven Pillars of Wisdom*, published after the war, Lawrence reflected upon how this end was achieved, whilst also aiding the British quest – and in so doing clearly defined the three levels of war below the political and how each sets the context to the one below, thereby ensuring coherence:

The Turkish Army was an accident, not a target. Our true strategic aim was to seek its weakest link, and bear only on that until time made the mass of it fall. The Arab army must impose the longest possible passive defence on the Turks (this being the most materially expensive form of war) by extending its own front to the maximum.* Tactically, it must develop a highly mobile,

* The theatre or operational objective.

highly equipped type of force, of the smallest size, and use it successively at distributed points of the Turkish line.

In this way he sought to make the Arabs 'an influence, a thing invulnerable, intangible, without front or back, drifting about like a gas'. In these words Lawrence shows that the purpose of Arab battle in the field was attritional, to win each local fight, rather than one of wills. Within this perspective the object of the battles was only to fight at the tactical level and to stretch the Turks at the operational level to the point of moral rather than material collapse. The Arabs undoubtedly needed their own will to do this, but the promise of independence was a sufficient spur.

Based on this strategy, Lawrence managed to convince Arab leaders to coordinate their rebellious efforts, and he was soon fighting with their irregular troops under overall command of Emir Faisal. Conducting operations mainly in the Arabian peninsula, with limited means, he focused on implementing his strategy of hindering the Ottoman war effort. Initially, for example, Lawrence persuaded the Arabs not to drive the Ottomans out of the town of Medina, thus forcing the Turks to pin down troops to maintain the city garrison. Lacking men and materiel to engage a regular army in major battle, Lawrence encouraged small-unit tactics, and favoured raids conducted by 100–200 tribesmen against substantial conventional Turk forces. He then directed his attentions towards the Hejaz railway line, which was the only major line of communication and supply for Ottoman forces as Britain's naval superiority in the Red Sea lay uncontested. With the Turkish army thinly spread across the empty vastness of the Arabian peninsula, Arabs found it relatively easy to strike and sabotage the railway, which ferried men, supplies and munitions across the peninsula.

Lawrence and his Arab irregulars focused on continuously destroying sections of the railway for two years. Small units of men were deployed to lay charges on tracks in various locations. They used sophisticated explosive devices that would inflict as much damage as possible so that the Turks would be forced to make time-consuming repairs. One of Lawrence's explosive devices was the 'tulip bomb', which twisted tracks to such an extent that they could not be re-straightened. Another way to disable a railway was to 'walk' a track out of service: groups of twenty men walked along the track, lifting rails and then discarding them. In a similar way, bridges were blown up to shatter rather than collapse as they consumed more man-hours to fix. Such was the Arab admiration for Lawrence and his use of explosives that they nicknamed him Amir Dynamite.

Such sabotage operations tied up increasing numbers of Ottoman troops, who were forced to protect the railway and repair the continuous damage. At the same time Turkish forces attempted to defend the Hejaz railway with outposts and patrols, but Lawrence's men formed large moving columns capable of rapid hit-and-run operations. The conflict did indeed soon turn into a war of attrition; but Lawrence always used far smaller forces to attack and sabotage tracks and infrastructure than the Turks used to conduct repairs. In 1917 he coordinated a joint action between Arab irregulars and forces which rebelled against their Ottoman master, serving under Auda Abu Tayi's command. In a daring overland attack, they seized the strategically important port of Aqaba; and in the final stages of the war, Lawrence was also involved in the capture of Damascus.

The Arab forces made a significant contribution to the British victory in the Middle East. They were credited with killing some 35,000 Turks and capturing or wounding a similar number. Every element of their fight reflected their part in the antithesis of interstate industrial war, much as the Spanish guerrillas and the Boers before them. By war's end they had achieved their strategic aim, with approximately 100,000 square miles of territory under their control that had formerly been under Ottoman rule. As such, their political aim appeared within their grasp – but the British and the French, their allies in war, failed them. In carving up the defeated Ottoman Empire, they did not honour the expectations of the Arabs, in spite of Lawrence's lobby at the Versailles peace talks in 1919, where he insisted this had been the understanding he had passed on to the sheikhs during the war. The Arabs were denied their regional independence, the provinces of the former Ottoman Empire became mandated territories ruled by the French and the British, and the House of Saud was left only with the sanctuary of the Arabian Desert. Within a matter of years this proved, quite literally, to be fortunate – since the largest reserve of oil in the world was discovered under their sands.

*

Interstate industrial war evolved through a combination of theory – with the enduring influence of Clausewitz – and practice. In contrast, its antithesis evolved far more through ideology and nationalism: given the very nature of the fight as a people's war against a larger enemy, there had to be an ideological commitment of some kind from the participants. However, it was in the interwar period that ideology really came to the fore. In the early 1920s, at about the same time Lawrence was writing his account of the war in Arabia and Palestine, a trend that had existed for some decades became linked with the tactical ideas of guerrilla war. This was the anarchists' idea of assassinating leaders in order to force their existence and ideas into the public foreground. Whilst often flawed in execution and totally flawed in concept – generally speaking people do not want anarchy, they want government, and will debate only leadership, purpose and parameters – the idea was taken up by, among others, Trotsky and many of his fellow Russian revolutionaries. The propaganda of the deed was born and became a line of operations in the revolutionary campaign. Its objectives were to force government, people and external agencies to pay attention, to make the 'cause' significant, to act or demonstrate against that which was unpopular, to gain recruits, and to gain at the least the population's tacit support of the 'cause'. In the UK, for example, such a deed was the murder of Lord Mountbatten by the IRA in 1979, on his annual holiday in the Republic of Ireland – which served no purpose other than to publicize the IRA.

Alongside the propaganda of the deed a second line of operations was developed: the strategy of provocation. In this case the idea was to use the strength and weight of the counter-revolutionary forces to advantage, rather as a judo fighter seeks to use the energy of an opponent's attack to throw them to the ground. Attacks or 'incidents' are carried out such as to invite, or possibly demand, response from the government, the objectives here being to reflect the government as a brutal oppressor to the people and external agencies, to instill within the people the notion of the security forces as the enemy, to gain sympathy for the 'cause' and to gain recruits. An excellent example of such provocation would be the marches in Northern Ireland that ultimately led to the events of Bloody Sunday in January 1972, in which thirteen of the marchers in Londonderry were shot by British soldiers.

The strategy of provocation also has further operational value, as a way of reconnaissance: if the security forces fail to react to a provocation at a checkpoint, for example, the level of their tolerance is established, at least locally, and other activities can be undertaken within that level. Such data informs the execution of the third line of operations: eroding the capability of the government to govern – both in terms of the means of government and the will to govern. A good example of this is the murder and intimidation of officials – in the case of Northern Ireland the murder of judges. These are the three major categories of operations, but it should be emphasized that whilst they each may be clearly defined, many acts serve more than one of these operational lines – and allow for exploitation as events unfold. Like the conventional and structured armies they face, guerrillas too must adapt and have organizational mobility if they are to use their force with utility.

In this formulation of the antithesis, revolutionary war, force is being used to form the people's intentions as to their governance: throughout all lines of operations the revolutionary is working to increase the acceptance of the people to be governed by the revolution. The strategic and theatre-level objectives are all to do with forming or changing the will of the people, not that of the opponent, and it is only at the tactical level, and at a time of the revolutionaries' choosing, that force is applied directly to achieve its destructive potential. These ideas gathered weight and were put into effect in both Russia and China. It was Lenin who drew on Clausewitz's thinking on weak against strong opponents, with his discussion of a 'people's war,' which should rely on popular support, and his argument that no single event could decide the outcome of such a war. In engineering the Russian Revolution there is no doubt Lenin applied this thinking in a very successful way. Indeed, the ideas Lenin derived from his own experience have had a major impact on modern guerrilla strategies.

Mao Zedong's revolutionary theories of war, as he and the Chinese Peoples' Liberation Army fought both the Japanese and the forces of Chiang Kai Shek, also centred on the use of guerrilla warfare tactics. He saw the concept of revolutionary war moving through three phases – and the war could be in different phases in different parts of the theatre, with the possibility (which materialized) of the revolutionary having to move back to an earlier phase in the face of a reverse. In simple terms the three phases were, first, to form cells in the community, ideally deep in the rural areas and on a border with a sympathetic neighbour, in order to achieve a local dominance by corrupting and replacing government through massive use of propaganda and indoctrination. In the second phase this local area was developed into a sanctuary by expanding the cell structure and linking with other liberated areas to form a region in which forces were prepared and food and weapons could be stored; this was coupled with the escalation of attacks on government institutions and military forces. In the third and final phase formed forces consolidated the sanctuary and operated against government forces in other areas where the cell structure could support them. This phase would continue until the government forces were defeated in the field and revolutionary government had progressively taken over rural area after rural area until the cities fell as well.

In both the Russian and Chinese cases the revolutionaries ended their campaigns with conventional formed armies in the field – which were necessary in the final phase to defeat the formed government armies that faced them in a trial of strength. However, the preceding clash of wills took different paths, according to the circumstances of the people and the theatre. In Russia, the revolution was centred on the urban proletariat whose labour fuelled the industrialization of the Russian economy and war effort. The revolution moved from city to city, through the countryside along the railway network. Trotsky's creation of the Red Army signalled the advent of an enormous war machine, which soon resembled the traditional armies of its enemies with its centralized staff structure and planning, its rigid adherence to orders and the paralleling of its chain of command with a political structure. In contrast in China, the revolution was centred on the rural population. The country was barely industrialized, riven by civil war and was in part occupied by the Japanese. The mass of people dwelled in the countryside, where they controlled the food supply and were the source of manpower. Nevertheless, in all but the final stages the revolution was fought amongst the people and for the people's minds. As Mao put it: 'the guerrilla moves amongst the people as the fish swims in the sea'. The Long March was proof of this: a massive military retreat by the Chinese Communist army, between October 1934 and October 1935, to evade the pursuit of the nationalist Kuomintang army. The communists covered some 9,000 kilometres until they reached a safe haven: the isolated north-western province of Shaanxi. En route, Mao Zedong established his leadership of the Communist Party, whilst his army confiscated both property and weapons from the more affluent and the nationalists, and at the same time recruited peasants and the poor. Out of an estimated 100,000 soldiers who began the march less than a quarter made it to the final destination. And yet, in the years that followed the Long March through China, Mao's army began consolidating its structure in its new safe haven in Yan'an. After successfully defeating Japanese occupation forces and the Kuomintang's nationalist forces, the People's Republic of China's army also became more like a traditional army, geared towards interstate industrial warfare. Ironically, in the decades that followed, in the western Muslim provinces of China and in Tibet, it became the prey of local guerrilla actions. Having already created conventional armies, once they took power the revolutionaries assumed all the trappings and powers of the governments they replaced, and often more. That is the true paradox of the antithesis of industrial war conducted by successful revolutionaries: it evolves to the point in which it merges with the conventional paradigm.

The Second World War saw a continued development of the antithesis with the Resistance and partisan operations in the German- and Japanese-occupied territories. From the point of view of the Allies these were 'deep operations' similar to those carried out by the Spanish guerrillas in the Peninsular campaign and the Arab irregulars in the First World War before them. For those involved there was always the political objective, if only in the early stages, of keeping the flame of freedom alight. It is notable that those movements that were based on the local Communist Party structure often did better than the others. This is not surprising, for a number of reasons: they had a vision of a better world, rather than just a return to the antebellum status quo, an existing cell structure and experience of the security measures to avoid penetration by intelligence services. They also had international links, primarily to Moscow, and as the Allies approached and victory was in sight, these invaluable guerrillas spent an increasing amount of effort ensuring their political position was secure for the future. To this extent Churchill's decision to back Josep Broz Tito's communist partisans in Yugoslavia instead of the royalists, on the grounds that the former killed more Germans, was undoubtedly the correct decision from the military strategic point of view. However, it carried political consequences, one of which became apparent towards the end of the war, when Tito's vision of a Greater Yugoslavia, including Slovenia and the port of Trieste, clashed with Britain's interests, namely of keeping the port at the head of the Adriatic in Western hands.

The Yugoslav partisans, headed from June 1941 by Tito, openly called for armed resistance to the occupying Third Reich. Tito soon became the chief commander of the Yugoslav National Liberation Army (NLA). His partisans staged a guerrilla campaign stretching right across the national territory. Lightly equipped irregular military forces set about opposing German control and began liberating swathes of territory in which they organized people's committees to act as civilian government. The Germans retaliated by punishing the civilian population and executing hostages, but this was not sufficient to break the partisans' will to resist. The NLA's activities were often supported directly by the forces of its allies – an inversion from previous models, when the guerrillas supported allied conventional forces. The Balkan Air Force was formed by the Allies in June 1944 to command operations that were mainly aimed at helping NLA forces. In late 1944 the NLA managed to expel the Axis from Serbia and, with the assistance of the Red Army, from the rest of Yugoslavia in 1945.

A less known but excellent example of the partisan formulation of the antithesis was the Ukrainian Insurgent Army (Ukrainska Povstanska Armiya or UPA), founded in 1942. Its goal was to establish an independent sovereign Ukrainian state. Although the German army retained control of the major cities, vast swathes of the mountainous western and northern regions of Ukraine were controlled by the UPA. One of its unique characteristics was that despite its huge local success – its membership peaked at a remarkable half a million men in June 1944 – it never received any foreign help. Indeed, the UPA is a good example of the political objective of a guerrilla group being different from that of the ally they are supporting, at least nominally. For together with other guerrilla groups, the UPA fought against the armies of both Nazi Germany and the USSR – their supposed ally. Moreover, in the early days of the war the Russians discovered their conscripted troops often tended to be sympathetic towards Ukrainian guerrillas. In fact, the UPA appealed to all who wanted to combat both Stalin and Hitler, and various nationalities could be found amongst its ranks including Tatars, Uzbeks, Armenians, and others. Because its propaganda efforts were also directed towards Red Army soldiers, Moscow had to make use of special troops such as NKVD (secret-service) forces or pro-Russian partisans to combat the UPA.

The Ukrainian guerrilla or partisan operation offers a good example of the difference between political as opposed to the military strategic objectives. The UPA had the objective of freeing the Ukraine from the Soviets, but just as long as the Germans occupied their land they fought alongside the Soviets to defeat them. Once the Germans were repelled the political and military strategic objectives merged into a single aim: their commander-in-chief, General Roman Shukhevich, kept the guerrilla war going against the USSR. He was killed in action in 1950, five years after the end of the Second World War. Undoubtedly brave, and successful in that he and his cohorts kept the insurgency going for nearly a decade, they none the less failed to learn one of the most important lessons from the more successful revolutionaries of the earlier Russian Revolution: that despite holding large chunks of the countryside, power ultimately lay with the people in the cities. For it was the Soviets who held the cities and thereby controlled the urban proletariat, who were the majority of the people and the means of production and distribution, namely industry and the railways, respectively. In the vastness of Russia and the Ukraine, small groups of partisans in the forests and swamps could not achieve sufficient critical mass to have an impact on the people.

A better-known example of the partisan formulation of the antithesis in the Second World War was the Resistance, a movement that fought against Nazi forces occupying France, and their collaborators. Resistance groups were of various political colours: some were Gaullists, others socialists (including Spanish republicans) and a large proportion were members of the Communist Party, especially after

Hitler's invasion of Russia. The French Resistance cooperated with Allied secret services and was especially useful in providing intelligence on the Atlantic Wall and coordinating sabotages and other actions, which contributed to the success of operation Overlord. The Special Operations Executive (SOE) in London began to help and supply the Resistance in November 1940, parachuting weapons, radios, radiomen and advisors. Both the Secret Intelligence Service and the Special Air Service continued its operations.

More in the classic mode of guerrilla fighters in the nineteenth century, the Maquis were predominantly rural guerrilla bands of the French Resistance. The word *maquis* is French for a type of mountainous terrain in southern France characterized by scrub growth. Armed resistance groups chose that type of terrain to hide. Members of those bands were called *maquisards*, and they used guerrilla tactics to harass German forces and the French Milice, the internal security force of the Vichy regime. Most Maquis groups relied on the support of the local population to supply them: the size of each could range from a cell of a dozen members to groups containing hundreds and even thousands of men at the end of the war. The Resistance provided assistance to the Allied invasion forces in the south of France during operations Dragoon and Anvil, and played a key role in preparing and supporting the invasion of Normandy by gathering valuable information on German defences and garrisons.

As war on the western front progressed, some Maquis groups rose up against the Germans and liberated parts of France, though at huge expense in human life since the Waffen SS responded with extreme violence. Local uprisings combined with sabotage actions could cut German forces off from their supplies and leave them stranded, surrounded by enemy forces. In the mountainous region of the Auvergne, 7,000 *maquisards* fought a pitched battle against some 22,000 SS troops in June 1944. In other words, a small force of guerrillas could tie down three times as many elite SS troops. SAS operations in collaboration with the Resistance in 1944 are credited with killing or wounding some 7,500 enemy and taking nearly 5,000 prisoners, destroying over 700 vehicles and, amongst other rolling stock, 29 locomotives, and directing bombers onto a further 400 targets.

In London the exiled leader of the Free French General Charles de

Gaulle created a command structure for these French partisan operations and gave overall command of the French Forces for the Interior (FFI) to General Marie Pierre Koenig. As Allied forces approached Paris in August 1944, Resistance cells seized control of the city. They fought with small arms, grenades and sniper rifles and set about arresting and executing collaborators. Most of the Paris police force joined them and the Germans soon began leaving the city. This enabled General Leclerc to enter Paris as a victor at the head of his Free French Division. Many members of the Resistance joined the FFI as they progressed through France and some were eventually incorporated into the French army when General de Gaulle decided to dismantle the Free French Forces and Resistance organizations on 28 August 1944. This shows the brilliance of de Gaulle. He provided a credible mechanism to formalize the informal, to neutralize it as a political force and then disband it. Unlike Russia or China or even Yugoslavia, the guerrilla force was not allowed to become a peacetime political force. In France the force that had proven utility was recognized on liberation for what it was, a threat, and therefore neutralized.

By the end of the Second World War the defining characteristics of the antithesis of industrial war had been established, as a combination of both guerrilla and revolutionary warfare. Both types of armed forces shared an evolutionary path, being formless in the initial stages in order to survive. To this day typically they consist of small, locally based cells that operate only on their own patch. There is no command chain but rather a general directing authority, which in the early stages may well be ideological and political, giving no orders as such but providing the ideas to which acts are directed. This authority and surrounding henchmen work by reinforcing and capitalizing on local initiatives where and when they succeed. The command is led by a Darwinian-like process of natural selection towards its goal. In time the movement has to gain some formal coherence to focus effort and to direct resources, and communication amongst the cells becomes more frequent. At this point it is particularly vulnerable to penetration by the security forces. A good indicator of a group reaching this stage is when a movement splits into armed and political wings. Finally, as in the Mao model, the armed wing takes on the appearance of a more formal force. However, whilst reflecting strength this development also encompasses vulnerability: the guerrilla force is about to take the security forces on at their own game. The weapons and the professional ability of the officers of the industrial armies to handle and manoeuvre mass are invariably superior to those of the guerrillas, who must therefore trade lives for experience. But if and when accomplished, the victory of the guerrilla or revolutionary over the established force will enable the final transition to an army of more conventional industrial form.

It is not merely method that makes this model of war a contrast or antithesis: industrial war has the overarching purpose of achieving the desired political outcome by the destruction of the opponent's ability to resist. It is essentially a trial of strength leading to a loss of will to resist. Its antithesis, however, allows the militarily weak to engage the strong to advantage. It is based on *only* using military force in tactical acts, with the object at the strategic level of winning the clash of wills: to erode the capability to govern, and to form the intent of the people. The proponent of this model of war seeks the tactical trials of strength on his terms and will wherever possible refuse battle under any other condition. If we use Clausewitz's triangular relationship of the people, state and army, broadly interpreted, as an analytical tool, we can contrast the two models. In industrial war the object is to destroy the opponents' army and to prevent his government from making war and protecting the people, thus breaking the triangular linkage. In the antithesis the object is to constantly and expensively undermine the stronger army and to thereby break the will of the government and the people to make war. Starting with the Spanish Peninsular War, the guerrillas represented both the army and the spirit of the Spanish state as an independent force resisting its occupier – and for this the people were a necessary element in their support. The French, not least because of the threat from Wellington's armies and their lack of forces to pursue the guerrillas in the countryside, could not break or unbalance this linkage. The same analysis applies to the Boers, only in this case the British did break the linkage. The Boer forces were harried and reduced to the point in which they were always on the run and unable to influence events, the people on the veldt were removed from contact with the commandos, and Britain offered a government for a peaceful future. The Boers in this way lost doubly: their own triangular relationship was broken, and they were unable to unbalance Britain's triangular relationship within itself.

But the trinity cannot be applied in the same way to both modes of the antithesis. In guerrilla war both sides clearly have their own distinct triangles. Revolutionary war, while still based on competing triangular relationships, has the characteristic that one of the sides is common to both triangles: the people. The government, the security forces and the people form the sides of one triangle; the revolutionaries, their ideology and their putative administration and the people form the sides of the other triangle. They both assume the people to be integral to their position and combat effort – and the revolutionary will expend much effort endeavouring to break the linkage of the government's triangle, so that his is dominant over the people at their choice. At the same time, the government will also expend great efforts to detach the fighter from the people – and one of the first signs of success for the guerrilla and revolutionary is when the established state against which they are fighting mounts a counter-operation. We have seen how in the Boer War the British countered the guerrilla war, and this example holds the major themes relevant to all successful counter-operations, including those of revolutionary war. In the main these are that the area in which the guerrilla or revolutionary operates, the sanctuary, must be progressively denied to him – whilst the established forces must enter and control it, and dominate communications both within and into the area. In this way the guerrilla or revolutionary is to be isolated, both from the geographical location and from the people within it, especially those who may offer him cover. Should the sanctuary be amongst the people, such as it is when the war is based in a large urban area, then this theme still applies, but the approach will necessarily be more difficult. None the less, the object remains to separate the people from the activist – not only physically, but to the point at which they refuse to support him and will therefore inform on him. The forces must be matched to those of the guerrilla or revolutionary in the tactical circumstances that prevail; they must not be over-matched, as one would seek to be in industrial war, since in this case one plays to the guerrillas' strategy of provocation and propaganda of the deed: a patently overwhelming force would be seen to be attacking a much smaller and weaker one. The tactical advantage is achieved by superior intelligence and information operations. Finally, the established government must hold out to the people a credible prospect for the future: only a viable and substantive programme, such as the one offered to the Boer population, will attract the majority of the people away from the ideologically driven guerrilla or revolutionary alternative.

This issue will be explained in greater detail in Part III, not least because both the problem of the guerrilla amongst the people and the manner in which he is to be fought have not changed in substance over the years. At this point, however, it should be noted that none of the themes is likely to be of value in isolation, and all need to be pursued to a common purpose and direction. There is one further method of counter-attack which is an exception to this rule, and that is a decision to terrorize the people or to drive them out. Notable examples of this method are the Roman solution with the Jews in AD 70, when they were both terrorized and driven out, or William the Conqueror's 'Harrowing of the North' in the 1080s, or Stalin in the Ukraine in the 1930s, when the local populations were terrorized and severely depleted. If decided upon, this deeply problematic policy can only ever be a 'one-shot' attempt: if it fails, and only some of the people are driven out or otherwise removed, the remainder will form the vengeful nucleus of the enemy. If the established force cannot or will not adopt the method of terror, as is now commonly the case – hence the revulsion at the genocide in Rwanda or ethnic cleansing in Bosnia and Croatia, in which precisely such attempts were made – then a force must mount a counter-operation with all the themes listed above, and persist in it until the challenge from the guerrilla or revolutionary group is completely diffused.

A classic example of a guerrilla group transiting all the way from its own operations through becoming established and finally mounting its own counter-operations is the Israel Defence Force (IDF). It started life in 1920, when Palestine was under the British Mandate, as the Haganah ('defence' in Hebrew), as a grassroots military organization to protect the Jewish settlement, and under full political supervision of a committee composed of left- and right-wing politicians. In 1931 a group broke away, not accepting the political leadership, and formed a classic guerrilla organization known as the Irgun (Etzel in Hebrew, which is the acronym of the national military organization). In 1940 there was a further splinter, with the creation of Lehi, also known as the Stern Gang, which broke away from the Irgun and basically adopted the tactics of terrorism. These distinctions are important since despite a short period of united resistance to the British in 1945–6, they reflect three clear gradations. The Haganah was illegal yet none the less always saw itself as a national armed force. Within a global context these were freedom fighters, even though for most of its existence the organization focused upon protecting the Jewish settlement in Palestine from Arab attacks rather than actively attacking the British occupying forces; indeed, at times the two actively cooperated, including throughout the Second World War, when they united in the fight against Germany. Moreover, the Haganah also collaborated with the British for a short while towards the end of the Second World War in hunting for Irgun and Lehi activists, since it disagreed with extreme violence; this was known within the Jewish organizations as the 'hunting season'. However, after 1945, in full commitment to establishing a Jewish state, the Haganah was at the forefront of the fight against the British, undertaking a wide array of activities from sabotage of the railway lines and radar installations within the country to blowing up the roads and rail bridges at the borders. At the same time, it continued to pursue its other activities, such as leading the clandestine Jewish immigration into Palestine, protecting the establishment of new settlements and pursuing the fight against the Arabs. As David Ben Gurion, head of the Jewish settlement in Palestine and subsequently the first prime minister of Israel, put it in October 1945, when the hard-line policy of the postwar British government became clear:

We must not confine our reaction in Palestine to immigration and settlement. It is essential to adopt tactics of S[abotage] and reprisal. Not individual terror, but retaliation for each and every Jew murdered by the White Paper [limiting Jewish immigration to Palestine]. The S. action must carry weight and be impressive, and care should be taken, insofar as possible, to avoid casualties.

*

The Irgun was more of a classic guerrilla organization, seeking to hinder the British forces, with activities such as blowing up the British headquarters in the King David Hotel in Jerusalem in July 1946, or raiding the Jerusalem British Officers' Club in March 1947. The Stern Gang, a terrorist organization, was ideologically driven, being anti-imperialist, and therefore actively sought to kill British forces as a cautionary example to others, in this way clearly following the revolutionary 'propaganda of the deed'. The most significant of these attacks were the 1944 assassination of Lord Moyne, a British government official deemed responsible for the policy limiting immigration of Jews to Palestine, and the 1946 assassination of Count Bernadotte, the UN mediator charged with the division of Palestine who insisted upon the Palestinian right of refugee return.

The three organizations reflect the gradations of forces within the mould of the 'antithesis': by 1939 the Haganah had created a full complement of professional military corps, including a strike force, and a general staff with its own chief. On 31 May 1948, just two weeks after the state of Israel was declared, the Haganah ceased to be – replaced by the IDF, to which all its structures were transferred. It had indeed been a national military organization in waiting. The Irgun and Lehi pledged to merge with the IDF, based on an agreement of March 1948, two months before the state was founded, and in the case of the latter there was little problem, since it was a tiny organization. However, the Irgun numbered approximately 3,000 fighters, and whilst most merged with the IDF throughout the country, there was lingering bad blood between the two organizations over the 'hunting season'. Matters came to a head in June 1948 over the arrival of an Irgun-financed ship, the *Altalena*, which held 900 overseas volunteers and a large cache of weapons. Ben Gurion, fearing the Irgun wished to arm its own men within the IDF, ordered it be handed over to the national army. A stand-off followed by a series of miscommunications led to the IDF opening fire on the ship, killing eighteen Irgun members and wounding ten. Despite his personal fury Menachem Begin, head of the Irgun, ordered his men not to retaliate. The organization thereafter folded into the IDF and ceased to be.

This example shows clearly how the partisan or guerrilla forces of the Haganah evolved to the point at which they became established forces, much as those they had fought for independence – and then had to assume the counter-operation immediately. At the same time, it reflects the crucial point made in the introduction to this book: that every armed force has to be made into a military force in order to achieve legitimacy. Thus in the newly formed Israel all armed forces had to become submerged in the national force or else be annihilated as a threat.

By 1946 there were clearly two models of war: the paradigm of inter-state industrial war, a trial of strength to force the opponent to our will, and its antithesis of revolutionary and guerrilla warfare, a clash of wills between the militarily weak and the strong, in which the weak, engaging only in tactical acts of its choosing, attempts to turn the power of the state against itself – aiming to win the clash of wills rather than the trial of strength. Interstate industrial war had already ceased to be, though was still the only model upheld by the militaries that had won the war, whilst the antithesis was beginning to evolve in new directions. The paradigm would be an integral part of the Cold War, and its antithesis the basis of all the parallel conflicts. The two would jostle along for over forty years, obscuring the new paradigm that evolved in the wake of the Second World War: war amongst the people.

5

Confrontation and Conflict: A New Purpose for the Use of Force

With the defeat of Germany and the eradication of fascism, the common purpose that had caused Russia and the Western Allies to work together disappeared. The ideological and geostrategic tensions inherent in their positions came to the fore, crystallized by Churchill's prophetic words at Fulton, Missouri, in 1946 about an Iron Curtain that had descended upon Europe, 'from Stettin in the Baltic to Trieste in the Adriatic'. This would quickly lead to the overarching period known as the Cold War – a title which I noted at the start of this book to be a gross historical misnomer, since it was never a war but rather an extended confrontation. Forces were structured and had the potential to be amassed and employed within the old paradigm, but no force was ever applied: the confrontation never became a conflict, definitely not at the strategic level of a full industrial war. And it is this dynamic of confrontation and conflict, rather than war and peace, which is at the heart of war amongst the people.

In the paradigm of industrial war the premise is of the sequence peace–crisis–war–resolution, which will result in peace again, with war, the military action, being the deciding factor. In the new paradigm there is no predefined sequence, but rather a continuous crisscrossing between confrontation and conflict, whilst peace is not necessarily either the starting or the end point; and whereas conflicts are ultimately resolved, this is not necessarily the case with confrontations. The Cold War is an example of a confrontation that was resolved – but only after forty-five years; the Israeli–Palestinian confrontation is still not resolved after fifty-seven years. Both confrontations and conflicts involve military forces and weapons, but their uses are invariably different: in a confrontation they will be *deployed* – positioned and postured to reflect force – and when *employed* they are used to achieve only sub-strategic objectives: they do not conquer a state or take territory so as to keep it, but rather attack a target which is important to the opponent in order to focus his attention and change his intentions. This is due to the main difference between confrontations and conflicts: their purpose. In confrontations the aim is to influence the opponent, to change or form an intention, to establish a condition and, above all, to win the clash of wills. In conflicts the purpose is to destroy, take, hold; to forcibly attain a decisive outcome by the direct application of military force.

A confrontation therefore includes the political and diplomatic agencies alongside the military – in fact, often in the lead of the military. The Cold War was never a military event, nor was it dictated by the military. It was, above all, a political and ideological confrontation, negotiated by politicians and diplomats and backed up by the appearance of military force. Much the same is true of the confrontations that took place in parallel to the Cold War, as indeed in many of our current situations. The overall objective of the military in all these was and is expressed as a condition: 'maintain law and order', 'ensure a safe, secure environment', 'maintain a no-fly zone'. These military activities in support of the political agencies are aimed at putting pressure on the opponent, to the point at which his will is broken or altered. Conflicts, on the other hand, are about trials of strength: military activities that may sit within a political or diplomatic framework, but do not involve these agencies in achieving the objective once the military activity is in process. In other words, if a confrontation has crossed over into a conflict, the military is in the lead and it is up to the other agencies to support it until the objective is attained – but at the same time they may continue working to resolve the confrontation that led to the conflict at another level. In essence, conflicts involve the application of force to attain a desired objective, whether at the tactical, operational or strategic level. And if the strategic level is reached, then a full war in the industrial sense is at hand. This has not happened very often since 1945, and then only in conflicts in which there was no threat of weapons of mass destruction.

Seen in this light, the paradigm of war amongst the people reflects a very different world from the one of industrial war: it is one in which the political and the military are both parts of the same continuum, often working together – with a main difference being that the civilian agencies do not take part in military action, though military representatives may be part of the political and diplomatic negotiations. Neither confrontation, nor conflict, nor the transformation of the one into the other, necessarily means that war will result. For whilst confrontations are essentially of the political and conflicts of the military, a confrontation is not just a political act just as a conflict is not just a military activity. The structure of the paradigm explains this well. The point of origin is always a confrontation: the core dispute, which is always political. Once an original situation of confrontation has been established – as, for example, the USSR and the US and the European Allies in the aftermath of World War Two, or between the UK and Argentina over the sovereignty of the Falkland Islands, or the Indonesians and the British over the formation of the Federation of Malaysia, or the IRA and the British over the status of Northern Ireland – it can either continue (notwithstanding resolution) as a confrontation or become a conflict. The USSR and the US with their respective alliances remained in perpetual confrontation during the period we know as the Cold War, whilst the confrontation over the Falklands became a conflict when Argentina seized the islands and the UK sailed to take them back. If the UK had accepted the fact of the Argentinean occupation but continued to argue that the islands were British the confrontation would have continued, albeit on a different basis. However, if they had ceased to lay claim to the territory the confrontation would have been won by the Argentinean deployment rather than employment of force – since no military engagement actually occurred, beyond a minor tactical skirmish with the tiny British force on the islands when the Argentinean force landed.

The best modern example of confrontation is the Cold War, since it was both all-encompassing and long, and saw all three levels being played out by both sides. At the strategic level forces were deployed and at high states of readiness; intelligence collection was a continuous and a highly developed activity, and there was an arms race in progress. When Russia sought to gain a strategic advantage by deploying missiles into the Caribbean theatre the confrontation nearly changed to conflict at a theatre or operational level, which could easily have spread to be total. This move of missiles to Cuba was an example of the importance of the operational level, in that if it had succeeded it would have materially altered the strategic situation to the disadvantage of the US. At the tactical level each side patrolled extensively, and intruded into each other's exercises in international waters and air space, and with special units into national waters and air space. However, whilst these were military patrols, no shots were fired or force applied: the confrontations never crossed into conflicts. Confrontations between such patrols in international space were regulated by means of extensive Rules of Engagement – an important topic in itself to which I will return in Part III – which were intended to prevent confrontations sliding into conflict without political approval. However, when they occurred in national space attempts would be made to engage them in tactical actions, an example being the US U-2 reconnaissance aircraft which entered Russian air space in May 1960 and was shot down. This tit-for-tat action was a cross into conflict, but as there was no follow-up there was an immediate reversion to the confrontation.

Alongside the military, both sides of the Cold War engaged in constant political and ideological confrontation, at all three levels, seeking to influence the other side and its peoples. Alliances were expanded, large sums were expended on developing weapons systems, particularly for operations in air and space, and major exercises took place to demonstrate credible alliance threats. Moreover, as communications improved so it was possible for the peoples of the West to show those in the East the disparity in their wealth and prospects. Whilst the military measures held the confrontation at a more or less stable state, they also maintained the Kremlin's intent not to attack but always to be prepared for total war. As a result, the Western Allies, who maintained their military capability but also prospered economically, ultimately won the confrontation by diplomatic, political and economic measures: they changed the intent of the peoples of the Eastern alliance, and thereby won the clash of wills.

When a confrontation cannot be resolved one or both of the opponents can decide to settle the matter by force of arms, a move to conflict, which also occurs at all three levels. The dispute between Britain and Argentina over the Falklands gives an example of a long-running confrontation that was moved to a conflict by the Argentineans in 1982. They made a decision at the strategic level to seize the islands and present a fait accompli to the British, whom they judged were neither able nor willing to react by fighting to take them back. To this end they mounted an operation amounting to a short skirmish between the invading Argentine force and a small British marine contingent. At this point the Argentineans expected the matter to revert to a confrontation, but one in which they possessed the islands and could deal from a position of strength. However, the British responded by remaining in conflict and actually going to war: Britain at the strategic level dispatched a force to liberate the islands, and committed its considerable diplomatic weight to establish a favourable context for the military action. It declared an exclusion zone around the islands, in effect the theatre of operations, and conducted a campaign, or operation, which despite the Argentinean air force's efforts succeeded in landing a force on the islands which after a series of battles liberated them. In this way we see a confrontation cross to a conflict and escalate to strategic level, through first the tactical level then to the theatre level, to achieve the strategic aim.

War amongst the people is not a paradigm of only linear evolution within either a confrontation or a conflict, since that is not the way of this world. Indeed, it goes much further and reflects that confrontations and conflicts rarely evolve in such a simple manner: the opponents can move from confrontation to conflict at any one of the three levels and back again. The various interventions into the region of the Persian Gulf over Iraq are a good example: in 1990 operation Desert Shield, deployed in response to the Iraqi invasion of Kuwait, was a classic confrontation at theatre level: there was a military build-up to support political and diplomatic negotiations, aimed at changing the intentions of Iraq to attack further south and seize the Saudi oilfields along the Gulf coast. This operation was then developed into operation Desert Storm, initially to support the diplomatic efforts to get Saddam Hussein to withdraw from Kuwait by posing a convincing threat. However, when Iraq failed to withdraw the coalition attacked, and the confrontation changed into a conflict at theatre level for the international coalition: operation Desert Storm in 1991. When this ended with a definitive victory for the coalition, the situation reverted to a confrontation. The coalition could possibly have made more of its new position at this point, given Iraq was weaker and its internal tensions were evident, by demanding more on the basis of the demonstrable and clear threat they could produce – but it settled for leaving Hussein in power and Iraq within its original borders. In time the confrontation was supported by the UN inspections of Iraq's nuclear, chemical and biological weapons facilities, UN economic sanctions and the setting up of two no-fly zones (NFZ), also approved by the UN. The NFZ were a military measure at the tactical level which supported the confrontation; they moved to conflict, albeit still at the tactical level, when the Iraqis chose to ignore the stricture or threaten a patrolling aircraft. However, when any such tactical conflict was concluded the situation immediately reverted to a confrontation at the tactical level. In December 1998, in reaction to Saddam Hussein's non-compliance with the UN sanctions regime, the air forces of the US and Britain patrolling the NFZ were reinforced and launched a series of punitive air strikes – still at the tactical level – that hit 100 Iraqi military targets: operation Desert Fox. This high-profile operation, which started on the eve of the holy month of Ramadan, was not UN sanctioned and resulted in international outrage – a case of force being used without utility, since Iraq came to be seen as a victim by many rather than the aggressor. From January 1999 the US and the UK continued to mount regular air strikes against Iraq as a consequence of its non-compliance with the NFZ, and more usually when attempts to shoot down their planes were perceived, without any international comment, thereby maintaining the situation as a confrontation with constant cross-overs to tactical conflict. In March 2003 the confrontation moved into theatre-level conflict with the invasion of Iraq, operation Iraqi Freedom, which successfully overcame the defenders, occupied the country and deposed the rulers and their apparatus. However, this operational-level military success did not lead directly to the strategic goal: the will of the people of Iraq had not been captured. Resistance continues at the tactical level, and the occupiers, the US-led coalition, react militarily while in confrontation with other parties as to the future of Iraq at theatre level. Taking these events as a whole since 1990, therefore, it should be clear that there has never been a war – definitely not a war in the industrial sense – in or with Iraq, but rather a lengthy confrontation that has at times crossed over into conflict, and then only twice (briefly) at the operational or theatre level.

This chronology is not coherent with the paradigm of industrial war. Though there have been constant attempts to explain it as such, and whilst the starting point in 1990–91 may have been a sequence of peace–crisis, there was never a full war in the region with the international forces, and following it and ever since there has definitely been no resolution or return to peace. However, if viewed within the paradigm of war amongst the people the chronology attains coherence and at the same time the reason for the crossing from confrontation to conflict and back again is explained: it is in the nature of the chosen objective. In 1990–91, as operation Desert Storm was being prepared, military force was used as a threat in the confrontation between the coalition and Saddam Hussein to try to make him withdraw from Kuwait: the objective was to influence his intentions. The threat was unconvincing in the circumstances and failed to work. The object at theatre level then changed to destroying his Republican Guard and forces in Kuwait, so as to liberate the latter and weaken Iraq. This was a clear cross from confrontation to conflict: from influencing his intentions to destroying his forces. For my part, the primary means of recognizing whether you are in confrontation or conflict rests with recognizing whether the objective is to change intentions or to destroy, and at what level of war this destructive act is to take place. The importance of doing this is crucial to conducting the operation as a whole, for each level of war is set within the context of its superior level – and so each conflict nests within a confrontation from which it derives. In this way, the lower the level at which conflict is taking place, the more must the factors that contribute to winning the confrontation – of which the military measures may only be a supporting part – be taken into account by the headquarters directing the military action. Without this confrontational context, the purely military acts of conflict serve no purpose in advancing to the overall objective or outcome, and frequently serve to reinforce the opponent's position. Furthermore, this analysis shows that in these circumstances the military have a difficult task to perform because the military acts to influence intentions are not necessarily the same as those to achieve the hard objectives of destruction. In the case of operation Desert Storm, it is possible that the security measures to conceal the nature of the coalition's capabilities and plan for conflict were too successful, and it therefore did not present a sufficiently visible threat. This could have been a crucial drawback, given the objective was to alter Saddam Hussein's intentions in the period of confrontation. But then again, whilst he may not have been scared, that confrontational objective might have been irrelevant; the coalition perhaps desired the conflict in any event.

This discussion of the paradigm of war amongst the people provides the background to the rest of this chapter and all those that follow. First, because it should reflect why force no longer has utility in the industrial sense: if the industrial sequence is peace–crisis–war–resolution, with massive military force applied in war in order to achieve resolution, in war amongst the people military force must be present and credible, and in many cases applied for reasons other than resolution. Moreover, applying massive force in the midst of a confrontation will not necessarily resolve it, especially if the political and diplomatic levers are not in play at the same time. Second, because it should now be clear not only that the Cold War was not a war but rather a lengthy confrontation – whilst the military operations, however large, that occurred in parallel to it and ever since, were mostly complex combinations of confrontations and conflicts. It is to these decades that we now turn.

By 1948 Russia and the West were in direct confrontation over the establishment of the West German government in the US, British and French sectors of Berlin. On 24 June the Russians blocked all movement into and out of Berlin. The Western Allies, using principally the

US Army Air Force (USAAF) and the Royal Air Force (RAF), established the Berlin airlift and supplied the city and their own garrisons until the blockade was lifted in May 1949. To give an idea of the magnitude of this effort and the impression it must have made on the Kremlin, the same total tonnage that was lifted into Sarajevo by the UN between 1992 and 1996 – considered one of the largest airlifts ever – was lifted every month into Berlin. At the height of this undertaking an aeroplane was landing in Berlin every minute. The Russians probably did not believe the airlift could supply more than the garrisons and when it supplied the city they could not interfere lest they started a war they did not want. Or possibly they did not want to risk a war before they were absolutely ready – as became evident in August 1949.

In the aftermath of the Second World War, the prosperous and triumphant United States felt safe in its monopoly of the atomic bomb. The Russians, however, were quick to catch up. They had begun designing their own atomic bomb in 1943. The quality of their research and the resources of the vast communist spy network meant that they probably knew as much as their wartime allies on the subject. Russia's backward industrial base and its lack of infrastructure slowed down progress. In August 1949, however, the newly defined Soviet Union surprised the world by detonating its own atomic bomb. In the same year the North Atlantic Treaty was signed and its implementing organization, NATO, established. A few years later, in 1952, the US built the first thermonuclear hydrogen bomb. The USSR responded a year later with its own H-bomb: the great arms race had already begun. From this point on world politics was dominated by the relationship between the leaders of two great power blocs, East and West, and based on nuclear deterrence.

The essence of deterrence, whether nuclear or not, is that the force which would be used in response to an attack is thought to be so destructive, and this consequence so certain, that the price to be paid is deemed too high for the gain sought by the initial attack. The important element to note is that the side which has to think the opposing force is so destructive and certain, and the price to pay is too high for the anticipated gain, is the side who is deciding whether to attack or not. You may think your weapon is just the thing, but for it to be a deterrent your opponent has to think it too – and, moreover, he has to think you will use it and use it effectively. In short, the real target of someone wishing to deter is the mind of the opposing decision maker, not in the first instance his forces or whatever else is of value to him. Of course, this man you wish to deter may think he is able to tolerate the effect you threaten and so may continue to try to achieve his purpose by force of arms. In this case, for deterrence to work you must be able, and be believed to be able and willing, to continue your attacks with increasing weight and effect: escalation. Alternatively your opponent may calculate that if he can achieve a devastating first strike you will be unable to respond. To really deter, therefore, he must believe you can endure an attack and retain the ability to strike back: to have a second-strike capability.

It was on this logic that East and West faced each other. Each believed the other had to be deterred from attacking. Each sought allies. The Soviets had the support of the Warsaw Pact countries and also China and Cuba whilst the USA had NATO, CENTO (Central Treaty Organization) and SEATO (Southeast Asia Treaty Organization), though as the confrontation continued support from all organizations other than the Warsaw Pact and NATO withered. Each side adopted the strategy of deterrence, which developed into mutually assured destruction (MAD): the creation and sustaining of industrial war machines according to the old paradigm, to be fuelled by conscription, mass mobilization if necessary, opposing mass economies and cutting-edge technology. Each had substantial forces deployed along the line of the Iron Curtain confronting the other. Each was prepared fully to transit to war at very short notice, and therefore developed comprehensive intelligence and surveillance operations to avoid being taken by surprise. All forces, on both sides, were organized and manned on the basis of industrial war. Should deterrence fail each envisaged a period of conventional war – read war in the old style, but done better with modern technologies and communications – followed by nuclear strikes as one side or another began to lose the conventional battle: 'strategic' on the opponent's homeland and 'tactical' on his forces. For the logic of deterrence rested on the certainty that the nuclear strikes would follow any failures of the conventional phase: that MAD really was assured.

It was also the flaw in the scheme, since the bomb meant that the ability to mass an army was made irrelevant by this single item of technology. The best defence against a weapon of mass destruction, short of preventing it being used, is not to mass and present the target; in such circumstances a large army is best used dispersed rather than concentrated. In this way each side cooperated in this deterrence strategy, holding large forces configured to fight a modern development of war in the industrial paradigm, all the time knowing this made them vulnerable to the nuclear weapons they both held. It was this necessity which kept the paradigm of interstate industrial war propped up. As we shall see, the West took advantage of this to hollow out their forces and prosper, whilst holding the capacity to destroy the guaranteed mass targets: the Soviet cities. In the meantime, the same forces were being used to conduct some of the parallel conflicts to the Cold War – which are the focus of this chapter and the following one.

Even with these immense military structures, each side played out the strategies of deterrence differently. The Soviets remained organized to move directly into a total war. They had learned how to do this and win during the Great Patriotic War, as the Second World War was known in the USSR, and had no intention of being caught out again in the next round: they intended to take the offensive from the outset of any attack on them. Equally, however, it suited the Kremlin's purpose to conduct the internal affairs of the Soviet Union on this basis: fully armed offensive deterrence fitted ideologically and it gave the political and military leaderships reason to control the population and the satellite nations of the Warsaw Pact. And it was to this end that the USSR bent its considerable scientific, industrial, military and intelligence capabilities, in two ways. Firstly, by establishing a strategic nuclear capability and a defence against that of the US and her allies, hence the race into space. The accurate delivery of nuclear weapons, the necessary surveillance and intelligence operations to be sure of the targets and the need to engage them, could not be achieved without establishing a presence in space. What is more, deterrence depends on your opponent understanding the extent of your capability, and so apart from testing your warheads what better way to achieve this than to show your technological reach? Secondly, the USSR sought to develop in the Soviet armed forces an offensive capability that would speedily destroy the opposing forces and take territories, particularly those of the European allies for whom in the end the US might not wish to trade Detroit and Chicago. In other words, to effect a land grab – much as the acquisition of Austria and Czechoslovakia by Germany in 1937–8.

The West – and I mean the West, because Washington never had the controlling influence over its NATO allies that the Kremlin had over the Warsaw Pact – adopted a defensive posture. It did not see itself as threatening to attack the Soviet Union, even if the Kremlin did see it in such a light. Because of this perception, and the Soviet offensive posture, every move the Kremlin made served to reinforce the view that the USSR was bent on assaulting the West at the first opportunity. In addition, the West did not stay on a total war footing. To be sure, many of the nations retained conscription and maintained large forces for their defence, but by the 1960s industry and commerce had reverted to a peacetime logic and the people began to prosper. In fact the people of Europe and America prospered as never before, and western Europe experienced the longest period without war in its history. Militarily, for the first time ever the armed forces of western Europe prepared to fight a common enemy rather than each other, their purpose being to blunt the Soviet assault and provide the trip-wire for the Western nuclear attacks. As a result, the armed forces of Europe, with the exception of some of those of Britain and France, were developed almost exclusively to defend the line of the Iron Curtain. And by each and collectively defending their national space, they could support the nuclear striking fleets and air wings of the US navy and air force, and enable their attack deep into the Warsaw Pact and Soviet territory. These strategic nuclear strikes were intended to destroy the capacity of the Soviet Union to make war at all.

Within these different strategies, which were mutually supportive as is often the case with long-standing confrontations, decades passed as each side, following the logic of deterrence, searched for evidence that the deterrent equation was unbalanced – and upon finding it, developed another weapon or deployment posture to rebalance the equation. The business of war, whether in the command economies of the East or those of the capitalist West, did well: militaries provided employment and underpinned nations, defence industries thrived and education and research centres that provided technology, and fuelled all elements of the war business, expanded heartily. There were moments of great tension such as the building of the Berlin Wall in August 1961 and the Cuban Missile Crisis in October 1962, but in all deterrence worked. Meanwhile other wars took place: Britain and France retreated from their empires, the US intervened in Vietnam and Russia in Afghanistan, and both East and West backed their proxies in the Middle East and Africa. But as we shall see, all of these took place within the known structures of deterrence: the two blocs constantly strengthened the structures, but never stepped out of them, especially not directly against each other.

It is worthwhile briefly considering the sheer magnitude of the structures – since once again it is the industrial aspect, in its size and output as well as technological capacity, that underpinned MAD. As the appendix tables on pp. 218–22 reflect, the bulk of capabilities, already strong in the early 1960s, just went on expanding and growing on both sides – until 1991. As a note of caution it must be emphasized that it is difficult to make a precise comparison of the statistics since the confrontation went on for a long time, the composition of the alliances changed and the battlefield systems were not always comparable, either with the opposition's apparently similar system or when a new system replaced an old one. For example, in broad terms a Tornado bomber can carry a similar tonnage of bombs to that carried by a squadron of Lancaster bombers in the Second World War, whilst its all-weather capability and precision bombing systems make it more probable that the bombs will hit the target. However, it lacks the range of the Lancaster and requires air tankers to refuel it to reach all but relatively close objectives. Another issue to be considered together with the statistics is that the two sides to the confrontation, NATO and the Warsaw Pact, were equipped and organized for different concepts of warfare. As noted, in broad terms the latter were organized for an offensive battle in Europe, which is why they had more tanks, but NATO land forces were configured to fight a defensive battle for western Europe while the sea and air forces established superiority in the Atlantic and over Europe, a prerequisite to bringing further

US forces into the war whilst sustaining Europe and launching nuclear strikes.

Keeping such provisos in mind, we can see that over thirty years of the Cold War the manpower available to both alliances throughout remained broadly the same and in the same proportions. The equipment increases in quantity during the period, with Warsaw Pact tank holdings rising from around 35,000 in 1961 to over 51,000 in 1991, whilst NATO held some 23,000. This was because the Soviet planning was based on a land invasion of western Europe. As against this, whilst both sides had more or less similar naval holdings, the US had double the naval aircraft – which was one of its main sources of global power. Missile systems increased from about 250 to 2,300, with NATO's holdings growing in proportion over the same period. The business of maintaining these inventories, in terms both of replacing old equipments and of matching the threat posed by the opponent's developments, was the basic stuff of the Cold War: the nuts and bolts that kept the vast machine in process. Whole intelligence departments on both sides were employed keeping up with the enemy, research and development (R&D) establishments spent millions on getting ahead of the other side and governments spent millions on equipping their respective industrial war machines. Then they employed them elsewhere, in conflicts such as Vietnam or Northern Ireland or Afghanistan: theatres of war where such equipment was not always very suitable or applicable.

Despite such parallel activity, there was a profound difference in approach between East and West. The Soviets remained geared for total industrial war, and the production lines to conduct such a war remained in being within their command economy. In the West the capacity for total industrial war was not maintained: prosperity came before guns. For some, the arms race was pursued with vigour, but in the main once the initial purchases were made their production lines were closed and limited stocks of munitions were held in the depots. If the West had failed to hold a Soviet attack, it would therefore have had to turn to the nuclear option, or else surrender. The Soviets, and in particular their intelligence services, trying to find out or deduce the intentions of NATO, chose the safe hypothesis that the West was planning a first strike. The more they searched for evidence of this, and the more they saw the lack of Western preparation to sustain a war, the more they assumed a first-strike plan on behalf of the West – in both offence and defence. And since an offensive first strike was the worst case for them, that was their working assumption. In truth, this was not correct: the West had no intention of making an offensive first strike, and indeed therefore its conventional forces could not be sustained as long as the Soviets': the standing forces were there to act as a trip wire.

And so the Cold War rolled along, costing billions; and whilst the sides engaged in both diplomatic posturing and negotiations, any true tensions tended to be played out, as we shall see, in the unrelated conflicts that occurred throughout the era. In this way the Cold War offered the deep security of predictability – until something else happened in parallel to the known confrontational activities of both sides: the Kremlin government and military remained strong, but it lost the people. The support of the peoples of the Warsaw Pact allies was never an absolute certainty, although their governments could be relied upon or else replaced as was Czechoslovakia's in 1968. However, slowly but surely the people of Russia as much as its satellites began to move away from the state, and its governments in particular; dissent, previously unheard of in the USSR, began to be voiced. And the crucial point was the Soviet adventure into Afghanistan in 1980, an interventionist venture to secure an unstable border region – in other words, an act of security rather than defence, and one therefore not absolutely essential to the survival of the state and the people. Worse still, it was an operation that failed to produce a quick decisive result whilst causing a steady and significant drain of casualties – and as a result the Kremlin began to lose the support of the Russian people. The essential trinity, the foundation of war, began to disconnect, and then became unravelled. As a contrasting example, with its intervention in Vietnam the US state lost its people's support, but only for the duration of the war itself. The people continued to support the defensive purpose of the military. As a result of this experience the US reorganized its army as a volunteer force, but placed considerable elements of its capability in the National Guard, which can only be committed with broad political support. The purpose of this reform was to distance the active army from the population at large while at the same time ensuring it would not be committed to any substantial venture without a strong base of popular support.

These examples reflect upon a development which has become increasingly relevant since 1945, and is so especially in our current circumstances: the primacy of defence over attack. This is not to say that in defence one sits inactive or supine in one position until one is assaulted, but as Clausewitz said: 'the defensive form of war is not a simple shield, but a shield of well-directed blows'.* In establishing the triangular relationship with the people and the army, the state will mostly favour defence, for a number of reasons. First, the people will pay for their defence; and the more the state and the military are aligned in their interests, the more the people will pay. Second, therefore, in defence there is the simplicity of matching the political object with the military. Third, and derived from the first two, is that defence enables the forming and sustaining of political will in a way attack or offence never does. Finally, defence enables a moral advantage, which is appreciated and sometimes necessary for the people, considered a bonus by the state – or at least its political leadership – and preferred by the military.

It is upon this conceptual background that one may understand the ending of the confrontation that was the Cold War: that the switch from constant defence to an offence into Afghanistan was unsustainable to the Russian people. The military and the state could no longer force the people back into the long-standing trinity, if only because elements of both actually supported the people. In 1985 Mikhail Gorbachev became general secretary of the Communist Party, and in an attempt to reform and re-engage the popular support of the people introduced the policies of glasnost (openness) and perestroika (conversion). In itself such an approach might have maintained the confrontation with the West, though in a relaxed and altered form. But during the late 1980s a weakening of links within the Warsaw Pact and the loss of popular support was reinforced by the realization, particularly by the east Europeans, of how much better off the people of the West were than they. Apart from the innate inefficiency of command economies, it was the consequence of putting guns before

* *On War*, section 1, ch. 1, bk 6 (Penguin edn, p. 357).

butter, or prosperity, for decades. The US-led diplomacy, based on its position of strength established by the successful execution of the deterrent strategy and the backing of the NATO nations, led to a series of measures to reduce tensions between the two blocs. In December 1988 Gorbachev announced the withdrawal of 500,000 troops from eastern Europe, and over the following twelve months, with the weight of the Red Army removed, east European state after state declared itself free of the Warsaw Pact. The Cold War was over.

The confrontation crumbled, but its military structures remained as a legacy: the institutions and the forces we have today are a product of the need to prepare for total war and to deter successfully. No one will ever know whether in the face of the enemy they would have been able to do what was intended, or whether the plans cast by so many commanders and their staffs – or the organizations and structures they developed – would have worked, but it is sufficient, for deterrence to work, that each believed the other could act effectively. But the forces equipped and organized for that purpose are in the main what we currently have to work with. These were never intended for use in non-industrial conflicts, but this in fact is where most of the men and equipment, when needed, have been applied. For soon after the ending of the Second World War they were fighting war amongst the people: non-industrial conflicts in which most current equipment cannot be used, conflicts based on political confrontations between state and non-state actors having many of the characteristics of the antithesis to industrial war discussed in the previous chapter. These conflicts took place in parallel to the Cold War. Indeed, the period 1946–91 could well be defined as one of an overarching confrontation (the Cold War) maintained by industrial structures, containing non-industrial conflicts, the parallel wars. It is within these conflicts that we see the first signs of the new paradigm, especially in the nature and objectives of the opponents, and in the constant adaptation of the existing means – the industrial military machines – to non-industrial conflicts. Within these situations force was applied in different ways, not always to the best utility. It was the beginning of a trend we live with to this day.

At the end of the Second World War, Japanese forces occupying the Korean peninsula surrendered to the Americans and to the Russians and Korea was divided into two zones separated by the 38th parallel. This dividing line was not the result of a ministerial or diplomatic decision: it was chosen for practical reasons following negotiations between officers of relatively junior rank. However, administrative convenience soon hardened into political fact, especially as the two former allies became enemies, and henceforth all attempts to equip Korea with a single government failed. In 1947 the US took this problem to the United Nations, which decided to appoint a commission (UN Temporary Commission on Korea – UNTOK) in order to reunify the country through elections. The following year, elections were held in the south but the commission was prevented from operating in the north. The government resulting from these elections, headed by Syngman Rhee, claimed to be that of all Korea but had no authority or existence north of the 38th parallel – where the Russians had set up a rival government led by the revolutionary communist militant Kim Il Sung.

Having failed to reach an agreement on the conditions of reunification, the Russians and the Americans both withdrew their armed forces. Korea became a country with two governments of opposing ideologies, each armed and supplied by one of the superpowers and both claiming sovereignty over the entire peninsula. This volcanic situation soon erupted. Launching a massive surprise attack, North Korean forces crossed the border and invaded South Korea on 25 June 1950. Two days later they had captured the capital city of Seoul. The invaders had Soviet backing, and they had also probably interpreted as a guarantee of impunity the famous speech given in January by the US secretary of state, Dean Acheson, in which he had excluded Korea from the Asian defence perimeter, which by implication the US was ready to fight to retain. Overall, therefore, we can see a confrontation moving into conflict – within the context of the wider confrontation between the blocs.

At the request of the United States, the UN Security Council met at once. The Russians did not attend as they had been boycotting Security Council sessions since January of that year in a show of solidarity with the new communist regime in Beijing (the Chinese seat was still held by the nationalists). The Council passed a resolution which requested members of the UN to support South Korea with all means necessary to repel the aggressor. President Truman had already instructed General Douglas MacArthur, the commander of the American occupying forces in Japan, to provide the retreating South Korean army with air and naval support. On 29 June he decided to move one step further: as South Korean forces lay on the verge of collapse, he ordered two American divisions to be transferred from Japan to Korea. A few days later, on 4 July, in the renewed absence of the Soviet delegate, the Security Council passed a resolution to establish a United Nations expeditionary corps to be deployed in Korea to restore international peace after repelling the attack. This resolution effectively endorsed the US action of meeting force with force. General MacArthur was put in command of the expeditionary corps – and thereafter it became a war conducted by a US general responsible to the US president acting as the agent of the UN. By September, around twenty other states, mostly allied with the United States for other political objectives, had contributed units to the UN army. However, Americans still represented half the ground forces engaged, 93 per cent of air forces, and 86 per cent of naval forces.

At first the fighting went in favour of North Korea, and the South Koreans and the UN forces that came to their rescue were driven to the tip of the Korean peninsula. But the situation was reversed in September 1950 when General MacArthur, drawing on his own and his staff's experience of the amphibious assaults of the Pacific campaign against the Japanese, and taking advantage of his maritime supremacy, landed troops in a bold attack at Inchon, 240 miles to the north and a few miles from Seoul. The success of this theatre-level assault unhinged the North Korean forces in the South: in a matter of weeks, UN forces were chasing disorganized North Korean troops across the 38th parallel. This astonishing success encouraged the General Assembly to pass a US-led resolution to ensure a stable situation in the whole of the Korean peninsula. This move was another example of the conflict being part of the wider confrontation: the Assembly possessed no legal power to pass such a resolution, but as the Russians had reclaimed their seat at the Security Council, the US chose to circumvent the Russian veto by granting the Assembly a decision-making capability which went against the UN Charter.

MacArthur reacted rapidly and on 9 October gave his forces the order to cross the 38th parallel. Three weeks later, after capturing the North Korean capital of Pyongyang, they were approaching the Chinese Manchurian border. With North Korean forces everywhere in retreat the war seemed to be over, but at the end of November China, deeply suspicious of American designs, entered the war. Frequent Chinese warnings to UN and US forces not to cross the 38th parallel had been ignored. However, the American decision to place the Seventh Fleet between China and Taiwan, where the last of the Chinese nationalist forces were established, combined with the speed of MacArthur's offensive deep into North Korea, acted as a trigger. On 26 November Chinese forces attacked on a wide front. Less than a month later the situation had been reversed: UN and South Korean forces were in full retreat as Chinese and North Korean troops marched down the peninsula. Seoul fell for the second time in January.

Chinese intervention altered the nature of the war and gave rise to a new debate about how it should be pursued. From June to November, although waged primarily by American troops, the war had been presented as an international punitive expedition. After November it increasingly appeared to become a Sino-American conflict. MacArthur wanted to recognize this fact and wage war on China using the most effective military means, from the pursuit of enemy aircraft across the border to the strategic bombing of Chinese territory, without excluding the eventual use of the atomic bomb. At home, in the era of McCarthyism, a boisterous segment of the US population supported this approach. The president, his civilian aids, as well as military chiefs of staff, shrank from the prospect of embarking on a long and costly war with China for the Korean peninsula, with the possibility that if they followed MacArthur's advice they could find themselves in conflict with the rest of the communist bloc and using the atomic bomb. Meanwhile at the UN, as the war was evolving into a conflict between China and the US, many members began to feel that the UN's political purpose for going to war had been lost sight of. And as the political aims diverged, the US began to feel a lessening in support from its allies.

The entry of China into the war gives an example, repeated frequently in the post-war period, of the difference in terms of the nature of forces between those based on manpower and those on firepower. The US forces had defeated and broken the North Koreans with a well-executed manoeuvre based on the rapid application of massed firepower. The Chinese forces succeeded because they had the man-power to face the UN forces with more targets than the latter could address simultaneously, which is why they attacked on a broad front. Wherever the attack succeeded they reinforced with more manpower and continued south. The US forces had been developed to fight industrial war, with emphasis on technology and the process for its effective application. In contrast, the Chinese had evolved through emphasis on manpower and the process of applying it en masse effec-tively. Faced with the prospect of defeat, MacArthur's proposal was to use his technological advantage to attack the sources of the Chinese manpower and prevent them entering the battle. However, doing this would in effect have altered the theatre and changed the strategic objective – thereby removing it from the political purpose. It was therefore not a viable option, and was rejected by Washington. This reflects the importance of the strategic objective always being firmly within the context of the political purpose, in order to ensure both coherence and its continuous contribution to the purpose. In this case the strategic objective being proposed by MacArthur, the destruction of China's ability to intervene in the Korean peninsula, did not match the political purpose. However much the United States might have wanted to neutralize communist China as a regional influence, they were not prepared to take the risks of doing this by military force. For in reality, the risks were of another, possibly atomic, world war, and the loss of allied support at the UN. Within this perspective the US forces – with their long-range, air-delivered, ultimately atomic, firepower – did not have utility.

The Truman administration opted to pursue operations only on the peninsula whilst attempting to reach a settlement. In effect the politi-cal and strategic objectives had been redefined: to fight to the point where the US on behalf of the UN could conduct negotiations to advantage, and accept some form of divided Korea. In short, force was not to be used strategically to achieve the political result directly but to enable its achievement at the negotiating table. MacArthur's well-publicized criticisms of the directions he was receiving eventually led to his dismissal for insubordination in April 1951. On 25 June the US accepted a Soviet proposal for a ceasefire to be followed by the beginning of armistice discussions. A settlement was not reached until July 1953. The final agreement provided for the creation of a demilitarized zone stretching along the frontier separating the states. The border was redrawn more or less along the 38th parallel, with South Korea gaining an extra 1,500 square miles of territory. And there matters have stayed; in the south the armies of South Korea and the US face those of North Korea, with China behind them. But now China has nuclear weapons, and the North Koreans say they have them too.

This was the first UN military operation, and also the last to be conducted in this unilateral way. As a result of the unsettling effect within the UN of the Security Council's endorsement of American actions, there was for a time a general rule that major powers should not be invited to make a fighting contribution to UN operations. This policy remained intact until the end of the Cold War, barring the Cyprus crisis a decade later, when the advantage of using British forces already present on the island appeared evident to most. Korea became the exception, although it was useful for a time in reinforcing the image of the UN as a body prepared to take action, as opposed to its weak predecessor, the League of Nations, in the 1920s and 30s.

The Cold War confrontation also provided the overarching structure for another kind of conflict: those resulting from the post-colonial withdrawals from empire. One of the most important examples of this trend, which emerged upon the model of the antithesis and came to show all the early signs of war amongst the people, was the Malayan emergency. The 1941 Atlantic Charter signed by President Roosevelt and Prime Minister Churchill, that would become the basis of the UN Charter, signalled that Britain would eventually grant its colonies the right to self-determination. But in addition, Japanese victory over British forces in 1942 had destroyed the aura of invincibility surrounding western European forces, whilst in 1947 the British departure from India set a precedent for waning colonial powers and would-be sovereign states. However, whilst this was accomplished relatively peacefully – notwithstanding the division into Pakistan and the ensuing dispute and wars over Kashmir – other colonies held the seeds of confrontation and eventual conflict.

The Malayan Peoples' Anti-Japanese Army (MPAJA) was formed as the military arm of the Malayan Communist Party (MCP) to resist the Japanese when they occupied Malaya. The majority of its members were of Chinese origin. The British had supported the MPAJA with weapons, training and advisors just as they did with other 'resistance movements' in Axis-occupied territories. After the war, the MPAJA was treated as a heroic ally, and a delegation was invited to attend the victory parade in London. However, the marriage of convenience between the MCP and the British did not last: they no longer shared a common enemy or political purpose, and the British vision of an independent Federation of Malaysia differed markedly from the MCP's. The MPAJA was renamed the Malayan Peoples' Anti-British Army (MPABA), but in a bid to attract support from different racial groups within the local population it was soon renamed yet again, to the Malayan Races Liberation Army (MRLA).

In June 1948 three British planters were murdered in Malaya. In a matter of months the 'Malayan emergency' escalated, as guerrilla units of the MRLA attacked plantations and sabotaged infrastructure to drive the British out and to prevent the colony from functioning – all the while terrorizing the local population into supporting them. In response Britain declared a state of emergency, and Malayan and British troops set about tracking down the communist terrorists (dubbed CTs). However, responding to force with force was understood to be insufficient to win. MRLA guerrillas benefited from years of experience of operations against the Japanese, and they were also in possession of stocks of weaponry hoarded at the end of the Second World War by the Communist Party. Moreover, they could rely on the jungle terrain for cover and were supported by a segment of the population, which included a sizeable part of the Chinese minority, although overall the people of Malaya were ambivalent about the insurrection.

Whilst international media attention was focused upon the Korean War, the British, drawing on their experience which reached back to at least the Boer War, decided to focus on removing guerrilla sympathizers from the field. Under a plan devised by Lieutenant General Sir

Harold Briggs, director of anti-bandit operations, a resettlement programme was launched in order to move hundreds of thousands of Chinese peasants living on the edge of the jungle into 500 'new villages', built for the purpose. The new villages were carefully planned in advance: roads, water, sites for shops, a school, a clinic and all other basic necessities were taken into account. On arrival, each family received some financial aid and construction material to build a house. The perimeter of each village was protected with barbed wire and a police post staffed by up to twenty men. As soon as the village was settled, home guards were recruited to reinforce the police at night, during which curfews were imposed outside the village, and sometimes within the perimeter itself. The main attraction for new arrivals was that they were given title deeds to their new property. To that point the Chinese minority was generally very poor and had few rights to speak of, having been denied land ownership and voting rights. The MCP had played to all these factors, which were now countered by the Briggs plan that gave the Chinese population a stake in the British idea of the future – they were now property owners, with a reason to support the future in which this standing would continue – and removed the people from the guerrillas, protected them from terrorism and politicization, and prevented them from being able to support the cadres in the jungle.

Once the resettlement programme had been fully completed in a district, strict food-control measures were introduced. Food brought into the villages had to be guarded and none was allowed to be taken out. Search parties prevented MRLA sympathizers from supplying the guerrillas. In some areas rice was even rationed and issued cooked so that it would become sour within a matter of days. These measures, like any blockade, took time to be effective but in the long run malnutrition began to have an effect on the guerrilla units, forcing them to take risks to gain rations and at the same time weakening their resolve. In parallel, the British pursued the CTs in the jungle. A jungle-warfare school was established, infantry units, still manned by National Servicemen – British conscripts – were trained and acclimatized so as to be able to operate as well or better than the CTs. Specialist units such as the Special Air Service (SAS) were reformed to conduct deep patrols of long duration. With the police intelligence operations in the villages and towns, and the intelligence from the deep operations in the jungle, the infantry patrols that had been trained for the jungle began to drive the CTs further and further into it with increasing success. British units were soon giving out medical aid and food supplies to Malays and indigenous Sakai tribes in the jungle, which all helped to remove the support of the people for CTs who shared the territory with them.

In October 1951 the MRLA ambushed and assassinated the British high commissioner. His successor, Lt. Gen. Gerald Templer, seized the situation energetically. Whilst following the Briggs plan, he speeded up the development of a Malayan army, and pursued administrative reforms within Malaya. He also pushed through measures granting ethnic Chinese residents the right to vote and handed key positions to indigenous leaders, pushing them on the way to self-government. Templer continued the development of intelligence gathering and analysis, and instituted rewards for those helping to detect guerrillas. Crucially he promised that Malaya would be independent when the insurrection was over. By the mid-1950s, with independence looming, the MCP realized that the insurrection was doomed to failure. Malaya became an independent state in August 1957. The last serious opposition by MRLA guerrillas ended in 1958 and the remnants of MRLA forces retreated to the areas close to the Thai border. On 31 July 1960 the Malayan government declared the state of emergency over, and Ching Peng, the guerrilla leader, fled to China.

The Malayan emergency is held up to this day in militaries around the world as a successful example of counter-insurgency and counter-revolutionary war. Briggs and Templer between them removed the principal political objective from the MCP's campaign. The depiction of the conflict as a liberation struggle from colonial oppressors that would never yield control lost credibility in the face of the promise of independence backed by the gift of land in the soon-to-be-independent state. They separated the people from the guerrillas' influence and then developed the forces and intelligence to hunt them down on their ground and on their terms. The British had won the will of the people while defeating the MCP's army – and this with a conscript army and within the tolerance of their own people, British public opinion at home. I understood the importance of this achievement when I was in

Zimbabwe in 1980, talking to the defeated white Rhodesians who had actually been the winners of most if not every tactical military engagement. They had copied and adapted to advantage almost everything that the British had done in Malaya – but for one essential difference to which they were blind. The British were clear they were leaving Malaya; the question was to whom to hand power. The Rhodesians were not leaving and were not about to hand power to anyone else. The British could herd people into 'protected villages' on the grounds that the villagers would inherit the village and the land; the Rhodesians were seen as corralling the people and denying them their land.

The Malayan emergency is also a classic example of a major party to the Cold War, Britain, that was building and sustaining an industrial army as part of the confrontation – and which then adapted and used forces from within it for a confrontation of a completely different nature. In purely operational terms, it is a clear example of organizational mobility, and the forces were indeed successful in their operations. What marks this, and other conflicts in parallel to the Cold War, as different is that they were conducted under the assumptions of industrial war, whilst in fact conducting war amongst the people: such an operation was seen as a temporary aberration from the real business of war, rather than a new reality of conflict. It was an early example of the paradigm: a long confrontation that constantly crossed over to conflict at the tactical level. Though guerrillas and British then Malayan troops were deployed across wide swathes of land, no engagement rose above the level of a company. It was therefore a series of tactical conflicts within a broad confrontation. And it was within this framework that the next stage of Malayan history was written: the Indonesian confrontation.

Malaya became independent in 1957, and the British began withdrawing from their other colonies in Borneo, which at the time was divided into four distinct administrative territories. Kalimantan, an Indonesian province, was located in the south of the island. In the north were the kingdom of Brunei and the two provinces of Sarawak and British North Borneo, later renamed Sabah. Britain planned to create the Federation of Malaysia, comprising Malaya, Sabah and Sarawak, leaving the Kingdom of Brunei independent. The Philippines and

Indonesia formally agreed to accept the formation of Malaysia after a referendum organized by the United Nations. In Indonesia, however, President Sukarno remained staunchly against the formation of the Federation arguing that it was a pretext to maintain British colonial rule in the area – but in addition, he wanted the whole of the island of Borneo, and in particular the oilfields of the Sultan of Brunei, for Indonesia.

In Brunei, the Indonesian-backed North Kalimantan National Army (TKNU) revolted on 8 December 1962. TKNU forces attempted to capture the Sultan of Brunei, seize the oilfields and take European hostages. The Sultan managed to escape and appealed for British help. British troops were sent over from Singapore and by 16 December the British Far Eastern Command could claim the principal rebel concentrations had been destroyed. In April 1963 the rebel commander was captured and the rebellion was over. However, in January 1963, Indonesia's foreign minister had publicly expressed his country's hostile stance to Malaysia by claiming a policy of 'confrontation' against it, and Indonesian irregular troops started to infiltrate Sarawak and Sabah. They were soon raiding, sabotaging and disseminating Indonesian propaganda in the villages whilst the Indonesian army commander General Suharto vowed to 'crush Malaysia'. The frequency of Indonesian raids from their bases in Kalimantan increased. Platoon-sized units roamed through the two regions, supported by Chinese communist sympathizers. The local population were slow to rally, not least because they were not of the same race.

In 1964 Indonesian troops began to raid targets within the Malaysian peninsula itself. Armed Indonesian agents were captured in August in the city of Johore. In September and October 1964 Indonesia launched paratroop and amphibious raids against Labis and Pontian, on the south-western side of the peninsula. Force levels were built up and by early 1965 some 15,000 British and Commonwealth troops were deployed together with considerable naval and air force contingents, the majority of the army units being sent to the threatened provinces in Borneo. From 1964 they were deployed in jungle bases to interdict Indonesian incursions and thereby protect centres of population. Once this essentially defensive measure began to take effect, and drawing on the experience of the campaign in Malaya, these forces set out to ensure the people of the tribes in the jungle along the border were actively loyal. A screen of patrols along the border, coupled with the information gathered from the people, provided valuable information. By June 1964 such data began to be sufficiently reliable for it to be acted upon, and the Commonwealth forces moved onto the offensive. Special Forces, which had honed their expertise in Malaya, launched secret cross-border operations with the purpose of obtaining intelligence and forcing the Indonesians to remain on the defensive on their own side of the border in Kalimantan. These raids were, of course, unpublicized, and were conducted as part of the highly classified operation Claret. Uncertain about where the Commonwealth forces might strike next, the Indonesians increasingly devoted their resources to protecting their own positions and correspondingly less on offensive operations. Parallel to these military measures a diplomatic offensive was undertaken on a number of levels. Britain used its position in the UN and the regional military alliance, SEATO (Southeast Asia Treaty Organization), to bring pressure on the Indonesians to cease their incursions and their claims to Borneo. More locally, they encouraged the Malaysian Federation to act and show its cohesion and independence. These military and diplomatic efforts exposed the inner tensions of the Sukarno regime: the Indonesian military were losing and being attacked in their own territory; there was no support for their campaign from the people in Sabah and Sarawak; and they were isolated internationally. In March 1966 President Sukarno was ousted from power in a bloodless coup and General Suharto took over. Operations on Malaysian soil decreased during this internal crisis and shortly afterwards, in May 1966, the Malaysian and Indonesian governments proclaimed the ending of hostilities at a conference in Bangkok. A peace treaty was signed on 11 August and ratified two days later.

The crisis is officially known as the Indonesian Confrontation, and it is clear how well the title describes the events: following on the Malayan emergency, every element of what was learned there was further honed and implemented with a high degree of exactitude. The overall campaign, military and political, had been conducted with finesse. The military actions complemented the political and were not designed to achieve more than tactical objectives. The people of Sabah and Sarawak were secured, and operations were conducted to gain information and intelligence. Once this foundation was laid, and the Indonesian objective denied to them, operations were conducted to bring pressure on their forces in Kalimantan which, together with the diplomatic pressures, caused the collapse of the regime. Britain drew on its considerable experience of jungle operations and made a number of organizational changes to create the patrol units that screened the border. We see here a superb example of the military actions, the tactical conflict, firmly within the context of the political and diplomatic activities, the theatre-level confrontation that occasionally escalated to strategic level. And all of these sat within the great political-level confrontation of the two blocs, the Cold War.

To this point we have seen two models of conflict sitting within confrontations: the Korean War, which almost escalated to the point of a nuclear war but remained limited to a theatre operation, and the two Malayan conflicts, in which tactical engagements sat firmly within the context of the political and diplomatic activity. Both models belong to the paradigm of war amongst the people, which as explained is one of combined military and political activity. As a result, the political-military relationship is both more complex than in industrial war, and absolutely crucial in ensuring a successful outcome. As I noted in the introduction, it is always at the political level that the decision to go to war – to cross over from confrontation into conflict – is taken, and it is also at this level that the decision to stop the fighting is taken. The military implement these decisions, at all three levels. At the beginning of a conflict, once the decision is made, activities will move to the military, starting at the strategic level. The context of the decision is always the broader discussion of strategy ongoing within any government, defined in continuous reassessment and debate amongst the various bodies of policy making: foreign and defence ministries, president or prime minister's offices, intelligence services and so on. In peacetime, policy debates tend to be general and focus on identifying threats – but these are only ever potential threats. It takes a real enemy to produce a real threat; and a real endeavour with a real object in an actual situation to judge risk. This point must always be considered by those deciding on policy, recognizing the potential enemy or highlighting the absence of such, since they are constructing the nest for those who will have to decide a specific strategy at some point in the future. Indeed, it is the appearance of a real enemy that brings the strategic level into play, for whilst it is possible to have a general policy identifying threats in peacetime, it is not possible to have a strategy until there is an opponent. Equally, the strategist of an operation must understand the nature and the limits of the policy nest he is in, and design a strategy in accordance. A strategy detached from the political and policy context stands little chance of working. As Clausewitz so excellently put it:

We see, therefore, in the first place, that under all circumstances War is to be regarded not as an independent thing, but as a political instrument; and it is only by taking this point of view that we can avoid finding ourselves in opposition to all military history. This is the only means of unlocking the great book and making it intelligible. Secondly, this view shows us how Wars must differ in character according to the nature of the motives and circumstances from which they proceed.

Now, the first, the grandest, and most decisive act of judgement which the Statesman and the General exercises is rightly to understand in this respect the War in which he engages, not to take it for something, or to wish to make of it something, which by the nature of its relations it is impossible for it to be. This is, therefore, the first, the most comprehensive, of all strategical questions.*

When the political level has made its decision to enter conflict, the policy debate should focus on three main issues: the end to be achieved, the way it is to be achieved and the means allocated to be used in this way to the end desired. It does not matter at what point one enters this argument – what does matter is that the three are in balance. You can decide the means and the way and accept the end they will achieve, but to set an end that the means and the way do not match is to court at the very least disappointment. Likewise to choose a way because it is available to you without allocating the means or, more critically, matching it to the nature of the end desired, will more likely than not

* *On War*, section 27, ch. 1, bk 1 (Penguin edn), p. 121.

confound one's efforts, however efficient they may be. I have found the use of this simple analytical tool of clearly identifying the end, way and means very useful in cutting through the mass of detail and conflicting interest that inevitably intrude into the debate of policy, and the same tool can be used in understanding the lower levels of war and their relationship with each other.

The end is really the outcome desired by the policy. This may be the re-establishment of the status quo or the creation of a friendly regime, or the removal of the threat in question. The way should be the general path along which the allocated resources – military, diplomatic, economic and others – will be used, and in what balance. The means are the resources, including such abstracts as political capital, allocated to achieving this purpose. In doing this the political level must understand, although they often do not, that these too will be at risk – that the means are being risked to achieve the end in the way intended. If resources, personnel, materiel, finance and reputation are directed towards achieving an outcome in a particular way they must also be at risk if the relationship between end, way and means is to remain balanced. If the end is not thought worth the risk to the means, then either the way or the end must be changed until a balance is achieved. For example, if the deployment of soldiers into a situation of human rights violations or even outright conflict cannot include the employment of force for fear of losing personnel, then there is either no point in the deployment or else the mode of its operation must be changed. Or, taking an historical example, we can see how the balance between ends, ways and means worked out in the Falklands War. The Argentineans invaded the islands in the belief that the British lacked the capability to take them back: lacked the sufficient means and in particular the will to fight for them. However, they misjudged both political will and perhaps the morale of the forces, and the available means were dispatched to liberate the Falklands. This they did, although outnumbered in the air and on the land, since the commander found a way to win both the trial of strength and the clash of wills.

The decision on allocation of resources is the most sensitive for the political level, and also the most crucial. As we have seen, typically since Napoleon the total power of the state has been harnessed to winning wars when the purpose has been the survival of the state. But fewer resources will be allocated to lesser political purposes, as apparent in the two Malayan operations. In our times, much removed from total war, we can see this issue played out in the parliaments of the world in one formulation or another. In every state there is a defence policy and a security policy: the former deals with the absolute imperatives of the survival of the state and the latter deals with the lesser imperatives – and both are within the international context. In other words, whilst it is the defence and security of the nation at stake within the policy, it is the survival of the state within the current international system that is being dealt with by the policy. In addition to the Ministry of Defence many other ministries have a part to play in the defence element of the policy, though in a somewhat dormant capacity – and they are expected to come into play in the event of industrial war; however, these same ministries – particularly the Foreign Ministry – are those that take the lead in the security element of the policy. The balance of resource allocation between the two and for a military intervention is usually decided, at least in democracies, by judging the popular political will to pursue the purpose and to bear the cost – both in the lives of the sons and daughters of their voters and to the exchequer, with consequent impact on the economy, education, health care and all elements of national life.

In the search for means, including abstracts such as legitimacy and moral force, nations often enter into alliances where they see their purpose being broadly in common. In so doing they not only increase the available forces, but also spread their risks. It should be noted there are marked differences, often ignored, between an alliance and a coalition: the former is of a more permanent nature and denotes equality amongst all members; coalitions are usually ad hoc affairs, led by one or two powerful members. However, maintaining the alliance or coalition requires hard diplomatic work and inevitably some compromise of the positions of its members, and the expenditure of material and diplomatic capital particularly by the principal members. And the less imperative and threatening the prospect, the less the commonality of purpose, the harder this is to do. NATO, for example, is a standing alliance – and it is maintained by permanent diplomatic interaction at its headquarters, where all members have ambassadors that meet regularly to discuss and negotiate alliance business. The international forces that conducted the Iraq wars of 1991 and 2003 were coalitions – and whilst the first was cemented by massive diplomatic efforts spearheaded by the US and especially the then secretary of state James Baker, the second appeared more cobbled together against the background of heated diplomatic dispute. The first greatly enhanced the political capital of all participants, the second diminished it for most.

Having decided at the political level the balance between the end, way and means, at the military strategic level we choose the objectives to be achieved by military force – and also decide their relationship to other objectives being achieved by, for example, diplomacy or economic aid. This selection, as indeed most aspects of strategy, is an art – as General Alanbrooke, British Chief of the Imperial General Staff during most of the Second World War, explained:

The art of strategy is to determine the aim, which should be political: to derive from the aim a series of Military Objectives to be achieved: to assess these objectives as to the military requirements they create, and the preconditions which the achievement of each is likely to necessitate: to measure available and potential resources against the requirements and to chart from this process a coherent pattern of priorities and a rational course of action.

Looking back to the Korean and Malayan campaigns, it should now become clear that the relationship to other objectives in both cases decided the final strategy and the outcome. In Korea, there was for a long time complete coherence between the political and military aims and the latter rested within the context of the former. But when the political context changed, and the military aim and way became out of step with it, the end or outcome of the policy changed and with it the military objectives. In Malaya, both military operations were balanced by the political, economic and diplomatic objectives, the military often serving as an enhancer rather than being the lead activity. It is crucial that the military objectives should be chosen for their value in achieving the political purpose or aim, not just because they are militarily possible: one must avoid the trap of confusing activity with outcome, as is so often the case with the 'something must be done' school of thought. Doing 'something' because it is possible or because a reaction, any reaction, is apparently needed to an undesirable situation will rarely achieve a desirable outcome and very probably incur a substantial cost, in human lives and materiel.

Having selected the military objectives the strategist must then allocate the military means from all the forces at his disposal, and in broad terms agree the way intended to achieve the objective in question. And the issue at stake is to agree rather than command, since in our modern circumstances the strategist is not the commander who is going to achieve the objective. This is not Napoleon or Moltke, who made the plan then executed it in the field: this is the modern strategic commander who sits at the head of a general staff in a headquarters, communicating with his commanders in theatre, and in many cases there are also multinational commanders. Finally, as always, the ends, ways and means must be brought into balance at the military strategic level, with priorities struck between the various military objectives. For these decisions provide the context for the theatre commander's decisions.

Throughout the conflict or confrontation, the relationship between the political and strategic levels must always be very close, to the point of engaging in a continuous discussion which does not stop until the overall purpose or aim is achieved. The political considerations provide the context for the strategy, and it must always be so throughout the entire conflict: the military considerations and action must always work within and contribute to the political purpose – and in harmony with all political considerations, since it is these that will keep the people within the trinity and enable the conflict to be pursued. State and people must always be in evidence, even for the smallest military operation. Particularly in the case of democracies, without this coordination there may be no political will to continue. In addition, the more the people of a state identify themselves as being directly threatened the more they will cooperate with the subordination of their interests in the name of survival and the expenditure of lives – and the more the state can demand, the defence of the people being its first political duty, and thereby its claim to sovereignty. This was clearly the case in most states in the Second World

War, or indeed as more recently apparent in the US Patriot Act passed in the wake of the 9/11 terrorist attacks: deemed to infringe to an extent upon civil rights, it none the less passed in both houses of Congress and was largely accepted by the US public, fearful of the threat of further terrorist attacks.

Given this correlate between fear of a threat and acceptance of state interference, it follows that one of the quickest ways a state or political leader can gain power over a people is for them to be threatened or for the leadership to create a threat. As we have seen, the Soviets throughout the Cold War were an example of this, using the deterrent strategies of the Cold War to keep the Soviet Empire on a total war footing. The intervention in Afghanistan then proved to be their undoing, since it could not be presented as a threat: there was no need for the war footing, and the people withdrew their support. On the other side, meanwhile, the states of the West had allocated means to achieve the end of holding their borders through a defensive strategy backed by nuclear weapons. Equally, however, they were able to allocate other resources to achieving economic prosperity. In so doing they retained popular support for the military effort, which could nest alongside other Western national aims.

This example demonstrates another important point, which is that the political objective and the military strategic objective are not the same, and are never the same. The military strategic objective is achieved by military force whilst the political objective is achieved as a result of the military success. For example, the political aim of Egypt's President Sadat in launching the 1973 war against Israel was to force it to negotiate the return of the Sinai peninsula to Egypt. The military aim of his forces, however, was to cross the Suez Canal and hold a minimal amount of territory in order to put pressure on the Israelis. The military clearly sat within the context of the political aim, but was distinct. Henry Kissinger reflected well on this matter:

What literally no one understood beforehand was the mind of the man: Sadat aimed not for territorial gain but for a crisis that would alter the attitudes in which the parties were frozen – and thereby agree the way for negotiators . . . Rare is the statesman who at the beginning of a war has so clear a perception of its political objective . . . The boldness of Sadat's strategy lay in planning for what no one could imagine; that was the principal reason the Arabs achieved surprise . . . Sadat, in fact, paralysed his opponent with their own preconceptions.*

Not only did the military act within the context of the political aim, but we see here an example of a statesman seeking to resolve a confrontation by initiating a conflict to alter minds.

It is the way in which the military success is achieved that directly affects whether or not it can be translated to political advantage. If the military success is achieved by bombing civilian targets and causing the loss of many civilian lives, which results in strong national and international public reaction, the chances are it will not be easily converted into political capital. As we shall see, to a certain extent the US experience in Vietnam reflects this reality: in technical terms the US was winning, but the manner in which this was achieved had a vast political cost both nationally and internationally, to the point at which the benefit of those victories became nullified by their cost.

Finally, in listing these characteristics of the political and strategic levels I am not suggesting some 'grand plan' is cast, with every aspect spelt out and worked through in detail. Rather, this relationship should produce a simple expression in broad terms of the end, the desired outcome, a statement as to the allocation of means to the end and a description of the general idea of the way the venture is to be prosecuted. If the end is to be achieved in a number of steps along different routes, military or otherwise, the statement should also include their priorities and sequencing. Simply sending out a whole range of missions at the same time will largely ensure incoherence, even if all objectives have been met, since it is difficult to gain political capital if a secondary target is attained before the major one or at its expense, for example. Moreover, it must be understood that these political and strategic decisions will and should be readdressed as events unfold in the adversarial circumstances of confrontation and conflict. The danger is always of making a local or specific change, without due consideration of the overall operation. It is only by hold-

---

* Henry Kissinger, *Years of Upheaval* (Boston: Little, Brown & Co., 1982), p. 460.

ing the overall aim constantly in mind that appropriate adjustments can be made.

So far I have dealt with the relationship between the political and military levels with regard to states that have a recognizable split between the political and military bodies. But this analysis applies to all confrontations and conflicts whether between states or not, with the exception of the purely criminal involving one or a few people. The dividing line between policy and strategy may be blurred; indeed, the thinking may all lie in the head of one man or woman. But understanding those thoughts and intentions is done best by dividing them out, the political from the strategic, and recognizing that the strategic rests within the political. On this basis it is always possible to make a plan and implement it to effect – to give utility to any force used.

APPENDIX: THE MILITARY
BALANCE 1961–1991

Some comparative estimates of strategic strength, early 1962

Category	Western Alliance (includes NATO, Western Alliances and US Treaty powers)	Communist Bloc (includes Warsaw Pact, China, North Korea and North Vietnam)
ICBMs	63	50
MRBMs	186	200
Long-range bombers	600	190
Medium-range bombers	2,200	1,100
Aircraft carriers	58	–
Nuclear submarines	22	2
Conventional submarines	266	480
Cruisers	67	25
Mobilized personnel	8,195,253	7,994,300
	NATO	*Warsaw Pact*
Total forces	6,061,013	4,790,300

The following is compiled from the core text of the Military Balance 1961–2, which was still more of a report than a statistical instrument. Although it is not really a comparative tool as powerful as tables, it provides estimates of the following type:

USSR

Land power
2,500,000 personnel
160 active line divisions. Infantry division at war strength comprises 12,000, an armoured division 10,500 plus supporting artillery and anti-aircraft units. Most of the active divisions are armoured or mechanized. Mobilization potential: 7,000,000

Airborne forces
100,000 formed in 9 divisions

Tanks
20,000 front-line and 15,000 second-line

Sea power
500,000 men
Navy: 1,600,000 total tonnage
Submarines: 430 units
Cruisers: 25
Destroyers: 130
Other vessels: 2,500,000

Warsaw Pact nations

Estimated to be able to muster 68 regular divisions
Total 990,300 under arms
360,000 in paramilitary formations
Satellite air forces: 2,900 planes (80% jet fighters)

North Korea
Total 338,000

North Vietnam
Total 266,000

Long- and medium-range nuclear systems for the European theatre, 1979–80

	NATO	Warsaw Pact
Ballistic missiles	326	1,213
Aircraft	1,679	4,151
US central systems (Poseidon)	40	–
Total	2,045	5,364
Warheads assumed available	1,065	2,244

Tanks and tactical aircraft in operational service in Europe, 1979–80

	NATO	Warsaw Pact
Battle tanks	11,000	27,200
Tactical aircraft	3,300	5,795

Ground forces available without mobilization and reinforcing formations available for the European theatre, 1979–80

	NATO	Warsaw Pact
Ground forces available (divisional equivalents)	64*	68
Reinforcing formations available	$52\frac{2}{3}$	$115\frac{1}{3}$

* These figures do not include the ground forces of Britain, France and Portugal.

NATO and Warsaw Pact armed forces (000's), 1979–80

	NATO	Warsaw Pact
Army	2,016.2	2,617
Navy	1,056.5	492
Air	1,103.9	729
Total armed forces	4,176.6	3,838
Estimated reservists	4,278.1	7,145

Ground forces: Atlantic to the Urals, 1990–91

	NATO	Warsaw Pact
Personnel	2,896,200*	2,905,700
Active divisions	93	$103\frac{1}{3}$
Reserve divisions	$36\frac{1}{3}$	100
Total divisions	$129\frac{1}{3}$	$203\frac{1}{3}$

* All service manpower except for naval forces but including marines.

Tanks and combat aircraft: Atlantic to the Urals, 1990–91

	NATO	Warsaw Pact
Battle tanks	23,022	51,714
Combat aircraft	4,884	6,206

US and Soviet strategic nuclear forces, 1990–91

	US	USSR
Total ballistic missiles	1,624	2,322
Total bombers	306	185
Total warheads	9,680	10,996

Maritime forces, 1990–91

	NATO	Warsaw Pact
Submarines	227	254
Carriers	20	5
Battleships/cruisers	51	43
Destroyer frigates	392	202
Amphibious	102	111
Naval aircraft	1,207	569

6

Capabilities:
The Search for a New Way

Withdrawal from empire, principally by Britain and France, provided the setting for the parallel conflicts that erupted during the Cold War confrontation – and yet, as we have already seen, they came to sit firmly within its context. Firstly, because they occurred concurrently with the Cold War. Second, because they were conducted with the same forces: the UK, the US or France, for example, when they were involved in Malaya or Vietnam or Algeria, were drawing from their standing forces – the industrial forces amassed and structured as part of the Cold War – and adapting them for the different nature of these operations. And third, because in many cases there were underlying political connections between the conflicts and the confrontation, as each bloc sought to expand its influence into ever wider spheres – but without actually coming into conflict with each other. These parallel conflicts therefore served in some cases as proxies: the dislike and distrust of the imperial power became subsumed either into pro-democratic rhetoric of popular political movements or else into anti-imperialist rhetoric espoused by underground communist movements. In turn, each of these was then embraced by one of the confronting blocs, thereby ensuring the local conflict took on far greater significance. In the previous chapter we observed this dynamic in both the Korean War and especially the Malayan operations, which came in the midst and the aftermath of the British withdrawal. The French withdrawal from Indo-China in turn held the seeds to the Vietnam War, which embroiled the US in its worst conflict since the Second World War – and the withdrawal from Algeria embroiled the French government and military in a confrontation that brought the state to crisis. These were the first clear conflicts of war amongst the people – yet whilst the French military understood the Algerian war to be a different form of conflict, Indo-China and Vietnam were fought within the concepts of industrial war.

As before, there were in these conflicts different kinds of enemies: non-state, lightly armed, ideologically charged. Enemies who used tactics that harked back to the antithesis of industrial war, but evolved them much further. To best understand these tactics, and the US and French response to them, there is a need to explore the basics of the term 'density', since it allows us to understand the dynamics of the modern battlefield on a large scale – which, given the breadth of the Indo-China and Algerian theatres, is important. Density is the modern manifestation and continuation of the tactical issue of mass manpower as against mass firepower, discussed in Part I in relation to Napoleon and Wellington. Imagine, for example, a battlefield where men with only clubs are engaged; ten on one side are attacking five on the other. Assuming all else is equal, the ten men are likely to beat the five since the larger side has the greater density of force. Now let us suppose the smaller side had positioned itself behind an obstacle, a ditch perhaps, such that the larger side could not get all its ten men into action simultaneously, perhaps because every other man had to help his comrade across and out of the ditch. In this case the smaller side might win, provided they had the speed to finish each fight quickly, the endurance to fight two or more times to the opponent's one, and the obstacle was of sufficient magnitude to slow the opponent's approach to a rate the defenders could address successfully. In this situation the smaller side, by providing themselves with an obstacle, altered to advantage, perhaps to equality, their density in relation to the opponent's. However, faced with the prospect of the obstacle, the attacking commander might decide to task two or three of his men to stay on their side of the obstacle and hurl stones at the defenders, to wound, distract and delay them in massing against his men as they crossed the obstacle. Provided the correct balance is struck between the number of throwers of stones and clubmen, and the throwers can see and hit the defenders, and they are skilled enough to sustain the rate of fire accurately, and there are enough stones of the right weight – another clear example of the importance of logisticians – the attackers might be able to achieve sufficient density of force over the obstacle and beat the smaller side.

So density is not simply a measure of the size of forces deployed, but of the force employed against the targets in range. Take all popular adversarial ball games such as soccer, rugby or American football – all of which may be understood in terms of density, as each side endeavours to engineer a situation in which one of its players can breach the other side's defence and score. The complexities of achieving this for an hour or so in a clearly defined area (the pitch) is what makes the game. A battlefield, especially the modern one, is infinitely more complex. In the pre-industrial battlefield, which was also clearly defined, British infantry squares defeated cavalry attacks because the square, although outnumbered, achieved a greater density of force than the cavalry. A cavalryman was effective only to the range of his lance or sword, and the infantryman with his musket to about fifty metres. But the horseman could cover that distance in the time it took the infantryman to reload, so two cavalrymen would defeat one infantryman. But by closing the infantry up into squares of three or four ranks the infantry could achieve a rate of fire of three to four shots per fifty metres by each rank firing in turn (as described on p. 44). Furthermore, they had reduced their size as a target by a factor of three or four, which meant that many fewer cavalrymen would be able to engage them with lance or sword if they did manage to close with the square. On the other hand, the square, a static group of closely packed men, was vulnerable to artillery fire, which is why Wellington tried always to site his infantry on the reverse slope of the hill to the enemy guns.

Keeping in mind the basic dictum that battle is an event of circumstance, it is now possible to see that density is a ratio of the force employed by each side in a particular set of circumstances. However, each side is free to alter the circumstances – which will alter the density, since it can only be measured in relation to the opponent and the circumstances. An excellent example was apparent in the discussion of the Korean War, when the Chinese attacked over the river Yalu and drove the UN forces back to south of the 38th parallel. The Chinese achieved a greater density than the UN forces: they were more numerous and advancing on a broad front, and they were prepared to accept considerable casualties. The UN forces were overextended after their rapid advance north, and could present a viable defence only on the main axes. These defensive positions were quickly outflanked by the Chinese moving on foot on secondary axes; moreover, the UN air forces were unable to locate the infiltrating Chinese columns, and in any event they did not have a suitable weapon with which to attack and halt them. Only when it had traded all its gains and some more and the peninsula had narrowed sufficiently for the density to reach something like parity did the Chinese advantage become attenuated. The only way MacArthur, with the forces he had to hand and with the technological bias of the forces he might call on for reinforcements, could have achieved a greater density without conceding gains was to attack the Chinese in their depth. But the consequences of doing this were politically unacceptable. As such, the UN force, with air forces and atomic weapons, lacked utility – and the desired outcome was adjusted accordingly.

In discussing density I have touched on another point that is closely related: technological and tactical innovation. The examples I have used make clear how each side has sought another weapon or tactic to alter the density of force to their advantage, be it the use of obstacles, or the square, or supporting fire with stones, or the destructive fire of the artillery, or concealment on the reverse slope. The British theorist General John Fuller wrote of the 'constant tactical factor' describing this interplay. Every technological innovation is in time countered by adopting a suitable tactic, which in turn spawns a demand for another technological innovation. The situation is far more complex in the current battlefield, which is much larger, amongst the people and suffused with technological innovations. The innovation of hijacking an aircraft and using it as a cruise missile on 11 September 2001, or of using artillery shells activated by a mobile telephone call as roadside mines in Iraq, and the technical and tactical reactions to these innovations, are precisely what Fuller meant by his 'constant tactical factor'. Indeed, these examples show it is doubly relevant now, and should be a caution to all commanders, as yet another new technological solution is proffered: take it, use it, but do not suppose the ingenuity that led to the technology is not matched by an equal ability to find the tactical solution, or vice versa.

This problem of density – and of military utility conflicting with political viability – was basic to the French and subsequently the US experience in Indo-China. Like the UK, France ultimately came to realize, through a combination of changed post-war international context, local unrest, and diminished resources, that there was no option but a withdrawal from its empire. The process of realization was slow and painful. In military terms, the French tend to see their war in Indo-China as falling into three distinct phases. First came the 1945–6 attempt to reassert total control. In the next three years, the French army – underestimating the developing insurgency – was engaged in a local colonial war. Finally, from the end of 1949 onwards, the war evolved into a large-scale conflict, which included a new international dimension: Vietnam became a stake of the Cold War for the two blocs.

Japan invaded Indo-China in 1940, but it remained under the nominal authority of occupied Vichy France for most of the Second World War, with the Japanese controlling it behind the scenes. In 1941 Ho Chi Minh, a trained communist revolutionary, returned to Vietnam and formed the Viet Nam Doc Lap Dong Minh Hoi or 'Viet Minh': an umbrella organization for all the nationalist resistance movements. It was active throughout the war against the Japanese, but was also preparing to fight the return of French occupation once it ended. In March 1945, the Japanese seized full control of Indo-China, though this was mostly effective in the south, where they had a concentration of troops. At the Potsdam Conference in July 1945, the Allies agreed that the Chinese would accept the surrender of the Japanese in Indo-China north of the 16th parallel and the British would do so south of that line. On 13 August the Viet Minh called on the Vietnamese to rise in revolution, and formally declared the independence of the Democratic Republic of Vietnam. On the 17th the Japanese forces in the north indeed surrendered to the Chinese nationalists, and to British forces in the south. The British supported the Free French in fighting the Viet Minh. In September 1945, under Ho Chi Minh's leadership, guerrillas occupied Hanoi, capital of the north, and proclaimed a provisional government. In France, Charles de Gaulle as early as June had

appointed General Leclerc de Hauteclocque to command an expeditionary corps to re-establish French sovereignty in Indo-China. However, months were needed before such a corps could be mustered and
shipped. As a result, the confrontation with the Viet Minh was more
of a political nature than of a military one until December 1946. These
two years were characterized by a series of negotiations between
France and the Viet Minh, as both parties lacked sufficient numbers
of troops to attempt to overwhelm the other. On his arrival in Saigon
in October 1945, with a handful of French troops supported by a large
British contingent, Leclerc swiftly re-established French control over
Cochin-China, the region south of the 16th parallel. By February 1946,
he had restored economic life and French forces had also penetrated
into neighbouring Laos and Cambodia.

The next move was a skilful combination of military and political
skill. In order to reassert French sovereignty over Indo-China, Leclerc
had to regain Tonkin and North Annam. These regions were Viet
Minh controlled and the French forces were too few to dislodge them.
The solution to the problem lay in using the common interest of both
parties, namely removing Chinese occupation forces, which were
behaving more as conquerors than liberators. Leclerc's plan relied on
a combination of pressure on the Chinese to remove their 150,000
troops, negotiations with Ho Chi Minh and a build-up to 65,000 men
to occupy North Vietnam. Negotiations with the Viet Minh eventually led to a preliminary agreement, in which Vietnam was recognized
as a free state of the Indo-Chinese Federation within the French
Union. In return, Ho agreed that French forces would replace the
Chinese nationalist troops, the latter much in need as reinforcements
against the Chinese communists in China by that time. In March 1945
Leclerc led French forces into Hanoi and then through all of Tonkin.

However, the situation soon deteriorated. In Paris, negotiations
with the Viet Minh faltered: Ho Chi Minh spent four months attempting to negotiate full independence and unity for Vietnam, but failed to
obtain any guarantee. Meanwhile, in Saigon, the high commissioner
set about creating a separatist client state in Cochin-China. As the Viet
Minh increased preparations for an upcoming conflict, Leclerc
resigned. In Paris, his warning that France was heading for a guerrilla
war it could neither ignore nor afford went unheeded. This was an

excellent example of incoherence between the policy context and the military strategy: Leclerc's theatre-level solution to the confrontation with the Viet Minh, based on an understanding of their motivation and ability to achieve independence, was not nested in the policy and strategy of France as a whole, which at that point still saw itself in control of its colony and believed it could negotiate an outcome short of independence. They were incoherent. In contrast, the Viet Minh used the period of negotiations to consolidate further their political position amongst the people, thereby strengthening their Clausewitzian trinity before conflict came. Their actions were coherent.

In November 1946, after a series of violent clashes with the Viet Minh – who, having failed to achieve their objective at the negotiating table, had begun pursuing the politics of terror – French forces bombarded Haiphong harbour whilst 1,000 French Legionnaires entered the northern provinces. This forced Ho Chi Minh and his Viet Minh troops to retreat into the jungle, their sanctuary. They soon retaliated by launching their first large-scale attack against the French at Hanoi. The phase of open colonial war had begun. The French immediately began a series of attacks on Viet Minh guerrilla positions in North Vietnam near the Chinese border. Although the Viet Minh suffered heavy casualty rates, most of their force slipped away through gaps in the French lines. This set the basis for a recurrent pattern as French commanders launched increasingly frequent attacks, which were often successful locally but never managed to eradicate the Viet Minh presence.

The Viet Minh focused on developing their sanctuary and the organization of their war effort: they intensified guerrilla operations to distract the French and to expand their area of influence, and set up a war economy based on support from the peasantry in order to gain supplies, arms, medicines and recruits for their growing armies. At this stage neither side of the conflict was seeking the annihilation of the other. Rather, they were seeking the military advantage so as to have the greatest access to the population and thus to exhibit the advantage of their idea of peace. By 1947 the French were prepared to grant independence of a sort, but not to the Viet Minh. They attempted to destroy the Viet Minh's credibility as a future government by setting up an alternative government headed by Emperor Bao

Dai, but since he had been so used by the Japanese in their proxy regime during the war, his administration was an evident puppet and it was never granted a sufficient degree of independence; it therefore had few followers. The Viet Minh were very clear as to their political purpose of total independence and the military acts to support its achievement, but they knew they needed to persuade the people and they were prepared to take as long as necessary to achieve their active support. For, as ever, the Viet Minh needed the people for all parts of the trinity: to provide the manpower and support for their forces, and to support their ideological view of the future of an independent Vietnam. To this end, and to sustain the fight against the French, they conducted guerrilla operations, albeit with ever-growing groups of formed forces, and set out to gain space and time in which to achieve their political purpose.

Between August 1949 and October 1950 the balance of power began to shift as French forces gradually saw their military edge and political position being eroded. In January 1950, the People's Republic of China and the Soviet Union both recognized Ho Chi Minh's Democratic Republic of Vietnam. China then began sending military advisors and modern weapons to the Viet Minh. These included automatic weapons, mortars, howitzers and trucks. With this influx of new equipment and the help of the advisors, General Vo Nguyen Giap, in command of Viet Minh forces, transformed his guerrilla fighters into regular army units. By the end of 1950 the Viet Minh had five light infantry divisions in the field, which went into combat with great skill, defeating two French columns during the Frontier Campaign (Cao Bang), which gave the Viet Minh control over 750 kilometres of the border with China. They had complete control of their sanctuary and were now conducting operations with formed formations in the field – they had entered Mao's third stage of revolutionary war, as explained on p. 169.

With Chinese involvement, the conflict slowly but surely became part of the Cold War confrontation, with the USSR also supporting the North and the US supporting the South. By October 1952, on the French side, 75 per cent of the costs of war were being met by American aid. To justify America's new financial commitment to this cause, President Eisenhower made great use of the 'domino theory', which purported that a communist victory in Vietnam would inevitably be followed by the fall of surrounding countries like a row of dominoes. This domino theory would be later used by a string of presidents and their advisors to defend ever-deepening US involvement in Vietnam.

In 1953, as the Viet Minh engaged in an intensification of guerrilla operations in all areas, the French general staff decided to seek a decisive result. Their concept was centred on the construction of a series of entrenched outposts protecting a small air base in an isolated jungle valley at Dien Bien Phu in the north-west of Vietnam, which lay astride important routes for the Viet Minh and close to their sanctuary. This supposedly impregnable aero-terrestrial base was designed to force General Giap to concentrate his troops and engage in a decisive battle. Operation Castor was launched in late November 1953, but the French had seriously underestimated both the military strength and the tactics of the Vietnamese. Giap responded to the challenge and immediately began massing Viet Minh troops and artillery in the area, seeing the potential for a decisive blow against the French. Viet Minh forces were concentrated to lay siege to the French base. Much of this concentration, which was achieved by forced marches on the jungle tracks mostly at night, went undetected by the French, and when information was available to indicate what was happening it was discounted because it did not fit what was assumed. The Viet Minh also dragged artillery, anti-aircraft guns and the ammunition supplied by the Chinese through the jungle. The guns were concealed in carefully prepared underground positions on the hills surrounding the base, each one manhandled into its elevated position in a night.

On 13 March 1954, Viet Minh artillery shattered the myth of the superiority of French firepower in a matter of hours. Giap began his assault by destroying the only runway, thus forcing the French to rely on risky parachute drops for resupply. From 30 March to 1 May, nearly 10,000 French soldiers lay trapped in the Dien Bien Phu valley, surrounded by 45,000 Viet Minh. French air power was not sufficient to support the defence: there was not enough of it, they could not locate the targets, and they lacked the technology to attack in low cloud and poor visibility. Nor were there the forces to spare to mount

a relief operation at that distance. Giap had established an advantageous density of forces. Faced with this inextricable situation, the
French appealed to Washington for help. The US Joint Chiefs of Staff
considered three possible military options: sending American combat
troops to the rescue, a massive conventional air strike by B-29
bombers, or the use of tactical atomic weapons. President Eisenhower
dismissed the conventional air raid and the nuclear option after the
British expressed their opposition to this plan. The Americans also
decided that sending ground forces would prove too risky, because of
the likelihood of high casualty rates in the jungles around Dien Bien
Phu. As a result, ultimately no action was taken. Giap's advantage
was overwhelming. On 1 May, eight days before the opening of the
Geneva Conference on the Indo-Chinese Question, Giap launched a
decisive attack on the French positions – an excellent example of a
military act directly supporting the strategic confrontation. The
French garrison surrendered on 7 May. In Geneva, the Great Powers
subsequently reached a compromise and Vietnam was temporarily
divided along the 17th parallel into two states, with general elections
scheduled to be held in 1956.

The French action in Indo-China was another example of a confrontation that crossed over into a military conflict, which was conducted
mostly at tactical level and occasionally escalated to theatre level. All
the while, however, it remained a political and ideological confrontation which became subsumed into the wider confrontation of the Cold
War. The French were defeated on both counts: they lost the political
confrontation and the military conflict. Giap, described by one French
general as a warrant officer learning to command a couple of battalions, had turned what had been seen by the French, with their industrial war training, as inferiority into superiority. What was the use of
having weapons that could crush the enemy if the enemy escaped?
How could you find him if he was invisible? How could you understand him if he did not live, think or organize like you? How could you
track him and interdict him if his logistic system was based on bicycles?
In 1963 Giap said to the French journalist Jules Roy, 'if you were
defeated, you were defeated by yourselves'.

Following the departure of French troops, and after eight years hiding in the jungle, Ho Chi Minh returned to Hanoi and formally took

control of North Vietnam. In the South, Bao Dai soon chose the anti-Communist Ngo Dinh Diem as his prime minister. The United States pinned their hopes on Diem to contain communism; he, however, had the acumen to predict that another, more deadly war over the future of Vietnam would soon erupt.

Ngo Dinh Diem was a Catholic who found a base of supporters amongst the minority formed by his co-religionists, many of whom had been part of the native elite under French rule. His staunch anti-communist stance attracted the sympathy of the United States and as a result, in January 1955, the first direct shipment of US military aid arrived in Saigon. The US also offered to train the South Vietnamese army. On the other side, on a visit to Moscow, Ho Chi Minh agreed to accept Soviet aid. American patronage, together with the arrival of some 900,000 mostly Catholic refugees from North Vietnam, gave Diem newfound confidence. In 1956 he refused to hold the unifying elections agreed to at Geneva. Instead he consolidated his power by calling for a referendum that gave the people of South Vietnam a choice between himself as president or Emperor Bao Dai as an elective monarch. Diem's supporters rigged the election and he obtained an easy victory.

From his first days in power, Diem was faced with stiff opposition from the plethora of his opponents: students, intellectuals, Buddhists and other dissatisfied groups in society were soon joining the opposition. His regime was repressive and unpopular, but Diem gambled on the United States' fear of the spread of communism to sustain his counter-revolutionary alternative. With American aid, he began to crack down successively on all his opponents, using the help of the US Central Intelligence Agency (CIA) to identify those who sought to bring his government down. He arrested thousands, but in the countryside failed to achieve much-demanded land reforms and was soon faced with guerrilla operations within South Vietnam. Diem claimed that the Democratic Republic of Vietnam (DRV) which Ho Chi Minh had set up in the North aimed to seize the Southern Republic of Vietnam by force. In fact, Ho Chi Minh's government tried to bring about Diem's collapse by exerting intense internal political pressure, and using the Communist Party as a means for unifying the state.

In 1959, the use of revolutionary violence to overthrow Ngo Dinh Diem's government was approved at a Communist Party conference in the North. This decision resulted in the creation of a broad-based united front in order to help mobilize Southerners in opposition to the Saigon government. The front brought together communists and non-communists in an umbrella organization that grouped together all those who went against Diem's regime. In December 1960, the National Liberation Front (NLF), or 'Viet Cong' (VC), as Washington later dubbed it (a derogatory abbreviation standing for Vietnamese communist) was formed.

To support Diem, the new US president, John F. Kennedy, dispatched a team of military advisors to South Vietnam in 1961 – the first of what quickly became a steady stream. As the scope of the guerrilla war against the increasingly unpopular Diem expanded, the US provided South Vietnam with more military aid, including American-piloted armed helicopters. Machinery, dollars and advisors poured in, but Kennedy remained reluctant to deploy American regular forces into the field. Washington and Saigon devised a counter-insurgency plan – the Strategic Hamlet Program – based more on the form rather than the substance of the British experience in Malaya. The aim of the programme was to cut the guerrilla away from his support. In order to achieve this goal, Southern forces, supported by the Americans, set about building fortified structures to protect villagers from VC influence. However, the sheer immensity of the task meant that Diem's partisans had to rely on conscripted labour. From the start, peasants were reluctant to leave their fields and dig out defences against a threat they knew to be directed at government officials rather than against themselves. Moreover the people were not relocated away from the guerrilla sanctuaries and onto land they were to own – on the contrary – whilst news of land reform in the North and in VC-held villages was common knowledge.

By the summer of 1963, Diem's government was tottering on the verge of collapse. The final stroke came when he initiated a violent crackdown on Buddhist monks: in a country where nine out of ten people were Buddhists, the consequences were immense. In the streets of Saigon, monks reacted through public self-immolation. The international outcry that followed caused consternation in Washington, where Diem was perceived to have lost touch with his people. As a result, the Kennedy administration decided to support a CIA-backed coup. In November 1963 Diem was deposed and later assassinated by a military junta. At the time of his death, the US had more than 16,000 military advisors in Vietnam. They knew of the inevitably approaching war.

On 2 August 1964, in response to US and South Vietnamese surveillance along its coast, North Vietnam launched an attack against the US destroyer *Maddox* in the Gulf of Tonkin. The Johnson administration seized the occasion to secure a Congressional resolution that granted the president extensive means to wage war, and air attacks against North Vietnam soon followed. The VC retaliated by attacking two US army bases in South Vietnam and, as a consequence, in March 1965 Johnson stepped up the pressure and launched sustained bombing raids on North Vietnam. Scheduled to last eight weeks, Operation Rolling Thunder would go on for another three years. A few days later, the first US combat troops set foot in Vietnam as 3,500 Marines were deployed to protect a military installation.

The introduction of US combat troops altered the stakes dramatically and forced Ho Chi Minh and his advisors to reassess their strategy. The North's strategy had been based on the assumption that it could defeat Southern forces in the field and then proceed to Vietnam's reunification; in the face of a US deployment they developed a protracted war strategy. The aim was no longer to attain a decisive victory in the field, but rather to avoid defeat at the hands of the enemy whilst creating unfavourable conditions for his political victory – in other words, to win the confrontation rather than the conflict. For the United States was perceived to be lacking a clear strategy of its own, and thus faced with a military stalemate would eventually tire of the war and reach for a negotiated settlement.

After three years it became apparent that the United States and its allies were bogged down. As the death toll rose and young American conscripts continued to leave for Vietnam, the government was faced with virulent criticism from anti-war protestors. Protests had first erupted on college campuses and in major cities, but by 1968 the whole country was experiencing a level of social unrest unseen since the American Civil War. The war became bogged down for a number of reasons. First and foremost because the opposing objectives were asymmetric: the US was seeking a decisive engagement at theatre level – following the logic of industrial war – in order to maintain their favoured regime in power. The North actively sought to avoid the decisive engagement, while at the same time causing maximum damage and cost to US forces. Second, the US and its allies were facing two types of forces: the guerrilla forces of the VC, drawn from, and local to, the people of the South, and the units of the North Vietnamese Army (NVA), who retained many of the characteristics of a guerrilla force but were trained and equipped to fight substantial engagements. And the third reason was that the US air attacks on the North were unable to break either the simple supply systems of the NVA or the will of the people to continue the war. Indeed, there is now some evidence that they served the contrary purpose, or were at least used by the Northern government towards that end. As the NVA gained in strength in the South, so the US increasingly concentrated on defeating it – but in so doing, the people of the South became more alienated, and the VC increasingly gained in strength, with the actions of the South Vietnamese government forces more often than not contributing to this alienation. Thus the people's will to support the US-favoured regime, a necessary component of the condition being fought for, was eroded further. And at the same time the will of the American people to continue to sacrifice their sons for the cause of South Vietnam was evaporating fast. Ultimately, the US failed to break the trinity of government, people and military that held the Vietnamese enemy together – whilst its own was put at peril.

In late January 1968, the armies of the Democratic Republic of Vietnam and the VC launched coordinated attacks against the major Southern cities in the Tet offensive, which was designed to force Washington to the negotiating table. It proved to be a costly affair for the attacking forces, who suffered approximately 32,000 killed and about 5,800 captured; however, it also proved to be a turning point. In March 1968, President Johnson began secretly negotiating with Hanoi to end the war. His successor, Richard Nixon, however, decided that the time for negotiations was not yet ripe. He opted to continue with a strategy of 'Vietnamization', which was intended to take advantage of America's technological superiority whilst limiting the involvement of its soldiers on the ground. The quantity of American forces on the field was gradually reduced and replaced by South Vietnamese troops. From a peak of around 500,000 in 1969, the number of American soldiers in Vietnam fell to 300,000 in 1971 and 150,000 in 1972. Meanwhile the air attacks were increased, and the conflict spread into neighbouring countries: in an effort to destroy VC bases and supply lines, US and South Vietnamese troops invaded Laos and Cambodia in 1970–71.

After a round of unsuccessful negotiations in Paris at the end of 1972, the US bombing campaign intensified again. North Vietnam's largest cities, Hanoi and Haiphong, were attacked, yet these attacks failed to have the desired effect. And while reducing the exposure of US troops to battle, in total these measures made little difference to the situation in South Vietnam. With the use of force at the theatre level proving to be insufficient, the US sought to destroy the capacity of the North to make and supply war by further bombing and attacks into neighbouring countries. In attacking sovereign states, they escalated the conflict because in effect they used force at the strategic level. But the escalation failed: the North's simple communications and industrial base were not wholly susceptible to these aerial attacks, and, as in Korea, the US was prepared neither to unleash its nuclear capability nor to invade. Furthermore, these attacks attracted international condemnation and increased domestic criticism. In January 1973, the United States signed a peace treaty with the Democratic Republic of Vietnam and began to withdraw its forces. The Paris Peace Agreement did not end the conflict in Vietnam, however, as the forces of South Vietnam continued the struggle against the VC for another two years. Saigon fell on 30 April 1975. The second Indo-China war had come to an end.

It had been a long and gruelling conflict which had effectively kept the people of Vietnam engaged for over thirty years, if the Japanese occupation during the Second World War is included. In military terms, it started with the resistance against the renewed French regime in 1945 as a classic guerrilla war in the framework of the antithesis to industrial war. But first the French then the US responded to these tactics with those of industrial war, using their forces, aeroplanes and equipment – designed to do battle in Armageddon – against the relatively simple and definitely simply armed local forces. And as the political divisions within Vietnam became more complicated, so did the conflict – which became an example of the new paradigm. For the Western forces deemed themselves in the midst of a technologically driven war within the industrial paradigm, and conducted themselves as such, when in reality they were caught up in a war amongst the people. It was an end-of-empire confrontation which started between the French and the Vietnamese, crossed over into a conflict and then became embedded in the greater confrontation of the Cold War. Once the French had been defeated, it was on the Cold War basis that the US became embroiled, crossing over into conflict at theatre level and even escalating to strategic level with the bombing of Cambodia and Laos. Throughout all the military activity, however, the ideological and political confrontation with the people of Vietnam persisted – both with those in the South who simply sought freedom from occupation and with the communist regime in the North – and it was on this count that the US were finally defeated: they never offered the people any alternative. On almost every occasion they achieved the density of force to win the local trial of strength, drawing on their technological advantage to do so – but in so doing they lost the clash of wills. The North Vietnamese, though the weaker side, so as to win the clash of wills used force to achieve their strategic goal of liberating the South and uniting the two parts of their nation under their rule. Their force had the greater utility: they understood how to use it both within the context of their political goals and, at lower levels, to enable the politicization of the people in support of the struggle for liberation.

A main lesson to be learned from the Vietnam War, as indeed from all the wars and conflicts described in this book, is that it is rarely possible to predict the outcome, especially on the basis of the known forces that entered it, or their inventories. The French were considered to be the superior force in 1870, but were defeated by the Prussians who were better led; conversely, the Germans deemed the Belgian, French and British armies reduced threats in 1914 – which on paper all three possibly were – yet none the less found themselves facing stubborn opposition from them, which undermined the Schlieffen Plan and led to the halt of the German forces and, four years later, to their defeat. In other words, the strength of a force is not merely a matter of numbers, of counting men and materiel. This matter of assessing a force has always been of importance, but became more pressing and more difficult as the twentieth century progressed and we arrived at our current era. For after the great industrial world wars, conflicts have more and more been of apparently asymmetric or grossly mismatched opponents – technologically armed industrial state forces against often poorly armed non-state actors – yet it is the latter that have often either prevailed or else turned a military victory into a political disaster for the victors. As we have just noted, both the French and the US forces were considered superior to any fielded by North Vietnam, yet both ended up defeated. None the less, we still tend to deem the conventional force the better and stronger, largely because we have a need for certitude of force strength, especially when entering into a conflict. In many ways this is a throwback to precisely the same trends of thought prevalent in public and military circles alike before the Great War, when numbers, technology and industry were deemed proof of superior military capacity. Such thinking was not useful then, and is no less a mistake now.

Still, our natural inclination is to measure: before commencing battle we want to know what we have, what the opponent has and whether or not we have enough to achieve our objective. We tend to measure potential military force by counting the men, ships, tanks and aircraft of all sides and we compare one inventory with another, measuring the balance of power accordingly. Quantifying is not necessarily an illogical method of assessment since there are few other objective measures, but comparing inventories can lead to dangerously simplistic judgements at the outset. Likewise, measuring the effect of the application of military force in or after a battle is nearly impossible, yet we tend to do so by counting the dead and destroyed equipment on all sides. Provided this is done honestly – the dead and destroyed are part of the opponent's inventory, and you know what they started with – this can be a good measure of local and tactical success, but it gives little indication as to the overall effect on the ability of any military force to either apply or resist an opponent's force. In other words, it gives little indication as to the true capability of a force – in which the opponents must be considered in relationship to each other not just as inventories but also, and probably most importantly, as dynamic bodies, each with imaginations, resources and above all a will to win. Again, these assessments can never be absolute: the power of a bomb may be known, but the power of the force applying it is different in each set of circumstances.

At base, therefore, because there is no such thing as a generic force, there is also no absolute measure of the strength or power of a force. First, because even with advanced technology, it is ultimately human: real people operate all the platforms, systems and weapons and real people direct them. A force is therefore an organic unit with a body, a mind and a will. You can count soldiers, weapons and equipment, but that will give you an idea only of the potential power of a force, not of its true capability. And that is due to the second issue, which is the very nature of battle as an adversarial activity, emanating from confrontations apparent and potential. There is always an opposing side, whether potential – as in the case of a standing army not engaged in a specific activity – or a real enemy. A measure of a force is therefore always in comparison to the one opposing, it is never absolute nor a possession. Or as the philosopher Michel Foucault discusses in *Discipline and Punish*: power is a relationship, not a possession. The power of a military force is composed of three related factors: the means – both men and materiel; the way they are used – doctrine, organization, and purpose; and the will that sustains them in adversity. In the combination of these three lies the true potential of a force, its overall *capability*, which can be assessed rather than measured – but it is not an exact science, for the two reasons given above.

In discussing Clausewitz in Part I of this book, we found that he effectively reflected on power as a relationship in war when he defined the trial of strength and the clash of wills as the two basic components. However, the quotation in full throws even more light on the issue:

If we desire to defeat the enemy, we must proportion our efforts to his powers of resistance. This is expressed by the product of two factors which cannot be separated, namely, *the sum of available means* and *the strength of the Will*. The sum of the available means may be estimated in a measure, as it depends (although not entirely) upon numbers; but the strength of volition is more difficult to determine, and can only be estimated to a certain extent by the strength of the motives.*

In this way the relationship is the balance struck in battle between the sums of the *available means* of the two sides and the strengths of their *wills*. However, for me the missing factor is the way the means are used in contrast to the opponent, and whether or not there is the will to use the means in that way. It is the business of the general to devise the way to use his means within the will of his political masters and his force so as to defeat his opponent. As Clausewitz notes, the trial of strength is really a matter of numbers, of examining the inventories of the opposing sides, but as we can see from the story of David and Goliath, the quantity, size and kinetic power of the means alone are not sufficient: it is the way they are used in relation to the opponent that makes the difference. As such, the potential strength of a force for the trial of strength can be understood as the product of its inventories – its means – and how they are used, the way.

Much the same applies to the clash of wills. The will to win is the paramount factor in any battle: without the political will and leadership to create and sustain the force and direct it to achieving its objective come what may, no military force can triumph in the face of a more determined opponent. On the battlefield we call this will morale, the spirit that triumphs in the face of adversity – and it is crucial. At the political and strategic levels the reward is defined in terms of the political purpose and the strategic objective: the grand prizes. However, as one enters the arena of the tactical battle, these objectives appear the more distant and relative. In battle men fight to kill before they are killed, and for objectives they think are worth losing their lives for. These tend in the extreme to be emotional and abstract objectives such as race, creed, honour, regiment or group. In the First World War, for example, trench life on the western front was totally detached from the outside world, and the comradeship between men was one of the most sustaining factors. In many battles it was this comradeship that propelled men or kept them in the battle, in support of their brothers in arms. The will to triumph in the face of an opponent in

* *On War*, ch. 1, bk 1 (Penguin edn) pp. 104–5; italics appear in the original.

adversity on the battlefield is called morale, and it is a product in the first instance of leadership, discipline, comradeship and self-respect. A high level of morale is a requirement of any battle-winning force. The difference in motivation between the political will and the morale of the force and the difference between the political objective and the objective that men are actually fighting for and are willingly dying for are potential strategic weaknesses. The more closely the motivation and the objectives between the levels can be aligned, the better. A clear example of misalignment in my lifetime can be seen in the Algerian war, which is discussed below. The morale, or fighting spirit, of the Foreign Legion and the *Paras* was never in doubt, but the will of metropolitan France to continue with the use of the means in the way they were being employed, evaporated. Political motivation and morale diverged to such an extent that de Gaulle withdrew from Algeria and the generals mutinied.

Throughout these pages we have seen how political will is an essential ingredient to success in war. The will to triumph, to carry the risks and bear the costs, to gain the reward of victory, is immense; as Napoleon had it, 'The moral is to the physical as three to one.' And indeed, in assessing capability we should weight this factor accordingly. But as with the means and the trial of strength, here too the way is important: the way the force is being used will have a direct impact on the will to take the risk, bear the burden and endure to the end. And once again the way is the business of the general: he must have the confidence of both his command and his political masters that he knows the way. And so, having analysed and understood the necessary components, we can finally attempt to assess the overall capability of a force as a product of the trial of strength and a clash of wills: the means multiplied by the way multiplied by the way multiplied by the will times three. For those of a mathematical bent I express it as a formula:

Capability = Means x Way^2 x 3 Will

But always remember Foucault's dictum: power is not a possession but a relationship. So we must only ever understand the capability of a force as being relative to that of its opponent. We must therefore assess the capability of each, and then compare the two.

I use the mathematical formulation to illustrate the complexity of judging a force's true capability as opposed to counting its inventories. It allows an assessment of the other factors, the role of the leaders in particular, in prosecuting a conflict or confrontation in the face of the opponent's actions. Indeed, seen this way it is clear that the capability of a force is the product of all three factors compared to the opponent's; if any one of them is zero there is no capability. As we will see, one of the endemic problems of our modern conflicts is the lack of political will to employ force rather than deploy forces – meaning will is close to zero – which is why many military interventions fail: the force capability is voided. Equally, the means of war, particularly the availability of manpower, are crucial: there must be at least one man or once again the capability will be zero. To go in the other direction it is well to remember Lenin's dictum that 'quantity has a quality of its own'.

If we now apply this formula to the Vietnam War, we can see that the North Vietnamese found a way to employ their relatively meagre means against the US forces in such a way that negated their far better equipped and trained industrial forces and technological capabilities. This led to the collapse of the US will, a factor that voided the force capability. In Malaya in the 1950s, the British found a way to use their means that not only matched the will of the forces and the people at home, but also the majority of the Malaysian people. Denied the support of the people, the communist terrorists found their way inadequate and abandoned their goal.

In overall terms, the capability calculation could be used to explain the outcome of a battle between two opposing forces – but probably no more, because it is very difficult to measure the way and the will before the event. Indeed, great efforts will be made by both sides to conceal this information from the other, by any means. For once at war, and as we have seen from Napoleon, pre-battle is part of war, the adversaries do not have to play by the same rules. And Napoleon, being a prime example of a true commander, systematically imposed his own rules and preferences on his opponents, to their disadvantage, forcing them to fight on his terms. That is a mark of real generalship, since it is based on the deep understanding that wars are not competitions: to be second is to lose. That is why a general must estimate the true capability of his force before he enters battle, even if he can only have total control over the way, being dependent on the political level above him for a proper supply of the means and the political will to win.

A classic example of the breakdown between the political and military levels, which absolutely voided the capability of the military force, was the Algerian war. Algeria had been made a French Territory in 1830 and in 1848 was made a *département* attached to France. In 1954, encouraged by the news from Indo-China of the French defeat in Dien Bien Phu and also of concessions made by France in Tunisia, the Comité Révolutionnaire d'Unité et d'Action (CRUA) set about planning a revolution to evict the French from Algeria. Their plan provided for the creation of a political front, the Front de Libération National (FLN), which would command a resistance army: the Armée de Libération Nationale (ALN). Their goal was to obtain full independence by creating a general atmosphere of fear at home through the launch of a nationwide insurrection, whilst appealing to world opinion abroad and building a political platform as the future nationalist government.

The FLN drew chiefly on the Viet Minh as a model for organization, as well as on some principles of the French Resistance (indeed, some of its fighters had fought the Nazis a decade earlier in the name of France): the leadership remained collective and fighting groups were small. Operations were directed by a zone *wilaya* command, which acted under the overall command of the centralized CRUA. The ALN was deemed itself too weak to secure and hold on to a large geographical area as a sanctuary, as the Viet Minh had done in North Tonkin; as a consequence the FLN's tactics were based on the classic guerrilla model.

On 1 November 1954, FLN guerrillas launched attacks in various parts of Algeria against military installations, police posts, warehouses, communications facilities, and public utilities. From Cairo, the FLN broadcast a proclamation calling on Muslims in Algeria to join in a national struggle for the restoration of the Algerian state, sovereign, democratic, and social, within the framework of the principles of Islam. The French authorities in Algeria were not fully prepared to meet this challenge, and believed they were faced only with a small-scale revolt. Their military response to the initial outbreaks of killings and bombings was limited but inappropriate, and a number of political leaders were detained and interrogated ruthlessly. This alienated many of them to the point of driving them directly into the FLN camp. During 1956 and 1957 the ALN successfully applied hit-and-run tactics according to the classic canons of guerrilla warfare. Specializing in ambushes and night raids, and avoiding direct contact with superior French firepower, the internal forces targeted army patrols, military encampments, police posts and colonial farms, mines and factories, as well as transportation and communications facilities. Kidnapping was commonplace, as were the ritual murder and mutilation of captured French military, *colons* (French settlers in Algeria), suspected collaborators and traitors. At first, the revolutionary forces targeted only Muslim officials of the colonial regime; later, they coerced or even killed those civilians who refused to support them.

In order to increase the level of international and domestic French attention to their struggle, the FLN decided to bring the conflict into the cities. The most notable manifestation of the new urban campaign was the battle of Algiers, which began on 30 September 1956, when three women placed bombs at three sites including the office of Air France. The campaign escalated in the period following, when the ALN carried out an average of 800 shootings and bombings per month through the spring of 1957, resulting in many civilian casualties, and mounted a series of political actions including a general strike. However, although the FLN was successful in engendering an atmosphere of fear within both the French and the native communities in Algeria, its reliance on coercive tactics suggested it had not inspired the majority of the Muslim people to revolt against French colonial rule. Furthermore, the loss of competent field commanders both on the battlefield and through defections, internal rivalries and political purges created difficulties for the movement. None the less, the FLN gradually gained control of certain sectors of the Aurès, the Kabylie and other mountainous areas. In these locations the ALN established a simple but effective – although frequently temporary – military administration that was able to collect taxes and food and to recruit manpower, even though it never managed to hold large fixed positions.

Despite complaints from the military command in Algiers, the French government was reluctant for many months to admit that the Algerian situation was out of control, and that what was viewed officially as an internal pacification operation had escalated dramatically. However, by 1956 two decrees provided for the recall of conscripts and the extension of compulsory national service, and by August 1956 the number of French soldiers in Algeria totalled 390,000, rising to a peak of 415,000 in late 1957. The French military, many of whom had fought in Indo-China, believed they understood the situation they confronted – and set out to apply what they thought they had learned there. In 1956, General Lorrillot introduced the system of *quadrillage* – a mix between static garrisons and mobile pursuit groups – to contain the ALN, which in time became very effective. He applied the principle of collective responsibility to villages suspected of sheltering, supplying or in any way cooperating with the guerrillas. Villages that could not be reached by mobile units were subject to aerial bombardment. The French also initiated a programme of concentrating large segments of the rural population, including whole villages, in camps under military supervision to prevent them from aiding the rebels – or, according to the official explanation, to protect them from FLN extortion. But it was in the battle of Algiers that their methods achieved the greatest prominence: General Jacques Massu, commanding the 10th Parachute Division, who was instructed to use whatever methods were necessary to restore order in the city, frequently fought terrorism with terrorism. Using his paratroopers, he broke the general strike and systematically eradicated FLN cells.

The French eventually won the battle in military terms, but the FLN had succeeded in showing its ability to strike at the heart of French Algeria. Moreover, the publicity given to the brutal methods used by the army to win the battle of Algiers, including the widespread use of torture, cast doubt in France about its role in Algeria. In 1958 the French shifted tactics from dependence on *quadrillage* to the use of mobile forces deployed on huge search-and-destroy missions against ALN strongholds. Within a year, major rebel resistance appeared to be suppressed. By the end of 1958 the ALN was approaching military defeat and by mid 1959 that defeat was almost total. However, in political and international terms the FLN remained unbeaten; indeed, political developments had already overtaken the French army's successes. In Algeria, military repression had destroyed any chances that might have remained of a dialogue between moderate Muslims and the French establishment. In France, public opinion was growing weary of this conscript war, whilst the constitution and the inherent weaknesses of the Fourth Republic prevented any liberal political solution. On the international level, France's major allies deserted it.

Increasingly, both in France and in Algeria, thoughts turned towards General de Gaulle, seen as the saviour figure that could resolve the Algerian problem. Having left office in 1946 and distanced himself from the politics of the Fourth Republic, in 1958 de Gaulle was asked to take up the premiership – and at his request was invested with full powers for six months, but his stance on Algeria was ambiguous. None the less, the colony was invited to vote on the new French constitution, which was approved by an overwhelming majority in both France and Algeria. The FLN responded by creating the Provisional Government of the Algerian Republic (GPRA), with the veteran nationalist leader Ferhat Abbas at its head. De Gaulle attempted to reach a settlement through a proposed 'paix des braves', but the GPRA held firm. The Constantine Plan, a detailed five-year economic plan for Algeria to reduce the gap between the Algerian French départements and those in continental France, was denounced by the GPRA as a new form of colonialism. In 1959, to avoid condemnation by the UN General Assembly, de Gaulle recognized Algeria's right to self-determination.

The severe drag on labour, morale and resources brought about by events in Algeria divided France as escalating tensions at home brought it to the brink of civil war. Meanwhile, the French had begun secret negotiations with the FLN. In Algeria, in April 1961, elements of the French army rebelled under the leadership of four generals. The 'generals putsch', as it came to be known, intended to seize control of Algeria and to topple de Gaulle in Paris. Units of the Foreign Legion offered support, and the well-armed Organisation de l'Armée Secrète (OAS) coordinated the participation of white colons. Although a brief fear of invasion swept Paris, the revolt collapsed in four days largely because the air force, the navy and the majority of French army units remained loyal to the government.

The generals putsch marked the turning point in the official attitude towards the Algerian war. De Gaulle was now prepared to write off the *colons*, and talks with the FLN reopened at Evian in May 1961. After several false starts, the French government decreed that a cease-fire would take effect on 19 March 1962 and in the Accords d'Evian, signed in March 1962, recognized the sovereignty of the Algerian state.

The Algerian war was a confrontation between French colonial rule and the people of Algeria. The French achieved tactical successes but at no stage did they win the people's will in sufficient degree to keep Algeria part of metropolitan France. Moreover, the tactical successes came at huge political cost, which ultimately nullified the utility of the military force. Unlike the other conflicts that occurred in parallel to the Cold War confrontation, it did not become subsumed within it – but it ultimately did evolve into a confrontation and near conflict between the French political and military levels. It was this confrontation, more than any local skirmish or military event, which voided the capability of the military force – and brought a rapid political resolution to both the confrontation and the conflict between France and the people of Algeria. For the second time in a decade, and despite their obviously superior forces and industrial capability, the French failed to triumph in a war amongst the people.

The parallel conflicts of the Cold War were many. The old imperial powers' withdrawal from empire did not necessitate military force in all cases, whilst in others it was used more or less within the parameters laid out in the conflicts discussed in this part of the book. These all reflect the evolution of the new paradigm of war amongst the people, but it is also necessary to note that at the same time there were a number of conflicts that remained firmly rooted within the old paradigm. To an extent this was so because, whilst in some cases nuclear capability on one side was either known or assumed, its use was not considered a serious possibility – meaning escalation did not pose a catastrophic threat. Chief amongst these were the India–Pakistan conflict over Kashmir, the Iran–Iraq war, and the ongoing Arab–Israeli conflict. And whilst there were definite attempts to subsume all three within the wider confrontation of the Cold War, with the two blocs taking sides, in essence they remained local if extremely malignant events. They also all share the distinction of failing to achieve a military strategic decision; indeed, as we shall see, in the Arab–Israeli case industrial war gave way to war amongst the people.

The Kashmir conflict, which erupted upon Indian independence and its division into two states in 1947, was and remains a confrontation over a specific territory which has risen three times to a strategic-level conflict, and has crossed over many times to conflict at the tactical level in local skirmishes. After 1998, however, when both sides tested their nuclear devices to deter the other, skirmishes largely ceased – though tension rose to the strategic level of confrontation once, in 2002, when a Pakistani-backed extremist bombed the Indian parliament. But tensions eased and the two sides then began serious negotiations over the disputed territory, realizing that war within the industrial paradigm can take place only if both or all sides within it accept the limits of *not* going nuclear. Both India and Pakistan have the manpower, the industrial base and the ideological bent for old-fashioned industrial war. However, neither can give a guarantee of not escalating to the nuclear level. They are therefore locked in a strategic confrontation, very similar to the Cold War, which may now be moving towards a resolution.

The appalling number of one and a half million dead in the eight years of the Iran–Iraq war (1980–88) bears witness to a true industrial-scale conflict, at least in terms of manpower. It was also conducted in a relatively small area, the easily defended ground of the Tigris–Euphrates valley, and in conditions which recall the western front in the First World War. Large volumes of materiel were expended over a lengthy period of time, and both states were totally focused upon the war and the search for victory. None the less, this industrial-style war also proved to be without operational or strategic results, and eventually petered out in a settlement.

Both the Kashmir conflict and the Iran–Iraq war can also be understood as industrial owing to the hard objectives at their heart: they were and are between armies over territory, rather than about the will and intentions of people. The third major confrontation, which has on occasion risen to strategic conflict of industrial nature, is the Arab–Israeli one; indeed, as noted at the very start of this book, probably the last battles in which armoured forces manoeuvred against each other were fought in 1973 on the Golan Heights and in the Sinai desert. This confrontation began in 1947 and is still in being. However, whilst it started out as a clear confrontation over hard objectives, it then evolved into a far more complex one over intentions – amongst the people. There are relatively short periods which we label 'wars', but the whole conflict from its inception to the present day has been a period of killing and violence, as each side has sought to advance its purpose by force of arms. This convoluted process is one of the more illuminating examples of the interaction of confrontation and conflict; and while I list it as having its roots in industrial war, the entire period from 1947 to the present gives an example of the new paradigm.

On 29 November 1947 the United Nations General Assembly endorsed a plan for the partition of Palestine, which provided for the creation of an Arab state and a Jewish state, with Jerusalem to be placed under international status. Heavy fighting immediately broke out as the local Arab leadership rejected the plan outright. On 15 May 1948 the United Kingdom relinquished its Mandate over Palestine; on the day before, in anticipation, David Ben Gurion had declared Israel an independent nation. The United States and the Soviet Union, followed by many others, granted diplomatic recognition to Israel. The Arab League, which had been founded in 1945 to coordinate policy between the Arab states, reacted promptly. Almost immediately the Palestinian Arabs, supported by Lebanese, Syrian, Iraqi, Egyptian and Transjordanian troops, opened hostilities against Israel's newly formed Israel Defence Force (IDF). The Israelis and the Arab League found themselves in conflict, the latter seeking a strategic resolution by force of arms: the destruction of the state of Israel.

Eventually the IDF succeeded in driving out the armies of neighbouring Arab nations and securing its frontiers through three major offensive operations, and in 1949 Israel signed separate ceasefire agreements with Egypt, Lebanon, Transjordan and Syria. The operational-level successes enabled Israel to draw its own borders, which included 70 per cent of Mandatory Palestine, instead of the 55 per cent it had initially been allocated by the UN plan. The Gaza Strip and the West Bank were occupied by Egypt and Transjordan, respectively. In spite of Israel's operational victory, neither side had gained a strategic decision, and the situation returned to a state of strategic confrontation. However, the confrontation was underpinned by tactical conflicts as each side raided across borders. In 1956 the number of skirmishes between Israel and Egypt increased, with Egyptian *fedayeen* irregulars making frequent incursions into Israeli territory and Israel responding by launching raids into Egyptian territory. Egypt, under the leadership of President Gamal Abdel Nasser, blockaded the Gulf of Aqaba and closed the Suez Canal to Israeli shipping. In July of that year Nasser nationalized the canal, a vital trade route to the east in which the British held a 44 per cent stake. In so doing he increased and expanded the confrontation at the strategic level to include Britain and France, the French fearing that closure of the waterway would halt shipments of petroleum to western Europe from the Persian Gulf. In the months that followed, and against a complex background of events, Israel, France and Britain entered into a secret alliance, planning to resolve the confrontation by taking the canal back and reducing Egypt's area of military influence.

On 29 October 1956 Israel invaded the Gaza Strip and the Sinai peninsula and made rapid progress towards the Canal Zone. The United Kingdom and France launched operation Musketeer to force the reopening of the canal on 31 October; Nasser responded by sinking all forty ships then present in the canal, closing it to further shipping until early 1957. On 5 November 1956, an airborne and amphibious assault by British and French forces seized the canal. The operation was decisive but it lacked a strategic context, and soon turned into a political and diplomatic disaster. The British and French came under intense criticism from the Third World nations and the Soviet Union. Moreover, whilst condemning Soviet repression in Hungary which occurred simultaneously, the US refused to condone the embarrassing actions of its main European allies in Egypt. In a Cold War context, the Americans also feared the conflict might escalate, especially after the USSR intervened on the Egyptian side. By exerting considerable financial and diplomatic pressure, the Eisenhower administration imposed a ceasefire on Britain and France, and the invading forces withdrew in March 1957. Their role was taken over by United Nations Emergency Force I (UNEF I), the very first United Nations peacekeeping force, established by the very first emergency special session of the General Assembly, which was held from 1 to 10 November 1956. Suez was not a war: it was two military operations, mounted by Israel and then Britain and France. The latter were defeated in the confrontation with Egypt, since force had no utility in the context in which it was being used. Force was used strategically with the intention of changing Nasser's intentions, and even to replace him for a more pliant leader. This failed. Operationally, force was used to occupy and safeguard the canal. It achieved the first of the operational aims and arguably failed in the latter, since forty wrecks in the waterway do not provide a free and open passage. The strategic context to give these acts value, which would have translated the hard objective of occupying the canal into an effect that achieved the malleable strategic objective of changing intentions, was lacking. On the other hand, Israel had relieved the confrontational pressure at the strategic level and with the imposition of the UN force was also free of tactical conflicts in the Sinai. To this extent its use of force had been successful since its objectives in both the confrontation and the conflict were related to the holding of the territory of the state – which they achieved.

In May 1967 Egypt requested the withdrawal of UNEF I and Nasser immediately began re-militarizing the Sinai. He then proceeded to close the Straits of Tiran to Israeli shipping, thus blockading the Israeli port of Eilat at the northern end of the Gulf of Aqaba. This was regarded as a *casus belli* by the Israelis, who were also threatened by Syria in the north. Negotiations with the US to reopen the Straits of Tiran failed. Both Egypt and Syria made preparations for war, but Israel executed a pre-emptive attack: on 5 June 1967 the Israeli air force destroyed the Egyptian air force, and gained air superiority for the rest of the war. In a matter of days Israeli forces scored amazing success: in the southern operation they occupied Gaza and the Sinai up to the east bank of the Suez Canal; in the centre, Jerusalem and the West Bank of the Jordan were taken from the Jordanians; and in the northern operation the Golan Heights that dominate the eastern approaches to the Sea of Galilee were seized from the Syrians. On 11

June a ceasefire was signed and the Six Day War was over – but the confrontation continued. Israel had won a series of stunning operational victories: the IDF's training, organization and equipment were models for the successful prosecution of high-speed-manoeuvre warfare. The forces opposing it had been destroyed. Not only had the state of Israel been defended by the strategy of an offensive defence but it had been expanded: its territory grew fourfold and included about 1 million Arabs in the newly captured territories. Approximately 300,000 Palestinians fled to Jordan, where they contributed to the growing unrest. These Palestinians in the occupied territories and in the refugee camps were in the great majority to become supporters of the Palestinian Liberation Organization (PLO), founded in 1964, whose 1968 charter called for the liquidation of Israel. Following the war, UN Security Council Resolution 242 was passed, which called both for a 'just and lasting peace in which every State in the area can live in security' and for Israeli withdrawal from the occupied territories. It has become the basic text of Arab–Israeli relations.

Israel's operational victories had returned the situation to the ante-bellum strategic confrontation, though with one profound difference: Israel was now in confrontation with a people rather than with defined states. Since the very core of the confrontation between Israel and its Arab enemies had been, and to a limited extent still is, the very existence of the Jewish state, up to the Six Day War it had been sufficient to have a strategy of existence to provide the context for all Israel's military actions: to attack, or if attacked to punish, any and every threat to the right of Jews to exist in a state of their own, and to conduct these actions both on or beyond the borders of the state. The military objectives of this strategy had been to defeat and deter guerrilla raids or to defeat the neighbouring Arab forces. Following the war such simple and hard objectives were no longer sufficient, since a substantial part of the confrontation was rapidly to become a competition with another people, not a defined state, over their existence in the same space as Israel. Winning the trial of strength had served very well up to this point, but from now on, with the new confrontation with the Palestinian people, winning the clash of wills had to be the primary objective. As of 1967, therefore, Israel needed a comprehensive strategy to handle this new confrontation, and to remember, as they for many years failed to, what the founding fathers of the IDF learned from their origins under the British Mandate: that it is the occupied who hold the military initiative.

For the next six years the confrontation between Israel and its Arab neighbours and the Palestinians continued, yet it also showed some signs of becoming part of the greater Cold War confrontation. With the help of Soviet supplies and advisors, Egypt managed to redeem its material losses from the Six Day War much more quickly than expected, and between 1968 and 1970 a war of attrition raged between Egypt and Israel: a constant crossing from confrontation to conflict at the tactical level. A ceasefire agreement was reached on 7 August 1970. Nasser died in September and was succeeded by his vice-president, Anwar Sadat, who respected the ceasefire but kept in mind Nasser's dream to liberate the canal. On 6 October 1973, the holy day of Yom Kippur in the Jewish calendar, Egypt and Syria launched operation Badr ('full moon' in Arabic), a coordinated surprise assault against Israel. As already noted, Sadat's aim in mounting the operation was to create a situation in which negotiations could take place to Egypt's advantage. Syrian forces attacked fortifications in the Golan Heights whilst Egyptian forces attacked fortifications along the Suez Canal and on the Sinai peninsula. On the Golan Heights, approximately 108 Israeli tanks faced an onslaught of 1,400 Syrian tanks. On the Suez Canal, hundreds of Israeli defenders were attacked by 80,000 Egyptians. Caught unprepared, the IDF initially lost ground and suffered heavy casualties. At least nine Arab states, including four non-Middle-Eastern nations, actively aided the Egyptian–Syrian war effort by supplying aircraft, tanks, troops and financial resources.

Israel mobilized its reserves and with the support of the United States, which organized an airlift to supply ammunition and critical stores, mounted a series of brilliant counter-attacks. By the time a ceasefire was called the IDF were on the outskirts of Damascus, and had crossed the Suez Canal and encircled the Egyptian Third Army. Despite the IDF's ultimate success on the battlefield, the war was considered a diplomatic and military failure in Israel, with nearly 2,700 Israeli soldiers left dead on the field of battle. In Egypt and Syria, despite the narrowly averted military collapse, the October war was perceived as a victory: the 'impregnable' Bar Lev Line along the Suez

Canal had been broken, Egyptian troops had taken a foothold on the eastern side of the canal, the Israeli air force had suffered serious losses, and the myth of the invincibility of Israeli arms had been smashed in the Sinai and the Golan Heights. The IDF had again triumphed operationally and preserved the borders of the state – yet the strategic confrontation still remained unresolved. Moreover, the fierce battles had shown the limitations of industrial war even to Israel, a society prepared to conduct it: manpower was not there to be consumed at industrial rates, nor were the equipment and ammunition available to sustain battle at high intensity for long. Both sides had needed their respective backers in the USSR and the US in order to sustain the war effort – and whilst both superpowers seemed willing to cooperate for their own Cold War interests, they were also wary since it was clear this confrontation was one that had the potential to spin out of control – affecting the entire Middle East and possibly further afield, whilst also endangering the supply of oil. It was the superpowers who therefore reined in the Arabs and Israelis, returning the conflict clearly to a more manageable confrontation. And in the months that followed the Yom Kippur War, US secretary of state Henry Kissinger mounted a diplomatic offensive in order to help stabilize the situation in the Middle East. On 8 January 1974, Egypt and Israel signed an initial military disengagement agreement. Egypt regained control of all territory west of the Suez Canal and of the whole of the eastern bank. Israel, although withdrawing thirteen miles east of the canal, was left in control of the rest of Sinai, including the town of Sharm el-Sheikh, which commands the Straits of Tiran. A second Egyptian–Israeli disengagement agreement was formally signed in Geneva in September 1975, in which Israel vacated further Egyptian territory and assets. Kissinger also managed to bring about an Agreement on Disengagement between Syria and Israel in May 1974, thus ending eighty-one days of artillery duels on the Golan front. Israel withdrew from the territory captured in October 1973 and from some areas occupied since the Six Day War, including the town of Quneitra. Ever since, the line has been policed by a UN force, to the apparent satisfaction of both sides.

During the next six years and with the active involvement of US diplomacy Israel and Egypt resolved their long-running strategic confrontation. In November 1977, President Sadat flew to Jerusalem, the first visit by an Arab head of state to Israel. This initiated peace negotiations between Israel and Egypt that went on sporadically through 1977 and into 1978, when the sides reached agreement in two areas. Israel agreed to withdraw from all of the Sinai within three years, and to dismantle its air bases near the Gulf of Aqaba and the town of Yamit. Egypt promised full diplomatic relations with Israel, and allowed Israel passage through the Suez Canal, the Strait of Tiran, and the Gulf of Aqaba. The second agreement was a framework establishing a format for the conduct of negotiations for the establishment of an autonomous regime in the West Bank and Gaza to settle the Palestinian question. These two agreements led to a negotiated peace between Israel and Egypt in 1979, the first between Israel and any of its Arab neighbours. For their efforts, Sadat and Prime Minister Begin of Israel were awarded the 1978 Nobel Peace Prize. In the Arab world, however, many saw Sadat's recognition of Israel and his rupture of the Arab front as an act of treason. He was assassinated in 1981.

Meanwhile the confrontation with the people of Palestine was gaining prominence. The PLO, having committed a series of terrorist attacks against Israelis abroad, including the murder of eleven Israeli athletes at the 1972 Munich Olympic Games and the hijacking in 1976 of an Air France plane to Entebbe, had established itself in Lebanon. From their bases on the southern border, Palestinian fighters mounted intermittent cross-border attacks against both military and civilian targets in Israel. In March 1978, after the hijacking of a bus by Palestinians, Israel launched a major military incursion into southern Lebanon, which prompted a formal US statement on the concern for the 'Territorial Integrity of Lebanon'. On 19 March 1978 the UN Security Council adopted Resolution 425 calling for Israeli withdrawal and establishing an international peacekeeping force for South Lebanon, the United Nations Interim Force in Lebanon (UNIFIL), which remains in Lebanon to this day. PLO bases in southern Lebanon remained active and the cross-border cycle of attacks and retaliation continued. In 1982, Israeli troops invaded Lebanon for a second time. The Israeli operational objectives were to destroy the PLO's military power in southern Lebanon and to create a security zone there. The strategic military objectives were to eradicate the PLO's military, political and economic hold over Lebanon, and evict Syrian forces, so as to facilitate the creation of a Christian-dominated Lebanon which would sign a peace treaty with Israel and thus end the confrontation over its borders.

On 6 June 1982, operation Peace for the Galilee was launched. Israeli troops soon reached Beirut and proceeded to besiege the city, where the seat of the PLO lay. Localized Syrian attempts to thwart the advance were quelled and both countries chose to avoid more than tactical-level conflict. In August 1982 Ambassador Philip Habib, the US special envoy to the Middle East, negotiated the withdrawal of Yasser Arafat and his PLO forces from Lebanon to Tunisia. A multinational force (MNF) was created to supervise the evacuation, which was rapidly completed by 10 September, and to provide protection to the Palestinian civilians remaining in Lebanon. Over the next few weeks the situation disintegrated. On 15 September Israeli military forces occupied the Muslim section of West Beirut after the assassination of President Bashir Gemayel, the recently elected Christian president of Lebanon with whom Israel had expected to reach a settlement. Two days later, some of Gemayel's followers massacred hundreds of Palestinians in two camps guarded by Israel at Sabra and Shatila. Since the US had pledged to Arafat that the Israelis would protect the Palestinian civilians remaining in Beirut after the evacuation of the PLO fighters, President Reagan hurriedly arranged for the return of the multinational military contingent to provide some level of security.

During the autumn of 1982 there were active negotiations amongst the United States, Israel and Lebanon over the withdrawal of Israeli forces and the terms of a possible treaty between Lebanon and Israel. An agreement ending the state of war between the two countries and providing for a phased Israeli withdrawal from Lebanon was signed by Lebanon and Israel in May 1983 but Syria declined to discuss the withdrawal of its troops. In June 1985 Israel withdrew most of its remaining troops from Lebanon, leaving a small residual Israeli force and an Israeli-supported militia (the so-called South Lebanon Army) in southern Lebanon. These forces established a security buffer zone three to five miles wide along the length of the Lebanese–Israeli border in order to protect Israel from attacks launched from Lebanon.

Israel had failed to resolve the strategic confrontation by the use of force. Initially, its operations had appeared successful, and the tactical engagements had all gone Israel's way, but the tactical victories did not amount to operational success. Over the years the IDF had developed as a force that attacked so as to rapidly defeat those threatening Israel's borders, and throughout its history it had been mounting tactical raids to pre-empt or punish raids against their settlements. Occasionally the whole military was committed en masse to achieve operational successes, as in 1948, 1956, 1967 and 1973. However, in 1982 in Lebanon the IDF was committed to achieve operational and strategic objectives that concerned the opponents' intentions rather than their forces. Its forces entered into a complex theatre of a dysfunctional state fighting amongst contending peoples as to its governance. This theatre also contained the forces of another state, Syria, with which Israel was already in confrontation, and of the Palestinians, who had no state and with whom there was another confrontation. None of these opposing forces engaged with the IDF at the operational level, whilst the tactical objectives and the manner of their achievement failed to amount to the theatre-level condition which Israel desired. Within Israel the invasion of Lebanon did not have the popular support of the earlier big operations out of the state, whilst to the enemy the IDF was shown to be less of a threat than before. The impressive armoured machine had first been restrained by the broken terrain of Lebanon and then, with its head firmly stuck in the urban area of Beirut, had proved to be more vulnerable than the street fighters had anticipated. And from a diplomatic perspective, the world at large did not see a small people defending themselves but a powerful regional player intervening and making an already dangerous situation worse.

After 1982 Israel remained in confrontations with its enemies, those with states around its borders remaining relatively stable but that with the people growing in intensity. In December 1987 collective Palestinian frustration erupted in a popular revolt against Israeli rule known as the *intifada* (uprising), which involved demonstrations, strikes, riots and violence. At first a spontaneous outburst, the *intifada* developed into an organized rebellion. The stoning of Israeli security forces and civilians by young men and boys and the reaction of heavily armed men in heavily armed vehicles often observed beating isolated and unarmed captives became the symbols of the *intifada*. The Israeli army, trained and organized to achieve the hard objectives of interstate conflicts and confrontations, lost many tactical engagements and every operational and strategic confrontation of the *intifada*'s strategy of provocation and propaganda of the deed.

The force was unsuited to its new purpose. Consider the infantry, an arm whose purpose is to close with the enemy and to destroy him. It has always been so, but in our times infantry is frequently carried into battle in armoured vehicles so that it keeps up with the pace of the battle fought with tanks, aircraft and modern communications, and is protected in this journey to its objective. But in the case of the *intifada* – and many other examples of war amongst the people – who was the enemy to engage and destroy? In technical terms it was the terrorists amongst the Palestinian people – but they were of and within the people. And if every Palestinian were to be treated as an enemy and subjected to the techniques of close combat, every Palestinian would undoubtedly become your enemy. The options were either meticulous intelligence-led searches for the enemy in a very hostile environment, or collective destruction. Having chosen the first option, the great strength of the IDF, its manoeuvrable armoured mass and its firepower, was of little value; instead it became dependent on the infantry, an arm that had been neither selected, trained nor equipped for the task. In the theatre of this war amongst the people the audience saw a brutal occupying force suppressing the legitimate desire of a people to rule themselves. Nevertheless, Israel's tactical measures to deal with this confrontation began to show success, but lacking a strategy other than to return to the status quo, and a comprehensive theatre or campaign plan to guide the choice of targets and to translate the tactical successes into victory, they suppressed rather than resolved the confrontation.

The *intifada* was remarkable for the organizing capabilities of its leadership. The successful Israeli pursuit of these leaders weakened their ability to resist the challenge of other Palestinian organizations such as Hamas and Jihadu al-Islamiyy, which were Islamic fundamentalist organizations – as opposed to the secular nationalist PLO – calling for the complete destruction of the Jewish state. Between 1989 and

1992, the '*intrafada*' between the opposing factions claimed the lives of hundreds of Palestinians. By 1992, with most of the Palestinian leadership behind bars, the *intifada* began to peter out. None the less, it had a marked impact on Israeli public opinion and policy making throughout the next decade, creating the impetus for the peace negotiations that were to take place in the following years. The *intifada* gave the Palestinians an identity they had not possessed before, either in their own minds or around the world, and the confidence to resist and to assert their identity in military acts. It also created a cadre of activists, some with extreme views, based in the West Bank and Gaza Strip, who were their own masters and not the servants of external agencies based in the Palestinian diaspora or in Arab states. This was reflected in the Madrid conference held in 1991 after the Gulf War, when all sides to the conflict and the wider Middle East were brought together to establish paths of negotiations – and the PLO was represented by Palestinian civilians acting on its behalf. The Palestinians thought they had won the clash of wills with Israel: to their thinking, their actions had collapsed the will of the Israeli people to continue on the path of conflict. They were correct in that Israeli public opinion had undergone a deep change, favouring a negotiated settlement over continued conflict. But they were also incorrect in that the victory in the clash of wills had not brought a victory in the trial of strength: Israel still had the massive force of an industrial army, and still saw it as the means for directly achieving its political ends.

The Arab–Israeli strategic confrontation continued in all its complexity. Thanks to considerable international diplomatic efforts and the willingness to negotiate, the Jordanians and the Israelis reached a resolution of their confrontation and signed a peace treaty on 26 October 1994. The situation in southern Lebanon continued to be one of tactical conflict, usually initiated by Hizbollah operating from Lebanese territory. The Golan Heights remained in Israel's hands with the small UN observer force maintaining the 'condition' of stability. The confrontation with the Palestinian people also moved, apparently toward resolution. In mid 1992 the Israelis contacted the Norwegian head of a European peace research institute in order to conduct a series of informal, secret talks between two Israeli academics and three senior PLO officials. The talks began in Oslo in January 1993 with the objective of drafting an informal document setting the basic principles for future peacemaking between Israel and the Palestinians. This willingness to negotiate made the prospect of a compromise possible. The Oslo meetings, upgraded to include senior Israeli diplomats and Norwegian foreign minister Johan Jorgen Holst, worked out the Oslo Accords, which were signed in Washington in September 1993. The Accords contained a set of mutually agreed-upon general principles regarding a five-year interim period of Palestinian self-rule. 'Permanent status issues' were deferred to later negotiations, to begin no later than the third year of the interim period. The PLO recognized the right of the state of Israel to exist in peace and security, and it also declared its commitment to the Middle East peace process and renounced the use of terrorism. In return, Israel recognized the PLO as the representative of the Palestinian people and declared its willingness to conduct negotiations with the PLO within the Madrid Middle East peace process. In May 1994, in Cairo, Israel and the PLO signed the Gaza–Jericho Agreement, which led to the establishment of the Palestinian Authority (PA). It looked as though the conditions had been created for the strategic confrontation to be resolved, but Israeli settlements continued to be founded and developed in the occupied territories and the terrorist organizations continued to develop their operations amongst the Palestinians. Worse still, the minds of the people on both sides had not been captured: their intentions did not wholly support developing the Accords into an agreed outcome. In November 1996 the prime minister of Israel, Yitzhak Rabin, was assassinated by an Israeli extremist. It was the start of another rapid downward spiral in the confrontation.

On the border with Lebanon the tactical conflict continued with a steady drain of Israeli casualties for no gain except that Israel remained in occupation of a security zone. There was a strong movement mounted from within Israel to withdraw, to cease the drain of casualties of occupation and to stand on the recognized borders of the state. Lebanon was recovering from its civil war and there was international pressure on Israel to honour its borders. Israel finally withdrew its forces in 1999, and the strategic confrontation with Lebanon was at an end. However, those with Syria, Hizbollah and the Palestinian-based terrorist organizations remained. Within the

Palestinian territories there was mounting public frustration with the corruption of the PA and its administrative ineptitude; at the same time there was anger and frustration with the continued expansion of Israeli settlements, despite promises to cease. In Israel there was waning confidence in the PA's ability to provide security on their borders and to deal with the terrorist groups operating from their territory. However, every time the IDF raided to secure Israel or imposed some measure or other in the name of security, it reinforced its negative image in the minds of the Palestinians and the world. The lame-duck PA was weakened further and the internal factions gained in power. Arafat learned, if he did not know already, to avoid accepting the identity of a state for his people, since to do so would have been to accept the responsibilities of state – responsibilities he and the PA were unable to discharge even had they wanted to.

In September 2000, sparked by Israeli prime minister Ariel Sharon's visit to the Temple Mount, a second *intifada* exploded. In two days it spread across Palestine and into Israel. Violence took hold in both state and territories, with suicide attacks in the former and IDF retaliation and clampdowns in the latter. The confrontation between the peoples of Palestine and Israel reached a new intensity of tactical-level conflict, with neither side able to turn the tactical successes to advantage operationally or strategically. By its tactical successes, Israel undoubtedly improved the security of its people, but in so doing it reinforced the opinion of those watching the theatre and the Palestinians that they were brutal occupiers. Equally, by using terrorism in the post-9/11 age the Palestinians reinforced negative images of themselves, especially in the US which is bent on the War Against Terror. As a result a stand-off has emerged in which the clash of wills is not being won by either side. Perhaps by retreating into the borders of 'Fortress Zion' with the Gaza withdrawal plan, and by leaving a stateless people without the infrastructure to manage or administer themselves, the situation will be created where the trial of strength, as long as it continues to be won, will serve to keep the strategic and theatre-level confrontations at the tactical level and on the other man's land.

The Arab–Israeli conflict has incorporated the three distinct periods discussed in this book: industrial war, the parallel conflicts of the Cold

War, and war amongst the people. Indeed, both *intifadas* are prime exponents of the new paradigm, and of the inadequacies of conventional forces and institutional thinking based on industrial war in dealing with such events. It is these matters to which Part III of this book is devoted.

PART THREE

War Amongst the People

7

Trends: Our Modern Operations

There is no specific date at which war amongst the people commenced. Its basic definition as a world of confrontations and conflicts emerged, as we have seen, in the aftermath of the Second World War, and assumed its forms from the antithesis to industrial war. But it became the dominant form of war at the end of the Cold War, although in reality industrial war had ceased to be a practical proposition with the invention of the atomic bomb. In the interim, as reflected in Part II, the parallel conflicts of the Cold War began to exhibit the trends of the new paradigm, each to a greater or lesser extent. It was only after 1991 that most conflicts reflected all the trends, for two major reasons. First, the end of the 'Great Confrontation' released the strictures within which nascent conflicts had been held by the interests of the two blocs. As we have already seen, many post-colonial confrontations within states or between the departing imperial powers and the local populations ended up being subsumed within the greater Cold War confrontation. But at the same time, other confrontations and conflicts had been kept in check by one of the blocs or a balance of power between the two. Once the blocs melted away these latent conflicts began to emerge – in many parts of the globe but especially in the Balkans and throughout great swathes of Africa – and in most cases they were intra- rather than interstate: amongst the people.

The second reason the new paradigm became dominant in 1991 was that it was the point at which the industrial army became effectively obsolete. For it was the Cold War, underpinned by mutually assured destruction, which had necessitated the maintenance of the structures and external appearance of the paradigm of interstate industrial war.

Once it was over, the true hollowness of the paradigm became evident: the West had won without a shot being fired. There had never been a war, only ever a confrontation which had never crossed over into a conflict, and at its end the Warsaw Pact collapsed together with the Soviet Union, and the prospect of total war between the blocs was removed from the international agenda. But the states of the two alliances still had industrial forces. All were relatively large, with many still resting on conscription, and all had industrial means of war – armoured fighting vehicles, guns, fighter bombers and in some states warships – and the defence industries to maintain them. In the subsequent fifteen years the armies have become smaller and essentially regular, since most states have abolished conscription and even Russia is contemplating such a move. But the weapons and equipment largely remain, either purposefully being replenished with much the same types and models, as in the US, or else ageing and bearing testament to wars of another age and another concept in most European states, where declining interest in defence spending had made replacement a low priority. This situation evolved initially because after the Cold War these states saw the end of the confrontation as the end of all threats and chose to take the 'peace dividend'. When their forces were deployed it was therefore only as 'peacekeepers'. At the same time, this concept fitted well with the growing interest in both the morality and the legality of the use of force. The concept of just war has been debated for centuries, but in modern times it has focused upon these issues, which began to emerge with the Nuremberg trials, and indeed lay at the heart of the entire notion of the UN, and definitely the UN Charter's definitions on the use of force to resolve conflicts. During the Cold War these had largely lain dormant, but once the confrontation was over they came to the fore – and have indeed retained a dominant position in public international discourse. The terror attacks of 9/11 shook the perception of a peace dividend in Europe, but did not provide a clear idea of the threats or enemies demanding a military response, other than the amorphous and ever-present miasma of 'terrorism'. And as noted at the start of this book, terrorism as such is not a formulated enemy: it is a threatening concept, occasionally implemented by individuals, some working together in loosely defined organizations. Yet without an enemy it is not possible to formulate a strategy, and without a strategy it is not possible to make anything but the broadest decisions on weapons and equipment. As a result forces in Europe have shrunk, but retain the form and equipment of another age intended for other battles.

It is with these weapons and armies that we now go into conflict – 'we' being all NATO nations as much as Russia, most former Soviet states and many others besides – organized to fight industrial wars whilst engaged in war amongst the people. Worse still, as we shall see, by applying these forces into our modern conflicts we can inadvertently contribute to the efforts of our opponents, thereby making our own aims all the more difficult to achieve. This may seem an anomaly – and it is not the only one. For many, the conflicts since 1990 with which people are familiar through the media are an anomaly too: there are planes dropping precision bombs, missiles fired from hi-tech guns, soldiers in helmets and flak jackets driving round in tanks, political leaders gravely committing men to battle and underlining the importance of the venture and promising success. In short, recent conflicts have all the trappings and iconic images of industrial war, but it seems these wars are never won. The purpose of the following chapters is to explain these apparent anomalies, based upon the historical analysis of Parts I and II and within the framework of the six basic trends that make up the paradigm of war amongst the people listed on p. 17 and summarized below:

- The ends for which we fight are changing from the hard objectives that decide a political outcome to those of establishing conditions in which the outcome may be decided
- We fight amongst the people, not on the battlefield
- Our conflicts tend to be timeless, even unending
- We fight so as to preserve the force rather than risking all to gain the objective
- On each occasion new uses are found for old weapons and organizations which are the products of industrial war
- The sides are mostly non-state, comprising some form of multinational grouping against some non-state party or parties.

It is now time to examine these trends more thoroughly.

THE ENDS FOR WHICH WE FIGHT ARE CHANGING

Industrial war had clear-cut strategic goals. It has been used to create states, destroy the evil of fascism and end the Ottoman Empire. In war amongst the people, however, the ends to which we use military force are changing to something more complex and less strategic. As we have seen, the driving idea behind industrial war was that the political objective was attained by achieving a strategic military objective of such significance that the opponent conformed to our will – the intention being to decide the matter by military force. These strategic objectives tended to be expressed in terms such as take, hold, destroy. In the two world wars both sides sought to achieve all of these on the battlefield, within the understanding that such an achievement would decide the political outcome – which in both wars it did. In contrast to these hard strategic ends we tend now to conduct operations for 'softer', more malleable, complex, sub-strategic objectives. We do not intervene in order to take or hold territory; in fact, once an intervention has occurred a main preoccupation is how to leave the territory rather than keep it. Instead, we intervene in, or even decide to escalate to, a conflict in order to establish a condition in which the political objective can be achieved by other means and in other ways. We seek to create a conceptual space for diplomacy, economic incentives, political pressure and other measures to create a desired political outcome of stability, and if possible democracy. The other party's objectives are also of this nature, since they do not have the means to fight industrial war; and those that thought they had, such as Iraq in 1991, have been defeated. They too therefore seek to establish a condition. As we shall see, the purpose of the international interventions in the Balkans in the 1990s was never to stop a war or destroy an offending side, but rather to use military force to create a condition in which humanitarian activity could take place, and negotiation or an international administration could lead to the desired political outcome. Similarly in Iraq, both in 1991 and 2003, military force was not intended to achieve the unconditional surrender of the state so much as the condition in which a new regime could be created by other means.

Overall, therefore, if a decisive strategic victory was the hallmark of interstate industrial war, establishing a condition may be deemed the hallmark of the new paradigm of war amongst the people. This trend occurred quite quickly after the Second World War, for two reasons. First, because both the way and the means of achieving the strategic military goal were politically unacceptable: a full industrial military response, often against poorly armed enemies, would mean a disproportionate use of force and cost a great deal whilst the ultimate escalation, to nuclear weapons, would be an unrealistic price in every way, not least because it could unintentionally also lead to another global war. Second, there was no strategic side to conquer: the enemy by design often did not present a target that was susceptible to strategic attack, since in most conflicts of war amongst the people the enemy is in small groups operating at the tactical level, against which the manoeuvres and mass firepower of industrial war are ineffective – as many examples in previous chapters have shown. These two reasons mean that, much as the political aims have changed, so has the use of force: the conflicts are fought for sub-strategic objectives.

The term sub-strategic arises from the confusion between deployment and employment. We may deploy forces strategically in terms of distance or in terms of the level at which the decision to do so is made. For example, to withdraw forces from Northern Ireland and to send them to Iraq would be a strategic deployment or redeployment: it is a strategic-level decision to reallocate forces between theatres of operations since it would require strategic transport resources to move the forces and a subsequent rebalancing of the strategic measures – men, materiel, weapons – to sustain the forces in both theatres to match the redeployment. However, none of this indicates the level or purpose to which force is to be employed. In fact, in Northern Ireland military force is employed reactively in support of the civil power and at the lowest tactical level. In Iraq in 2003 military force was used initially to achieve an operational objective: the destruction of the Iraqi forces and the removal of Saddam Hussein and his Ba'ath Party apparatus. Subsequently the application reverted to the tactical as the coalition grappled with the insurgency that followed. In neither case has the employment of force achieved the strategic objective of a democratic Iraq, nor could it have done since that requires the willing cooperation of the majority of the people. In both Ireland and Iraq, therefore, force has been applied sub-strategically: the effects achieved by military force do not themselves either directly or in aggregate amount to achieving the strategic objective.

The political rhetoric that accompanies any modern conflict does not reflect this shift in aims – which is itself indicative of our confused understanding of the utility of force. As conflict is entered, the declared intentions all tend to be of hard strategic objectives, of 'going to war' in the industrial sense, but the actions and outcomes are entirely sub-strategic, relating to the world of confrontation and conflict. For example, in the Korean War the US crossed from confrontation into conflict in 1950 not least because President Truman was under severe domestic pressure for being too soft on communism, and his ability to appear bellicose against the Soviet-backed North Koreans was therefore useful in the circumstances. However, when conflict escalated in 1953 to the point at which the use of atomic weapons was being mooted, and this option was ruled out, a strategic military decision became unattainable at a price the allies, and in particular the US, were prepared to pay. A condition was therefore arrived at, the ceasefire and a divided Korea, in which it was intended to find a solution by diplomacy. Over fifty years later such a solution has yet to be found, and since North Korea claims to have tested its own device, the confrontation is now nuclear.

The various wars of colonial liberation during the old imperial powers' retreats from empire illustrate the enemy's ability to avoid strategic attack. Again, whatever the rhetoric at the time – which was usually a determination to either leave or stay at any cost – the imperial powers actually sought to establish a condition of sufficient stability in which they could hand over government and depart while retaining some influence. In these cases the enemy was usually a guerrilla force operating within the concepts of revolutionary war, for example in Malaya, or a terrorist organization, such as EOKA in Cyprus. In any event, as we have seen, such an enemy was not and is not susceptible to strategic defeat by military means. To do this requires the suppression of the people – counter terror – to the point where out of fear they reject the terrorist in their midst, or are so controlled that the terrorist is unable to operate, or else they are transported elsewhere. The political costs of taking these actions are strategically high in terms of morality, legality, manpower and finance. Moreover, they are of doubtful operational value since, as we have seen, the methods often serve the opponent's strategy. The French attempt to counter terror with terror in Algiers discussed on p. 246 was an example of precisely such a failure: the method was militarily effective in the city, but it created a political condition that broke the will of metropolitan France to continue. As a result, the French withdrew and the generals mutinied in the face of that decision. However effective the use of force had been at one level, it lacked utility at the higher levels.

The Falklands War in 1982 is the only one I can think of that occurred during my service in which the strategic objective of liberating the islands from Argentinean occupation was achieved directly by military force in a single campaign: it was an old-style industrial war between states. In so doing Britain restored the antebellum status quo – yet the political issue of sovereignty remains open to this day. At a first glance, the 1991 Gulf War looks similar, since Kuwait was liberated swiftly with military force. However, that was not the whole story, since apart from the liberation and restoring the regional status quo, the strategic intention was to create a condition in which Saddam Hussein's behaviour was much modified, or better still his people deposed him. The final outcome was that the objective of liberating Kuwait was achieved, but the strategic condition was hardly decisive and subsequently had to be maintained by no-fly zones and the other means of UN sanctions and inspections, until 2003. At that point a US-led coalition force invaded Iraq with the intention of deposing Saddam Hussein and his Ba'athist apparatus, and creating a theatre condition in which a democratically elected government established a rule in the state to the satisfaction of the US. The theatre-level objectives of occupation and the removal of Hussein and his apparatus were achieved very quickly and successfully; however, these were but enabling objectives to the achievement of the strategic condition. That condition has yet to be met, and until it is the strategic goal of establishing a sympathetic democratic government in a stable state is unlikely to be achieved.

In truth, such a condition of democracy is militarily difficult to achieve when occupation is involved, as Israel has discovered in the occupied territories and as the imperial powers discovered after the

Second World War, when the colonies sought independence. The reason is simple: upon occupation the military force loses the strategic initiative. Once all the tangible objectives have been taken or destroyed, and the land held, what is there left for force to achieve strategically, or even operationally? The initiative moves to the occupied, who can choose to cooperate with the occupiers or not. And if they have popular support, those that choose not to cooperate are in the classic position of the Spanish guerrillas who fought Napoleon: they can mount their own destructive tactical offensives, whenever and wherever they choose, which drain and exhaust the stronger military occupier.

The interventions of forces under the UN and NATO flags have also been to establish or maintain conditions in which a strategic decision might be reached. During the Cold War the UN evolved a type of military operation called 'peacekeeping' whose purpose was to maintain – not establish – a condition. Typically this occurred when two warring parties agreed to stop fighting, but neither trusted the other and they therefore needed a third party to stand between them. Usually the UN was requested to provide the third party because such action came with the authority of its charter, and the force provided was composed of contingents from nations with no stake in the dispute. The UN force was not expected to use force except in self-defence and even then not to alter the situation as it stood between the two parties – which makes the use of the term 'force' in the title somewhat misleading. Long-running UN operations such as those in Kashmir and in Cyprus are classic, and successful, examples of peacekeeping. Possibly the best reflection of this particular brand of open-ended condition-maintenance may be found in the many UN missions created within the complex chronology of the Arab–Israeli conflict.

The very first mission was established on 29 May 1948, when the Security Council, in resolution 50 (1948), called for a cessation of hostilities in Palestine and decided that a UN mediator should supervise the truce, with the assistance of a group of military observers. The first group of military observers, which has become known as the United Nations Truce Supervision Organization (UNTSO), arrived in the region in June 1948 – and has been there ever since. In resolving the

Suez crisis in 1956–7 the Security Council established the UN Emergency Force (UNEF I), with a mandate to secure and supervise the cessation of hostilities, including the withdrawal of the armed forces of France, Israel and the United Kingdom from Egyptian territory and, after the withdrawal, to serve as a buffer between the Egyptian and Israeli forces and to provide impartial supervision of the ceasefire. Following the Yom Kippur War, the United Nations Disengagement Observer Force (UNDOF) was established by Security Council resolution 350 (1974) of 31 May 1974 to maintain the ceasefire between Israel and Syria, to supervise the disengagement of Israeli and Syrian forces, and to supervise the areas of separation and limitation, as provided in the Agreement on Disengagement. The mandate of UNDOF has since been renewed every six months, with both sides appearing on appointed dates to sign on the dotted line – from which one may deduce that they want the condition maintained. As noted on p. 256 above, on 19 March 1978 Resolution 425 established an international and still-extant peacekeeping force for South Lebanon, the United Nations Interim Force in Lebanon (UNIFIL). It was mandated to confirm the Israeli withdrawal – which took place in June 1978 – restore international peace and security, and help the Lebanese government restore its effective authority in the area.

Most of these missions have been successful within their narrow remit of maintaining a ceasefire line and whatever general condition was required in the mandate – the most unsuccessful being UNIFIL, since the cross-border raids between Israel and Lebanon have continued regardless of its efforts – a 'failing' often decried around the world and especially in the media. However, this is more a case of misunderstanding the unfortunate conjunction of the words 'force' and 'peacekeeping' – since all are known as peacekeeping forces – which has often created expectations of intervention and enforcement that could not be fulfilled, since the sole purpose of these missions was to maintain the condition of a ceasefire agreed by the parties. The worst examples of this miscomprehension – or indeed public cognitive dissonance – may be found in the long saga of the UN interventions in the Balkans, which will be explained in the following chapter. Suffice it to say at this point that naming the mission that began its life in 1992, and was deeply involved in the horrors of the Bosnian war,

UNPROFOR, an acronym for the UN Protection Force, can be seen as somewhat ironic in retrospect. More significantly, and despite the 1995 UN operation and NATO air strikes that ended the Bosnia conflict and the bombings in 1999 in Kosovo, neither confrontation was resolved through the use of force – and the ongoing international forces in both are mandated to maintain the condition of a ceasefire until such a resolution is found.

This trend of changing ends – of a forceful search for a condition – highlights another aspect of our modern conflicts: we do not respect the enemy. As emphasized throughout this book, battle is an adversarial activity with an enemy, and that enemy is not inert, waiting for us to attack him and falling in with our plan. He is a very alert and sentient opponent, who seeks constantly to foil our plans and do unto us that which we seek to do unto him – and worse. None the less, in our approach to modern conflicts we persist in the unspoken assumption that our opponent, and in particular the people amongst whom he operates, will conform with our plan and share our idea of the future condition. When matters do not go according to our plan we tend to leave the assumptions unchallenged and blame 'rogue elements' or 'foreign fighters'. Yet practically by definition the opponent is always fighting for a different outcome and will resist the imposition of our vision of the future. Failing to respect the existence and use of his free creative will, which is not the same as respecting his values or motivation, is to set yourself up for defeat. Worse still, he will use you to serve his ends of getting the people on his side, and then humiliating and defeating your force. In fighting amongst the people the enemy is deliberately choosing to keep the level and nature of the conflict where our advantages of numbers and equipment are neutralized. He develops his operation precisely upon the lines established in the antithesis to industrial war: creating disorder, advancing his cause by very public acts (propaganda of the deed), and by provocation tests our willingness and ability to act or causes us to overreact (strategy of provocation). The ill-fated UN operation in Rwanda (UNAMIR) gives an example of an assessment of the willingness to act by provocation. It was meant to stop military assistance reaching the Rwandan rebels – and, inter alia, ultimately create the condition in which humanitarian suffering could be alleviated and democratic elections could be held. However, though approved in 1993, the troops were only properly deployed in February 1994, and it took but a few minor provocations from the rebels and other parties to establish it as a paper tiger with very little – if any – international political will behind it to use force. Indeed, as the situation deteriorated some contributing nations withdrew their troops, so that at the height of the crisis there were fewer than 400 UN personnel on the ground. The rebels came to understand that the threshold of international tolerance was very high and ultimately massacred nearly a million people in a hundred days.

The actions of the 'insurgents' in Iraq after the end of the official conflicts in May 2003 have also been provocations of the coalition forces, not only to harm them but also to establish their threshold of action. In either case, however, the underlying purpose is really to provoke a violent reaction, or preferably an escalation of violence, which could be used to show the people of Iraq what a ruthless lot the US-led invaders are. As such, the provocations are part of the insurgents' strategic method. The strategic aim of the coalition forces is to show the same people how bad the insurgents are and how good they themselves are. Both are fighting each other amongst the people, over the will of the people – which is the final aspect of this first trend: in seeking to establish conditions, our true political aim, for which we are using military force, is to influence the intentions of the people. This is an inversion of industrial war, where the objective was to win the trial of strength and thereby break the enemy's will. In war amongst the people the strategic objective is to capture the will of the people and their leaders, and thereby win the trial of strength. The dangers and costs of coercing the people have already been discussed, and if, as history keeps on showing, they are used, then the coercive measures must be maintained, or the spirit of freedom and independence will break out.

Capturing the will of the people is a very clear and basic concept, yet one that is either misunderstood or ignored by political and military establishments around the world. The politician keeps applying force to attain a condition, assuming the military will both create and maintain it. And whilst for many years the military has understood the need to win the 'hearts and minds' of the local population, this is still seen as a supporting activity to the defeat of the insurgents rather than the overall objective, and it is often under-resourced and restricted to low-level acts to ameliorate local conditions and the lot of the people. This brings us back to the relationship between the trial of strength and the clash of wills. Since the overall objective we seek by employing force is to win the clash of wills, it follows that every trial of strength must be won in such a way that each success complements and supports the measures to win the clash of wills. Only then will the forces we send have utility and deliver the political result desired.

WE FIGHT AMONGST THE PEOPLE

The second trend is of course that increasingly we conduct operations amongst the people. The people in the cities, towns, streets and their houses – all the people, anywhere – can be on the battlefield. Military engagements can take place against formed and recognizable groups of enemy moving amongst civilians, against enemies disguised as civilians, and unintentionally and intentionally against civilians. Civilians can be the targets as much as the opposing force. In the first instance this is because they are mistaken for the enemy or are in close proximity to the enemy, and in the second to terrorize them. This occurs because moving amongst the people is the guerrilla fighter's proven method of neutralizing the strength of his stronger opponent. Secondly, civilians can be targeted because the will of the people is the objective, and the direct attack on the people is thought to assail that will. And finally, there are the media that bring the conflict into the homes of millions of people: people who vote and whose opinions influence their politicians – those who make the decision on using force.

As we have seen, the people had become an objective during the Second World War, when the cities of Europe and Japan were bombed to terrorize the people into changing their will. It has since continued to be an objective, with 'ethnic cleansing' such as in Bosnia or Rwanda, and terrorist attacks on the people, for example by the IRA in Britain or ETA in Spain. The people being attacked in the Second

World War were those of the enemy government: they were understood to be the support base of the opposing force. The post-war bombings are different, since the attackers depend on the people to be able to prosecute their attacks, whether they cooperate or not: they are carried out both on and amongst the people. The main and significant similarity between the two forms of attack is the political objective, which both in the war and ever since has been the intentions or will of the people – as already noted above in the first trend.

The guerrilla fighter needs the people for concealment. He moves amongst them like the trees of the forest and to this end he will endeavour to appear as normal as he can to those he moves amongst, even if he and his kind are a minority within the society as a whole. He needs the people in their collective form to sustain himself. Like a parasite he depends on his host for transport, heat, light, revenue, information and communications. The Russians understood this and before attacking the Chechen capital Grozny in 1994–5, in an attempt to bring the Chechens to a decisive battle, they removed the people before levelling the city. And in Kosovo in 1998–9, in their direct and simplistic logic, the Yugoslavian army worked to the same principle: no people, no threat; hence ethnic cleansing – which is what led to the NATO bombing over the province. Or indeed, the US forces, who in their attack on Fallujah in 2004 waited until it had been more or less evacuated before commencing a major assault on the local insurgents. But these solutions are based on two often flawed assumptions: first, that the opponent will give battle on your terms, which he will not if he can avoid it, and second, that the people are powerless to react to what is done to them, which in the long run they are not.

In order to understand operations amongst the people, and to capture their will, we must first understand 'the people'. The people are an entity but not a monolithic block. They form entities based on family, tribe, nation, ethnicity, religion, ideology, state, profession, skill, trade and interests of many different kinds. Within these entities the people's position is incoherent, and their views and opinions are varied and various; only with political leadership do their positions cohere. The family will discuss a matter; when, where and how depends on the family, but a member of the clan will lead and this small and specific entity will form a view. The chairman of a club committee – political or social – will perform a similar function in a more formal way. And the political leaders of states are clearly there to lead, guide and represent their states' political discourse and position. Within these many circles, the guerrilla fighter needs to have an entity supporting him, an entity whose position he controls. To this end he must know the needs of the people – and appeal to them in a way the state or other leaderships do not.

At base, people want things that may be divided into 'freedom from' and 'freedom to'. They want freedom from fear, hunger, cold and uncertainty. They want freedom to prosper and do what they reasonably want. And they want the society of their families, friends and those of like mind. They will follow the leader who in their judgement in the circumstances is the most likely to provide these things. Even in totalitarian regimes, where the people have little or no choice of leader, it is interesting to note that leaders use the rhetoric of fulfilling needs and wants – knowing that ultimately the people can rebel, even if it takes a long time and the cost is high. If the circumstances are those of fear and uncertainty then the people will look in the first instance to the leader whom they believe can alleviate, or better still, change the circumstances. Their readiness to compromise their other wants will be in direct proportion to the extent of their fears. Understanding this, the guerrilla fighter wants to create a situation where he or his man is the leader who best satisfies the people's wants. The more he can represent his opponent as the aggressor directly threatening the people, the more they are likely to cleave to him for protection.

Short of a situation where they face a direct armed threat, the people want an administration that they understand and relate to. This is much more important to urban than rural people. In rural areas people usually wish to be left alone to provide for their own needs; in towns and cities, lives are so interconnected and dependent that an administration is necessary to provide for those needs. In practice the boundary between urban and rural is far from clear, and the more developed the society the more the rural area is a dormitory and recreational area for the urban. In general terms, the administration need not be that financially efficient or run to democratic standards when the requirement for it is more to do with providing the essentials of life, the 'freedom froms'. But as these basic wants are satisfied so the people will come to desire more, and it is when they are focused on the 'freedom to' that people want efficiency, high ethical standards and so on. It is important to understand this issue well, because at the outset people's needs are often satisfied best by a consistent and fair administration in which the minorities are seen to have an equal share; an equality that is recognized by all to be guaranteed by the forces of the administration. The unspoken but essential assumption on which democracy rests is that the minority trusts the majority not to take unreasonable advantage of their position. For democratic values to prosper this foundation has to be laid from the outset. In many of the areas in which our modern conflicts have erupted, either the majority genuinely did not respect the rights of the minority, or else the minority perceived itself to be unfairly dealt with. When this sense is matched with fear as a result of attacks on one or the other party, you have a potential explosion waiting for a spark.

I realized this first in 1980 in the newly independent Zimbabwe, where I was involved in forming their new armed forces. The African population was composed in the main of two tribes, the majority Shona and a sizeable minority of Ndebele. The forces that had fought the 'Liberation Struggle' were composed of the armed wings of two political parties, each firmly based in its respective tribe. Initially the two parties and the leadership of the two armies were represented in government and the newly forming Zimbabwe National Army; but neither trusted the other and both distrusted the Rhodesians. Each of the guerrilla armies kept reserves of men and weapons in their respective sanctuary areas of Zambia and Mozambique. Over the next two years ZANU, the Shona-based majority party, established itself firmly in power and with the aid of North Korea was able to form the 5th Brigade, an extra to the four we were establishing. Gaining access to observe this extra brigade's training was not easy, none the less it became clear that the Ndebele were being discharged and it was becoming a nearly all-Shona force. At about the same time the reserves of weapons held by the Shona began to be brought openly into the country. Whether as a result of these moves or in anticipation, the Ndebele had been bringing their own weapons into the country covertly and building some form of movement in Matabeleland. About two years after independence the government, mainly ZANU, struck. Ndebele leaders were marginalized or arrested and a little later the 5th Brigade was committed into Matabeleland, where it crushed the 'revolt' with a series of atrocities in the Ndebele tribal trust lands. Mugabe and ZANU have held and reinforced their power over the Zimbabwean people ever since.

What happened in Zimbabwe is an example of the people dividing openly and fighting amongst themselves. In other areas, as we have seen in many of the parallel conflicts of the Cold War and ever since – the situation in Iraq being a prime example – the opposing force, the insurgents, are not only of the people but are fighting amongst them to attack the occupier and also to establish a dominant position at least locally for their own faction or ethnic group. In conducting operations amongst the people the insurgent, terrorist, guerrilla, freedom fighter etc. follows a somewhat generic pattern, always adapted for the particular circumstances that face him. He has a 'sanctuary area' where he feels sufficiently safe to associate with others of a like mind. He will not go so far as to avow his identity and purpose, but he will move in close proximity to, perhaps even amongst, those who represent the movement in its overt form. For example, al-Qaeda in Afghanistan under the Taliban felt safe to move about in their own circles, though not necessarily openly declaring themselves in society. The guerrilla will then have a 'preparation area', where he will conceal his weapons, assemble his bombs and plan and rehearse his attacks. Here his real purpose is at risk of being discovered, and he will take great care over his security, adopting techniques such as operating in cells, where only three or four people are known to each other. Communications will be limited and will be conducted as much as possible to avoid attribution and intercept, for example by using public phone boxes at random and cash rather than traceable credit or debit cards. The 'preparation area' for al-Qaeda's attacks on 11 September 2001 appears to have been in Germany and Florida. Finally there is the 'operational area' in which the target lies: the guerrilla aims to be in this area for the minimum of time, since he is armed and formed for the attack, and his intentions are evident to all who see him for what he is. Timing, disguise and deception are his main aids to achieve surprise – and it is surprise that secures the attack and makes escape more likely.

The guerrilla is at the greatest danger as he moves into the operational area because his behaviour will change as he executes his plan, and the alert defender may see this in time to react effectively. He will aim to be in this area for as little time as possible, and to leave in such a way as to confound those who seek to follow him either literally or forensically. Suicide attackers, who can be likened to a V-1 or cruise missile, are particularly effective in that they can be launched from some distance from the operational area and their extraction does not have to be considered. The 9/11 attacks had these characteristics, as well as the double utility of using the aeroplanes as weapons. This meant that in the first instance the operational area was the interior of the aeroplanes. The attackers were in transit from preparation to operational areas as they went through the airport, and even if one or two were prevented from boarding there were sufficient conspirators and aeroplanes being seized to do the job, and the arrested men or man would not have given sufficient evidence of the enormity of what was about to occur.

Although I have described these three areas in a spatial sense one must not suppose that is necessarily the case, particularly when the conflict is taking place amongst the people in an urban area. The three areas can be defined in time; for example the guerrilla in question only carries out activities related to each area at certain times of the day. Perhaps for him the preparation area is when he is going to work, and on the commuter train he can meet up with his comrades as though they were strangers. Alternatively they may be defined by activity, meaning perhaps an area would be when he is in the golf club or church. Even down to the lowest level, where the guerrilla does not move from his village or commune, the three areas are evident. He will appear to the outsider as the herdsman or delivery boy, he will meet in discrete groups at discrete times and his weapons will be concealed. He will only show his hand when the target presents itself, perhaps the military patrol or government official. Movement from area to area is a time of vulnerability for the guerrilla or terrorist. He is moving from one form to another, from one milieu to another, and exposing his intentions as he does so.

I do not want to suggest these patterns of behaviour are planned in advance, except possibly by the most astute individuals; rather, they evolve by a process of trial and error. As apparent from this discussion, the guerrilla fighter usually initiates an attack only on his terms, and the security forces react to it. A Darwinian process then occurs as the guerrilla learns, by surviving and even profiting from the engagement, which tactics and techniques work. As it does with the people of an occupation, the operational initiative lies with the guerrilla. However, once he is in operation, the security forces become party to this process, and herein lies an opportunity. If the security forces design their operations to learn about their opponent, instead of trying to defeat him in the first instance, they will gain the intelligence and penetration to take the operational initiative. Until this vital knowledge is available, the guerrilla cannot be separated from the people, and until this is done all tactical acts by the security forces carry the risk of serving the guerrilla's overall strategy of provocation and propaganda of the deed.

We now come to the other manner in which we fight and operate amongst the people in a wider sense: through the media. Television and the internet in particular have brought conflict into the homes of the world – the homes of both leaders and electorates. Leaders are influenced by what they see and by their understanding of the mood of the audience, their electorate. And they act on these perceptions, often for reasons to do with their own political purpose rather than the one at issue in the fight itself. Indeed, confrontations may end up crossing into conflicts, or escalating in levels of fighting, or indeed crossing the other way and de-escalating owing to perceptions formed from the media. Whoever coined the phrase 'the theatre of operations' was very prescient. We are conducting operations now as though we were on a stage, in an amphitheatre or Roman arena. There are two or more sets of players – both with a producer, the commander, each of whom has his own idea of the script. On the ground, in the actual theatre, they are all on the stage and mixed up with people trying to get to their seats, the stage hands, the ticket collectors and the ice-cream vendors. At the same time they are being viewed by a partial and factional audience, comfortably seated, its attention focused on that part of the auditorium where it is noisiest, watching the events by peering down the drinking straws of their soft-drink packs – for that is the extent of the vision of a camera.

I have come to certain principles for conducting operations in this theatre, based on the view that the media is just that: a collective medium. In this case it is a medium in which you operate, like the weather. To a large extent the media is common to all parties in the theatre, whether they are in confrontation or conflict or allied. It is a means of communication, although one must expect the message one wants transmitted to be ignored for a better story, distorted by personal or editorial bias, misinterpreted from a lack of knowledge or misrepresented from a lack of contextual information. Above all one must never forget that the interest of a journalist or producer – which is usually genuine – is driven by a need to fill space with words and pictures. I used this understanding in the Gulf in 1990 when considering my method for conducting operations against the Iraqis. I realized the need to make particular arrangements for handling what I called 'presentation' in order to ensure the continuing support of our people and allies, to impart to the enemy a specific impression we wanted him to have and for my command to feel it was well presented. The position of 'war correspondent' has a legal standing: one who volunteers for this position accepts and obeys instructions from the military as to movement, wears uniform if ordered and submits copy to censorship; in return the war correspondent receives access, information, an advantageous viewpoint, food, shelter and security. I decided that once battle was joined we would deal only with accredited war correspondents; they would be allocated to units in the division and my staff would censor their copy. Since every other journalist's copy had to pass through a US Central Command process in Jubayl I offered my correspondents an advantage over the others, the British censorship process being a great deal quicker than the official US one. Within these mutually beneficial parameters we had the basis of a relationship, and in order to ensure its smooth running I formed a new External Relations branch in my HQ. The head of this branch, Chief External Relations, was responsible for dealing with everyone who was not directly in the operational chain of command, from the Prince of Wales when he visited, to the local sheikh, to the media. Since the Chief was informed of all developments, and was indeed party to some, the media in this way had a constant contact, which made both their lives and ours much easier.

In the theatre the forces of all sides, and in particular the political leaders and military commanders, have a symbiotic relationship with the media: the media needs the military because they are the cause and source of the story; the commanders need the media to tell the story to their forces' advantage, but also to tell their own people and government how well they are doing, or at worst, how gloriously they are losing. In addition, commanders and leaders alike need the media in order to learn the perceptions of the other side, and to explain their own versions of events. To this extent the media is a crucially useful element in modern conflicts for attaining the political objective of winning the will of the people. It has also become the medium that connects the people, government and the army, the three sides of the Clausewitzian triangle. In the simple situation of two states at war the medium in one triangle could be considered as independent of the medium in the other. Indeed, in the days of industrial war most governments had a Ministry of Information to direct and control their own media. But our complex conflicts and modern communications have changed this: with twenty-four-hour news broadcasts and global networks, the media is to a large extent common to both or all of the triangles of all the sides; a common medium. Despite the symbiotic relationship, the relationship between the journalist and the subject is weak and liable to break down, since the subject – the military commander or the political leader, which includes the insurgency leader – sees it as being based on an implied promise that is most unlikely to be satisfied. The political leader and the commander expect the reporter to tell his story as he would wish it to be told and as he told it to the journalist. But the journalist sees them as a source of his story, and the events and meetings of the day are presented to support this story rather than that of the political or military leader. I am not suggesting either party is deliberately twisting or spinning the story (although that happens). Rather the media claim to be objective, and tend not to be, whilst political and military leaders persistently expect the objectivity of a shared perception where one is most unlikely to exist. In other words, they know the media is not objective – yet they still speak to it, use it, become disappointed and complain. This is

mainly because they seek a platform or at best a conduit, not understanding that the media is a medium in which all events are mixed,
presented as if happening concurrently and all of the same importance, reported in tiny digestible chunks – then discarded. Attempts to
control this relationship and prevent it from going wrong have ranged
from the tight control of those permitted to speak to journalists and
about what, to censorship, to giving journalists 'minders' – and various other measures too. All of these, of course, have the opposite
effect from that sought, since they imply to the journalists that there
is something to hide, so setting them off in pursuit of a conspiracy, to
find the skeleton in the cupboard, or to find the 'whistle blower'. In
this way the measures feed into the journalistic story rather than shap-
ing it – but it is this story that is told to the people, both those amongst
whom the fight is taking place and those in the audience.

The media is not part of the operation, but since it is everywhere in
the theatre its presence must be calculated – especially in one's
choice of method as to how to achieve surprise. The business of concealing one's intentions and presence while endeavouring to establish
those of one's opponent is as old as conflict – and definitely mattered
to Sun Tzu, who devoted several chapters of his *Art of War* to the subject. For the past few hundred years the media in various forms has
been scoured for information for this purpose; indeed, Napoleon was
an avid reader of the British press. Nowadays we have an international media that cannot be controlled, whose communications are
frequently better than those of the military and that acts to inform on
the theatre as a whole to both the players and the audience. Within
these circumstances, and in order to achieve concealment, I think it is
better to practise illusion rather than deception. In the latter one
attempts to lie and deceive, in the former one seeks to have the opponent deceive himself. As an example, in 1990 in the Gulf we did not
want the Iraqis to realize that the main attack would be into Iraq
rather than Kuwait. We thought they would be looking for the British
division on the grounds that there was only one, and being one from
a principal ally it was likely to be on the main axis of the attack. It was
important therefore to conceal the fact that we had moved from
the coast opposite the Iraq–Kuwait border up into the desert to join
the two US army corps on the main axis. Working on the basis that

the TV channels rarely declare when they use library pictures, we gave many facilities for television shots before the bombing started, always trying to have the sea in the background. When the bombing started we moved into the desert and stopped the facilities. Months later, when watching a tape of the news broadcasts of the period before we attacked, I was interested to see how frequently there were clips of film with the sea in the background. Perhaps this had helped to form the picture in the mind of the Iraqi general, one of seven, I recall, that we captured in the attack. He remarked to his captors that he did not know the British were in front of him; he thought the Challengers were on the coast.

Finally, the media stories or depictions are also a strong reason we still see conflicts within the interstate industrial model, since they are usually told from the perspective of the conventional military forces sent in by nation states. Like the political and military establishments, the media is still caught up with the concept of industrial war, not realizing or understanding it is now war amongst the people. At the same time, because the media has little time or space to convey information – a minute or three on screen or on air, a few inches in the daily press – so it must work with cognitive images and jargon in order to be appealing to and understood by its audiences. These images and jargon are all of individuals and situations involving conventional armies in industrial war. This has now created a new loop, since much of the audience and even segments of the media realize there is a dissonance between what is being shown and experienced and what is being explained – the former clearly being other forms of war, the latter being desperate attempts to use the framework of interstate war to interpret war amongst the people. Taking an example from our daily TV news flashes, we often see heavily armed soldiers patrolling in tanks through streets full of women and children, whether in Iraq, the Israeli-occupied territories, or elsewhere in the world, or else we see ragged civilian men and children attacking heavily armed soldiers in tanks. The pictures themselves clash with our cognitive understanding, but the interpretation then laid on them by the reporter or studio commentator – attempting to explain the military actions of the soldiers – confuses us further, for they are mostly explained from a conventional military perspective, as if two equal forces were engaged in a skirmish on a battlefield. In other words, a new reality is being restructured around an old paradigm, for the most part unsuccessfully.

In sum, this second trend, of fighting amongst the people, reflects both the specificity of our current conflicts and yet also their all encompassing nature: the individual guerrilla of all descriptions or alternative political leader moves and fights amongst the people, the specific people of his interest, whilst the audience of these conflicts has become, courtesy of the media, the people of the world. The people of the audience have come to influence the decisions of the political leaders who send in force as much as – and in some cases more than – the events on the ground. Those making the war amongst the people have also come to use the media to influence decisions, and above all the will of those people they seek to lead and co-opt. This is not so much the global village as the global theatre of war, with audience participation.

OUR CONFLICTS TEND TO BE TIMELESS

There are no quick fixes or solutions for war amongst the people, particularly when faced by an opponent of any stature. Moreover, action at the right time is more important than action per se, which brings me to my third trend: our operations have become increasingly timeless; they go on and on. All the confrontations and conflicts mentioned in the previous chapter reflect this well, from the continuing Korean confrontation to that in Cyprus to the thirty years of conflict in Indo-China. More recently, operations in Iraq have been ongoing since 1990, whilst the international community first intervened in the Balkans in 1992 and there is no end in sight. This open-ended and timeless trend occurs for three reasons. The first is to do with the chosen objective or end, the second is to do with the method or way (these two are combined) and the third is to do with the shift between paradigms.

The first trend of war amongst the people, the changing ends, reflected that we are conducting operations more often than not to achieve a condition in which the strategic military objective to gain the political purpose is achieved by other means or in another way. Sometimes the condition is achieved quickly in a single campaign, such as in the Falklands, but more usually it is attained as the result of a long operation against opponents using the method of the guerrilla or terrorist. One of the fundamental tenets of the guerrilla or terrorist is that he fights only when the time is right for him. He gives battle when the conditions for success exist, and not before, avoiding the decisive engagement except on his terms. Even when he fights, the 'decisions' are almost always tactical rather than operational. As we have seen, such an opponent is hard to beat quickly. However, what would in any event be a slow process is made even more so when one has to consider the people amongst whom the fight is taking place. Since both the theatre and the strategic objectives involve gaining their support, or at least denying their support to the opponent, the speed at which their will is captured is the measure of progress towards the goal. Rushing to achieve a quick victory against an opponent who refuses to cooperate in having the fight on your terms, particularly when operating amongst the people, is likely to alienate the people rather than to win them over. Evidence of this undesirable outcome may be found in many of the post-1945 conflicts, the Russian assault on Grozny to quell the Chechen rebellion being a particular case in point. I am not suggesting that one does not want to win quickly the fight one chooses; that is always the preferable way, especially since fights cost less when fought rapidly, and a high tempo of telling blows allows one to dictate the course of the battle. But the guerrilla knows this, which is why he picks small fights on his terms. But these small fights, even if they occur daily and rapidly, do not in themselves aggregate into a battle; they are not in themselves decisive. It is the overall fight to establish the condition that is therefore that which provides a decisive decision.

Once the condition has been attained, in all cases it then has to be maintained until the strategic objective is achieved. In Korea, for example, there has been an impressive presence of US troops since the signing of the ceasefire in July 1953. Indeed, even after a significant reduction resulting from a general reorganization of the US military in 2005 there remained 25,000 troops in South Korea proper – and there they will remain, at whatever strength, until a final settlement is reached. The long-running UN operations also reflect this trend in simple terms. For example, UNFICYP, the UN mission in Cyprus, was established in 1964 as a stabilizing measure following violence between the Greek and Turkish communities in the island – and it remains there to this day as a result of the inability to agree on a solution to the confrontation; yet until one is found the Green Line between the two communities has to be maintained by a small military force. The force has become smaller over the decades, but the operation nevertheless continues into its fifth decade. Where forces have intervened forcibly, and to a greater or lesser extent made the changes required to create the condition, then they still have to maintain it. In 1999 NATO was used again to establish a condition by bombing, this time in Kosovo. In this case it was a condition in which Slobodan Milosevic, president of Serbia, would hand over the administration of Kosovo, a province of Serbian sovereign territory, to the UN backed by a NATO force. The immediate aim of the condition was to remove the threat of oppression and ethnic cleansing from the majority of inhabitants in the province, the Albanian minority of Serbia. However, at no point before or during the bombing campaign was there a clear expression of the long-term political purpose. Was this action to create an independent Kosovo? Or was it to cause Milosevic to be deposed, to change the regime in Belgrade to one that could govern Kosovo to the UN's satisfaction? As has been noted several times in this book, without a clear political purpose it is not possible to have a military strategic objective. As a result, the NATO and US attacks were a series of tactical events coordinated by the daily Air Tasking Order, which decided on targets that were thought to bring pressure on Milosevic to withdraw from Kosovo. The condition was achieved after seventy-eight days of bombing and a series of diplomatic exchanges between the US, Russia and the OSCE on the one hand, and Milosevic on the other. After protracted negotiations in a tent on the Macedonian border with Serbia as to the modalities of occupation, NATO occupied the province and the UN began administering it. This deployment and administration, and therefore the condition, have remained precisely the same ever since: no strategic solution has been found.

In sum, the trend of our recent military operations is that the more the operation is intended to win the will of the people, the more the opponent adopts the method of the guerrilla and the more complex the circumstances, the longer it will take to reach the condition in which a strategic decision can be made and a solution found. And while it is being found the condition has to be maintained, and since in part at least it has been arrived at by force it must be maintained by force for want of the strategic decision. This situation is enabled, however, by the third reason for timelessness cited above: the switch between paradigms. In industrial war there was a need for a quick victory since the whole of society and the state were subjugated to the cause. All the machinery of state focused on this undertaking, whilst society and the economy completely halted their natural flow and productivity and became harnessed to the cause. War therefore had to be completed as soon as possible in order to allow for normal life and commerce to resume – the price to nations being exceptionally high when this did not happen, as in the two world wars. In the new paradigm military operations are but another activity of the state; indeed, they are designed specifically to be so – as the examples of the wars in Korea and Vietnam well reflect: as soon as there was a significant danger of the military operation expanding too much and invading civilian society beyond certain barriers, it was effectively halted, by either changing the objective or withdrawal. In other words, modern military operations are in practice dealt with as one amongst many activities of our states and can be sustained nearly endlessly: they are timeless.

WE FIGHT TO PRESERVE THE FORCE

The fourth trend brings us back to the pre-Napoleonic era, in which the warring armies could not fully commit to the definitive fight since, lacking a system of cheap manpower such as conscription and given the expense of materiel, they could not afford to replace their forces. These issues have once again become relevant in our modern times, for different reasons but with the same effect: we fight so as to preserve the force. A reason often cited now for this is the 'body bag' effect: democratic governments conducting operations for 'soft' objectives are uncertain of the support of those at home, and as has been shown repeatedly in these pages, every state and military must maintain the support of their people. The extent of the leaders' uncertainty is measured approximately but accurately in their degree of casualty aversion. This is undoubtedly the case, but I think the reasons for this trend go deeper than the need to maintain popular domestic support, critically important though that is.

Firstly, seeking to preserve the force is not only a characteristic of democratic leaders uncertain of their popular support. Guerrilla and other unconventional and non-state forces conduct war on this basis too, because it is difficult, time consuming and costly to replace men and materiel. The same reasons apply to the conventional armies of the post-war era – the Soviet army probably being the one exception, given its call upon vast numbers of conscripts and the extensive defence industries controlled and funded by the state. Yet even that army eventually came to consider the need to preserve the force, a trend strongly reinforced by its much-impoverished successor the Russian army. The armies of those nations that no longer have conscription – probably the majority in the Western world – have to compete with the other professions, commerce and industry for their share of national manpower. As a result, in order to pay a competitive rate and to have money in the budget for equipment and training, they tend constantly to reduce their numbers. Yet even with these much smaller armies, and in order to compete well on the national labour market, a significant proportion of the defence budget is usually allocated to pay and allowances; in Britain's case it is in the order of 50 per cent. Leaving aside the effects on morale of operations where men have a high expectation of being a casualty, wasting the lives of these expensive assets, particularly those with several years' experience, is bad economics.

For those countries, especially in Europe, that still have conscription, matters are no better. Often the law prevents the conscript from being employed on operations short of those defending the homeland, so when forces are required for other operations the conscript must volunteer. Sometimes for domestic political reasons this is done even if the law does not demand it. In addition, because of wanting to give every chance for the national manpower to be educated and in gainful employment, the conscript has a relatively short period of service and is trained for one task in one set of circumstances. So when he does volunteer he is likely to be volunteering for a longer period of service to cover the extra training required for the specific operation. In short, the volunteer conscript is a scarce asset and one not to be wasted, especially if volunteers are scarce owing to the high likelihood of becoming a casualty.

The situation is not much better regarding materiel: it is too scarce and expensive to waste. Much as the industrial-war personnel production line no longer exists now that conscription has largely been eliminated in most parts of the Western world, neither do the heavily subsidized wartime production lines for materiel. Therefore, apart from weapons or systems which are still being made for other customers – other armies – there is no commercial argument to keep a line open exclusively for a single army, except perhaps on a small scale to produce components for major overhauls. Indeed, the Soviet Union's attempts to maintain its wartime production lines when the force was not employed, and at the expense of the overall advance of material benefits to society, contributed to its collapse. And so our current reality dictates that lost equipment in any great quantity could be replaced only slowly and at great expense – neither of which are acceptable in any state that has set other issues of civilian betterment as national priorities. Indeed, it appears that the US alone in the Western world can commit forces, or at least materiel, on a more open-ended basis, but even there strong reservations in political and civil society exist. Moreover, given the cost of many items, even with a vast budget there is still a limit: US and British forces in Iraq in 2003–4 complained of shortages ranging from flak jackets to suitable communications. Finally, the source of many major items of equipment for most armies everywhere is not national but international, and few nations if any have complete control over their industrial defence base. The states with large economies and an inclination to sustain large militaries, such as the US, China and Russia, probably have the most control over their defence industries, but even US defence production is made cooperatively with other industries around the world. Any nation that sought total control over its industrial defence base would have to invest billions, and even then would probably have to tolerate a limited array of capabilities.

All this leads to the reality of our modern forces and commitments: the armies, both men and equipment, are often earmarked for a number of eventualities. In the Gulf in 1990–91, commanding the British Armoured Division, I felt these pressures palpably. I had all the up-to-date tanks in the British army, and because the engines were unreliable I was also given very nearly every tank engine in the inventory. The rest of the army had been stripped of its equipment in order to give me a sustainable force. I was conscious that I had the bulk of the army's modern assets in my command, that there were no production lines standing ready to replace losses, and that we had other commitments that might require them. I thought at the time, and still do, that I was the first British general for a long time who had to consider how to fight so as not to lose the army. I am not suggesting my predecessors were careless of their commands; they were not. But when faced with the prospect of battle they knew there were reserves of equipment elsewhere in the service, and an industrial base behind them capable of rapidly producing replacements. None of my superiors ever said to me directly that I had the train set and they would like it back as near complete as possible, but I was struck at the time how, when I was visited by any senior military commander or official from Britain, many of their concerns were to do with the equipment. In fact, the understanding that I needed to fight so as not to lose the force in part shaped the way I planned to use my command in our attack into Iraq. As it happened, the enemy proved to be a poor lot and we managed to bring almost everything back.

In our current circumstances forces in many countries are in a similar position. They are over-committed, and cannot afford to sustain any losses. Taxpayers pay their taxes for a force to defend hearth and home; they may approve of it being used for some other venture but they expect their defenders to be ready and available in case of need. A judgement has to be made, therefore, as to how much the capability to defend is mortgaged so as to engage in other ventures. And these, as we have seen, are timeless: a nation may commit forces to a new operation, but still have a commitment of forces to maintain the condition elsewhere. Taking the major international operations since 1991: Iraq was followed by Bosnia and Croatia, which were followed by Kosovo, which was followed by Afghanistan, which was followed by Iraq again, and whilst each of these operations was in motion other forces were staying behind to maintain those still in process. In addition, there were quite a few smaller operations in Africa throughout this period, including Rwanda, the Congo and Sierra Leone, to name only the obvious, to which many of the nations with forces already involved in the situations listed above also sent forces. This is triple earmarking, or worse – and in most cases with small armies and reduced resources. Moreover, if a new crisis were to arise, then further forces would have to be found to undertake and sustain them.

The lack of forces and resources is a major contributor to the situation in which we find ourselves, having difficulty in sustaining the forces we have committed already. The US, despite its comparatively large forces, is finding it difficult to sustain its current commitments. The forces of the European states when added together would appear to be of a comparable size to those of the US, yet fail to produce anything like the same number of deployable forces. This is so even allowing for the manpower overheads carried by the separate infrastructure of each nation, such as a general staff and HQ, a Ministry of Defence and so on. The reason is that in many cases such forces are still structured for industrial war: their reserves of manpower are trained, organized and held until needed on mobilization to expand the army, and to give it the ability to carry out a range of tasks needed to be done by or for the military only in war. For example, most armies differentiate between the military engineers that make or cross obstacles, such as laying minefields or bridging rivers, and those who construct buildings and roads. The former are usually field units, the latter are usually reserve units, to be called up in an emergency and with an understanding that civil society will not be able to use these men during their period of military call-up. In our modern wars we need the civil engineers more than we do the military ones, who are required for the manoeuvre of large forces on the battlefield. But to provide these building and road engineers means calling up the reserves for a long period and reducing the capacity to maintain, for example, the motorway system at home. From a political perspective, such discomfort to the civilian population would be disastrous – and so it is rarely attempted. As a result, many forces that deploy into war amongst the people lack both the necessary skills and the materiel for the tasks they face.

At root, therefore, our forces are still structured within the industrial paradigm, and we are constantly reorganizing them to conduct these modern operations. And when we do not reorganize, we find we have large forces in theatre that contribute little to achieving the objective but none the less need guarding and feeding: the force has no utility. Moreover, without reorganization we have difficulty sustaining the operation. This is the most endemic organizational feature of our modern operations – and as I noted in the preface to this book, it has come to be regarded as normal. But unless we stop seeing this situation of constant flux in this light, and start making fundamental reorganizations of our forces, we will find that rather than a difficulty in sustaining our forces in theatre, the entire situation will become unsustainable. And whilst reorganization for an operation in the face of specific circumstances is undoubtedly part of the important concept of organizational mobility, which is critical to any use of force, our current situation is none the less different. This is not simple adaptation in response to the actions of the enemy but a conceptual failure, since it is a continuous attempt to draw forces from organizations structured in a specific way and for a specific purpose – industrial war – for a completely different concept of conflict – war amongst the people. If our forces in action are to have utility, we need to organize our standing forces to reflect the change in paradigm and accommodate the need to form an appropriate force for each operation.

ON EACH NEW OCCASION NEW USES ARE FOUND FOR OLD WEAPONS AND ORGANIZATIONS

Following on from the basic flaws in the structures of our forces, the fifth trend is that we are using weapon systems in ways for which they were not originally designed and purchased. The bulk of the equipment we have today was acquired to defeat the Soviet threat in industrial war – but the enemies we face today are of a completely different nature, usually armed with much lighter weapons. Indeed, the most effective weapon of the past fifteen years was the machete, with which nearly a million people were slaughtered in Rwanda over three months in 1994. In purely numerical terms, that is a higher ratio than any of the industrial wars. The AK-47 and the suicide bomber have been equally effective if not as efficient, and are absolutely central to most of the current conflicts in which a variety of states and coalitions are and have been engaged since the end of the Cold War. Moreover, the sides that use these weapons are most often exceedingly adept with them. I am not proposing that we equip forces with just machetes, but we now have to adapt our own industrial, high-technology weapons to these circumstances.

Each state has a slightly different process for acquiring or procuring the equipment its armed forces need, but they all share common characteristics. The process is founded upon the logic of industrial war: that there must be an identifiable threat, in terms of an enemy and his weapons, which must be matched by weaponry operated and organized in such a way as to defeat it. The key is to gain the technological edge over the threat. Operational concepts and organizations tend to be adjusted to take advantage of the technology rather than to fight in a different way. The business of war is closely linked with this process: there are always budgetary difficulties, and as a result equipment tends to be acquired to improve existing measures of proven requirement rather than to bring into service a new equipment type altogether, or to deal with anything but the primary threat. If a case had been made for the fighter-bombers we have today on the basis they would be used to patrol no-fly zones over Iraq or Bosnia, or to drop small quantities of bombs on small tactical targets, I doubt they would have been purchased. And when new equipment is designed, its cost is kept down by limiting it to the specific threat. For example, the Challenger tanks and some of the aircraft I had under my command in the Gulf lacked any or adequate sand filters because they were designed to face the Soviet threat on the plains of north-west Germany. When commissioned, the budget did not allow for any extras, so when the tanks were finally needed they had to be rapidly adapted to the new threat. Much of the reported comment about General Wesley Clark, the NATO Supreme Allied Commander Europe (SACEUR) at the time of the Kosovo bombings in 1999, and well covered in his book *Fighting Modern War*, concerns his search for a way to use the means or weapon systems available to him in the face of the Serb defences – to achieve the end he had been set. This search for a new way to use the means that had been acquired and organized for a different purpose and enemy, and the frictions it caused, underpins much of the story he has to tell.

The major reason for this trend is that the opponents have learned to drop below the threshold of the utility of our weapon systems. They have learned not to present a target that favours the weapons we possess and the way we use them. When they make a mistake out of pride or overconfidence they suffer, but unless the blows they receive are catastrophic they learn from the experience and seldom repeat them. Consider the case of General Aideed, the Somali warlord in Mogadishu in 1993, where he faced a US force operating in support of the UN. If we compared the inventories of both sides, the US force was qualitatively and probably quantitatively superior. But whether by accident or design Aideed found a way of operating at the tactical level that offered the US force little option other than to engage on his terms – and some eighteen dead and seventy wounded men later, the US force was withdrawn. In theory, of course, the US had the option of bringing its full military industrial weight to bear, but this was not judged to be practical for international and domestic political reasons: the difficulty of finding the targets and the high probability of large numbers of civilian casualties, set against doubtful support for the venture at home, decided the matter in Washington. It might have been different if Aideed had refused to hand over the bodies of the US dead, but he understood the threat very well – and in any case had no further use for them. Certainly Aideed operated as he did because he had to find a way to use the weapons he had, but primarily because his objectives were to gain control of the distribution of food, and thereby gain power and control over the people. He wanted the US force to leave – to change intentions; he did not want to defeat it. On the other hand, Saddam Hussein in 1991 showed the world that co-operating with the US concept of war, particularly in an open desert, was not a recipe for success: his armies were badly beaten. But he had got himself into a position from which he could not retreat without being seen to be forced out; therefore the bigger and stronger the force doing the forcing, the more he could be seen to be outnumbered and out-forced, the better for his purposes.

Those who depend on the tactics of the guerrilla or terrorist tend to avoid presenting themselves as a target suitable for attack by the weapons and tactics of the industrial war, at least until they are ready to compete on those terms, as General Giap did with the French at Dien Bien Phu. The guerrilla trick is to force the conventional military opponent to fight on his terms, where he is likely to have the advantage, or else to force the military to react in a full industrial manner against the guerrilla fighting amongst the people, and so reinforce the strategy of provocation and the propaganda of the deed. The IRA, who see themselves and to a large measure run themselves as an army, have been very careful to operate below the threshold of the utility of the British army's weapon systems, and the army, in turn, has been careful not to introduce those systems into the Irish theatre. Infantry battalions are reorganized before deployment, and the support company, which mans the heavier infantry weapons such as mortars, is re-roled as a rifle company whilst the numbers in the surveillance and reconnaissance units are increased. When large numbers have been needed to sustain the operation, artillery, armoured and engineer units have also been re-roled into rifle companies. All units are put through a training regime before deployment to ensure that they are practised in the tactics that have been developed to counter those of the IRA.

The business of war influences this trend in another way too: the industries that create the weapons and the platforms tend to persist in manufacturing them within the model of industrial war. And so, even when equipment is replaced – either massively, as in the case of the US, or else on a more piecemeal basis elsewhere – it is done within the assumptions of the old paradigm. This means that once again it usually needs to be reorganized and adapted for every conflict; and if the reorganization is not successful, the force will not have utility. The US forces in Iraq, for example, complained in late 2004 about the lack of suitable and adequately armoured vehicles, and apparently needed to scrounge for metal in rubbish heaps to provide additional protection for their vehicles. This was not only a shortage of armoured vehicles necessary to patrol in the hostile environment so much as an abundance of 'soft skinned' vehicles, which are a standing mode of transport behind the front in industrial war. Once again, therefore, it is clear the change of paradigm has not been acknowledged, and it is this conceptual gap that is influencing the production of new equipment, which is often not suitable for the current forms of military operations.

THE SIDES ARE MOSTLY NON-STATE

The final trend is that we tend to conduct our confrontations and conflicts in some form of multinational grouping, whether it is an alliance or a coalition, and against some party or parties that are not states. Indeed, in many of our modern conflicts it is only the soldiers that are representatives of states – yet they are operating within groupings and environments that are either sub- or supra-national. From an international perspective, this trend is to an extent a consequence of some of the others: the choice of ends and the timelessness of our operations. The more the objectives are 'softer' and pertain to achieving a condition, and the longer they go on, the greater the imperative for interested states to join together.

We enter into these arrangements for a number of reasons: we need more forces, or more space; we want the legitimacy of numbers; we want to spread the risk – of failure, to resource, of responsibility; and we all want a seat at the table. As noted in Chapter 6, an alliance is of a more permanent nature and denotes equality amongst all members; coalitions are usually ad hoc affairs, led by one or two powerful members. An alliance is formed in anticipation of the event, in an attempt to deter some course of action, and there is usually some coordination of planning and training to make it the more useful. The main difficulty with alliances is agreeing the common purpose, and hence the strategic objective, when the case in point falls short of the event for which it was formed. Coalitions are products of a specific event, with the allies joining because they have a shared objective. Coalitions need not be formal: in effect the 2002–3 US operation in Afghanistan was in coalition with the Northern Alliance, and NATO's 1999 operation in Kosovo was allied with the Kosovo Liberation Army (KLA) for as long as the bombing continued. In those operations of a more humanitarian nature, informal coalitions are formed also with the many non-governmental organizations (NGOs). However, these informal coalitions need sensitive and careful handling, since by definition the purposes of the two organizations – military and NGOs – are mostly disparate, and they have joined together owing to circumstance and necessity rather than a shared ideology. Whether formal or informal, one must always bear in mind that the glue that holds a coalition together is a common enemy, not a common desired political outcome. There must, therefore, be measures put in place to cover the loss of cohesion that results from victory. Examples of the absence of such measures are the deep divide between Russia and the Allies after the Second World War or NATO and the KLA in Kosovo after the success of the bombing campaign in 1999.

The commander of an international military force, especially one formed within an international organization, must always be aware of the political factors behind the makeup of the alliance or coalition. Indeed, the nature of the relationship between allies is an important factor in the context of the operation: the basis of the collaboration, whether practical or moral or legal, must be absolutely clear at the highest level and transmitted down, since it will ultimately define the limits of the shared activity. And when military force is intended to be used at the lower levels then this contextual understanding has to be found at those levels too, most especially for the commander at the level at which military action is contemplated. He needs to understand that his force is not a whole: each national contingent will have been sent for different reasons, and its government and people will have a different balance as to the risks and rewards. Each contingent will have to some degree different equipment, organization, doctrines and training, and each will have a different source of materiel as well as varying social, legal and political support. The result of these differences is that allies usually agree on objectives that tend towards the lowest common denominator of the options available. Each of the allies is in it for their own reward and the nature of this reward must be understood by the commander.

Such multinational groupings of states are opposed by groupings that are also not states. They might be the parties to a civil war or an insurgency, whether operating as formed armies or guerrillas or terrorist groups or the band of some warlord. In contrast to the formality of the multinational organization, and its dependence on the formulas and procedures that states impose on it so as to manage their affairs at the least risk to themselves, the non-state actors appear formless. They often use political and military titles borrowed from the terminology of states, and use the nomenclatures of formed industrial armies to describe the organization of their forces, but they are not states in either law or fact. Moreover, even if one or more sides appears to have a just or moral cause, one must not be fooled into assuming it is a formulated side, representing a position that is coherent with the majority of the population and with the structures and procedures to provide accountability. Such an unfounded assumption was the case with, for example, the US support of the KLA in 1999.

Clausewitz's trinity of state, army and people is a useful tool with which to analyse the actors' purpose and activities, despite their not being states. As I have already noted, the aim of all sides, including the intervening international force, is to win the will of the people. Therefore the non-state side will also have some dependency and relationship with the people, there will be an armed force of some description and there will be some political direction to the use of that force. It is very possible, particularly in the early stages of the life of one of these organizations, that both the military and political decisions lie in the hands of one or a few men, but nonetheless they will be separate decisions. A warlord whose primary purpose is to profit from the diamonds mined in his area will have to establish political relations with his market, with other warlords and with neighbours through whom he can move his goods and proceeds. He will be dependent on the people at least as a source of labour, and probably as a source of supply and military manpower. He will probably have considerable military forces more or less organized to do his bidding. He will use them to defend his interests and possibly to expand them, and they will probably be used to coerce the people into supporting the warlord's policies. It does not matter that he is apparently formless: he will have a form, but as discussed elsewhere it will be one that operates to his logic, not ours. In searching for his form, assumptions are made which often lack foundation. I remember during the London conference in 1995 that ultimately led to the military operations that stopped the war in Bosnia, the then SACEUR, General Joulwan, briefed the conference that the Bosnian Serbs had three corps massed around Sarajevo. In fact they had no such thing. His intelligence officers had assumed apparently that the Bosnian Serb Army was organized as a NATO army and had interpreted the unit titles accordingly, assuming a corps was a formation of manoeuvre rather than a static organization for territorial defence. Following upon this logic, one must also be careful not to legitimize the opponent or to make him more powerful than he is. Just because he says he is a general or the local party leader, or because he is gaining a lot of international or local media time, does not of itself require one to cooperate with what is often something of a fiction. Doing so tends to bolster such fiction, whilst at the same time establishing the importance of this person in the eyes of the people, thereby reinforcing his position. When entering into operations where the objective is one of establishing a condition one has to be particularly careful of making a wrong move. The 1999 operation in Kosovo was a case in point. The aim was to rid the province of ethnically based violence, particularly Serbian aggression against ethnic Albanians, by taking it under international administration. In using military force to achieve this end, common cause was made with the KLA, which became legitimized as a result. Regrettably, during the fighting and in the immediate aftermath of the international occupation, Serbs, a minority in the province, were driven from their homes. Moreover, in 2005, with the international administration still in place, the democratically elected prime minister of Kosovo, a former KLA leader, was indicted by the International Criminal Tribunal for the former Yugoslavia (ICTY) for crimes committed during the 1999 fighting; he resigned and flew to The Hague to stand trial.

This leads to the final reality reflected by this sixth trend, in which it is the soldiers of the international force who are the only clear representatives of defined states. There is no such entity as an international soldier, even if he or she dons a blue helmet or fights under the NATO banner or is part of an 'international coalition' as in Iraq. Upon recruitment each soldier swears allegiance to the state to which the army belongs, and he or she remains within that allegiance and legal framework – whilst the state loans them to an alliance or a coalition for a limited period or for an operation. On the ground, therefore, it will be a national soldier representing a non-state coalition or organization, fighting a formless or non-state opponent. In these circumstances the commander of a multinational force, himself representing a state, has a very difficult balance to strike and maintain as he strives to reach his objective.

The absence of a formulated enemy is a main reason for the unlikelihood of conducting interstate industrial war, and is therefore a strong underpinning element of the new paradigm of war. This absence also reflects the near completion of a circle: interstate industrial war saw the subordination of the individual to the nation state for the purpose of victory on the battlefield; the strategic bombing of the Second World War, and the Holocaust, saw the nation state attacking the individual and the blurring of the defined borders of the battlefield; in the new paradigm of war the individual has turned on the nation state, whether through terrorist attacks or the use of force outside the framework of the state, against the totems (including the armies) of the nation state. Whether we are living in a post-nation-state world remains to be fully clarified, but it is possible to believe that the nation state is fighting for its supremacy. And it is within the context of this fight that it sends out its forces on operations, seeking to preserve and advance its interests as a state but within non-state formulations. It is for that reason that the forces of the state often lack utility. What must now be examined are the political and military mechanisms within which such forces operate – and how they might be improved.

8

Direction: Setting the Purpose for
the Use of Force

Taken together, the six trends discussed in the previous chapter show that we cannot now be practising industrial war. Rather, we are engaging in conflict for objectives that do not lead to a resolution of the matter directly by force of arms, since at all but the most basic tactical level our objectives tend to concern the intentions of the people and their leaders rather than their territory or forces. As a result we often find ourselves battling with these leaders for the will of their people, hoping to sway the latter towards our intentions. We are not using the weapons we procured or produced for the purpose or in the way we intended, and we fight with forces that we cannot afford to lose; indeed, we have difficulty in sustaining the forces we have committed already. In short, we are engaged in a different paradigm of war, one that is patently based upon confrontations that cross into conflicts – yet we persist in viewing them as either potential industrial wars or else deviations from them. So much so that there is now a fashion of referring to 'military operations other than war' or 'warfighting capabilities' as well as 'peace enforcement' and 'stabilization and implementation operations', whilst troops and soldiers have become 'warfighters'. All of these suggest a change in reality is being acknowledged, but when closely examined it is clear these phrases, which have even led to official military doctrines, are formulated entirely within the vision and understanding of industrial war – yet as an adjunct, which is why it is necessary to define these activities and actors as something other than war. There seems to be no acknowledgement whatsoever that it is the vision that is in need of change rather than operational scope or nomenclature.

In this light it becomes clear that the six trends actually reflect not only the characteristics of the new paradigm, but also the endemic flaws in our approach. These manifest themselves in both the political and military spheres, and especially in the relationship between the two. For it is not just the military that is still caught up in the paradigm of industrial war, since it is the political leadership that sends out forces in search of a solution to a problem, assuming it can be definitively resolved by the deployment of force. It is also the political leaders who allocate the funds to the military and are responsible for creating and maintaining the political will for military operations, and also the sustainment of each nation's standing forces. Equally, it is the political leaders who create coalitions and alliances, and multinational military missions with the inevitable convoluted chains of command. Finally, it is the political leadership that, in seeking to use the forces available to it, endeavours to do so without risk to its asset – the force itself – and without ensuring the military actions are coherent with the actions of its other levers of power. In other words, it seeks to use force like a tool out of a box, without a blueprint for the item under construction. Nevertheless, it is still the military that is caught up in outdated concepts of war, and persists in organizing forces according to that end. It is also the military that is still engaged with seeking the technological solution to threats of an industrial-warlike nature – even if the existing and emerging threats are clearly different.

At base, therefore, the civil–military relationship that underpins the current paradigm is deeply problematic and shapes its application in many ways. The institutions of both are at the heart of the matter – as are also deep misunderstandings, and possibly ignorance, as to the different purposes for which force can be used and the way in which it can be used, especially amongst the people. Such decisions are made on the basis of intelligence and data on the enemy, yet I would suggest that here too the concepts of industrial war have made such a deep mark upon the institutions dealing with these matters that the different realities posed by war amongst the people have yet to be properly assessed. Understanding these different elements of decision making, and the world of the force commander who has ultimately to bring them together in the application of force, is the purpose of this chapter.

As already stated, the political leadership is the source of power in which the purpose of entering into the conflict is decided – as also the process of formulating the aim and the overall political guidance. This is done in the institutions of the nation state that govern the use of military force – ministries for foreign affairs, defence, legal affairs and the military services – which are themselves the product of the development of the state and the application of industrial war. Their very being, and therefore world vision, is predicated on industrial war. Even those states whose beginnings lie with the antithesis to industrial war, such as China with Mao's Revolutionary War, adopted the forms and institutions of industrial war as they became states. As a result of this conceptual genesis, the process of committing military forces to achieve objectives that fall short of a strategic military decision of industrial war pose difficulties to these institutions. These difficulties unfortunately relate to five areas endemic to any military operation:

- Undertaking and maintaining analysis of the opposing force, including the collection of information and intelligence to support the analysis.
- Identifying and stating the aim and objectives of an operation.
- Limiting the risks of the chosen course of action to achieve the objective.
- Directing and coordinating the overall effort.
- Forming and maintaining the will to succeed.

These difficulties of comprehension, which are constantly apparent in current military operations, be they national or multinational – the latter being composed of national forces more or less directed by their own institutions – are the result of the policy-making institutions viewing all situations as either war of the old industrial type or as something unwarlike for which armed force is of doubtful value. Possibly the best example of this can be found in the six principles of the Weinberger Doctrine, and their aftermath. After the Vietnam War, which had enmeshed the state in controversy both internally and internationally, much military and political thought was dedicated to the issue of US involvement in conflicts around the world. The most notable and propagated thought came from the then secretary of defence Caspar W. Weinberger, who in 1984 outlined six conditions which a conflict should meet before the US should consider becoming involved:

1. It should be of vital national interest to the United States and its allies.
2. Intervention must occur wholeheartedly with a clear intention of winning.
3. There must be clearly defined political and military objectives.
4. The relationship between the objectives and the forces must be continually reassessed and adjusted if necessary.
5. There must be a reasonable assurance that the American people and Congress will support the intervention.
6. Commitment of US forces should be the last resort.

Weinberger defined these conditions as an 'intervention test' that, in his mind, would prevent the US from becoming entrapped in another quagmire. Subsequently, General Colin Powell, when he was Chairman of the Joint Chiefs of Staff during the Gulf War 1990–91, added a further principle: that should the US intervene, the operation should be short, occasion few casualties to US forces, and the force used must be decisive and overwhelming.

On first reading these principles may seem thoroughly sensible and straightforward, which they are – but not for our current conflicts, since individually and taken together they describe a set of circumstances where the political tenets of industrial war are satisfied. From the point of view of a system with a tools designed for a specific purpose, industrial war, they are reasonable as a means of ensuring the tool is not misused. But armies are not tools; the means they possess and use, the weapons, are the tools – it is the way the means are used, and to what ends, that characterizes armies and their relationship to their political masters. On closer examination one can see that many of the issues the Weinberger principles seek to define before the event can be clear only during or after the event, and are open to multiple interpretations. And General Powell's addition supposes the enemy can be defeated quickly, and that such a defeat will lead directly to the achievement of the political purpose. But for situations where the object is the will of the people, where the enemy is operating as guerrillas, or where conditions of acceptable governance are to be created and maintained, these assumptions are unlikely to be satisfied. And as is amply evident in conflicts around the world, from Iraq to Haiti, from Kosovo to the Congo, in which US and other international forces have become involved, the conditions are decidedly not satisfied.

For a brief period that lasted from the point at which they were formulated in the mid 1980s to the end of the Cold War, Weinberger's principles appeared to have validity, because the institutions could argue with justification that the primary purpose of deterrence required them to have the credible appearance of a force capable of industrial war on a massive scale. With the end of the Cold War this reason evaporated, yet we have continued to conduct our analysis within the industrial model. Indeed, the principles and the ethos they represent have become an obstacle to using military force with utility, since they are based on flawed assumptions that have none the less become written in stone. Take as an example the idea that 'commitment of force should be the last resort'. Is it? The assumptions on which such an assertion rests seem to be as follows:

- That there is an orderly process recognized by both parties in which force is the last act.
- That force is an alternative to other options rather than being used in concert with them.
- That when all other options have been exhausted force will provide the solution.

The assumptions are satisfied generally when one considers the peace–crisis–war build-up to an industrial war in pursuit of a strategic military decision. But what if force cannot provide the solution? Does one just pile on more force? And if this might work, will the price be too high to bear? What other options are there other than to accept defeat? And if not, how do you terminate the engagement if your last resort is not working – or is defeat an exit strategy?

As shown in previous chapters, US forces have continued to become engaged in conflicts around the world in spite of the

Weinberger principles. For as former secretary of state Madeleine Albright said when a general was using the principles in arguing against deploying US forces into some conflict: 'What is the point of having all this army if we don't use it?' And lest it be thought I am being particularly critical of the US, I can only emphasize that I refer to many governments that have sent out forces, whose deployments in almost all cases have been marked by characteristics that stem from the understanding of conflict born of industrial war and embedded in our institutions. I have heard arguments running along the lines of the Weinberger principles in other capitals, including London, particularly when I was the Assistant Chief of the Defence Staff for Operations and Security in the Ministry of Defence in 1993–4. Take for example the genocide in Rwanda in the summer of 1994. There was a debate between the policy-making institutions – Foreign and Commonwealth Office (FCO) and Ministry of Defence (MOD) officials – which unfolded over the weeks of the massacre. The starting point was a political recognition that appalling events were happening – and, to be absolutely clear, a sensible sense of the fact too: the human need to act in the face of appalling events. The UK, not having any people on the ground in the inadequate UN mission in Rwanda described in the previous chapter, had been surprised by the news, and had an incomplete picture of what was happening. Against this background, a sense of the institutional debate based upon the assumption that military force could and should be used may be derived from the following:

FCO: What can we do in the face of events in Rwanda?

MOD: What do you want us to do?

FCO: We ought to act. Something must be done. We can't have people being massacred. As a permanent member of the UN Security Council we cannot be seen to be doing nothing.

MOD: So you want us to use military force?

FCO: Yes.

MOD: To do what? To stop the killing?

FCO: Yes. Exactly.

MOD: Who do you want us to fight? We are not clear who is doing the killing: is it tribe on tribe, or is it a force found from a tribe? And

Rwanda is a big country. Where do we start? Kigali, presumably, it's the capital and we would want an air-head.

FCO: Well, there must be an international force, of course.

MOD: And what would be the British aim in joining the force?

FCO: To play our part as a permanent member of the UN Security Council.

MOD: Is Britain to lead the force?

FCO: No, it should be led by the UN – a proper UN mission.

MOD: That will take some time to assemble, so it will probably be too late to stop the killing.

FCO: Then the mission should be aimed at bringing post-conflict order.

MOD: OK. But we need to be clear how many British troops are currently available. Given our deployments in Ireland, Bosnia and a few other places, not many.

FCO: What do you suggest?

MOD: What are our government's priorities? Is contributing to this force a higher priority than these other tasks we are already undertaking?

FCO: Probably not.

MOD: In that case, these UN forces always lack expeditionary logistic support. And if we want to speed up the deployment of this force, offering a logistic unit would probably be the most valuable contribution.

FCO: Will that put our soldiers at risk?

MOD: Hardly any.

The conclusion of the debate was put into action, and the outcome was that the fighting was not stopped, the genocide unfolded, a new UN mission was eventually assembled to help restore order – the hapless UNAMIR had by then been drawn down to under 400 troops – and the UK contributed the logistics. From the perspective of this chapter, however, it is the underlying ethos that is most important. If we take the six Weinberger principles, we can see them all at play – or not, which is why there was no military intervention: the conflict was not a vital national interest; there was absolutely no wholeheartedness or intention of winning; it was not possible to define political and military objectives; as events unfolded, and the awfulness became apparent, the relationship between the objectives and potential forces were continually reassessed, reinforcing the option of not intervening since too many would be necessary; there was at the time little public interest or support for intervention; and the UN presented an option which meant a last resort was not reached.

The principles are a useful way of understanding these events, but it is also important to emphasize that, at base, both sides to the debate were examining whether a war – old-fashioned industrial war – could be fought and, coming to the conclusion it could not, lost interest. Or rather, sent out a UN peacekeeping mission to sort out the mess rather than stop it – though if there ever was an example of a situation that might have been resolved or at least greatly ameliorated by a short, sharp intervention at the start it was Rwanda in 1994. By which I mean, the employment of force with the object of making it abundantly clear to those leading the rebels that ethnic violence in the face of a UN resolution would be punished. Given the rebels' limited armament, machetes and AK-47s, this would not have involved any heavy lifting of a massive force. But this did not happen, for the corollary to the Weinberger formulation is that if war is not possible, it is also not possible to apply force, since force can be applied only in war. In other words, peacekeeping must be – and is – a derivative of industrial war, and as such is toothless.

A hallmark of modern warfare divided between political and military levels is the not infrequent complaints of political interference in military affairs. The Duke of Wellington was assumed to have been his usual blunt self on this matter in a letter he is supposed to have addressed to the secretary of state for war during the Peninsular Campaign:

My Lord,
If I attempted to answer the mass of futile correspondence which surrounds me, I should be debarred from the serious business of campaigning . . . So long as I retain an independent position, I shall see no officer under my command is debarred by attending to the futile drivelling of mere quill-driving from attending to his first duty, which is and always has been to train the private men under his command that they may without question beat any force opposed to them in the field.

Another example is Moltke the elder's general staff resenting Bismarck's interference. I can also think of occasions when I too have been irritated by what appeared to me the unreasonable demands of politicians. However, as will become evident in the discussion in the following chapter, since my experience as Commander UNPROFOR in 1995, when I operated in a political vacuum, I have no doubt that any form of political involvement is better than none. Proper and ongoing political involvement is an ingredient vital to the success of an operation, in a confrontation no less (and possibly more) than a conflict, since both the political and military acts must be closely aligned. This is especially true in our modern confrontations and conflicts, although the fact that these are often pursued within multi-national organizations or ad hoc alliances unfortunately makes such coordinated involvement exceptionally difficult to attain, since all the nuances of relationship between the political and strategic levels, and also the political and military entities, are multiplied several times over. In theory, there is a core mechanism in each organization or coalition that should allow for coherence of thought, plan, command and action to be sought and decided. In practice this does not always happen. In NATO there is a standing forum of ambassadors and senior military representatives to negotiate all issues, especially during a crisis; each is briefed and instructed by the foreign ministry and highest political levels in their own capitals, and between them they will evolve the political guidance for the strategic level: the military headquarters of the allied command in Mons. This in turn is made up of officers from all NATO nations, forming a staff that can order and direct the deployment in theatre. However, while each officer in principle and in practice is supporting the Supreme Allied Commander Europe (SACEUR), each also remains linked to his or her paymasters at home. The more senior the officer, the more must the national link be expected to be open and working.

Whilst these frameworks function quite well on a general basis, this is not always the case in time of crisis. Capitals speak to each other whilst also briefing their ambassadors and officers; equally, they also seek direct contact with their deployed forces rather than going through the NATO chain of command. It is an extremely delicate and often complex web. The UN is an even more complicated proposition, since it lacks a strategic military structure. As a result, nations deal directly with their contingents on the ground, sometimes confounding the theatre commander who is attempting to employ them within his plan. For ultimately, each contingent remains under command of its parent state, since this is the source of its legitimacy and administrative support. To this end it hands a limited authority of command, depending on the circumstances, to the multinational commander. The national contingent commanders find themselves reporting to both their national and multinational commanders. This duality of command demands careful management, particularly in view of the ease of modern communications and the ever-present media. Indeed, the handling of an allied command can be considered as another confrontation: a collaborative confrontation that is held together by the shared intent of all the nations involved. The commander must take great care that he understands just how far the shared intent will stretch. He must set out to establish a relationship with capitals whereby rather than seeking their permission through consensus one gains their consent to employ and deploy their loaned national force. This is difficult to achieve because the political decision to act together is consensual, and one wants the national political authorities to consent to military decisions that may have a national political impact. The strategic-level commanders should make every possible arrangement to facilitate this translation from consensus to consent. But in the end the degree to which this will be achieved is a direct measure of the confidence each capital has in the multinational commander – that he understands their position, is not careless of their interest and knows when and what to ask. This characteristic of command will exist as long as we have multinational forces, particularly when the forces are drawn from democratic states. The politician who decides to provide the force is responsible to the people, the electors; the degree to which risk to the force can be tolerated is in direct proportion to the value of the endeavour to the people, and confidence in the commander – a man perhaps known only by reputation – weighs heavily when assessing that risk. In this regard I always think it best to remember the old saying that fame has no present and popularity no future.

As of the Gulf War 1990–91, when in command of an operation in these circumstances I have been guided by three rules, the effects of which are interrelated:

- *For every endeavour ensure there is an objective or purpose in common.* Especially when capitals are involved and wish to limit the risk to their forces, this can be difficult to achieve. As a result, one may have to allocate a particular endeavour to one or two contingents, but this limits one's capability, is a weakness the opponent can exploit and is bad for an alliance in that the burden is not shared. Such an option should therefore be avoided if at all possible.

- *Ensure there is equity in risk and reward.* By this I do not mean that every ally should expect to carry the same risks and gain the same reward, but rather that each ally should be rewarded in proportion to the risk it carries. This is as much a matter of presentation as anything else, and should be in the forefront of a commander's mind when considering his public information policy, in which the proportional share of the burden is established in the most positive way. This is much more important, and not the same thing at all, as mentioning one's 'superb allies' at the start of every address to camera.

- *Conduct command on the basis of goodwill to all allies.* If the commander and his staff do this, then others will follow. The moment the corrosive attitudes of mistrust, envy and dislike are loose in the command, its fragile morale is doomed. One's best advocates in the capitals that supplied the troops of the command are their own commanders.

In the past years there has been much talk of interoperability and the search for standardization of common procedures and equipment amongst the militaries of many nations. Interoperability means the measures necessary to work together effectively with the different national organizations and equipment as they are; in short, sorting out the mess. Standardization means the measures necessary to avoid the mess in the first place. However, important though these issues are, they depend utterly on the value of the three human factors I list above. And a commander of a multinational force that does not incorporate them will probably have problems in and with his command.

The organization of the multinational force must be understood for what it is capable of rather than abstract aspirations such as 'bringing peace' or for other such goals for which it is neither equipped nor especially staffed. I call this understanding the 'level of the fight'. As I have already noted, the national components of the force are all connected to a different source or capital and have different restraints and constraints on their actions. It would be nice if this were not so, but the reality must be taken into account by those setting the context for the operation as much as by those conducting it. Each fight or specific tactical engagement can only be undertaken by a national grouping; to do otherwise in the stress of the moment is to ask more of the language skills, training, military cultures and the interoperability of equipment than can be borne safely. This is true of all services. For example, in an air raid the package of aircraft types and functions – bomber, fighter, electronic warfare, anti-radar, command and control – might be multinational, but all the aircraft attacking a specific target at a particular time will be from the same nation. The land battle is more complex, since even in a small grouping such as a company of tanks there are between nine and twelve vehicles engaged over a large area. Except in a flat desert this means that the tank commanders all have a different understanding of the battle, depending on the nature of the terrain they are in and its relation to the objective. Add some supporting artillery and infantry, and of course enemy fire, and matters become even more complex. It would be absurd to expect commanders to be translating orders into another language at this point.

Understanding the 'level of the fight' can be applied in two circumstances. The first occurs when one is already in the situation, as happened to me in Bosnia in 1995. My force was composed in the main of battalions from different nations; each was deployed in its own area, carrying out its mission and with a base to secure. As a result no battalion could be manoeuvred as a whole, which meant the level of the fight I could have was at best that of a reinforced company, a subdivision of a battalion.

However, the opponent I ultimately came to fight, the Bosnian Serbs, were operating in company and battalion groupings supported by artillery – and so to have any prospect of winning I needed under my hand battalions from single nations that I could manoeuvre together with an artillery group. As events in that year unfolded these assets were provided by France, Britain and the Netherlands. With this ability I could then plan to use my force to advantage, choosing objectives of an appropriate size accordingly and sequencing all the individual national battles so that each, or at least their sum, achieved the overall objective. Without such an understanding of the available 'level of the fight' one is likely to use the force to disadvantage and find it crumbling under one's hand. It will not have utility.

However, it is best that the analysis is conducted before the event, which is the second circumstance, when the operation is being considered at the outset, at the strategic level. For example, in 1999 when we were planning the NATO entry into Kosovo, I appreciated that the Serb defences were based on battalion-level groupings. In order to be convincing as a deterrent or coercive force, the NATO forces entering Kosovo would therefore need to be able to fight at brigade level. And as the officer responsible for actually creating the force, 'generating the force' in NATO parlance, I went to the nations of the alliance for brigades, which were found by Britain, France, Italy, Germany and the USA. By considering this in advance of the event, we were able to provide the subordinate commanders with a force they could use.

This discussion of the 'level of the fight' involves understanding the organization of the multinational force in relation to the opponent so as to establish in the event what enemy force it is capable of overcoming, or else before the event what it should overcome. But whether one fights at all, the nature of the fighting, the choice of targets and objectives and the weapons and methods used to achieve them are also governed by legal considerations. When the Security Council initiates a UN operation, it does so either under Chapter VI of the UN Charter, which allows use of force only in self-defence, in other words reactively and not as such to gain the objective, or Chapter VII, which authorizes 'all necessary means . . . to achieve the mission', in other words proactively. Political control in all forms of multinational deployment – UN, NATO or coalitions – is also exercised by Rules of Engagement (ROE), which came into being in their modern form during the Cold War in order to govern reactions to the adversary in every possible contingency, even the most minute, and covered when force was to be used, in what circumstances and to what degree. Above all, the purpose of the ROE was to prevent any contingency causing a slippage into a nuclear war. ROE therefore proscribe action, and we are now applying this proscriptive logic to circumstances that are not remotely similar, which is an inhibiting factor in the appropriate and timely use of force in our modern circumstances.

At a more practical level, the ROE and the designation of an operation under Chapter VI or VII of the UN Charter must be coherent with each other, since there is little point in, for example, having a Chapter VII mission in which the ROE allow only self-defence. There must also be a degree of coherence with a third legal instrument common to modern international deployments, the Status of Forces Agreement (SOFA) by which a force is present in any state, other than by a forceful intervention. Whilst most of the public assume – if any thought has been given to it at all – that the international community or indeed any nation can simply park its forces in another country so long as it has guns to enforce its stay, the truth is entirely different. UN missions, and any legal military presence of a foreign state, have to be agreed by the host government, and the manner or status in which the guest forces are accommodated is detailed. In the Balkans, for example, the UN in the name of all the national troops under its command had SOFAs with all the governments of the former Yugoslavia from 1992 onwards. These laid out explicitly where UN forces could be located, what they could do there and how much the UN paid for its stay, amongst other things. Conversely, in Kyrgyzstan, for example, following the US invasion of Afghanistan in 2002 a force made up of several nations took up residence at the airfield outside Bishkek, the capital. Since it was not a coherent multinational force operating under a single command, all the participating nations signed separate SOFAs with the Kyrgyz government – and it was these instruments that allowed their troops to remain in the air base and use force from it. In contrast, the government of Uzbekistan allowed only humanitarian operations to be mounted from its soil – thereby dictating a SOFA of a different content.

All these instruments are part of the factors that shape and define the nature of the theatre – and the international and multinational force commander must be aware of them, and the manner in which they work together, in order to be able to plan and execute the use of force. To this end he must be very clear as to the goal to be pursued and the desired outcome – and the way to achieve it.

*

In 1993, working in the Ministry of Defence in London, I decided there were only four things the military could achieve when sent into action in any given political confrontation or conflict: ameliorate, contain, deter or coerce, and destroy. I subsequently gave a lecture to a NATO audience to this effect, though I am not sure it made a deep impression. More significantly, in all my activities in the following eight years of service I operated within an understanding of these four functions:

- *Ameliorate* This function does not involve the use of military force in any way. Here the military deliver aid, put up camps, provide communications, build bridges and all other such constructive activities in aid of civilian life, or they train the soldiers of other armies, or they observe. The military are used in the more humanitarian cases because they are at hand, are capable of looking after themselves and have some of the necessary skills. In short, they are self-starters who can create a semblance of civil life in any space and support it. If force is used at all it is only in self-defence. However, it should be noted that whilst the military may often be the quickest way to react to an emergency, not least because it is under the hand of government, it is expensive and often lacks the range of skills to do more than a quick fix, such as observe, which borders on the following category of containment. Military observers and monitoring missions also perform this ameliorating function by virtue of their presence and their ability to report what is going on to other external parties or the parties to the actual conflict. However, if nothing is done as a result of these reports the observers lose their value and can quickly become part of the problem. Training or advising other armies, even providing 'advisors' as the US did in the early stages of their involvement in Vietnam (and as did the Soviets in places such as Egypt or Syria), is more like the military's core business. But even in this case force is not being used directly by those deployed, since their only intended purpose is to improve the ability of the force being trained.
- *Contain* This function involves a certain use of military force, since here the military prevent something from spreading or passing through a barrier. Typically such operations are those to prevent trade sanctions being broken, or arms to be supplied, or no-fly

zones to prevent certain weapons from being used. The military have the intelligence systems and weapons to conduct these operations. Force is used locally and in response to attempts to breach the barrier either in self-defence or to enforce the exclusion zone or barrier. Control of the use of force is achieved by deciding certain ROE which will enable the specific operation, but usually no more.

- *Deter or coerce* This function involves a wider use of force, since here the military deploy to pose a threat to some party or carry out a threat against a party, to change or form that party's intentions. Examples of such operations are the entire confrontation of the Cold War, or the deployment to the Gulf in 1990 of operation Desert Shield to deter Iraq from seizing the Saudi coastal oilfields, or the international activities related to Kosovo, such as the NATO threats of bombing in 1998 to deter the Serbs from harassing the Albanian minority, and the 1999 bombing to coerce them into withdrawing from the province. In deterrence the military are deployed in a threatening posture and take active measures to prepare to carry out the threat, and in coercion employ force. In the case of deterrence the employment of force is usually closely controlled at senior political levels by means of ROE, and in the case of coercion by close political attention to the target lists as well as ROE.

- *Destroy* This function involves the employment of military force, since here the military attack the opposing force in order to destroy its ability to prevent the achievement of the political purpose. In modern times, the Falklands War of 1982 and operation Desert Storm in 1990–91 are examples of this employment of force, as was its use in classic industrial conflicts such as the two world wars. Military forces are trained and organized to do this, and as discussed this is what we see as the primary purpose of military forces and to this end developed the political, legal and military institutions to form, control and employ this force accordingly.

These four functions fall into two pairs. The first two, amelioration and containment, can be put into play without knowing the desired political outcome, though it is preferable this be determined in advance. Even the most altruistic motives in response to a natural disaster such as an earthquake or tsunami will have political over-tones when the armed forces of a state are deployed. Neither function will lead to a decision; each may well create a condition in which a decision may be found, but the condition is unlikely to contribute directly to the decision, largely because the political leadership of the parties can continue to operate within the containment or even benefit from the amelioration. UN operations almost always fall into these categories. To achieve the two other functions, deterrence and destruction, the actions taken must nest within a strategy, which in turn requires knowledge of the desired political outcome. If they are carried out without the guiding logic of the strategy, then the effect achieved is at best one of the other two. Many of the conflict situa-tions current around the world have unfortunately followed this inef-fectual path. For example, as part of the so-called 'War on Terror' the invasion of Afghanistan in pursuit of Osama bin Laden and al-Qaeda, intended to deter and destroy, ultimately became an operation of strategic containment at best. Another example would be the imposi-tion of the no-fly zone in southern Iraq in 1992. Its purpose was to deter the Iraqis from persecuting the Marsh Arabs. It achieved the containment of the Iraqi air force and prevented it being used against the Marsh Arabs, but it did not prevent their persecution.

The four functions can be achieved at any of the three levels of mil-itary activity – strategic, theatre and tactical – and different functions may be achieved at different levels. For example the strategic function may be to coerce while the theatre or tactical function is to destroy in order to carry out the threat. An example of this is the Kosovo bomb-ing in 1999. The strategic function required was to coerce Milosevic into withdrawing his forces from the Serbian province of Kosovo so that NATO forces could occupy the province and the UN could administer it. Note that this in itself is not the political outcome desired, since that has yet to be defined – six years after the fact. The threat was to bomb his forces and his infrastructure; the nature of the threat, the forces available and the constraints on their use, together with the lack of a defined political outcome, meant that the theatre-level function was the same as the strategic, to coerce, whilst the threat, the destructive function, was carried out at the tactical level. And having occupied the province the UN, other organizations such as the EU and the Organization for Security and Co-operation in Europe (OSCE), and the member states continue to search for the political outcome, whilst NATO achieves the function of containment at all three levels. In the case of Desert Storm 1991, as discussed already, the destructive function lay at theatre and tactical levels, but again for want of a clear strategy to achieve a stated political outcome the strategic military function reverted to containment.

Understanding matters in this way is helpful to all involved in decision making on the use of force, civilian and military alike. It is also increasingly important now that many in the military on both sides of the Atlantic talk about 'effects based operations'. Each of the four functions makes clear what is expected by the specific use of force at each level, and the relationship of these effects one with the other. However, in order to decide correctly on the necessary function of force and its purpose within the circumstances, the decision makers must be in possession of good and sufficient information; and in order for the force commander to implement their orders, he must have as much knowledge as possible of the enemy and the environment. All this demands proper data.

Intelligence and information are crucial elements in any decision on the use of force, and subsequently throughout the operation. Consider the background to operation Iraqi Freedom in 2003, in which the main *casus belli* appeared to be the possession of weapons of mass destruction by Saddam Hussein. A significant part of the debate was based on UK and US intelligence reports, which were then proven to be unsubstantiated. None the less, on the back of such data massive force was applied at the theatre level: the confrontation with Saddam Hussein became a conflict, and whilst he was toppled, no weapons of mass destruction were ever found. As already discussed, the gaining of good information is essential to the effective use of force at any level, whether to choose the course of action or to prosecute the attack. Information is available from many sources: intelligence services, the military, diplomats, international bodies such as OSCE, NGOs, the institutions in the region in question, commerce and the media. Ideally, the intelligence services would have agents in place beside the opponent's principal decision makers. Of course, the opponent will be operating to prevent such an occurrence, but in the case of a long confrontation against a formed and recognizable opponent it may be possible to achieve such an advantageous position – though you will never be told if this is the case. This reflects upon the very essence of intelligence operations, as dependent upon time, chance and the vagaries of human nature; these dictate whether or not the opportunities occur, and whether they are taken. The very nature of war amongst the people, particularly its conduct between non-national bodies when 'intelligence' is quintessentially national, makes this desirable situation most unlikely in advance of the committal of force.

For my part, in dealing with the mass of often non-specific information which constitutes intelligence I came to realize how important it was to understand which questions you had to answer, and that you could know these only when you knew what it was you wanted to achieve. If I did not know what I was to achieve or the questions needing answers, then this did not preclude analysis or action; it told me I had to collect the information to decide what to do. In addition, one should make a conscious decision as to the collection: there is an abundance of data surrounding us all now, most of it freely available, but there is only so much time and so many resources to handle it. Effort must therefore be focused on the specific items and issues necessary for you – and you must make these absolutely clear to your staff and information services and sources. Each decision maker should do this, otherwise he or she will be in the position of acting on information collected to answer a different question.

In the foregoing I have used the word information rather than intelligence quite deliberately. For me, intelligence has two meanings. The first is to describe the product of the assessment or analysis, one's understanding or intelligence. This should be held securely and be concealed from your opponent except when you wish him to know what you know. You should conceal your intelligence because your opponent can deduce your intentions and actions from that knowledge, and by keeping him unaware you can surprise him. The second use of the word is to describe information collected secretly: you wish to conceal that you have the information and how it was collected. The information collected must be assessed with the rest to produce the intelligence or answers to your questions. This applies to political and civilian activities as much as military, since they are all connected. Above all, one must avoid the trap of assuming information is correct or valuable to you just because it is secret.

For the military commander, information is then required to answer questions on two broad subjects: items and intentions. Information on items falls into two broad categories: the battlefield or environment, and the opponent's men and materiel. By collecting information about items we can deduce the probable intentions of our opponent and by finding the items we can attack them and frustrate his intentions. I wrote 'probable' intentions since the assessment is only as good as the assumptions on which it is based; assumptions must always be challenged. Israel being taken by surprise during Yom Kippur in 1973 gives an example of state institutions failing to challenge the assumptions: despite all information pointing to a major troop build-up on the borders, the assumptions remained that neither Egypt nor Syria had the capability or will to attack and definitely not in concert. The increased activity was therefore attributed to regular if possibly enlarged troop rotation, a theory that suited the assumptions rather than reality. Collecting information about intentions is much more difficult. The intentions one wants to know are those of commanders and statesmen, they are protected and few in number, and intentions can change quickly if only as to timing. It is well to remember that Napoleon's opponents were confounded by his ability to change his form rapidly and move his *corps d'armées* accordingly, thereby causing confusion as to his intentions: when his enemies found an item, one or more of his corps, they were unable to assess his intentions; moreover, lacking a well-placed agent or source, they did not know his mind – which in any event he tended to make up at the last practical moment, which he could afford to do because of his organizational mobility.

Indeed, the collection of this information is as old as time, and most certainly biblical times. Men are dispatched to scout the ground to find the best routes, forage and water. Other men are sent to find the enemy positions, and to provoke them into declaring their reactions. Still others are sent to intercept the messengers that carry the communications of the king. Spies are sent into the enemy camp and cities to seek out the strength of his positions, to penetrate the council of the leader, to report on his intentions and ideally to influence them. And each commander in conflicts of any fluidity has found that his ability to collect this information is limited by his need to keep the target under surveillance once he has found it. For once a target is under surveillance the unit or asset tasked is unusable for another mission. Each side is doing the same to the other and each is trying to prevent it. Sun Tzu's *Art of War* is in many ways one long treatise on the use of information and spies, preferably to achieve one's aim without the use of force, or else to enable force to be used most effectively. And for all the technology, agencies and acronyms of today, nothing has changed except for the detail of the questions that need to be answered.

In industrial war the emphasis is on collecting information on the items. We assume the intention of the opponent is to achieve the strategic decision by defeating us using force of arms, and that his desired outcome is directly opposed to our own. On the basis of these assumptions and by collecting information about items we make our plans to thwart his intentions – unless, of course, there is very good information to the contrary, and even then we may not react in order to conceal the source of the information. If we attack, we attack the things our information indicates will defeat the opponent. In essence, we seek to direct the opponent's actions by destroying his capability to adopt alternatives until surrender or destruction are his only options. Our intelligence capabilities are very well developed to answer questions about items and to find and attack these items. We want to know time, place, amount and activity; our systems provide such data in profusion and usually in greater quantity about ourselves than about the opponent. The information is objective, can be assessed by calculation, and lends itself to presentation in tabular and graphic forms. The staff procedure in the headquarters supports the process for making the decision and then acting on it.

Besides the items, there are intentions. If, as is the case today, the opponent does not join with us in seeking a strategic decision on the battlefield, if our shared objective is the will of the people, if he fights amongst the people and below the threshold of the utility of our weapon systems, endeavouring to provoke us into reinforcing his position by our actions, then our questions are mostly to do with intentions rather than things. In essence our objective is to form the people's intentions, and thereby the opponent's leaders' intentions by deterring them from the options of conflict because their subordinates judge there is a high probability of being exposed and destroyed. The information required to answer questions in these circumstances is to do with intentions, timing and consequences rather than items. This is subjective information that deals with probabilities and sentiment; it requires judgement and an understanding of the opponent's logic in assessment. It does not lend itself to simple displays. Information about items is still required but at particular levels and about different things. The environmental information concerns the way the society in question is working, how its infrastructure functions, who administers society, where and when children go to school and so on. The information about the opponent's items, men and materiel, will not be easily obtained; in many cases, as described already, the opposition forces reveal their identity only when it is thought safe to do so. To be able to gain information about the opponent's items it is best to understand the pattern of life in the environment and then when abnormalities occur to seek their cause. Sometimes the causes are not innocent. In industrial war the equipment is the critical item in war-making and is manned by people; if you know where the equipment is you therefore know where the people are. In war amongst the people the person is the critical item, if necessary he will make a weapon of whatever is to hand and in any event he usually carries weapons only at the last practical moment. It is he who must therefore be identified as separate from the people.

Forces organized for industrial war have relatively small numbers of reconnaissance and surveillance units and equipment in proportion to the numbers of units and equipment for attacking the opponent. These units and their equipment are often unsuited to operate amongst the people: the equipment is designed to look for things that the opponent does not possess since he does not have a formed army, and the units are trained to operate within the concepts of industrial war. The need to locate people rather than items, together with the need to develop information by further reconnaissance and surveillance, can quickly overwhelm the small number of specialized units.

The remedy lies in recognizing that the balance of effort lies with the gaining of information, mostly low-level information in large quantities, and not with conducting large-scale tactical or theatre-level manoeuvres. To do this, these military units, as also the civilian intelligence services, must develop a much deeper understanding of the enemy in war amongst the people: the active opponent against whom the application of force is being considered.

The new enemy does not have a formed or formal army. He may have operatives throughout a land, but he cannot operate at the theatre level. Because he depends on the people, because the people will feel the effect of his attacks, we must see all his operations as 'local': there is no manoeuvre of forces, no design for battle and no immediate connectivity with an operation elsewhere. Each engagement is particular unto itself and in its setting, but connected together through a nervous system by an overarching political idea.

The nervous system is unlike that of a conventional armed force. Conventional forces evolved their nervous or command system as part of the developments of industrial war, and most were well established before the radio came into service. The conventional system is in essence hierarchical: information flows up from the bottom, being aggregated at specific points in the chain of command, and orders and instructions flow down, being disaggregated into detailed tasks at each point in the chain. In this way the whole force is concentrated on achieving its singular military strategic objective, with every individual action and achievement contributing coherently towards that end. But the system is vulnerable to the loss of a point of command – in which case the chain is broken. Modern communications have been applied to this basic model, but the model is still the foundation. Guerrilla, and in particular terrorist, nervous systems do not work in this way, mainly because of their dependence on the people and their lack of strategic military objectives. As a result they tend to have characteristics specific to the locale in which they are operating. To use a botanical analogy, their nervous system is 'rhizomatic'. Rhizomatic plants can propagate themselves through their roots; nettles, brambles and most grasses do this. They can increase by spreading fertilized seed, or vegetatively through their root systems, even when the root is severed from the parent body. This allows the plant to survive a bad season or seasons and the disturbance of the soil.

A 'rhizomatic' command system operates with an apparently hierarchical system above ground, visible in the operational and political arenas, and with another system centred in the roots underground: the true system. It is a horizontal system, with many discrete groups. It develops to suit its surroundings and purpose in a process of natural selection, and with no predetermined operational structure; its foundation is that of the social structure of its locale. The groups will vary in size, but those that survive and prosper are usually small and organized in discrete cells whose members will not necessarily know their relationship with, or the membership of, other cells. The cells operate by getting others to do the dirty work as much as they can, either directly, as a badge of entry or belonging, or indirectly through some front organization. In all cases the need for security is paramount. A cell will do a minimum of three things: direct and sometimes lead military action, collect and hold resources such as money and weapons, and direct and sometimes conduct political action, which can range from funding schools to electioneering. Different people usually carry out the different functions.

These cells operate to the centre of the root system by a process of franchisement. The centre provides the idea and driving logic; it also directs the overall effort by means of this conceptual outreach, often ruthlessly purging subordinate cells that do not understand the purpose of their tasks, or else follow their own selfish path. The centre will reinforce successful cells with funds, skills and weapons, seeking to establish an area of sanctuary from which to develop. It will allow cells considerable latitude in the method they adopt to suit the local circumstances – provided that security is not breached and that the cell is both successful and in its actions no more corrupt than condoned by the movement. This latter point is always a potential weakness and in assessing it one must understand that the judgement of corruption is that of the local community. If the guerrilla fighter can show himself to the people as their defender, risking his life for the greater good of all, then they will support him; and if his attacks are advancing a cause the majority actively support at the risk of his own life, they will also support him. But the more the people see the guerrilla gaining a personal advantage, the more his actions appear as a 'protection racket', the less their support is given willingly. The point at which support ceases to be given willingly will vary from person to person, culture to culture and cause to cause, but it can be assessed. Those who would benefit from a continuation of the existing regime and a stable society are less likely to support change: their risks are highest and they often earn the most. Such people will support the cell or guerrilla if they see change as inevitable, or desirable for ideological reasons. Those cultures where it is expected that each will take his cut, or where power is exercised absolutely and restrained only by specific proscriptions, are more likely to tolerate individual gain than others. For the security forces seeking weakness, if it can be seen that the guerrillas are going further than their people can tolerate, and their support is being provided in part at least from fear, then an opportunity exists for attacking the rhizomatic system.

The rhizomatic command system is difficult to attack, just as rhizomatic weeds are difficult to eradicate. As any gardener knows, the way to grow a good lawn is to, amongst other things, cut and roll the sward while maintaining a moist and fertile soil. This encourages the root system to spread and put forward more shoots. Equally, gardeners know that if you want to make a flower bed you need to remove all the grass roots from the soil or they will sprout again. Rhizomes are eradicated by one of three methods: digging them up, poisoning or removing the nutrients from the soil, or by penetrating the roots with a systemic poison. Cutting off their visible heads causes them to lie dormant for a season – at best. Much the same is true of organizations with a rhizomatic command system such as guerrilla and terrorist networks, in which the people are to the organization as the soil is to the rhizome. I tend to find this analogy more helpful than Mao's known dictum: 'The people are to the guerrilla as the sea is to the fish.' Unlike the attack on rhizomatic plants, where one or other method can be used, the attack on a rhizomatic command system is done best from all three directions, operations in each direction being conducted so as to complement the others. It is important to remember that the outward and visible elements of the system, particularly those involved in low-level actions, are to an extent expendable. While their death or capture limits their actions and acts as a deterrent to others not to act in that way again, it does not necessarily deter the resolve to act; indeed, it is often a spur to action in another direction. As a result, any use of force against these opponents must be carefully calculated.

War amongst the people is a paradigm of confrontations and conflicts, defined by the six trends discussed in Chapter 7. It is fought against enemies firmly embedded in the people, who do not present a strategic target. Our institutions, civilian and military, have yet to adapt to this new reality – each within itself and the intertwined world that leads to any decision on military action. Much the same is true of the international organizations that feed off the member states. They are all still embedded in the world of industrial war, seeking information and intelligence towards making decisions – on using force as much as the way it is used – without properly considering the enemy against which they seek to operate, or the consequences of the actions. Even if force is used to stop violence, it will not deliver the strategic decision sought by those who decide to apply it. For unlike industrial war, in war amongst the people no act of force will ever be decisive: winning the trial of strength will not deliver the will of the people, and at base that is the only true aim of any use of force in our modern conflicts.

9

Bosnia: Using Force Amongst the People

The time has come to talk of the Balkans – primarily as an illustration of the six trends discussed above and of all the surrounding issues that have been raised, especially in the previous chapter. I was a multi-national commander working with institutions structured to collect information, make decisions and use force in industrial war; but I was commanding a force engaged in war amongst the people. This discussion is also of use because the events in those areas of south-east Europe, tragic in themselves, have shaped and changed the way we understand the use of force, at least on a multinational basis, and mostly not for the better. Worse still, despite applying force in Bosnia in 1995 and Kosovo in 1999, we have learned little of the utility of force from these experiences. Moreover, it was events in Bosnia that taught many of the troop-contributing nations (TCNs) that a UN force was extremely difficult to use and possibly an ill-advised option to choose in the face of conflict, whilst the NATO bombings in Kosovo taught the US that control of force on a communal basis was not viable for the sole superpower in the world. These perspectives have not changed, thereby making the multinational use of force ever more complex – which is paradoxical in itself, since we are more and more inclined to deal with situations on a communal basis, as reflected in the sixth trend of the paradigm of war amongst the people.

I was involved with the Balkan operations of the UN and NATO for seven of the last ten years of my service (from 1996 to 1998 I was GOC Northern Ireland). As the Assistant Chief of the General Staff for Operations in the MOD I was privy to the many debates that followed the UK's initial contribution of a medical unit to the UN Protection Force, UNPROFOR, being formed in Croatia in 1992, the extension of the force into Bosnia as that unhappy place collapsed into civil strife, the involvement of NATO and the formation and work of the Contact Group after the efforts of the US ambassador Cyrus Vance and Britain's Lord Owen – respectively representing the UN and the EU – to negotiate a resolution were dismissed by the US government in 1994. I commanded UNPROFOR in Bosnia through-out 1995 and from late 1998 until I left in the autumn of 2001, as the DSACEUR I played my part in NATO's continuing Bosnian operation as well as those in Kosovo, Macedonia and Albania. I do not intend to tell the story of all these operations: they are not yet over and others have written of them at length, but I do wish to use them to illustrate the complexity of our current world of confrontation and conflict, from the perspective of one involved at a senior level. And whilst I reflect on the wider Balkan situation, my focus is upon Bosnia, in a chronology reflecting the six trends of war amongst the people.

THE ENDS FOR WHICH WE FIGHT ARE CHANGING

The starting point to understanding all operations in the Balkans in the 1990s, including the NATO bombings of 1995 and 1999, was that they were without strategies. At best, events were coordinated at theatre level, but on the whole, especially with regard to the inter-national interventions, they were reflexive – or functionalist, to use a term coined to understand the workings of the Third Reich. Each event was a function of the one preceding it, rather than part of a plan, and whilst theoretically underpinned by UN Security Council resolu-tions (SCR) which laid out mandates, on the whole the forces deployed and employed, whether UN or NATO, were used in response to events on the ground rather than with a view to attaining a strategic objective. In fact, whatever political purposes the forces deployed into the Balkans served, they were not supporting goals directly related to a resolution of the conflict or confrontation in question. And this was apparent from the start.

UNPROFOR was originally deployed in February 1992 in order to deal with the conflict between the Croat majority and Serb minority in Croatia, and was based in the then 'neutral' and safer Sarajevo in Bosnia-Herzegovina. The circumstances were deemed to be similar to those of a classic UN peacekeeping mission – a neutral body to implement a ceasefire agreement between warring factions – and so that formula was applied. The mandate of the force was as 'an interim arrangement to create the conditions of peace and security required for the negotiation of an overall settlement of the Yugoslav crisis within the framework of the European Community's Conference on Yugoslavia'. The Security Council did not perceive, or perhaps did not place in the balance, that the minority of Croat Serbs were not a state and were not empowered to negotiate with Croatia as a state, or that the situation had arisen because of the break-up of Yugoslavia, as the various ethnicities sought to avoid becoming part of Slobodan Milosevic's Greater Serbia, or that Serbs in Bosnia and Serbia might support their brethren in Croatia. Nevertheless, UNPROFOR did contain the situation, and the Croats of Serbian ethnicity remained in their homes in what the mandate defined as 'UN protected areas'.

In June 1992 the mission was expanded to cover Bosnia-Herzegovina when war broke out there, and by the autumn of that year it was this crisis that became, and remained, the focal point of international interest – and not by chance. As the newly independent Bosnia-Herzegovina collapsed into a three-sided interethnic war, scenes of fighting, in which apparently well-armed and often uniformed Bosnian Serbs attacked unarmed or lightly armed and disorganized Croats or Bosniacs – Bosnian Muslims – were on television screens all around the world, with refugees streaming out to all surrounding states. In its initial response in June, UNPROFOR had deployed Canadian and French units to Sarajevo, and whilst these could not simply stand by and watch these scenes, it was unclear how they should respond, and to what end. After much debate between capitals and in the Security Council, UNPROFOR was mandated

to support efforts by the United Nations High Commissioner for Refugees (UNHCR) to deliver humanitarian relief throughout Bosnia and Herzegovina, and in particular to provide protection, at UNHCR's request, where and when UNHCR considered such protection necessary . . . [and] to protect convoys of released civilian detainees if the International Committee of the Red Cross (ICRC) so requested and if the Force Commander agreed that the request was practicable.*

In other words, it was not intended to create the condition for peace but rather to 'ameliorate' the situation. Passed under Chapter VI of the UN Charter, and with matching ROE, force could be used only in self-defence, but it was not to be used to change the situation.

Britain deployed a battlegroup to this operation. We knew that this unit would be operating amidst a war, and an armoured infantry unit with its fighting vehicles for their protective armour was sent. Others did the same, and the overall force was composed of units of battalion strength drawn from different nations: a force of TCNs. Most nations had only one battalion and the Scandinavian countries made up a single battalion between them. Each battalion had its own area and task, and this became the focus of attention of the capital that provided that unit. The logistic support of the units lay in the main with their nations. For the force commander, and the perspective of the use of force, this structure meant the force could not be manoeuvred as a whole, since in practice once a unit had established itself in a position, there it would stay. In other words, even if the use of force were possible, it would have to be designed as series of sub-battalion-level engagements in fixed areas, with no mobility as a force.

The UN arrangements for direction and command of the operation were those of a classic peacekeeping mission, where the combatants want peace and accept, indeed have requested, the presence of the 'Blue Helmets' and white vehicles. Unfortunately, in Bosnia the combatants did not want a collective peace so much as their three distinctive ideas of peace, and were bent on fighting for them. In itself this was an entirely incoherent situation, with the theoretical mission and the reality into which it deployed being of two very separate natures. Put in other terms, the UN Security Council understood

* UN Department of Peace-keeping Operations (DPKO) website, background to UNPROFOR: http://www.un.org/Depts/dpko/dpko/co_mission/unprof_b.htm.

the situation to be a confrontation and sent a mission for this purpose – into a full conflict at the strategic level between the warring factions. But this was not the only incoherence. The negotiations to find a definition of peace acceptable to all were in the hands of Ambassador Vance and Lord Owen, who reported directly to the UN Secretary General and the EU, but there was no direct linkage between their negotiations and UNPROFOR's actions. The UN mission itself was a joint civilian–military effort, headed by a Special Representative of the Secretary General (SRSG) and officers of the UN departments of Political Affairs, Peacekeeping and Administration, who worked together with the overall force commander's military staff, all of which were sent by the nations since the UN does not have a standing multinational command structure in the way NATO does. The two staffs comprised the main UN HQ in Zagreb – and whilst this was not a totally incoherent structure, it none the less demanded much effort on behalf of both sides to maintain. The subordinate UN headquarters in Bosnia were based on various national military head-quarters, to which civilian staff were attached. The only multinational headquarters was the force commander's, which started out in Sarajevo but moved out to a small town outside it, Kiseljak, for the first two years of the war; in 1994 General Michael Rose, the then force commander, moved it back to Sarajevo, into one of Tito's former residencies, and it was this headquarters which I took over from him in 1995 – known as BH Command, or the Residency.

Within these structures, the greatest incoherence was in the reality unfolding on the ground, in which the UN, as a result of having such a widespread presence, had become inextricably bound up. Though it was not a participant in the conflict, it was clearly there, albeit with a humanitarian mandate. This mandate dictated the conditional nature of the military objective in Bosnia, which was then also reflected in the ROE and the actions of the various contingents. The international rhetoric regarding the downward spiral of events and the interna-tional deployment within it was always strong and determined, but this translated into very little other than reinforced camps of interna-tional troops attempting to defend the delivery of humanitarian aid, and often themselves. There was no strategic direction, there was no strategic military goal to achieve, there was no military campaign, there were no theatre-level military objectives: all acts were tactical. UNPROFOR opened up routes, secured and ran Sarajevo airport and guarded convoys of aid. Yet over the years, and always in response to the events on the ground between the sides, more and more troops were sent in. By the time I assumed command in 1995, there were some 20,000 (the original deployment in 1992 was 5,000), all bound to their respective national headquarters and all prohibited from using force except in self-defence by the mandate and the ROE.

The events leading to the establishment of the 'safe areas' in 1993 give a good example of the weakness of this arrangement. During 1992 the Bosniacs in the east of the country had maintained control of substantial areas of territory centred on the towns of Srebrenica and Gorazde and the village of Zepa. The humanitarian situation inside these areas was bad, a fact that was used as part of the political play of the warring factions. As a UNHCR official explained to Lord Owen:

The Muslim pockets were used by the [Bosniac] Sarajevo government in November (1992) as pressure points on the international community for firmer action. The longer that aid convoys were unable to reach them, the greater the pressure on the mandate. When convoys did succeed, calls for firmer action were unwarranted. Two weeks after the first successful delivery Muslims [Bosniacs] launched an offensive towards Bratunac [a Serb-held town just outside the besieged Srebrenica]. Thus the integrity of UNHCR and UNPROFOR was undermined, further convoys were impossible, and the pressure for firmer action resumed.*

This explanation, as indeed the situation it reflects, shows how the UNHCR and UNPROFOR became caught in the first of what I came to call the hostage or shield situations that marked the story of UNPROFOR: they had no good choices. Lacking any form of strategic or theatre direction, nobody appears to have noticed the danger in which UNPROFOR stood.

The Bosnian Serbs attacked the eastern Bosniac area in January 1993 and the defenders were driven into enclaves centred on

---

* Jan Willem Honig and Norbert Both, *Srebrenica: Record of a Crime* (Penguin, 1996), p. 80.

Srebrenica, Gorazde and Zepa. By mid February the situation in the enclaves was dire: there was little food or medicine and people were dying of malnutrition and from minor wounds. Convoys were denied access by the Bosnian Serbs. The pressure on the 'international community' to do something intensified. During the next few weeks the USA put its finger in the pie by air-dropping supplies into the enclaves, and France, Germany and Britain followed their lead. Then in early March the Security Council requested the Secretary General to increase UNPROFOR presence in eastern Bosnia. In response General Morillon, the Frenchman then commanding UNPROFOR, personally led a small detachment into Srebrenica, composed in part of British troops operating a considerable distance from their base in southern Bosnia. From the middle of March General Morillon, sometimes a hostage of the people packed into the town of Srebrenica and sometimes a hostage of the Bosnian Serbs, acted to discharge his orders. He personally led a convoy of relief supplies into Srebrenica on 19 March, and the next day the trucks evacuated some 750 refugees to the Bosniac-held town of Tuzla. He negotiated with the Bosniac commanders, and with General Ratko Mladic, the Bosnian Serb commander, seeking always to support the UNHCR and the other humanitarian agencies, to protect the refugees and to bring them aid while not intervening with force.

The idea of having a zone in which combat does not take place is not new, and was being voiced in relation to the Balkan crisis from about 1992 onwards, with its proponents drawing on the recent use of 'safe havens' in Kurdistan in 1991–2 in the aftermath of the Gulf War. In Kurdistan the idea had worked, it was thought, because after the war the US and UK allies were not neutral and had demonstrated their willingness to use force; the terrain allowed for the use of air power and the areas in question were not isolated and could be reached by crossing the border with Turkey, an ally. These criteria did not apply in Bosnia; nonetheless, during the negotiations the idea of demilitarizing the area around Srebrenica was introduced by General Morillon, and the proposal began to be discussed again in capital cities and at the UN. In itself this three-cornered dialogue – which became four-cornered once the overall UNPROFOR headquarters in Zagreb was included – reflects the immense complexity of formulating policy within international circumstances, and then implementing it.

On 26 March, in a meeting with Milosevic and Mladic in Belgrade, a ceasefire was agreed and on the 28th another convoy reached Srebrenica. These vehicles evacuated some 2,400 refugees the next day, to the evident approval of the Serbs who later announced that only empty trucks could travel to the enclave. The Bosniac government reacted to these evacuations by denying access for the sixth convoy of refugees. They wanted the people to stay, not only to retain a Bosniac presence and to maintain a base for military operations but also to pressure the UN into supporting the enclave. The UN faced a dilemma: did it evacuate the refugees and stand accused of ethnic cleansing by the Bosniacs, amongst others; or did it seek to supply the enclave in the face of Bosnian Serb resistance? It attempted to do both, but on 5 April the ceasefire collapsed. In spite of General Morillon's personal intervention it was not reinstated and fighting broke out anew. On 16 April, as Bosnian Serb forces were moving ever closer to the town of Srebrenica itself and the defenders' ammunition was running out, Security Council Resolution 819 was passed. It declared Srebrenica a safe area, defined as 'one which should be free from any armed attack or any other hostile act'. Despite such phrasing, at base the real problem was that no one was completely clear what a 'safe area' was, and in absolute and real terms it was not supported. Few nations offered troops to enforce the resolution.

At the time I was working in the MOD in London, where news of these events arrived from four directions. There were reports from the British contingent in UNPROFOR that were drawn from the reports of their detachment in the area of Srebrenica. They were timely and factual but suffered from the relatively narrow point of view of a small unit taking part in a bigger affair. We had, as troop contributors, HQ UNPROFOR's reports, but they were often less up-to-date than those on the national diplomatic channels, partly because the process of producing them took longer and partly because the UN's communications were based on the civil network and were poor in comparison to those supplied to our military contingent. We had reports from the various British embassies and missions, particularly those at the UN and at NATO. And finally, we had the media, whose coverage I came to find essential: apart from being a source of information, it gave me a context within which to have some understanding of how others would interpret what was happening and thus the value of the other reports, most of which focused on completely different aspects of the same events. I learned quickly how persuasive this contextual media reporting could be, and how on occasions it could cause other reporting to be ignored or discounted, especially when the viewer was presented with visual information that contradicted a view previously formed from the other reports. I therefore took to listening to the radio and not watching television until I had read all the other reports.

We were dealing with three matters. There were the reports about the events around Srebrenica described above, although our focus was on the small element of the British contingent. This points to one of the characteristics of multinational operations of this nature, which is that the institutions of each state are not responsible for the collective outcome, but only for the national assets committed to achieving it. The national reporting together with the media reporting, and when it reached us the UN reporting, all helped to produce a more or less coherent picture on which advice could be given – which was my role as ACDS for operations. And whilst the big picture was of great interest, our primary concern was with the British deployment and how extended it was, stretching as it did from Split on the Dalmatian coast to Srebrenica. The second matter concerned the safe areas and the third the use of air power, initially to supply the enclaves and then to impose a no-fly zone (NFZ). At the same time there was growing pressure to act on behalf of the refugees, as a direct result of the harrowing pictures on the TV screens. In light of these imperatives, and in retrospect, it seems to me that the most coherent imperative was the need to be seen to be doing something – 'Something must be done' was a catchphrase of the times, used exhaustively by politicians, diplomats and media as much as by the UN. It was this approach that blotted out a considered debate on the true dilemma facing the UN, which was caught between the sides in a hostage and shield situation, and the need to analyse why UNPROFOR was consistently failing to achieve its stated purpose.

It was against this background that the national representatives at the UN worked hard to draft a SCR that would appear strong and decisive, while at the same time avoid exposing their own national troops to risk. One has only to read the 'constructive ambiguities' of SCR 819 of 16 April and 836 of 4 June to see how well they did. Shashi Tharoor, then special assistant to the undersecretary of state for peacekeeping operations, analysed the matter well in noting that the resolutions

required the parties to treat them as 'safe', imposed no obligation on their inhabitants and defenders, deployed UN troops in them but expected their mere presence to 'deter attacks', carefully avoided asking the peacekeepers to 'defend' or 'protect' these areas, but authorized them to call in air power 'in self defence' – a masterpiece of diplomatic drafting but largely unimplementable as an operational directive.*

The concept expanded: in short order Zepa, Gorazde, Sarajevo, Tuzla and Bihac were declared safe areas – yet UNPROFOR was never provided with the forces that the UN DPKO assessed were necessary for this new task. Worse still, the force was now in an impossible situation: it was responsible in the eyes of the Bosniacs for the supply of food and medicines into the safe areas, and when this failed they used the fact to berate the UN for its failure and to demand more robust international action. But in the eyes of the Bosnian Serbs UNPROFOR was responsible for keeping the safe areas demilitarized, and when the Bosniacs mounted operations from them the inhabitants and the UN were 'punished' by the Serb denial of convoys. This was truly the hostage and shield situation.

If 'Something must be done' became the main approach to the Balkan crisis, it was further complicated by the 'something' being the desire to use air power which emanated from the US. Washington was increasingly involved in the debate as to what to do about the Balkans, not least due to a powerful lobby by the Bosniacs and the Croats. The US stance was clear: it did not want to be involved on the ground, and equally saw no need to be neutral with regard to the sides. The TV pictures of Bosnian Serb aircraft attacking refugee

*Shashi Tharoor, 'Should UN Peacekeeping Go "Back to Basics"?' *Survival*, vol. 37, no. 4, p. 60.

columns was enough to have an NFZ declared over Bosnia by the UN in October 1992, and in April 1993, led by the US, NATO undertook to police the zone aerially and mounted operation Deny Flight. The motivation for this initiative was as much to ensure the protection of the US aircraft dropping supplies as to prevent the Serbs strafing refugee columns. However, this initiative created a command-and-control dilemma. If a student at any military staff college in the world produced a plan that had forces operating in the same space answering to two different chains of command he might, if he was lucky, be told to try again – but more probably he would have his cards marked 'fail'. Having a NATO NFZ over and within a UN operation created this very situation. The NATO planners therefore had to find a way to link the two command chains so that UN-authorized flights were not attacked, and when NATO attacks were made UN units were alerted to the possibility of retaliatory attacks. NATO's solution came to be called the 'dual key' procedures, within which both the senior NATO and UNPROFOR commanders in the region had to approve a NATO operation. In the summer of 1995 I became the commander who turned the UNPROFOR key.

These events in the spring of 1993 held within them all the components of UNPROFOR's involvement in the sorry tale of the subsequent two and a half years. From this point on the situation was set for repetition in a downward spiral reflecting all six trends, but especially the first, of changing ends. For whatever the rhetoric or even the honest expectation of the decision makers, for most of the time military force achieved no more than amelioration: ameliorating the worst effects of the war in Bosnia and Croatia. The UN force was not expected to use force to change the situation, but only to protect itself; and the states that sent in their forces did not intend them to fight except to defend themselves. As a result commander after commander stood between the parties to the war, attempting to discharge his orders to support the delivery of aid, yet finding himself in one variation or other in the position of General Morillon in Srebrenica: the inevitable hostage and shield situation. With clear instructions not to fight and to be neutral, each commander, in trying to discharge his orders, made agreements that slowly but surely weakened the position of UNPROFOR. On each occasion the lack of readiness to fight was demonstrated to all the warring factions, and more and more positions were adopted that were in effect hostages or shields to one or other of the parties. I did not understand this dynamic fully until I inherited these well-intentioned efforts as the commander of UNPRO-FOR in January 1995 and found myself besieged in Sarajevo, with the Bosnian Serbs denying my forces all movement and under the cosh of the vociferous complaints and pressure of the Bosnian government and the representatives of the US government. What is more, I would very probably have done much the same as my predecessors if faced with the situations they had been in, since the objective of the force – to protect humanitarian aid – had no direct bearing on the desired political result of creating a condition for negotiation.

There was also the matter of the differing ends to which the UN and NATO were working. The NATO-enforced NFZ contained the level of violence in theatre by preventing the Bosnian Serbs from using their air force to any effect. And as the fighting continued and UNPROFOR appeared increasingly useless, attempts were made to use the alliance air power more assertively. Not long after the NFZ came into effect UNPROFOR was able to call on NATO for close air support for its self-defence. For this purpose the command arrangements devised by NATO were workable, provided the threatened UN force had the communications and competent men to guide the aircraft onto the target. If the contingent in question came from a NATO nation then this could be expected, since they were used to working together, but a UN force is not only found from NATO nations and I was never confident that these other contingents were covered adequately.

The NATO capability was subsequently used after a particularly murderous attack in early 1994 on the Markale market square in Sarajevo. The aim of the operation was to reinforce the safe area by declaring exclusion zones around it: each zone was to be empty of all the Bosnian Serb heavy weapons, and if not would be attacked from the air. From the point of view of NATO, and in particular the US advocates of this idea, this was a simple proposition, and one that would relieve the pressure of terror instilled by the frequent shelling of Sarajevo. But from the UN and UNPROFOR points of view such an action would be partial; it would also prevent the Bosnian Serbs from defending their people in, for example, their part of Sarajevo. These differences led to two weeks of intense debate between NATO and the UN, which was much more difficult than it might first appear since it was carried out in four layers: between commanders on the ground and their national HQs, within capitals amongst the departments that deal with the UN and NATO, then among capitals, and finally in discussions in the two international organizations. On all occasions these were often lengthy events, in which the nations reflected all their reluctance and inability to decide on the issue, other than the unspoken one of protecting their own troops. Field Marshal Lord Vincent, former Chief of the Defence Staff and chairman of NATO's Military Committee at the time, once described such meetings as 'a hotbed of cold feet' – a description that I also found fitting throughout all my subsequent years of service in NATO. The meetings went on and on, but in the end the agreed result was another variant of the hostage and shield: weapons would be collected at collection points and held under UN 'control' – a word which subsequently became open to interpretation – but the Serbs were able to maintain them in case they were ever needed for self-defence, in which case they would be returned. The threat of NATO air power worked and coerced the Bosnian Serbs into removing their weapons or putting them into the collection points. The Russians, who were contributing troops to UNPROFOR, took the prospect of NATO using air power so seriously that unilaterally and overnight they moved a battalion from Croatia into Sarajevo, rather as a footballer marks the player with the ball – and they were to do the same in Kosovo in 1999. But progressively the Bosnian Serbs learned that NATO – which, for the Russians, meant the USA – could be restrained by the UN, and that the shield and hostage trap could be equally applied to NATO. For NATO sought to coerce and deter and the UN sought to contain and ameliorate, and there was no unifying strategy to give coherence to these differing ends. With many of the nations contributing troops to UNPROFOR being also NATO members, national considerations, especially of troop safety, always reigned supreme.

Apart from the differing ends to which NATO and the UN were

working, air power can only be used effectively to coerce or deter if it is used in accordance with these ends. It can be called in to support a force on the ground and attack the targets indicated by the force as threatening it; and it can react to any aircraft ignoring the NFZ and shoot it down. But if it is to deter or coerce, then the opponent has to believe that targets that matter to him will be struck effectively, even if they are not necessarily those that he is risking in battle. He must also believe that you will escalate if you do not succeed in getting him to succumb at first, and that the outcome will be to his disadvantage. One is in effect negotiating by threatening or using force, in confrontation not conflict. Technically, both NATO and the UN were in confrontation with the Bosnian Serbs, but NATO was focused only on the Bosnian Serbs, whilst UNPROFOR was dealing with all sides to the conflict, and their respective positions. But even if the two organizations and their ends had been aligned, to be fully effective in executing such a policy there is a need to select targets which will affect the intentions of those one is opposed to rather than necessarily the specific incident at hand: a bridge in village A may be attacked by the opponent, but it may be more useful to respond by hitting a road in village B which is of greater significance to him, and would therefore have greater coercive value. Though if an attack has taken place, one must above all recognize that deterrence has failed. The attack may also demand a response in the place it occurs because of its imperative, but one must recognize the different effects required: namely defending the position and also reinstating by coercion the deterrent state. In the Bosnian context, the threatened NATO action was to attack the weapons inside the exclusion zones and outside the collection points, in short to attack the weapon or weapons involved in an incident. This was the equivalent of defending the bridge in village A without reinstating the deterrent state. For any such incident initiated by the Bosnian Serbs with knowledge of the threat – and there were a number of such incidents – meant they had for whatever reason discounted it. At base the nations, and therefore the international organizations, were not willing to act forcefully with the measures they had put in place, nor to create the overarching diplomatic and political structures which would have given them substance.

WE FIGHT AMONGST THE PEOPLE

When I took up command of UNPROFOR in January 1995, Sarajevo was covered in snow and relatively serene, since a cessation of hostilities agreement (COHA) amongst the three sides had been signed on 31 December 1994, brokered by former US President Jimmy Carter and the civilian UN head of UNPROFOR, Yasushi Akashi. I spent my first weeks acquainting myself with my international command, and there is no doubt the ceasefire was of use in allowing relatively easy access to all parts of Bosnia not controlled by the Serbs, known as the Muslim–Croat Federation and created following an agreement between the two sides in 1994. I also travelled to Zagreb to meet Akashi, whom I had already encountered in the preceding year whilst dealing with Bosnia at the Ministry of Defence in London, and his military counterpart, Lieutenant General Bernard Janvier, the overall force commander. Within the UN chain of command, I reported to him; I had known and liked him since we had met during the 1991 Gulf War, during which he commanded the French Division. Whilst the COHA was agreed for a period of four months during which the sides were meant to be negotiating further, past experience taught me, and many around me, that the chances of this were slim: as winter waned, the sap of battle would return. In the interim, having relative freedom of movement, I visited all the international headquarters and many of their units. I also gained access to Srebrenica in Bosnian Serb territory, though the Serbs did not allow me access to the other enclaves. In fact, by February the Serbs were limiting both UNHCR and UNPROFOR access to the safe areas, particularly Srebrenica, and by March sniping incidents by both sides in Sarajevo were on the increase. That month the Bosniacs mounted two large attacks, one in the north-east and the other in the west. On 8 April the Serbs closed off access to Sarajevo airport, thereby halting the humanitarian airlift, and by the middle of the month it was clear the situation had deteriorated to general warfare.

I first met General Mladic within a week of my arrival in theatre. I drove up to the Bosnian Serb capital, Pale, a village some miles outside Sarajevo, where we held my introductory meeting which followed what we came to know as a standard pattern. On my side, I had with me my military assistant Jim Baxter, the UN chief of civilian affairs Enrique Aguiar, my spokesman Gary Coward and a couple of interpreters. Opposite us were the three Ks: Karadic, Krajsnik and Koljevic (classified in my head as the mad, the bad, and the loony), who were the political leaders of the Bosnian Serbs; and of course Mladic with one of his chiefs of staff. The meeting opened and continued with a long harangue on the history of the region, dating from the medieval appearance of the Turks in the fourteenth century and passing very slowly through the intervening centuries to the events of the Second World War, all of which was cast to justify and make entirely reasonable the position adopted by the Bosnian Serbs in going to war in 1992, and throughout the hostilities ever since. Meetings with Bosniacs or Croats followed a similar pattern, but with their own specific cause being justified. Eventually, the history lesson over, and I having introduced myself, I was told what they expected of me and UNPROFOR, namely to police the Bosniacs and Croats in keeping their side of agreements made with the Serbs. If we failed in this, they said they would have to respond to their opponents' provocation (over time I came to learn that provocation was a term the Serbs were very fond of, and used repeatedly), and it would be the UN's fault – mine personally and UNPROFOR's – if the agreement or ceasefire broke down. In turn, I told the Serbs of my own expectations of them: I wanted access to all the safe areas, for both UNHCR's convoys and UNPROFOR's, and explained that there was an agreed procedure for dealing with any breach of any agreement to which they were signatories, and it did not involve – or allow – taking punitive action. The denial of aid in itself violated both the agreements and the UN resolutions – and in addition, it was also a punitive measure. My words produced a further history lesson, although of more recent events, where it was claimed their opponents were denying them their human rights, and other such abuses. Positions having been staked over a period of three hours, we then adjourned to partake of the Balkan lunch, a mid-afternoon meal of standard format involving a large quantity of lukewarm, rather greasy meat, accompanied by slivovic.

Over the next two months I met Mladic on two more occasions, which led me to form a view that he was very much in charge of his army, and command appeared to be centred on him. He was respected by his subordinates, and it was evident his orders were obeyed to the letter; this seemed to be as much because they were recognized as appropriate and well thought out as because of any fear of punishment for not doing so. He had the following of his army, a mark of a commander. I also gained the impression that the Bosnian Serbs themselves saw Mladic rather than Karadic as the personification of their struggle. Towards me and the UN, he appeared a confident, arrogant bully who rated UNPROFOR as a hindrance rather than a threat. One of these meetings took place in Vlasenica on 7 March, when I was on the way back from Srebrenica. The content of the meeting was well reflected in a subsequent UN report:

At the meeting, General Mladić indicated that he was dissatisfied with the safe area regime, and that he might take military action against the eastern enclaves. He also said that, should such attacks take place, he would nevertheless guarantee the safety of the Bosniac population of those areas. The UNPROFOR Commander warned him not to attack the enclaves, stating that such action would almost certainly lead to international military intervention against the Serbs. General Mladić was dismissive.*

It was on my journey through Bosnian Serb territory, and my meeting in Vlasenica, a small town on an important route in eastern Bosnia, that I came to what I called 'the thesis', since it started from a theoretical premise. If you are trying to ascertain the intentions of an opponent, you need to focus your collection of information on some hypothesis. As the information is acquired, you build either an antithesis, or you reinforce the hypothesis into a thesis. In Bosnia, the latter happened. My hypothesis was based on the knowledge that none of the three warring factions, including the Serbs, could form, manoeuvre and sustain a formed force of any size in the field for any length of time, owing to a lack of either suitable training, structure, arms or men – or a combination of them all. The original pre-war Yugoslav army (JNA) had been organized on a territorial basis, to defend the national territory once an invader had penetrated the

---

* *Report of the Secretary General Pursuant to General Assembly Resolution 53/35 (1998)*, 'V. Events of January 1995 to June 1995', para. 180; available at http://www.un.org/peace/srebrenica.pdf.

borders. It had not been organized or trained to manoeuvre large formations. Each formation had an area to defend and control, and a
superior HQ could order elements from one formation to reinforce
another and build a concentration in a particular location if required.
The supply and maintenance of the force was based on local depots
and resources, which were spread all over the country. The very senior HQ could detach a small command HQ to go forward and conduct a particular battle. Conscription was universal and all men had
a reserve commitment in a local unit in defence of their area.

Of the three factions the Bosnian Serbs had gained most from the
break-up of the army: the most trained officers and the most equipment, but the fewest men. This reflected the dominant position the
Serbs had in the former Yugoslavia – which is a main reason the other
republics wished to cede from a union with it – in which they had a
disproportionately large number of ruling positions in government
and the military. They therefore had many officers, who also had
greater access to the weapons as Bosnia disintegrated into war. On the
other hand, their relative paucity of manpower reflected the fact
that the Serbs were a numerical minority in Bosnia before the war, and
therefore by definition had fewer enlisted men to call upon. This particular combination of officers, weapons and men meant that the more
territory the Serbs took the more thinly their limited manpower
became spread, and that this reduced density had to be compensated
with increased firepower. Moreover, the more men they had to call up
to man the line, the fewer were available for farming and what passed
for the economy. In commanding this force, Mladic – a corps commander in the JNA – used the methods he had been trained in. Units
from a number of areas would be grouped together and he would send
one of his senior staff to oversee a particular battle or incident. The
other two sides adopted similar methods, though they lacked the
weapons and the trained manpower to be as effective as the Serbs.

Coming back to my thesis, and the trip through Serb territory, it
became evident how empty it was: how few men they had to secure
what they held. The collapsing COHA was also evidence that both
the Bosniac-Croat Federation and the Serbs wanted to finish the issue
between them with a fight – they wanted to cross back from confrontation into conflict. The Federation, by receiving arms from

abroad despite a UN embargo and by having more men, was gaining in strength while the Bosnian Serbs were at best standing still. This meant both sides would be seeking an early decision by force of arms since neither position was sustainable over time; the siege of Sarajevo had to be lifted. For the Bosnian Serbs to generate the necessary forces to meet this challenge, they would have to reduce the number of troops containing the eastern enclaves. I anticipated that the Serbs would squeeze the enclaves by denying the UN aid convoys and by driving in the perimeters to positions where the Bosnians could not easily attack their movements.

It was against this thesis that I continued to seek information, and make my subsequent judgements. In the fullness of time, much of the thesis was proved correct. However, none of my thoughts or analysis at any point envisaged the collapse of the Bosniac defence of an enclave. The Bosnian operations from the enclaves were such that I thought their forces to be capable of mounting an adequate defence. Indeed, so robust were these that the Serbs saw them as a threat and demanded the UN control them. Moreover, at no point did I imagine the wholesale murder of over 7,000 men and boys in Srebrenica. For there is no doubt that for UNPROFOR the operation came to a head with the murderous loss of the safe area of Srebrenica in mid July 1995, and the subsequent loss of the safe area of Zepa in early August. These losses were a disaster, one that only grew in size as we came to realize the awful consequences. It was a disaster whose seeds had been sown with the decisions made in the spring of 1993: decisions to threaten with no intention to act, to deploy forces with no intention to employ their force; decisions made in no political context except fear of the consequences of action to the force; decisions that were incrementally reinforced by word and deed over the intervening period. The events from May 1995 illustrate this.

In May I attempted to reimpose the exclusion zone around Sarajevo, which had been violated with the breakdown of the COHA when the Serbs resumed shelling the city and withdrew some weapons from the agreed collection points. To this end I used NATO to bomb Bosnian Serb ammunition supplies. Whilst I did not see this in such terms at the time, I was in a confrontation with Mladic over this matter. My confrontation sat within the context of the greater one between the international community and the Serbs, which had given birth to the ideas of safe areas and exclusion zones. The previous threats of military action had failed to deter Mladic, and the exclusion zones were ignored and the safe areas shelled. I put the threat into effect; I moved from confrontation to conflict. The first attack, which destroyed the target, showed that the threat was insufficient; Mladic shelled all the safe areas, killing over seventy civilians in Tuzla. In response I attacked again. Again the targets were destroyed, and again Mladic countered. He took hostages and threatened their lives. I was ordered by the UN to stop using force and all efforts in capitals were devoted to hostage recovery. Subsequently the decision not to use air power except in self-defence was held by the Secretary General in New York, and I received a directive from the UN in late May 1995 that made the position of all the nations clear: 'the execution of the mandate is secondary to the security of UN personnel. The intention being to avoid loss of life defending positions for their own sake and unnecessary vulnerability to hostage taking.' The safety of the force was more important than achieving its mandate. Mladic had won the confrontation.

UNPROFOR was seen by all – the three warring factions, increasingly the US and NATO, and all the international media – to be without utility. What little political direction that existed before these events evaporated. My only source of advice and comment came from Carl Bildt, appointed in the aftermath of the crisis to recover the hostages and as the EU negotiator replacing Lord Owen. I had lost a battle (or confrontation). In thinking this through I came to the conclusion that I had to understand the use of force in a different way, that it had to be applied to alter a decision maker's mind, and that this understanding must affect my choice of targets. For by now three points were clear to me: first, that Mladic needed to control UNPROFOR, and by doing so he had us as potential hostages. Second, that his guns were important to him, because their fire compensated for his lack of infantry. And third, that air power, as we were using it, was not the threat we thought it was; it did not overcome his need for his guns. Based upon these understandings, and whatever the decision as to UNPROFOR's future, I decided I needed to appear to Mladic as being unpredictable and out of his control. To this end I planned to enforce our mandate: to use the Bosniac's route over Mount Igman into Sarajevo and to react forcefully in self-defence if attacked, and to supply the safe areas, particularly Srebrenica, by helicopter – and if these were attacked, to defend them with air attacks. These plans were not put into effect, since the political will to risk the forces for the objective of ensuring supply was lacking. I was unable to explain, not least because my ideas were unformed, that Mladic was conducting a battle of minds and intentions, not events. The other reason was that to many in the international community and the media we were part of the problem, not the solution. Nevertheless, I took every opportunity to try to regain a position of security for the force and freedom of movement. I would need both of these whatever was decided.

All the fighting in Bosnia – interethnic, and with the international community – took place amongst the people. The Bosnian Serbs did not wish to live amongst the Bosniacs nor have them living with them, nor did the Croats want to live together with the others. The Bosniacs, even if they did have initial feelings of coexistence, were of a similar mind. It was a very personal conflict. The majority of those who fought in a particular area were local to it; in many cases they knew their opponents in person. Neighbour drove neighbour from his house. Local forces, with local leaders, empowered by local people because they could protect them, dominated the fighting for local objectives. Force was used to terrorize, to ravage and to lay waste in a manner that medieval princes would have understood. Hostages were taken, corpses were bought and sold and populations displaced in what came to be called 'ethnic cleansing'. I believe this phrase actually originated through inadequate translation at the beginning of the war in 1992. A reporter witnessing people fleeing a village soon after its defenders had been defeated and the Bosnian Serbs had entered it asked a Serb what was happening. 'We are mopping up', he said in Serbian. This was translated as 'cleansing'.

The conflict also took place amongst the other people: the people of the world. Bosnia was a true theatre of war. Long before arriving in Bosnia I had realized the crucial importance of the media in forming international public opinion – and therefore their position in the conflict. In the theatre of war, they were the medium conveying the war amongst the people to the global audience. As a result, the media had become indispensable to the warring factions and the dynamic of the conflict. On the stage of the theatre the players were given visibility: petty officials and thugs, the vast majority of leading actors on all three sides, took centre stage and became stars of the show, whilst international statesmen and generals fluffed their lines or appeared to be following a different script. Personalities rather than the actual issues at stake became the basis of analysis and commentary. The parties each played to the cameras: the Bosniacs by both pleading their desperate case and morally blackmailing the international community for allowing it to deteriorate, and the Croats by arguing their historical right to live a separate existence. Above all, the Bosnian Serbs, in their arrogance and overconfidence, seemingly unaware that however much the coverage of their deeds might please them and their domestic audience, it revolted the external viewer. The theatre also dictated when and what decisions were made in the international fora. Each major decision was triggered by the TV coverage of some gross incident, such as a larger than usual number of deaths by shell fire in Sarajevo, the bombing of refugees or the evidence of a massacre. The visual image and the ensuing questions of the commentators to politicians provided the stimulus for capitals to engage again. This usually resulted in imposing on the UN another task for which it was promised forces and resources that arrived late, if at all. All the increasingly complicated structures of UNPROFOR resulted from these reactive and ill-resourced measures: the initial deployment from Croatia into Bosnia, the NFZ, the safe areas and the exclusion zones, all were triggered by a particular event transmitted into the capitals of the world. There is nothing wrong with that – but for the fact that in reacting to each event without the logic of a strategy and a context, the operation was and became increasingly incoherent.

By the time I arrived in theatre it appeared that the media unanimously held UNPROFOR in exceptionally low esteem, blaming it for all the weaknesses of the mission, regardless of its own precarious and exposed position devised by the member states that sent it there to start with. This situation had been aggravated by a series of stormy relationships between the media and previous UN commanders and their spokesmen, who sought to justify and explain their actions in light of the mandate. On the whole they were factually correct, but given that the context of these explanations was usually the continued suffering of the Bosnian people, reflected in endless footage of innocent people being shelled and blown up, the reflection tended to be of narrow and uncaring people seeking to rid themselves of any responsibility. I knew this was not the case: even without the benefit of hindsight I have now, I knew the commanders were all good soldiers who were put in an impossible situation with absolutely no political backing, trying at once to implement their mandate, help the local populations and control and protect their forces – and all without the ability to use force. Given this background I sought to establish a clear media policy as soon as I arrived in theatre. As with the use of force, it seemed to me the key lay in the ability to escalate. I therefore decided I would rarely if ever make public media appearances unless necessary to underline a message. Instead, I had two chief spokesmen, Gary Coward, later Chris Vernon, and Alex Ivanko, military and civilian respectively, who were authorized to speak on my behalf. To this end I ensured they attended every daily briefing for senior staff and were kept fully informed of all developments. They were backed up by a multinational staff of spokespersons, both military and civilian, who could brief the world's media in a variety of languages. In addition, I started a system of meeting the press informally about twice a week over dinner, when each time three or four attended my table at the Residency. In this way I maintained constant contact with this important body, and was able to explain the background to the situation in general and UNPROFOR's actions in particular. With all these measures I sought to establish a positive relationship with the media, based on reliability of information and interpretation.

WE FIGHT SO AS TO PRESERVE THE FORCE

In the aftermath of the hostage taking of May 1995 I had formed a battlegroup, based on the British battalion, in case I needed to rescue hostages. In the event I was forbidden any offensive action, but the idea of a rapid reaction force (RRF) gathered momentum in London and Paris and in early June it was agreed that such a force would deploy. It was to consist of French and British armoured infantry battlegroups, and an artillery group of units from Britain, France and the Netherlands. The RRF was to be commanded by a French brigadier general with a multinational HQ. Subsequently Britain deployed an airmobile brigade to the Dalmatian coast and this too was available to me on request. The force was not to adopt the UN blue helmets or paint their vehicles white: it was an unmarked UN force. This was fine by me: they were to fight and I did not want them to look like the UN. I particularly wanted the guns. In comparison with aircraft, guns with the appropriate target-locating and fire-control systems apply fire as accurately, can maintain the fire for longer, are not weather dependent and would be under my command. They could, in the right quantities and deployment, defeat the Bosnian Serb artillery.

If this RRF were to be used successfully its employment had to come as a surprise and yet its deployment was going to be in full view. It seemed to me therefore that I should avoid being seen as the com-mander of the force; it should be thought of as being under the hand of others: NATO, the nations, or even the UNHQ in Zagreb. If Mladic had thought the force was under my hand, especially after the bombing in May, he would have made sure he had potential hostages at hand to seize and guns in range of vulnerable UN positions. I decided to share this understanding with no one and played my cards accordingly. It took a long time for the force to deploy, not least because the Bosniacs and Croats viewed it with extreme suspicion, believing it might be used against them. The guns were not in position until about mid August. The next problem was that in the minds of the capitals in question this force was for the better protection of UNPROFOR. The French had their UN forces centred on Sarajevo, and having taken more casualties than any other contingent were insistent that their element of the RRF, in particular their guns, remained in range of Sarajevo. So if the RRF was to be used it was to be used best around Sarajevo.

By the end of June the hostages taken after the bombing in May had all been recovered, the RRF was beginning to deploy, I was clear that I was not to risk the force and General Janvier had negotiated a delivery of aid into the enclaves via Serbia. I went on leave. I handed over to my deputy, General Herve Gobillard in command of Sector

Sarajevo, took a small detachment with a radio with me and arranged a series of daily calls. During the week I was briefed over the radio that the safe area of Srebrenica had been shelled, and there had been some fighting around the southern corner of the enclave. This was a known point of tension, since the Bosniac positions overlooked a road used by the Serbs, and there had been a series of recent Bosnian attacks in the vicinity. I agreed with the assessment that this attack was in reaction to these 'provocations' and might amount to further squeezing of the enclave. I was then recalled from leave to meet the UN Secretary General, Boutros Boutros Gali, Yasushi Akashi and General Janvier in Geneva on 8 July. On that day we discussed the Secretary General's report to the Security Council on UNPROFOR and the future of the mission. As the meeting was ending we were informed that Bosnian Serb forces were attacking Srebrenica again, and that a Dutch soldier had been killed by the Bosnian defenders in circumstances that were not clear. This was assessed as evidence of further squeezing coming up against the defenders' positions. It was decided that I should go back on leave.

By early on 10 July I understood that the attacks on Srebrenica had continued, the defenders were falling back, the Dutch were establishing a blocking position and air attacks were planned to support it, and some thirty Dutchmen had been taken hostage by the Serbs. I was told that Akashi and General Janvier were in contact with the Bosnian Serbs and Belgrade, and that they agreed that air power should be used. Later on that day I learned it had not been used and early on the 11th I was asked by my Chief of Staff to return from leave. It took some thirty-six hours to complete the journey back into besieged Sarajevo – by which time Srebrenica had fallen. We had failed again. Another confrontation lost, and it had hardly come to conflict. If we were to recover from this, it was even more important to extract our people and to pick the confrontation we wanted and to have it on our terms.

It took some time to gain a picture of the situation. Communications were poor and reporting was confused. As far as we were able to ascertain in BH Command, the Dutch battalion were held with over 20,000 women and children in their camp in the enclave; there were about 2,000 Bosniac men who had been taken away we knew not where, and it looked as though some Bosniac fighters and some young women had broken out towards Tuzla and Zepa. Finally, we had still to recover the thirty Dutch hostages. And throughout all these assessments I did not think there had been the massacre of about 7,000 people. We now know how events actually unfolded; indeed what was happening whilst I was assessing the situation – yet at no stage did it occur to me that mass murder had been committed. Such knowledge was yet to come. In the meantime I considered I had three tasks: to assist the UNHCR with the reception of the Srebrenica refugees, to demand access for the ICRC and UNHCR to the Bosniacs held prisoner and to recover the Dutch battalion and the hostages.

Dealing with the refugees was a massive task: the Serbs had agreed to allow buses to take the women and children from the Dutch camp to Tuzla. The operation was made harder by the Bosniacs' desire to 'punish' the UN for its failure at Srebrenica by refusing to help in looking after their own people – until we were able to make the point that in principle they were behaving as badly as their enemies. The logistic arrangements were swamped and it took the UNHCR and the other agencies time to deal adequately with the mass of shocked and uprooted people. I decided the Dutch battalion would not be withdrawn until all the refugees were clear. Late on the 14th Carl Bildt asked if I could get to Belgrade by midday on the 15th for an important meeting with Milosevic and Mladic. We started travelling almost at once: out through the defences along the Igman trail, then at dawn by helicopter to Split, by plane to Zagreb where we picked up Akashi and General Janvier, then to Belgrade and the meeting.

This was my first meeting with Mladic for about three months and the first time we had spoken since the bombing in May. We were sent away by Carl and Milosevic to discuss the modalities of extracting the Dutch battalion from Srebrenica, which we did after a long discussion about the bombing in May and at Srebrenica. The officer taking a note of this meeting recorded it as being forceful and argumentative. From it I formed the opinion that Mladic did not fear the bombing itself, since he could not see how it would prevent him from doing what he pleased; rather, he feared not being in control of the UN commanders. He had enough on his hands with his Bosnian enemies; he did not need another group of commanders altering the situation,

possibly to the advantage of the Bosnians. The question was, therefore, how to test my judgement and how to play on this fear if I was
right?

In the negotiations over the Dutch battalion Mladic promised
access for the UNHCR and the ICRC to the prisoners and the general
area. Medical and supply convoys were allowed, the thirty Dutch
hostages would be released, on 21 July the Dutch would withdraw,
and freedom of movement into the enclaves by the UN was granted.
Finally, it was decided that on 19 July Mladic and I would meet again
in Bosnia, and Carl Bildt and Milosevic would meet concurrently in
Belgrade, with the two meetings linked by telephone. By the time these
meetings occurred we had still not been given access to Srebrenica and
it was clear that atrocities of some scale had occurred. Once again
both Mladic and Milosevic promised access. At the end of the meeting my staff informed me I had been summoned to London and was
to fly the next day.

No nation that sent forces to join UNPROFOR, or for that matter
NATO in support of UNPROFOR, had any intention of committing
those forces to battle or indeed of risking them at all. The ROE
were there to control the use of force for defensive purposes only.
Even the coercive measures of the exclusion zones to prevent the guns
firing into the safe areas were essentially defensive. No nation wanted
to put a force at risk. Most contingents were equipped with armoured
vehicles for the protection of the occupants rather than to take the
fight to the enemy. The difficulties the UN had in finding a contingent
to fulfil Security Council Resolution 836, defining Srebrenica a safe
area, is a case in point: it was nearly a year before the Dutch battalion
deployed into it. And in June 1995, after NATO lost a US F-16 to a
Bosnian Serb missile, they withdrew their flights to orbits over the
Adriatic. But if there was any doubt about the matter the directive
issued to me by the UN in late May 1995, clarifying that the safety of
the forces was more important than implementing the mandate,
made the position clear: it represented the lack of political will of all
the nations to risk the deployed forces – and its instructions were not
countermanded by any capital. Within the convoluted international
logic of deploying forces but not employing them, the directive was

not illogical. But, as the lady said, you can't be a little bit pregnant, and you can't be a little bit interventionist either. If you stand in the middle of someone else's fight you must expect to be pushed around; and if you do intervene, decide if you are fighting one or all of the sides and get on with it – and be prepared to risk the forces allocated to achieve the object.

ON EACH OCCASION NEW USES ARE FOUND FOR OLD WEAPONS AND ORGANIZATIONS

The London conference of all TCNs and the wider international community had been called because none of the troop contributors, particularly Britain who had troops in the remaining eastern enclave at Gorazde, wanted another Srebrenica. I landed at Northolt in the late afternoon of the day before it was to be held and was taken straight to see Prime Minister John Major. He explained that it had been decided that the next time the Bosnian Serbs attacked Gorazde, NATO would bomb the Serbs until they stopped; we would be thoroughly partial and not mind upsetting the balance between the factions, escalating as necessary. The two 'keys' would be held by the military, General Janvier for the UN and Admiral Leighton 'Snuffie' Smith for NATO. On the event there was to be no political decision, that had already been taken; the military alone had to decide that an attack was taking place. A senior air-force officer was to be sent to make it plain to Mladic what was threatened. I asked about the other safe areas, wanting to know whether the threat applied to attacks on these as well. No, I was told; only Gorazde. I knew that London was worried about the British battalion in Gorazde, but I had not expected this complete change of policy or its sole focus on the one enclave, and what was more upon the soldiers in it rather than the besieged Bosniacs.

I argued that this threat had to apply to all enclaves. How was I, a UN commander, to differentiate between enclaves? How was I, a British commander of a multinational force, going to deal with all my subordinates when a different reaction was threatened if British forces were attacked rather than those of other allies? What about my

French, Egyptian, Russian, Ukrainian, Bangladeshi and Scandinavian battalions, I asked. I also saw pragmatic problems. I doubted that we had the targets to quickly shock the Bosnian Serbs into stopping an attack, and I doubted we had the collective resolve to bomb on in the face of retaliatory shelling of the UN's camps or hostage taking. Having made the threat we could be sure Mladic would take measures to counter it. I explained I was quite happy to fight the Bosnian Serbs, but not on only one pretext, defence of the British, and in the one place where they had the initiative and I was unable to reinforce and had no weapons other than air power in range.

After a while we were joined by the foreign secretary, Malcom Rifkind. Both men were surprised by my lack of enthusiasm for the plan, but insisted that it had been decided. The discussion lasted for about an hour and ended with the prime minister asking me to have breakfast with Michael Portillo, the secretary of state for defence, before the conference. I went back to the hotel were I met and compared notes with General Janvier, who was also surprised by the change in policy. We agreed that at the conference we must make the facts on the ground clear to all.

By breakfast next morning I had collected my thoughts on the conference. I decided that the most important thing was to have all the enclaves included in the threat, which at least would help me as a commander to keep the force together. I did not expect this would be decided in the conference, since I realized the outcome had been pre-cooked in the corridors, and I did not know which other nations had been in on the cooking. I also wanted during the conference to have the rapid reaction force mentioned as much as possible, and whenever possible in relation to NATO.

Michael Portillo and I met for breakfast. He was new to his portfolio and I had not met him before. Nevertheless, he had been briefed, so it did not take long for me to explain my position as a multinational commander and that my whole command must be covered by the threat, not just the British and Ukrainians in Gorazde. He said that this could probably be arranged but that I must not expect it by the end of the conference. It also became increasingly apparent during this short breakfast that London had a very different picture of the situation from the one I had; it came as something of a surprise to Portillo that Zepa, another eastern enclave, had not fallen (it was to do so on 25 July). The intelligence and information we were all receiving was not of the same nature – yet decisions were being made on the back of this unclear picture, decisions about the use of force at theatre level.

The conference was held on a very hot day in a crowded Lancaster House, and it was grim. Every UNPROFOR troop contributor was represented, as was NATO, the UN and the US. The overall mood was one of sympathy with the Dutch – indeed, during the conference it was announced that the Dutch battalion had arrived safely in Zagreb and everyone applauded – largely from a sense, I thought, of 'there but for the grace of God go us all'. Everyone had their say, including General Janvier and I, and at the end of a long day there was a press conference in which it was announced that any threat to Gorazde would be met by air strikes of hitherto unseen intensity. Thirty-six hours later, on my way back to Sarajevo, I learned that the Bosniacs and Croats had met and decided to act together: this was the decision that initiated the Federation's subsequent successful attacks on the Bosnian Serbs. A week later it was announced in the press that all the enclaves were covered by the threat of bombing issued at the London conference.

Apart from making a plan to further the London conference decision, I was trying to prevent the people of Zepa going the same way as those of Srebrenica. Despite the new announcement, it was clear there was no intention of initiating intense bombing in their defence; the most that was practical was to get as much of an international presence into Zepa as possible, including myself, to 'mark' the Serbs. The last of the UN withdrew on 3 August: another retreat from a lost confrontation. The majority of the inhabitants either escaped or were escorted to safety.

The pressure on Zepa was lifted on 29 July when the Bosnian Croats and the Croatians attacked in the south of Bosnia and some 10,000 Serb refugees started to move toward Banja Luka. This attack was the precursor to operation Storm in Croatia, a general offensive by the Croatian army that drove the Croatian Serbs from their homes in the Krajinas. As a result a further 200,000 refugees moved into Bosnian Serb territory and some went on to Serbia; in turn, the remaining Croats and Bosniacs in the Banja Luka area were driven from their homes. The Croats laid the Krajinas waste. UNPROFOR in Croatia had failed in its original purpose. But suddenly the Serbs were on the back foot.

The ethnic cleansing of the Croatian Serbs from Croatia was a prime example of the dynamics of the 'theatre of war'. While recorded and displayed at the time, the act was never attacked in the media for what it really was: the expulsion of a minority by a state from their homes on the basis of their ethnicity, and the failure of the UN to protect them, particularly as this was the original purpose of the UN deployment. To my mind the reason for this deep failure was that the victims were Serbs. Over the years of the conflict in the region and the besieging of Sarajevo and the enclaves, and particularly after the fall of Srebrenica and the gathering evidence of the atrocity that followed, the Serbs were seen as the cause of all ills in the Balkans. The fact that these people were not the Bosnian Serbs who had committed those crimes, but actually Croatian citizens who had been in possession of their lands ever since the Austrians had planted them there in the sixteenth century to guard their border with the Ottoman Empire, was ignored. From the international, and especially the media perspective, they were Serbs – and it was time Serbs got a taste of their own medicine.

The pace of events and their impact on the Serbs led the US secretary of state, Warren Christopher, to announce a new initiative to negotiate a settlement. The assistant secretary of state for European and Canadian affairs, Richard Holbrooke, was to lead the negotiations. At the same time, my staff and I were planning with NATO and the RRF for the day when I would be faced with my post-London-conference exam question. I did not know where or when the question would be posed, and we had to carry on apparently as usual until it was. I expected the Bosnian Serbs to pick a time and place that suited them. Apart from knowing that I was to react in a certain way I had to recognize that as a consequence I would be in a new relationship, a coercive relationship, with the Serbs. Finally, I had no idea of the political objective, other than to prevent the Serbs' attack from succeeding, to which this military effort was to be directed. What positive outcome did we seek beyond that of the status quo? These issues went to the very core of our military planning, since the choice of targets to bomb is difficult without such an overall objective.

I did not want the Serbs to have the initiative. In essence I wanted to be the one who chose when and where we fought, and what about. And so the preparations continued. We made plans for what we would do for attacks on each of the safe areas, and the RRF continued to deploy, always making itself look as much as possible like part of NATO. In parallel we had been slowly reducing the size of the British contingent in Gorazde, and in July the British announced they would not be replacing the battalion when its tour ended in early September, and no other nation volunteered for the job. After the fall of Zepa and the withdrawal of the small Ukrainian force that had been deployed there it was easy enough to withdraw the equally small Ukrainian detachment from Gorazde. I felt I had to assume that in the eyes of both the Bosniacs and the Serbs it would be in their 'hostage and shield' interest to keep the British there, but I also thought that in the light of the London conference decision and their recent successes in south-west Bosnia, the Bosniac government could be brought to agree on the British withdrawal. Furthermore, they had sufficient control over their military in Gorazde that they would do what they were told even if they did not agree with losing their shield. Mladic and the Bosnian Serbs were another matter, if for no other reason than that the battalion would have to move through their territory.

In truth, by this time Mladic had a host of problems. In addition to the increasing threat of a Federation attack in the south-west, the Serbs also had an acute refugee problem and he needed the UN, and in particular the UNHCR, as never before. I decided that I would deal with the withdrawal of the British battalion as though it were a routine administrative exercise, and therefore wrap the discussion as to its modalities in the wider one of our UN assistance to the Serb refugees. Mladic went along with this approach. He did not see UNPROFOR or me as a threat; on one occasion during this period my interpreter overheard him referring to me as the 'blue lamb', which I was. He agreed to a meeting with all the local commanders, including the British. At this meeting I got him to issue orders for the withdrawal to his commanders in front of me and the British battalion commander, John Riley, in the expectation that they would be obeyed unless directly countermanded by Mladic himself. We did not set a specific date for the withdrawal; it was to be decided by John Riley nearer the event in late August or early September.

The RRF continued to deploy and, after considerable obstructions placed by the Croats and Bosniacs had been overcome, we had an artillery group on Mount Igman overlooking Sarajevo. The French were still adamant that their artillery units were there to support the French units. Since the French were all in Sarajevo and I had only enough helicopters to lift elsewhere from the British artillery regiment one six-gun battery and supply it with ammunition, the place I could have a fight and employ the greatest firepower was in the Sarajevo area. So in the end the decision taken at the London conference came down to this: if I was to use the forces available to me, NATO and the RRF to best effect I had to seize the first opportunity presented by an attack on Sarajevo and, if at all possible, ignore attacks on the other safe areas. Having done the planning with NATO, I was aware there were only so many targets suitable for air attack. The more we could mix the mode of attack – air, artillery and the battle groups – the greater our options and effect; by a wide margin this was achieved best around Sarajevo. My RRF was an ad hoc force of two armoured infantry battlegroups from different nations, supported by an artillery group with a wide mix of equipments from three nations; it was under UN command and supported by NATO's 5th Tactical Air Force, itself a mix of nations and equipments. This force was about to go on the offensive for a purpose unimagined when those equipments and organizations were designed.

THE SIDES ARE MOSTLY NON-STATE

On 28 August five mortar rounds landed in the Markale market place in Sarajevo killing twenty-three people. We immediately set in hand the investigation as to the probable perpetrators of this attack. The Serbs were already claiming it was nothing to do with them and that the Bosniacs had fired on their own people, but there was no evidence to support this contention. None the less, I wanted it established beyond reasonable doubt that the shell was fired from Serb territory before our attack was initiated. General Janvier was on leave at the time and the key was mine to turn, but I have no doubt he would have done the same if he had been on duty. I could not at first announce my

intention to turn the key, since the British battalion had yet to withdraw from Gorazde. The date for this had been set for the next day.
After checking with the commanding officer I told him to withdraw
as soon as he could. Meanwhile it was important to conceal my intentions from Mladic, so telephone calls continued to be made as we
investigated the incident. Mladic wanted a joint commission, I said we
would have to consult my higher HQ. I was stalling.

That evening the British battalion crossed into Serbia and drove on
to Croatia and Zagreb. I approved the route through Serbia for a simple reason. Despite the apparent political advantage to Mladic to have
the British move in that direction and not towards the UN position in
Bosnia, if successfully extracted the route gave the unit the least time
in Bosnian Serb territory. I am not sure Mladic knew that the battalion had gone until I told him in a telephone conversation on the 29th
that I had decided the mortar rounds had been fired by his troops. He
immediately threatened what he would do to the battalion and I
ended the conversation. I would like to know what happened in his
HQ when he learned they had already left under cover of his orders;
the thought gave me pleasure at the time. I then turned the UN key,
and Admiral 'Snuffie' Smith, the NATO Southern Region commander,
turned the NATO key. Smith to Smith, as it was known. Force was
finally about to be applied according to a plan. But the strategy
remained unclear. I was still in doubt as to the positive political outcome desired, as opposed to that of 'drawing a line', 'showing we
mean business', or 'being credible'. I called Richard Holbrooke. His
negotiations were well under way and I wanted him to know what
was going on. I thought he would want to provide some political
input, since I was sure what we were about to do would affect his
negotiations. To my surprise he saw the intended action as a separate
and disconnected activity and apparently of no consequence to him.
As a result I decided my tactical objective would be to lift the siege of
Sarajevo, so as to supply the population and fulfil UNPROFOR's purpose; and my operational aim was to attack Mladic's sense of being in
control, in order to support the negotiations.

During the period of planning following the London conference, I
had agreed with General Mike Ryan, NATO's air commander, that
he would choose the targets in Bosnia for his aircraft to suppress the

Serbian air defences – known as SEAD targets (suppression of enemy air defence). This had to be the first order of business if we were to establish air superiority. On my part, I would choose the targets that achieved the objectives I had set myself – and as part of my overall plan for the use of force. For in addition to NATO's air power, I also had the artillery and battle groups of the RRF to employ in concert with the air attacks.

The targets and attacks can be thought of in three separate but related groups. The first were of course the SEAD targets: the necessary enabling activity, but one that also affected the overall capacity for command and control within the Bosnian Serb army. Their communications, and some other assets, would be deeply affected, as would, therefore, Mladic's ability to control. The second group were the Serb artillery positions and armoured vehicles around Sarajevo: the specific causes of the siege. These were attacked successively by the UN artillery and NATO close air support, and the results then exploited by my battle groups. At the same time, my artillery attacked the Serb air defences in the immediate vicinity of Sarajevo. As a result of these combined attacks, within three days the siege of Sarajevo was broken. The third set of targets were those intended to change Mladic's intentions by attacking his personal sense of control. Clearly, the combined effects of the first two categories of targets impacted on this too – all the bombing was aimed at undermining him as a commander – but I also sought to attack specifically his need to control. An example of such a target was a military facility in the village where his parents were buried. It was attacked repeatedly, in the knowledge that in Mladic's culture a failure to protect the bones of one's ancestors is something of a shameful dereliction of family duty. (Matching these attacks, and to increase the pressure, we told the Bosniac press that Mladic could not look after his parents' remains.) Another example is my attacks on Mladic's links, electronic and physical, with each of his corps spread throughout Bosnia, in which I tried to make the physical cut of communications as close as possible to the boundary between each formation. I wanted him to have, at his daily briefings, a sense of progressive communications failure, and thereby loss of control. The context of all these attacks for me was my understanding of Mladic, formed over the months, that we were conducting a mental rather than physical battle. I brought heavier weapons to this battle of minds than hitherto within a plan, and had the ability to exploit the results.

The siege of Sarajevo would not have been lifted with only air strikes and artillery; it was the battlegroups on the ground that exploited the effects of this targeting, and gave confidence to the people of the city. NATO air power was crucial to this, but without the UN land component, both artillery and battlegroups, the bombing could not have made the breakthrough: it was the combined forces that gave it rapid utility. It was not long before Richard Holbrooke was in almost daily contact, now seeking to exploit the impact of our military actions in his negotiations. He was being asked by the Serbs to stop the bombing. We allowed a three-day pause, during which some Bosnian Serb weapons were withdrawn from the reinstated Sarajevo exclusion zone as the Serbs tried to convince us they were complying with our demands. We were not convinced, and so the bombing started again. And it was now firmly linked to the negotiations, not by design but by the juxtaposition of events.

With the start of the second phase of the NATO–UN action, the Croatians and the Federation launched a joint offensive towards Banja Luka from the positions gained in south-west Bosnia and the Krajinas in August. They made rapid progress, aided no doubt by the effects of the bombing. By 14 September we were beginning to run out of targets to attack, but Richard Holbrooke had brought the negotiations to the point at which that same day Milosevic pressured the Bosnian Serbs into a ceasefire. During the next few days, Sarajevo airport was opened, the Bosnian Serbs withdrew all their weapons from the exclusion zone and people began to move openly around the streets of the city. I also received some evidence that we had been successful in concealing the identity of the true commander of the RRF. In a meeting with one of Mladic's chiefs of staff, General Milosevic, on 17 September – where he was given the arrangements for the withdrawal of the Serb forces – he expressed great surprise when he discovered first that the RRF was under my command, and that I had been choosing many of the targets. Our ploy had been successful. On 20 September the UN and NATO commanders announced that 'the military mission had been accomplished' and 'the resumption of air strikes is currently not necessary'. International use of force in Bosnia was then at an end.

In writing of the decisions taken in the weeks immediately after the London conference I must emphasize that I had no idea of what was to be their political outcome, let alone how to get there. What I did was to establish a position where I had the greatest freedom of action, so that when the opportunity occurred I was able to use the force available to me to the greatest effect or utility. Tactically we broke the siege. Unfortunately our direct effect politically, our support for the negotiations – the confrontation – is harder to judge, primarily because the UN had come to be part of the confrontation only gradually rather than being part of it from the outset. This was the first real use of force, and it had no previous or planned context. At the same time, the political outcome was also influenced by other activities: the Croatians and the Federation were also using force for their own ends, taking advantage of the joint UN–NATO actions. I think it was their successful assault, in which Serb territory was actually lost rather than bombed, that ultimately decided the matter.

None of the individual Bosnian sides to the conflict – Bosniac, Croat or Serb – were operative states, though the international community recognized Bosnia-Herzegovina as an independent state in 1992, and therefore the Bosniac-Croat government that was in Sarajevo. On the other side, there were the UN and NATO, international organizations, their contradiction of purpose – the UN seeking neutrality whilst NATO directed its efforts against the Bosnian Serbs – remaining apparent until after the fall of Srebrenica in July 1995. Moreover, in their responsive stance to events, both approaches had the effect of giving credibility to the Bosnian Serbs' position that they were in effect a state and should be treated as such. And both approaches combined gave added vulnerability to UNPROFOR, and to the trap of hostage and shield. Before the events of September 1995, when previous crises brought the contradictions to a head, the Serbs soon learned to play on them, to threaten the positions they held hostage or to take more; and to the frustration of the US and NATO the default position of the TCNs was always that of preserving the force: denying or at best severely restricting the use of any force that could come to harm their troops on the ground, either directly or by Bosnian Serb retaliation. These frustrations resulted in considerable transatlantic tension. The reality of this situation was that one force (NATO) had been superimposed on another force (UN), which was not intended to be forceful, in such a way that it could not be used to effect. The two forces had differing objectives. The UN was in confrontation with all the parties to the conflict, and in each crisis arrived at an immediate result but weakened their position in the long term. NATO was in confrontation with only the Bosnian Serbs, but after an initial success its credibility was quickly eroded: the Bosnian Serbs saw that NATO air power was restrained by UNPROFOR and constrained by the choice of targets, and therefore that the alliance aircraft could not successfully attack the targets that mattered to them. It was only when the UN and NATO coordinated properly on a defined plan that the international position was represented coherently as a side in the conflict: the ultimate non-state side.

OUR CONFLICTS TEND TO BE TIMELESS

The deployment of a multinational force into Bosnia started in the spring of 1992 under a UN flag. Thirteen years later, at the time of writing, a multinational force is still there under an EU flag. The UN–NATO military action in Bosnia, which brought about the cease-fire in 1995, then led to weeks of negotiation in Dayton, Ohio, and in December to the signing of the resulting Dayton Peace Accords. These Accords, which in effect are a very detailed ceasefire agreement, amount to another condition in which a solution should be found. It is still being sought, and until it is found the international community must maintain the condition with a military presence. This started with the 60,000-strong NATO force which replaced UNPROFOR's 20,000 in January 1996: over the years it was scaled down, and in November 2004 the EU took over with a force of 7,000. In truth, it is essentially the same force: when the UN force became NATO's, most of the troops already on the ground remained, swapping their blue berets for national ones and the UN flag for NATO's. When the EU took over from NATO, the same troops largely remained once again, swapping their NATO flag for the EU one. We only have one set of forces, which are always double or triple earmarked for all the different organizations and purposes in which they are used.

In September 1995 the forces I commanded performed well: they achieved all their objectives. But in overall terms this must be understood: force was used to attack and achieve tactical objectives, but it did not attain a strategic aim or a definitive political outcome. In Bosnia, military action together with Holbrooke's political negotiations brought the conflict to an end – but the confrontation still remains.

Conclusion: What Is to Be Done?

War amongst the people is not a better paradigm than interstate industrial war, it is simply different – and understanding difference, and accepting it, must become a central part of our way ahead. For confrontations and conflicts will not cease, and we will continue to become involved with and in them, either as individual nations or, increasingly, in coalitions or alliances, probably on behalf of the international community. It is therefore imperative that we begin to assimilate the trends and implications of the new paradigm, and begin a process of deep change. NATO nations are currently focused on 'transformation', as are many others outside the alliance – and this is a positive step. However, at the moment it does not encompass a cognizance that we are living in a world of confrontations and conflicts rather than one of war and peace, nor does it encompass the idea of change as a constant factor rather than a single step. Indeed, the world of 'transformation' is constructed upon the clear understanding that the circumstances have changed, but not the overall concept of this event called war. By this I mean that there is an acceptance in many circles that we now conduct operations rather than wars, but we still expect them to deliver a definitive military victory in its own right that will resolve a political problem, rather than one that contributes and supports the resolution of the matter by other means. There is no understanding that we live in a condition of continuous confrontation and conflict, and that therefore these operations are conflicts derived from confrontations, and that even if military action is successful the confrontation will remain, to be resolved by other means and levers of power. To be clear, we read of senior officers stating that a given problem cannot be solved militarily, and they are of course correct –

and are recognizing the change in paradigm. But it is one thing to recognize change and quite another to act on it – and such action is not yet apparent. Until this need for a deep change to our institutional thought patterns and structures is understood and acted upon, there can be no real transformation – neither in our forces nor in the way we expect them to attain the results we seek. In short, our military forces will lack utility.

What is to be done? This was the title and subject of one of Lenin's more significant pamphlets, and whilst I do not suggest his radical approach, I do advocate a revolution in our thinking, within the framework of war amongst the people: that our confrontations and conflicts must be understood as intertwined political and military events, and only in this way can they be resolved. As such, it is no longer practical for the politicians and diplomats to expect the military to solve the problem by force, nor is it practical for the military to plan and execute a purely military campaign, or in many cases take tactical action, without placing it within the political context, with both politicians and the military adjusting context and plan accordingly throughout the operation as the situation evolves. This is no longer industrial war: the enemies are no longer the Third Reich or Japan, who posed absolute and clear threats in recognizable groupings, and therefore provided stable political contexts for operations; as we have seen, our opponents are formless, and their leaders and operatives are outside the structures in which we order the world and society. The threats they pose are not directly to our states or territories but to the security of our people, of other peoples, our assets and way of life, so as to change our intentions and have their way. Above all, they are not located in a single place that can be easily defined for battle. They are of and amongst the people – and it is there that the fight takes place. But this fight must be won so as to achieve the ultimate objective of capturing the will of the people. If we are to face and defeat those who confront us and threaten us with force, who are demonstrably operating amongst the people to capture their will and change our intentions, then we must adapt and be prepared to adapt again to face this reality. These facts must become the basis of our approach to the use of force, as also the understanding that whilst conflicts may be won not all confrontations, including those that started the conflicts, may be resolved by the use of force, or even other levers. Indeed, some may have to be managed. This approach can be achieved; indeed it must, since without it there will be no utility of force. Establishing the way to approach these necessary changes is the purpose of this chapter.

ANALYSIS

The starting point to changing our approach must be a change in our concepts of analysis, which is the basis of all political and military activity. At present the tendency is to analyse situations in terms of industrial war, and when the circumstances do not fit to declare a case of asymmetry or asymmetric war. As I noted at the start of this book, I have never cared for this description since I think the essence of the practice of war is to achieve an asymmetric advantage over one's opponent; an advantage in any terms, not just technological. If your opponent has found a way to negate your industrial and technological advantage, and for whatever reason you are unable or unwilling to change your own parameters so as to regain the advantage, then you must fight on the battlefield he has set and on his terms. And on the whole, it is this outcome we are watching in Iraq, the Israeli occupied territories and many other hotspots of the world.

With this starting point one needs to understand in considerable detail the nature of the desired outcome of the strategy being formed – political, military, economic, structural, regional and other such basic concepts – as also a sense of what may be resolved by conflict and what will remain in a state of confrontation. I have argued that the strategic object cannot now be achieved through the singular use of massive military force alone; in most cases military force can only achieve tactical results and to have more than passing value these must be stitched into a greater plan. Hence the analysis of the outcome desired must be in sufficient detail to see what to attack, and to link these applications of military force to the applications of other levers of power.

When faced with a direct threat to one's own existence and way of life the desired outcome is clear, but other circumstances are harder to assess, especially when there is also some prospect of material gain, in assets or territory for example, rather than the moral dividend from humanitarian relief or the security resulting from stability of the international order. These matters are complex, and require prioritization and adjustment of the desired overall result as the practicalities of achievement become evident. In reality the priorities tend to be set on the urgency of action – what can I do now? – rather than setting the highest priority on the issue or item that has the greatest value in achieving the desired outcome. To use a medical analogy: faced with a patient with a bad skin disorder, caused by a poor diet resulting from an overstressed work and home life, the doctor must decide where his priority lies. The priorities for action are probably in the order of the three listed, but the priorities for effectiveness in achieving the object of lasting good health are probably the reverse. However, in real life the doctor is a practical man and he knows he can do little about the patient's job or marriage, and anyway he wants the patient to be able to pay his bills, so he settles for a change of diet as the highest priority, explaining matters and recommending a diet accordingly, and gives the patient some ointment to reduce the symptoms, which is what the patient came in for. In international affairs we tend to place the highest priority on what we do rather than on what will achieve our ultimate object. This is because we sometimes have not defined our object in sufficient detail, and sometimes because in taking action we forget there are higher priorities. The decisions made in 1990–91 over Saddam Hussein's seizure of Kuwait give an example of a failure to prioritize correctly. It was clear that the seizure and occupation of Kuwait was a symptom of Saddam's rule: that he was the problem. The priority for action was clearly to liberate Kuwait, but the priority for the desired outcome was, at the very least, a neutered Ba'athist regime governing Iraq. As events unfolded we became absorbed in the action and on achieving our priority for action, the liberation of Kuwait and the destruction of much of Iraq's armed forces – and we failed to take advantage of the position we had gained to achieve our desired outcome.

I must emphasize the importance of understanding the desired outcome before deciding whether or not military force has a part to play in achieving it. Only by knowing what you want can you frame the questions to ask of the analysts and intelligence services; and only by knowing what you want in terms of the political outcome can you decide what it is you want the military to achieve. In plain terms the strategic military objective should describe the result of the military action. In the Second World War it was simple to express the military objective as, for example, 'the unconditional surrender of Germany', but in our modern circumstances we are not seeking such strategic outcomes for the use of military force, not even in the invasion of Iraq in 2003, to take the most current example. Various terms are now used to apparently define what it is the military are expected to achieve – terms such as 'humanitarian operation', 'peacekeeping', 'peace enforcement', 'stabilization operations', 'achieving a stable and secure environment' – yet these are in reality more of a description of the activity rather than the outcome. None the less, many people, including senior decision makers and policy makers, use and understand them as descriptive of a good outcome, and this can lead to confusion of purpose.

It is therefore possible to see the vital importance of conducting an analysis based upon the desired political outcome, since it will reveal whether military force can and should be used, and if so to what degree and purpose. In an ideal situation one would start by deciding the desired outcome in sufficient detail that it becomes possible to describe what must be achieved to realize it. If this cannot be done to the point of resolution, perhaps because not enough is known to decide or because a decision is to be reached democratically, then the intermediate political objective becomes that condition in which this decision can be reached. For example, if it is desired to have a democratic government in a particular state, one cannot describe its final form, it being the nature of a democracy that the people decide, but one can decide the condition in which the people of the state are most likely to make a decision one would approve of. The intermediate political outcome therefore becomes this condition. Having reached an understanding of the outcome and the political objectives on the route to achieving it, one must then decide which of the four functions of force listed in Chapter 8 – amelioration, containment, deterrence or coercion, destruction – is best suited in the circumstances to contribute to realizing it. One can then decide the degree of force required.

Of the four functions, deterrence/coercion is the one that if achieved alters directly the opponent's intentions, so making it possible to win the clash of wills rather than the trial of strength. For deterrence or coercion to work the threat of military action must be directed at a target or targets of sufficient value to the enemy that their preservation is thought to be of greater importance than achieving his original intention against you. The military actions to make the threat effective can be decided only when the target is known. For the threat to be effective, the threatened party must believe it will be carried out. This belief is formed in the mind of the threatened by his judgements of your military ability to carry out the threat, leading him in turn to believe there is no alternative course of action to that threatened open to you and that you have the will to execute it. He has to be convinced that even in the face of his own counter-measures the targets he values will be found and destroyed, and that even if he can bear their loss you will escalate by attacking targets of even greater value to him. For escalation is measured in the value of the target to the threatened, not the tonnage or quantity of force used to destroy it. Military forces intended to achieve the effect of forming intentions have two objectives – of both deployment and employment – that are all too easily forgotten. They must be deployed within the confrontation, and act to contribute to the opponent forming the beliefs outlined above, so as to achieve the desired outcome: the primary political objective. And they must be ready to be employed in conflict as a force to attain the threatened objective in such a way that, having achieved it, the primary political objective can be gained.

What tends to happen is that for various reasons – such as a lack of political will and domestic support, or lack of forces, or lack of a clear idea of the outcome, or all of these – we settle on the military achieving amelioration or containment: we deploy force. Then, when other civilian measures and agencies – political, diplomatic, legal, economic – fail to resolve the matter as we wish, we seek to use military force or its threat to achieve the result we want by deterrence or coercion: we employ force. There is nothing wrong in this gradual response provided one knows the desired outcome by the time deterrence measures are taken; for if such knowledge is absent then, as already described, one will achieve no more than containment. The reason for this is that the opponent, who is amongst the people, is also using military force to deter or coerce – but he does so knowing his desired outcome. He knows that the threat he is making or acting out is directed towards achieving a particular goal, and he acts in such a way as to advance towards that goal. If one is using force only to defeat his actions, without a goal of one's own to give direction to one's efforts, then by virtue of his strategy of operating amongst the people, of provocation and propaganda of the deed, one's actions are as likely as not to reinforce the opponent's position rather than weaken it. The opponent, with a different outcome in mind, will also have an idea of the characteristics of the outcome he seeks and intends. In conducting the analysis before an operation, or indeed as the situation evolves throughout it, the two opposing visions of the future should be examined with care to see where commonalities lie, in the first instance because there is no need to have a fight about what one can agree on, and secondly to provide what all want in the way that suits your desired outcome, and to show it is to the people's advantage. As noted already, all people desire security and order, and this characteristic is most likely to be common to the desired outcomes of both sides. For make no mistake, even the Maoist revolutionary or the fundamentalist theocrat usually understands the need for establishing security and order. The questions will be who is providing security and from what, whose laws and regulations prevail, and who are the judges.

LAW AND CONFLICT

In all the examples of war amongst the people discussed in this book, the desired outcome has been expressed in one way or another as a stable state, governed democratically, in which the rule of law functions within international norms, society is developed with due reference to human rights and the economy is run in such a way that the fiscal and monetary arrangements are reliable. The precise nature of a state that satisfies this broad description will vary with the circumstances and defining these characteristics in the particular case is difficult, particularly in advance, as just discussed. Nevertheless, it can be deduced that the rule of law must pertain.

For centuries we have debated the concepts of the justice and morality of going to war and the manner in which it is fought. After the last great industrial war, the Second World War, we adopted the United Nations Charter that describes when it is legitimate to go to war, although in recent years as we have seen its strictures are open to interpretation. We also tried and punished those of our enemies we found guilty of war crimes and in so doing did away with the defence of obeying orders. And we built on previous work to develop a body of international humanitarian law (IHL), starting with the Geneva Conventions to govern the conduct of war, particularly in regard to the protection of the non-combatant and those rendered *hors de combat*. This body of law is not in itself concerned with the morality of the use of force or whether or not the conflict is legitimate, for example by the passage of a UN Security Council resolution. All the legal measures developed since 1945 were in the main understood and created within the premise of industrial war between states. Now we are fighting wars amongst the people we are confusing the legality of our actions with their morality, whether in considering entering the war or in its conduct. Indeed, as seen in the international public outcry surrounding the US-led coalition's invasion of Iraq in March 2003, operation Iraqi Freedom, there exists a perception that the legality of engaging in combat also establishes its morality – and vice versa. Within this, we are unclear as to the standing of the soldier in law and in relation to what law. As a result we are often confused as to the utility of force in a particular situation. It is a difficult debate which is made even more complex when operating amongst the people, since there will already be some existing law in the society of those people, and at the same time, the intervening multinational soldiers will bring with them another set of laws: as already noted, there are no international soldiers and each is answerable to a different national law. This complex reality reflects upon two aspects of law and conflict: establishing the rule of law amongst the people, and the relationship between the military and the law.

Regarding the first, if one is operating amongst the people, and the object is to achieve and maintain a situation of order in which political and economic measures are to take hold, then by implication one is seeking to establish some form of rule of law. Indeed, this may be defined as a strategic objective – which means that to then operate tactically outside the law is to attack one's own strategic objective. This is effectively what happened with incidents of abuse by US soldiers in Abu Ghraib prison in Baghdad or British soldiers in Basra in 2004 – or of course the US-administered camp in Guantanamo Bay, Cuba, in which terrorist suspects captured during the war in Afghanistan were and are detained. Moreover, such acts and policies provide evidence to one's opponent to support his strategy of provocation and the propaganda of the deed, which will only assist him in gaining support from the people and turning their minds against you. This leads us back to the crucial point that the objective of all our operations amongst the people is the will of the people, and if we want a stable state and to remove our forces from maintaining a 'condition', they must be sufficiently content with the outcome that it remains intact. Undoubtedly the defeat or neutralization of those advancing the opposing view by force of arms is a necessary step, but it must be done in such a way that the people at large reject them or at the least no longer support them.

The circumstances in which military force is deployed will necessarily dictate the laws to be enforced and the powers of those enforcing them. There is no reason in principle why specific laws or decrees should not be enacted in the event, but they will need to be applied fairly and equally to all. At its most basic the carriage and use of weapons by unauthorized non-uniformed people, concealment of weapons, failure to stop when ordered and resistance to search of self and property are all proscribed by law to some degree in all societies. In any event those conducting the operation and the people amongst whom they move must be clear as to the law being applied, which should at the very least be the body of IHL.

I have found it helpful when operating amongst the people to hold in mind that the military are there to impose order. To this end there is a good principle in English common law which is that when you are faced with violent disorder and it is your duty to quell it, then you are to take the course of action with the least likelihood of causing loss of life and property. And while of course the military must fight and defeat their armed opponents to best advantage, they must do so within this guiding principle. In the worst cases of fighting and disorder the imperative for firm action will tend to result in casualties, destruction, crude judgements and rough handling; nevertheless, the controlling measure remains the law, and the military should be accountable to it. To this end I think there is considerable scope for a form of international customary law to develop. The sooner order is established then other, more regular police work can begin.

For the rule of law to be supported and enhanced such that the people support it, the military measures must be focused on the lawbreakers. This demands good information and intelligence, precision in the attack or arrest, and a successful prosecution. Every time the innocent, even if they support the lawbreaker, are attacked or arrested, killed or imprisoned, the law is diminished and the ultimate objective of the people's will to support it is made more difficult to achieve. The more the measures to impose order involve terrorizing the population the more the position of the opponent as their defender is enhanced – and the less likely you are to gain the strategic objective, the will of the people. It is difficult to apply military force to this objective, since by its nature it is lethal, massive and tends to be arbitrary. Its practitioners have in the main been trained for a war they are not fighting.

The military achieve their deterrent effect because they represent a credible threat: that they will see you breaking the law and kill or arrest you. This effect must be planted in the minds of the majority for military deterrence to be in place. But this situation has to be sustained by the military presence and does not describe the outcome desired. To reach the desired outcome the currency of deterrence must be changed from that necessary to achieve order under law, the aimed bullet, to that necessary to achieve justice within the law, evidential information leading to a prosecution and sentence. To this end the military can be of great assistance to the civilian authority in establishing itself: they have the manpower and systems to collect information, and the systems to handle and communicate information. The sooner this ability to handle large quantities of data is put to supporting the police in developing the deterrence of evidential information, the sooner the military deterrence can be withdrawn into the background.

I have argued as a principle the need for the military action to support the development of a sustainable rule of law. The application of the principle and the degree of military effort allocated will vary with the circumstances, and will of course take time to apply effectively in the face of the opponents' measures to the contrary, but as long as the outcome desired has amongst its characteristics a sustainable rule of law then all efforts should be directed towards this end, the utility of force being to establish the rule of law.

And so there is the second aspect of the legality of the use of force: the relationship between the military and the law. The standing of those employing military force and their use of it in law should be understood from the outset. The more we establish courts to deal with cases of the breach of international humanitarian law, such as ICTY (International Criminal Tribunal of the former Yugoslavia) or the ICC (International Criminal Court), the more we must be sure of the position of those we commit to operations. Initially we should be confident both of the morality of the operation as a whole and of its legitimacy. These are not simple judgements, especially in a multinational setting, but consider the position of the senior commanders: are they to commit men to an operation that they believe lacks legitimacy? Our institutional thought patterns based on the past say yes: you do what you are told, out of loyalty and discipline; your country right or wrong. But since Nuremburg and more recently at The Hague, the defence of obeying orders has failed. To my mind this matter cannot be taken too seriously. For example, in early 1999, we awaited the decision as to whether or not NATO was to bomb Serbia and Serbian forces in order to coerce Milosevic into withdrawing his forces from Kosovo, a province of Serbia, where they were oppressing the Kosovars. This was to be done without the licence of a UN Security Council resolution, and I was in some doubt as to the legitimacy of our intended actions – and whether I, the DSACEUR, should be taking any part in the operation. I reflected deeply on the matter and finally decided that it was legitimate simply on the moral grounds that if I, a strong, fit man, was walking down a road and saw and heard in a house evidence that a violent crime was in process it would be my duty to break in and stop it, using sufficient force to do so.

And then we have the laws of the states that send the servicemen to the theatre and the law of the state or states that comprise the theatre. In one way or another these bodies of law will govern the use of armed force; usually it is permitted in self-defence and to create order when disorder is threatening life and property. In both cases the use of force will be governed by the concept of a demonstrable and imminent threat and proportionality in response.

Because of the nature of war amongst the people the use of force is usually initiated at a relatively low level. It is the citizen and soldier who are affected, not just leaders and commanders. All parties therefore need to know where they stand: the people, since it is they who suffer most in lawless circumstances and it is they whose will we seek to win. Our servicemen need to know too: it is they who are held accountable in law when matters are considered after the event. IHL, most especially the Geneva Conventions and the laws of war, is supposed to be a standard text for all soldiers and officers in the military forces of those states who are signatories; it must become an international aim to ensure IHL is propagated and understood in all forces, regular and irregular, around the world. The soldier is being held accountable to the law for his actions in these campaigns, and it behoves those who send him to ensure he has an adequate understanding of the law and his position in relation to it. He also needs to know that those setting the context for his actions are doing so in such a way that he can operate effectively within the law. To this end the law and its establishment should be central to the directing logic of campaigns amongst the people from the outset – the law at a minimum being the body of IHL and that to do with establishing order and self-defence.

Ultimately, therefore, establishing the legality of the use of force is an imperative, whilst ensuring the morality of the use of force cannot be over-emphasized. However, it must be made clear the two are not synonymous, either with each other or with the utility of force. If the aim is the creation of the rule of law, using force outside legal and moral parameters will not have utility – since the purpose of the application is confounded by its circumstances. Albert Camus put it well in his *Chronique Algérienne*:

While it is true that in history at least, values – whether of the nation or of humanity – do not survive unless we fight for them, neither combat nor force suffices to justify them. The fight itself must be justified and enlightened by those values. To fight for the truth and to take care not to kill it with the very weapons we use in its defence; this is the double price to be paid for restoring the power of words.*

PLANNING

And so we come to the plan – which is not a detailed programme, but a broad outline, an intended pattern of events, based on the information and analysis to achieve the desired outcome, enumerating the objectives to be achieved; and allocating responsibility, authority and resources accordingly – so that effects achieved are coherent, focused and networked. This is difficult to do, particularly with the institutional structures we have developed for conducting industrial war rather than war amongst the people. On the whole we currently employ the 'check list' approach to planning, which is all very well provided the matter is simple and confined to a single competence or at higher levels to a single institution. To avoid confining one's thinking within the institutional structure, I have found the approach of asking questions of myself a helpful way of analysing the matter, setting objectives and organizing my effort. In particular it helps prevent me taking action on a false prospectus while at the same time avoiding delay, by indicating the actions required to gain information. I have never had the opportunity to use the questions that follow *ab initio*, but I have used them to understand why something was not working out satisfactorily, or to argue a point, or to decide what to do in a particular set of circumstances as events have unfolded.

There are two sets of questions to be asked in making a plan. The first set deals with the context of the operation as a whole, at the political and strategic levels, and the second with the context of its conduct, at the theatre level. I shall describe them as though military

* Albert Camus, *Actuelles III, Chronique Algérienne (1939–1958)*, in *Oeuvres Completes, Essais* (Paris: Editions Gallimard, 1965), p. 898.

force is being considered, but they apply in large measure to all other forms of power and influence and will show that these efforts all need to be drawn together at the appropriate level. The questions in each set are iterative in that each answer must be coherent with the other and the answers to one set must be coherent with the other.

On being faced with a situation where you think you may need to intervene with military force in your own interest, the first set is to define the outcome and the effort to be set to achieving it, in what is understood to be the specific circumstances of the time:

Who are we opposed to? What is the outcome they desire? What future do they threaten? How is this different from our desired outcome?

Are we seeking order or justice? On a scale between them, where is our outcome? If we are seeking justice, who is it for?

Who are we going to deal with, their present leaders or do we want others in power? If so, who are they? Are we changing the present leadership entirely? If not, who stays?

Are we using their law or ours? If ours, do we want theirs to change?

Who is administering the state, them or us?

Do we know the outcome we want in sufficient detail that we can set objectives to be achieved? If not, the most we can achieve is a situation likely to be conducive to an outcome we will approve of. Can we define this 'condition' so that we can set objectives to be achieved? If not, the most we can do is to ameliorate and contain, whilst we find the information to answer the foregoing questions.

At what level can we in theory achieve objectives directly by force of arms? Should we do this? Can we do this? Will we do this? When do we do this?

If not, what are we prepared to threaten and promise in order to achieve the objectives we have defined? What does the opponent most value that we can threaten? What does he want most? (Remembering always that threats are expensive when they fail and bribes are expensive when they succeed). When do we do this?

The second set of questions is answered on the basis of the circumstances in the theatre as understood at the time, and the answers to the first set of questions. However, before listing them it is important to emphasize the close correlation between the use of force and the threat of its use. Towards the end of the first list of questions one is establishing at what level it is possible to expect military force on its own to have utility, or the point at which confrontation moves to conflict. Should the theatre commander be expected to use force directly then he is clearly not merely threatening its use, and he can approach his objective on a purely military basis – just as he would in industrial war. However, should this not be the case – and even if it is at the outset it is very rarely so overall, since with success the situation changes – then the theatre commander must consider the nature of his threats at the outset so that his military action reinforces them. Upon this basis we may turn to the second set of questions:

How do we show the threat is credible, that we will carry it out, that we will succeed even if we have to escalate to do so? Are all other courses of action open to us perceived as being less attractive to us than carrying out the threat?

How do we show our desired outcome to be more in the people's and opponent's interest than us carrying out our threat?

How do we show the opponent's threats are insufficient and that we will reject their alternative outcome?

How do we ensure our promises are credible in the eyes of the opponent and the people?

How do we ensure the opponent and the people can be trusted?

In considering the plan, it must be clear that the answers to the questions lie with a wide range of agencies, of which the military are but one, and maybe only a minor one at that. Assuming only one state is involved, the agencies are, amongst others, the Foreign Office, the intelligence services, the Treasury and those organizations through which international aid and development is dispersed – both governmental and non-governmental. If a coalition-led or alliance-led operation is being planned, then these agencies in each contributing state are relevant, as are the internationally mandated organizations such as the UN family. And depending on the nature of the intervention, there may be a utility in involving agencies in the target state – indeed, a need to do so.

The true institutional difficulty is in bringing the agencies together to answer all the questions. Nevertheless this must be done if the use of force is to have a result that leads to the outcome rather than reinforcing the opponent's position. By establishing the context for the endeavour in answering these questions, what is not known or decided is as clear as what is, and objectives – including those of gathering the information to answer the questions – can be set accordingly. Any operation, but particularly one of war amongst the people, is an exercise in learning about the opponent and the operation should be conducted towards this end. In answering these questions the difference between the opposing or competing desired outcomes – our own and that of the opponent – is held in mind from the outset. Inter alia this allows the consideration of whether the military endeavour is just or not. By holding the difference in outcome in mind, the use of force and all the other pressures can then be focused on resolving the difference to advantage. For it must never be forgotten that such planning is for the advantageous ending of a conflict emanating from a confrontation, and its aim is absolutely to end the former in such a way that the possibility of resolving the confrontation to advantage is increased. Therefore, whilst one seeks to capture the people's will in conjunction with defeating the opponent amongst them, this is often very difficult to achieve in circumstances where the two – opponent and people – are of one nation or ethnicity faced by some intervening force. The underpinning confrontation is too easily reduced to one of 'them and us'. In these circumstances it is particularly important to decide who one is dealing with early in the planning. For example, when it is the existing leadership, one is recognizing that in order to bring the confrontation to a peaceful state it is necessary to cooperate with the leaders of the people so that it is they who lead their people from the opponent. The use of force in these circumstances requires a delicate touch, but if you get it wrong – whether too much or too little, too soon or too late – the local leaders are shown to be but ciphers in the hands of the intervening military.

INSTITUTIONAL THINKING

The difficulty with the conduct of our modern operations is in harnessing the efforts of all the agencies in theatre to the single purpose. In answering the second set of questions within the context of the first one knows what information and intelligence are required, the public information and media output, the military, economic, political and administrative objectives and, most importantly, the relationships between these activities. To take the case of the military, the level at which it can act as an independent group is that at which you intend to seek a decision directly by military force. If the level of such engagements is typically that of a company then all levels of military command above that should be closely linked with the other agencies and understand their mutual dependency. In other words, above the low tactical level of company action, it must be understood the military will not be the sole or probably even lead player, and in order to achieve the best effect it is important to establish the roles of all those agencies and coordinate between them. As ever, a main consideration in doing this is constantly recalling that this is war amongst the people. An example which shows how much has to be changed becomes apparent when one examines the military staff structure for dealing with the people during conflict. In industrial war the idea is to clear the civilian from the battlefield and to manage the rear area of one's force so that the civilians do not get in the way. To this end staffs were organized and trained to deal with this effort. In NATO they are called CIMIC staff (Civil Military Coordination staff) and are held by the armies of most states on the reserve, being required only on mobilization and encompassing functions which are the stuff of daily civil life. Within this perspective, dealing with the civilian population is a secondary and supporting task, and as a general rule selection for this branch would not be considered career enhancing. However, in our modern conflicts, dealing with the civilian population is directly associated with the objective and is a primary not secondary activity. Furthermore, it is also the nexus for cooperation with all other agencies and levers of power in theatre. In practice such staff is in constant demand and in short supply, throwing a strain on the reserves and demonstrating their importance – yet they are frequently ill prepared for the task, drawn at random from other branches of the services, and on short tours in theatres that often demand the establishment of trust and good relations with the people over time. Once again we have a prime example of the need to acknowledge the change in paradigm and adjust our militaries accordingly.

But it is not merely the militaries that need to be reformed for war amongst the people. We must adapt all our institutional patterns of thought and logic. Our institutions, for example the ministries, armed forces and alliances, have processes that are founded in the experience of industrial war, which structure thinking and tend to lead information to be marshalled and assessed in terms of that model of war. The institutional pattern of thought needs to change to one in which the use of military force is routinely considered as one of the possible supporting measures for other endeavours and vice versa. In these circumstances force may not be an act of last resort, and it will need to be applied precisely within the greater context of the measures it is intended to support. Presently our institutions are structured like stovepipes, from the tactical to the strategic, and except in particular cases there is little interaction between them – a fact particularly evident when dealing with multinational organizations. We need to have the ability to bring them together, at least at theatre level and probably lower, so that their actions are directed by one set of hands and their actions are coherent. This applies to all ministries and military staffs: to persist with institutional thought patterns that lead to the defence ministry or department being responsible for conducting the affairs of an occupied state is folly.

The directing set of hands may be of one man or a few, but they must be of one mind and have the authority to act to achieve the desired result. The director may be a senior diplomat, politician, administrator, or military officer, but he must have a senior representative of the other agencies necessary for success grouped with him, answerable to him and with resources to call upon. We must develop a structure that increases the ability of those charged with winning the clash of wills to direct their collective efforts to a single purpose in the theatre: to win the confrontation by ensuring that any act of force supports the achievements of the others and vice versa. This need for structural change is particularly important in the case of the multinational operations – which we must increasingly anticipate being the usual case – where the different institutions link back to different capitals. In fact, with the UN and NATO it is more complicated, in that national contingents link back directly to capitals and to the organization's HQ, in New York and Brussels respectively, where national representatives then also link back to capitals. Furthermore, NATO deals only with military matters, so when NATO is deployed another organization has to be found alongside but separate from it to handle, for example, law and order, governance and the economy.

Essentially what is required is a strategic-level body that sets the context for the operation as a whole, and is the source of guidance and sustainment for the theatre. I think the EU has great potential in this regard. Its institutions cover the full range of governmental activities and it is developing a common foreign and security policy with a capacity to commit military forces to support it. If these efforts are guided towards developing a capability, including the will to act, for confrontation and conflict rather than industrial war then the EU will be well placed for the twenty-first century.

But for such organizational changes to work there must be a change in the way we think about the campaign. We need to think of the campaign as a whole, not as a sequence of discrete events, for example preparation, invasion, occupation, nation building, withdrawal. By thinking of it as one confrontation in which conflict has a role the actions that are taken in the early stages are conducted so as to contribute directly to, or at the least to avoid the confounding of, the achievement of later ones. Answering the questions listed earlier helps to clarify the matter as a whole, as also the connection between various actors. As different agencies have a greater or lesser part to play as events unfold so they must all be involved in these considerations, and these considerations will affect the choice of targets and objectives to win the clash of wills.

The theatre of operations must also be understood as a broader concept than the spatial one of industrial war. Of course, events and actions take place in specific geographical locations, but the locations include the people and by virtue of modern communications they resonate differently and in different places depending on the people in those places. For example there are US and NATO operations taking place in the Afghanistan theatre of operations, but where is the theatre for the counter-terrorist campaign or the counter-narcotics campaign? And how are those campaigns connected to the operations in Afghanistan? Until these relationships are understood we will not be able to define well what is strategic and what is operational, nor will we be able to handle the collection and assessment of information, let alone its dissemination to influence and inform.

And for the commanders in particular we should understand that the priority design determinant of the strategy and campaign is the acquisition of information, to learn about the enemy and the people and to find out what separates the one from the other. This will allow our efforts, whether forceful or not, to be applied with precision and for us to exploit the advantage. War amongst the people is conducted best as an intelligence and information operation, not as one of manoeuvre and attrition in the manner of industrial war. Most of this information is necessary to comprehend the context of the operation and the actions being taken, for without this contextual setting the tendency is to act as though each event is separate and in doing so fail to realize that tactical success is leading to operational failure. Much of this information is available for collection and is not in itself of a military nature; the skill lies in the assessment and the decision as to what action, if any, to take. Finally, we need the information so as to achieve the deterrent of the law, evidential information in sufficient depth for a successful prosecution. Without this the overarching objective remains unrealized, thus the longer armed forces must stay in order to maintain stability. To win the clash of wills we must change or form the intentions of the people; the pressures and factors that bring about this change of will are communicated by the passage of information of other deeds, of growing confidence in the rule of law, as well as demonstrations of and the use of force.

THE MEDIA

The media and its role must also be an integral part of planning – if only because it will pitch up in any event, and tell a story, so it is best to consider the story and the role of the media from the start. On the basis of this understanding I see the media as being to a large extent the source of the context in which the acts in the theatre are played out: they do not make the facts, but it is they who express and display them. In the theatre of war those on the stage and watching in the stands judge actions in the theatre within this context, and it is up to the planners to ensure the audience via the media always remembers there are at least two producers and companies on the stage – not one mixed-up large one. That is why establishing the context of the event and getting the story right from the start is so important. To act effectively one is trying to gain a position where the majority of the audience and people on the stage are following your script in the context, and not that of the opponent. If you are fighting for the will of the people, however many tactical successes you achieve they will be as naught if the people do not think you are winning. It is by communicating through the media that this understanding is in large measure achieved.

In my opinion it is the business of the political and strategic levels to take the lead in establishing the context for the theatre commander to operate in to advantage. If they cannot or will not do this, which can be the case particularly in a weakly supported coalition or alliance operation, then the theatre commander must do what he can to set the context. But on the whole he is not well placed to do this, and in any case will have other priorities – though he must always design his operation to work within the context that exists, regardless of how it is represented in the media. To link the actions in theatre to the context and to exploit them to the next act there is a need to capture the story – to which end a 'narrator' is necessary, one who explains to the audience what has happened, its significance and where events might lead. This person is more than just a spokesman: he is telling the story, by linking the events as they occur, constantly recalling there are two sets of players and two scripts, into the most convincing story in the circumstances. All must know that he is speaking with the authority and is in the mind of the commander. In a multinational force it is well to have narrators who are at least representative of the principal language groups, so that native speakers who understand their audiences serve the national media. A prime example of successful narration would be the evolution of media management in NATO during the Kosovo bombing, during which it was some time before NATO and the capitals began to speak to the media coherently. The reasons for this were a combination of geographic, technical and procedural. The bombing was taking place in Europe, one hour ahead of London and six hours ahead of Washington. London's procedures produced an authoritative press briefing, often by ministers supported by the Chief of the Defence Staff, before the daily NATO briefing, with the result that the NATO briefers would find themselves being challenged by the media with questions based on the London briefing. In addition, the technical reach of the BBC, ITV and B Sky B was such that the British briefing was being followed in Europe and being used in the national political discourse in European capitals. On the back of all this, Washington was waking up each morning to find that its agenda, at least as far as the media was concerned, was being dictated by Europe. It was a media mess, which held the seeds of political strife. Eventually, in mid April, Prime Minister Tony Blair sent Alistair Campbell, his communications director, to pull the strings together – which resulted in a procedure to coordinate the content of briefings. Matters improved thereafter and it was Jamie Shea, the NATO spokesman, who became firmly established as the narrator of the conflict. He was so successful in the position that when NATO entered Kosovo it was his name, as much as any of the leaders, that was on the local people's lips.

The starting point for any commander should be that he has only himself to blame if facts are incorrectly reported, and if they remain uncorrected. The reporters and journalists in the theatre want to know what authority is about. They want a steady source of reliable information, preferably with coffee and communications to hand – although with the advanced equipment of today the latter is less important – and reliable data pertaining to their own security. They should be provided with these basic facilities, whilst the narrator should be readily available to them and prepared to talk to the audience at any time. Never lie to the press, whether to deceive them or the opponent. You will in time be found out, with the result that your ability to communicate with the people will be jeopardized. On the other hand you can practise illusions: not every armoured vehicle need have its infantry in the back.

The commander should avoid the temptation of cooperating with the journalist in becoming the story. The journalists will always see him as one: to pump him up and to deflate, to set him in contrast to others for good or ill, to personify and simplify what is a collective complex activity. He should remember that 'fame has no present and popularity no future'. The commander should, in my opinion, engage directly in public with the media only when he has a message to send to an audience that only he can transmit through the media. On the other hand he should be closely engaged in the background. His role is to explain the story of the operation. Just as the narrator is linking events so that the audience gains an understanding of the story, so the journalist briefed by the commander should understand the more complex linkages between events and the context. The commander is the producer, and he should want the journalist to understand the story's plot, but the producer is not the story until it is a success or failure.

The journalist has a difficult job to do, particularly if working on the TV; he usually has very little time to put the visual images on the screen into a meaningful context. The images will mean something in their own right but will only be explained fully when seen in their true context and from a stated perspective. In the time available the journalist has to appeal to mental images to provide the context, and our mental images of war are in the main founded on the industrial wars of the past. After the Gulf War in 1991 I had occasion to view a recording of all the BBC and ITV news coverage of my command during the period, from our deployment to the ceasefire. I had seen none of it before, and was struck by how similar the visual images were, with tanks and aeroplanes predominating, and how the word pictures were appealing to memories of pictures of the trenches of the First World War or the bombing of the Second. In most cases the journalist, perhaps in attempting to be impartial, reported from his or her individual perspective rather than explaining the perspectives of those engaged. As a result, the reality of what I had experienced with my command was lost or not conveyed. It was after viewing these tapes that I formed the view that a narrator was required in our modern operations – and ownership of the story claimed from the start.

Finally, do not expect anything like perfection in this presentational endeavour. There will be disasters, genuine differences of view and mistakes – with the opponent also working hard to make it so. One must take the long view, and beware the seduction of the short-term gain and effect offered by the journalist to achieve journalistic ends. The job of the military alongside all agencies conducting the operation is to defeat the opponent and win the will of the majority of the people for the future, not to sell a newspaper that is tomorrow's cat litter.

WAR AMONGST THE PEOPLE

The purpose of this chapter has been to examine the way in which to analyse and plan an approach to modern conflicts. It should be clear this approach is based upon a view of the world as one of confrontations and conflicts rather than war, and therefore one in which military force has a role to play; but that role is not a detached one, nor one which will achieve the strategic objective by itself. Above all, I strongly believe this approach is both possible and necessary if we are to apply force with utility – and I am equally sure force has a role to play in achieving political objectives. Take as an example the US plan for operation Iraqi Freedom, referred to earlier. With all the benefit of hindsight, and with no involvement in the actual planning, I compare what happened with the analysis I recommend.

Based on the political rhetoric at the outset, the desired outcome was a democratic state operating to the norms of Western democracies and open to free trade with the West. Such a state would be purged of Saddam Hussein and his regime, and pose no military threat to its own citizens, the region or the world, including that of putting weapons of mass destruction in terrorist hands. Given this desired outcome, which is both political and military in nature, one would construct a strategy by working back in considerable detail from it whilst never forgetting the basic dictum that your enemy is a reacting, thinking being; he is not sitting still waiting for your onslaught but actively creating his own strategy both to foil yours and probably to attack you. Furthermore, within the idea of confrontation and conflict, the opponent is both a military and a political being – meaning that focusing on and overcoming the resistance of the one without reference to the other will not lead to the desired strategic outcome. With this in mind, the analysis and planning would have started with the understanding of the strategic objectives – the will of the Iraqi people and their leaders, and the necessary measures to capture it, or at least keep it neutral. This means the proper process should have been to start to define the successful outcome of the occupation before the occupation actually commenced – before the invasion. The lead agency for this planning should therefore not have been the military specifically but rather those responsible for reaching the desired outcome and conducting the occupation. It appears from the evidence available that this was not the case.

The construction of a strategy and its theatre-level execution could and should have been done following the two sets of questions posed above, especially the five basic groups posed at the start of the first set and repeated below – and the need for coherence in attaining answers to them:

Who are we opposed to? What is the outcome they desire? What future do they threaten? How is this different from our desired outcome?

Are we seeking order or justice? On a scale between them, where is our outcome? If we are seeking justice, who is it for?

Who are we going to deal with, their present leaders or do we want others in power? If so, who are they? Are we changing the present leadership entirely? If not, who stays?

Whose law are we using, theirs or ours? If ours, do we want their law to change?

Who is administering the state, them or us?

Given the desired outcome, the answers to these questions for operation Iraqi Freedom suggest one had clearly to get to the capital in the face of opposition, and depose the leadership, for which military force was necessary. But did one destroy and remove the capacity of Iraq to administer itself? If the answer was in the affirmative, there should then have been the question of what or who would administer the state; if the answer was in the negative, the question should have been what must be destroyed and what must be left in place – in organizational as much as material terms. For example, if the Ba'ath Party, which was the regime, was to be destroyed, what was to replace it in administrative, not political, terms, keeping in mind that the only other organized structure in Iraq was that of religion, the mosques and imams, many of which were radicalized by sectarian rivalry. In destroying the Ba'ath Party, therefore, did one seek to empower this only viable alternative structure? And if so, what controlling measures were to be put in place?

In conducting such an analysis, one starts to identify the objectives that can be achieved only by military force, and the limitations on the use of force beyond them – including, for example, infrastructure that is necessary for the good administration and order of the people. There is then the question of the level at which you wish force to be used. By this I mean, is the use of force meant to achieve a strategic, theatre or tactical result? It is obvious the nature of the desired outcome could not be achieved by military force – the most that it could achieve was the condition in which other levers of power could create the desired outcome. Therefore it could not, and did not, have a strategic effect. Furthermore, over two years after the initial attack, it was uncertain that it had achieved the theatre condition to effect the desired outcome.

The questions of administration and law and order should have been raised – and therefore questions as to whether all Iraqi forces, including the police and internal security forces, should have been destroyed or dismantled; or should one have seen the need to differentiate between those who had to remain as part of a confrontation in a new administration rather than those who were part of the conflict and therefore had to be destroyed? Alternatively, it might have been anticipated that the leadership, particularly at lower levels, and the security and bureaucratic echelons they led, would melt away amongst the people to await events. In this alternative scenario, such people would have remained as part of the confrontation after the conflict was ended, to be treated in a way in which they saw it as being in their interest to cooperate with the coalition. For example, perhaps the promise of the continuation of their pay and benefits, with the threat inherent in the evident and comprehensive dispatch of their senior leaders, would have been sufficient to win this confrontation. This may have been especially so if alongside the application of military force other levers of power became quickly and effectively evident. For example, the rapid inclusion of police support from coalition countries would have supported and begun the process of reorientating the internal security forces. Such an analysis should also have foreseen where military and security forces needed to concentrate their efforts to support the civilian effort. Equally, the introduction of expert civilian administrators to existing structures of governance would have enabled an ongoing administration, and therefore a sense of normalcy in daily life, whilst at the same time continuing the process of reorientation at another level.

Underpinning all these options and solutions would have been a deep understanding that the arrangements for command fused the political, economic and military actions into one concerted effort – from the strategic through theatre headquarters to the lowest levels of administration. In addition, one must always revert to the basic point made throughout Part III of this book: that the people are not the enemy. The enemy is amongst the people, and the purpose of any use of military force and other power is to differentiate between the enemy and the people, and to win the latter over to you, which leads to a further point about the approach. In deciding the method of operation, once one has gained initial entry, the primary purpose must be the acquisition of information so as to identify the true target from amongst the people, to understand the context in which the target is operating, and to be able to exploit a successful attack upon that target. This means that in all but a few cases the deployment of forces and the use of military force is to result in the collection of information and in support of the other levers of power: it is they that can exploit the successful tactical action. And the more the military is in support the nearer one is to the strategic goal. If this approach is not adopted one runs the risk of having one's tactical actions turned against one by the astute practitioners of the propaganda of the deed and the strategy of provocation. This leads to the final point, since there remains the question as to the relationship of the operation – Iraqi Freedom – with the war on global terrorism: where does the strategic-level act fit into the strategy of securing the US and perhaps the allies from terrorist attack? Or is it providing fuel, high-octane strategic fuel, for those who operate to the tenets of the propaganda of the deed and the strategy of provocation?

At base therefore, an analysis of operation Iraqi Freedom starting out from the desired outcome, rather than seeing Iraq as a whole, or all Iraqi forces as a whole, would have made it possible to identify where military force was needed to destroy – and where it was needed to be applied alongside other levers. This would have been done within an understanding that military action would eliminate specific obstacles, and others would remain in confrontation, to be resolved over time by a combination of all levers. However, it is but an example, which reflects the crucial importance of changing our approach to conflicts – and attaining a utility of force.

UTILITY OF FORCE

In writing these words I do not suggest that armed force cannot be used, and used effectively, to achieve a political purpose. One has only to see how effective a few men armed with simple weapons can be, and how hard it is to defeat them and prevent them advancing their political agenda by force of arms to realize this. Force does have utility – for all purposes: defence, the security of the state and its people, and in keeping the peace on an international basis. By this I mean putting the teeth into our international efforts that range from keeping the peace to peace enforcement to defence. But for force to be effective the desired outcome of its use must be understood in such detail that the context of its use is defined as well as the point of application. For the general purpose of all interventions is clear: we seek to establish in the minds of the people and their leaders that the ever-present option of conflict is not the preferable course of action when in confrontation over some matter or other. This applies as much to the state with nuclear weapons, rogue or otherwise, as it does to the terrorist or the machete-wielding rebel; each is posing an armed threat to the people to establish a condition in which to achieve its political goal. To do this, military force is a valid option, a lever of intervention and influence, as much as economic, political and diplomatic levers, but to be effective it must be applied as part of a greater scheme focusing all measures on the one goal.

Just as I continue to think there is still utility in military force, provided it is applied correctly to support the winning of the clash of wills, so I think our forces are still useful. The relative size of the land, air and sea services, and the nature and quantities of their equipment will undoubtedly evolve to the new paradigm, but the most urgent need for change is in the organization of forces. And the strategic organization of the means must reflect the way the force is used strategically. As I have argued throughout this book, the emphasis has shifted from organizing our forces to defend our territory to using them to secure our people and our way of life, and conducting these operations at a distance from our borders. The possibility of a direct attack on some states by missile, nuclear tipped or not, exists, and if the security measures to prevent proliferation of weapons of mass destruction fail then the possibilities will increase; these attacks will always need to be deterred. To do this will require, in the case of most states, defensive alliances to provide a credible counter-strike capability with the necessary intelligence coverage and an effective missile defence system. But these defensive measures should not be seen in isolation: it is all very well building a castle, but to prevent yourself from having to live in it under siege it is as important – indeed, it is the first consideration – to secure your interests, as narrow or as wide as they may be, and to be seen as able and willing so to do. To mount the security operations we can identify certain constants: they will be expeditionary, they will be multinational to some degree and involve non-military agencies, and they will last a long time. Each nation will arrive properly at slightly different organizations according to its history and circumstances; however, the more these organizations are congruent with those of other nations the better the fit when grouped together in some multinational force. This is the challenge facing the European nations, particularly with their armies, which are well armed to deal with any enemy equipped with ex-Soviet equipment. It is making sufficient of these forces available and sustaining the availability outside their borders that is the organizational problem at the strategic level.

Operationally the way the forces are used and thus organized must reflect both the strategic constants and the war amongst the people. In this regard we must take every advantage that technology offers, particularly in space, in the air and at sea to gain an edge in communications, reach and command. But in seeking to do this it must be understood that our opponents have gone amongst the people to neutralize these advantages: in our modern circumstances having the technical advantage is not in itself sufficient; it does not stand as such in its own right. We have to engage our opponents amongst the people and in these circumstances technological advantage is achieved only when the technology is in direct support of those engaged amongst the people. Achieving this essentially organizational change will require us to develop different relationships from those for industrial war between the deployed elements of the three services and within their components. Despite the need to use technology in every way, one must beware of seeing it as it was in industrial war: it is no longer a question of two or more sides seeking to outdo each other with technology. For example, great advantage is presently expected from the 'digitization of the battlefield' and 'network enabled warfare'. However, we must be careful to understand where we seek to gain this advantage and over what. There is a danger of knowing more and more about oneself and proportionally less and less about the enemy. Information technology should be harnessed to support the information operation being conducted to understand and find the opponent and separate him from the people, and to network the effects of our actions so as to complement one another.

To this end I anticipate an increase in the means to gather information and their wide deployment about the theatre and amongst the people. This collection is as much to ascertain intentions as it is to find things and particular people. This reconnaissance and surveillance network must have at least some operatives who are familiar with the people they move amongst, who speak their language and understand their norms of behaviour. All the operatives will need the training and character to move comfortably amongst the people conscious that their enemy is proximate and yet avoid as much as possible falling into the traps of the opponent's strategies of provocation and propaganda of the deed.

The increase in collection will probably be marked by a decrease in those elements that strike on the basis of the information gained, whether they are infantry, artillery, fighter-bombers or warships. Their weapons and techniques will become more sophisticated. They will be held centrally and be committed appropriately to attack targets that exploit and support the information operation, using our technological advantage to gain the necessary reach and sophistication in our weapon design. The supporting arms and services must be kept to a minimum so as to present the fewest targets and to reduce the operational overheads that have to be sustained, not least in the numbers required to guard and patrol to secure the bases. Of course, some must exist but each one of these facilities and its attendant guards and supply convoys is a set of targets waiting to be attacked, which gives the opponent an advantage; each one and in particular its security patrols is evidence of an oppressive presence. When this is realized and it is withdrawn one faction claims a victory, and just as likely another faction will declare a lack of confidence and demand the base remains. The art is in seeing the campaign as a whole from the outset and thereby avoiding unnecessary exposure to such risks, and when they are unavoidable to establish the context in which to take the action to advantage. Again our air and maritime advantages may allow many of these activities to be conducted out of harm's way. I think we must conceive of the application of force, in contrast to the intelligence and information operation, as a raid at theatre or strategic level rather than a sustained operation. Here too advantage might be taken of multinationality, although this will require a measure of political will, for example if the people of the EU can move about Europe covered for medical emergencies on a simple form, the E111, why can't the same nations pool their medical arrangements in the field?

The desire to protect the soldier so as to maintain his morale, which I wholeheartedly support, often manifests itself in measures that isolate him from the people. He appears helmeted, armoured and armed amongst them, or in his heavy armoured vehicle on the street.

His behaviour as he patrols is threatening. His bases are heavily fortified and often sited to overlook the people. These measures, while most necessary in particular cases, do not have my general support. They all define the soldier as 'the other'; the opponent amongst the people is gaining advantage every day they are in place. Other ways should be adopted: organizing differently, using different equipment and lowering decision levels as to when such measures are adopted, reduce the numbers exposed and the visual impact to the necessary minimum.

The staffs that support the commanders on these operations will need to be multidiscipline as well as multinational, when necessary, and headquarters and their procedures organized accordingly. Just as there is a need to see, plan and direct the operation as a whole from a strategic point of view, so must this be done in the theatre. A military HQ may provide the framework for this multidiscipline HQ simply because it usually exists before the start of the operation, but it must do more than accommodate the representatives of the other disciplines – it must incorporate them. The staffs and systems need to be able to cope with the differing information requirements of confrontation and conflict. In the fight or conflict the information required is objective and about time, space, amount and effect. In a confrontation one is dealing with subjective information of intentions, timing and consequences. At the risk of over-simplification, one plans a fight rather like one plans to build a bridge; actions are sequenced in a logic of construction, resources assessed in advance and provided to a schedule, and so on. In handling a confrontation one seeks to build a 'portfolio of options' to be called upon as events unfold, each chosen so as to advance towards the desired outcome. In war amongst the people the context of each fight or conflict is a confrontation. The commander and his staff in the theatre and their subordinate commanders must recognize which of the two they are conducting at the time and the part their subordinates have to play. One of the consequences of this is that hierarchical chains of command can be a hindrance, particularly when the engagements are at low tactical levels; they lead to layers of headquarters between those actually engaged in conflict and those conducting the confrontation. If we are to be effective, this too will lead to change in military organizations.

Finally, we must develop the confidence to grant authority to those we send to conduct these complex operations commensurate with the responsibilities laid on their shoulders. This confidence will come only with the selection and training of the right people, and achieving this on a multinational basis will be difficult to do and will take time. Nevertheless, until this is achieved we will not gain the full potential of the deployed forces and resources.

When I originally described the levels of war in the Introduction I made the point that each level sits within the context of the superior level. It is the business of the commander at each level to provide the nest or context for his subordinates to have the best possible opportunity to achieve the objective he has set them. In all circumstances he needs to set the objective in terms of the size of the enemy force, allocate forces and reserves to achieve it, and to define the subordinate's battlefield.

These judgements are taken in advance of action. The test of the senior commander when it comes to taking action is to ensure that in the face of his opponent's actions he maintains the validity of his judgements. In addition, however, the more we wish to use force sub-strategically to achieve military objectives to win confrontations, the more we need to understand that the other organs of power – economic, diplomatic, politic, humanitarian and so on – are part of the context of such an operation: they define the confrontational battlefield. The commanders at these sub-strategic levels need to have their actions firmly nested in a context that includes the political, economic and social factors local to the achievement and exploitation of their objective. Without this wider context commanders at all levels will not be able to achieve their objectives, nor therefore enable the final attainment of the desired political outcome – the overarching purpose of all activity. In other words, the force will not have utility.

Such changes will help give the organizational mobility necessary to make best use of our limited forces deployed and employed on these long operations amongst the people, and to do so coherently with other agencies. For it must never be forgotten: war no longer exists. Confrontation, conflict and combat undoubtedly exist all round the world and states still have armed forces which they use as a symbol of power. None the less, war as cognitively known to most non-combatants, war as battle in a field between men and machinery, war as a massive deciding event in a dispute in international affairs, *industrial war* – such war no longer exists. We now are engaged, constantly and in many permutations, in *war amongst the people*. We must adapt our approach and organize our institutions to this overwhelming reality if we are to triumph in the confrontations and conflicts that we face.

Index